IMBROGLIO

*Rising to the
Challenges of
Borderline
Personality
Disorder*

IMBROGLIO

Rising to the Challenges of Borderline Personality Disorder

Janice M. Cauwels

W. W. Norton & Company

New York   London

The text of this book is composed in 11.5/13 Bembo
with the display set in Bembo Regular and Medium.
Manufacturing by the Haddon Craftsmen, Inc.
Book design by Margaret M. Wagner.

Library of Congress Cataloging-in-Publication Data

Cauwels, Janice M.
    Imbroglio : rising to the challenges of borderline personality
    disorder / Janice M. Cauwels.
        p.   cm.
    Includes index.
    1. Borderline personality disorder.   I. Title.
    [DNLM: 1. Borderline Personality Disorder.   WM 190 C375i]
    RC569.5.B67C38   1992
    616.85'852—dc20
    DNLM/DLC
    for Library of Congress   91–32092

ISBN 0–393–03349–X

W.W. Norton & Company, Inc.,
500 Fifth Avenue, New York, N.Y. 10110
W.W. Norton & Company Ltd.,
10 Coptic Street, London WC1A 1PU

1   2   3   4   5   6   7   8   9   0

*To Jack L. Katz, M.D.,
and B. Timothy Walsh, M.D.*

Contents

II   WHAT CAUSES BORDERLINE PERSONALITY DISORDER?

III   WHAT CAN BE DONE ABOUT BORDERLINE PERSONALITY DISORDER?

Preface

*A*t a point well into her topic, Dr. Cauwels writes:

> Borderlines worry about exposure not just for the obvious
> reasons but because they know that *other people can't understand
> their illness*. While the stereotype of BPD tends to be taken
> very seriously, its reality often is not. The whole situation is
> incomprehensible.

*P*erhaps this all too elusive, all too present malady labeled
borderline personality disorder is indeed incomprehensible, but
this book carries us well beyond the stereotypes and ex-
poses us to much of its reality. To help readers understand
the incomprehensible appears to be Dr. Cauwels' agenda.

Imbroglio is an extensive and up-to-date report on the
clinical, scientific, and political status quo of this old new-
comer to the mental hygiene arena. It is a comprehensive
and thorough presentation, certain to inform and guaran-
teed to challenge the reader, whether he or she be a patient, professional, relative, or curious layperson. In ap-
prehending her subject, Dr. Cauwels draws upon multiple
perspectives: the "observable" (phenomenologic), the
"measurable" (empirical), and the "intuitive" (psychologi-

cal/psychodynamic). Didactic and scholarly sections are balanced cumulatively with vivid personal accounts of the illness from patients, families, and therapists. Clinical objectivity is well represented here, but so too are the existential sufferings and strivings of patient and professional alike.

Over the past year I received phone calls from the author loaded with questions about the topic of this book. The calls were always fun, informative to me, and, I hoped, of some use to her. Having now read how Dr. Cauwels put together all this material, I am even more impressed. She has quoted me accurately and in context, not an easy undertaking with a topic this complex. I sense that she has handled all of her informants with equal care and taken their perspectives seriously. Certainly the result grapples head on with the conundrums of BPD and avoids regression to oversimplifications or polemics.

Section I introduces us to prototypic patients with BPD and carries us through the tortuous history of American psychiatry's attempts to understand them and their disorder. This includes biological as well as developmental and psychological approaches to the illness. No major theories have been left out, nor have the primary contributors, many of whom are quoted offering their most recent opinions and speculations. The relationship of BPD with affective disorders, dissociative disorders (like multiple personality disorder), post-traumatic stress disorder, "newly" rediscovered childhood histories of physical and/or sexual abuse, and other frontiers of investigation and controversy receive special focus.

Section II elaborates on the psychoanalytic, biological, and temperamental theories of etiology. Perhaps of particular interest to the professional clinician/investigator, this encyclopedic section is also written to be comprehensible to those unfamiliar with science and medicine. If you're looking for glib post hoc explanations of "borderlineness" in the disintegration of modern society, then don't read Chapter 21. There the author uses Charles Dickens' descriptions of two Victorian "borderlines" to highlight that the malady predates the time when we thought social order began eroding. The concluding chapter of this section, on the final common pathways that produce the disorder, calls for more research into the nature of this bewildering condition. I could not agree more.

Section III deals with what to do for people with BPD. It provides an evenhanded review of the variety of psychotherapeutic approaches that have evolved for treatment, ranging from psychoanalysis to investigative psychotherapy to cognitive behavioral therapy to supportive/eclectic therapies. Other modalities such as pharmacotherapy and hospital treat-

ment are covered with equal rigor, as are the long-term follow-up studies offering insights into the natural history of this condition. Dr. Cauwels finishes with a plea to temper—and tolerate—passion with perspective in one's attempt to bring this uniquely difficult disorder under
control. Whether we are someone who has the disorder, whose relative
or friend has the disorder, or who tries to treat the disorder, we can trust
that Dr. Cauwels has modeled such an effort with this book.

The author has organized and presented an incredible amount of
work in an eminently comprehensible and interesting fashion. If you are
looking for diatribes and divisiveness, select another book on the borderline. If you prefer balance and integration, turn the page.

Thomas H. McGlashan, M.D.
New Haven, Connecticut
September 3, 1991

IMBROGLIO

Rising to the
Challenges of
Borderline
Personality
Disorder

Introduction:
The Borderline
Imbroglio

"My father saw me skimming through a book on borderline personality disorder that I found at the mall bookstore and said, 'Hey, I want to read that.' I told him not to waste his time. The book is so superficial and the case histories so unborderline that I was afraid it would give him the wrong idea."

"ALICE"

One dictionary definition of *imbroglio*[1] aptly summarizes not only the subject of borderline personality disorder (BPD) but also the predicaments of the people involved with it personally and professionally:

A confused mass; an intricate or complicated situation (as in a drama or novel). Besides being complex, BPD itself is as fascinating as the most gripping performance or fictional work.

An acutely painful or embarrassing misunderstanding. The families and friends of borderlines know that the illness is devastating but not what it is all about. Borderlines themselves are trapped in a chaos of disturbed thoughts, distorted perceptions, raging emotions, and humiliating behaviors that seem well beyond all sense.

A violently confused or bitterly complicated altercation. Theoretical attempts to tame BPD have resulted in much controversy and mistrust among therapists.

This book therefore explains how to "rise to the challenges" of BPD in several respects. The challenge to therapists, of course, is effectively to treat this often intractable illness. BPD can be treated successfully—in fact, many borderlines proceed to help other sufferers. Another challenge to them, and to those who care for them, is to understand the illness as much as possible.

Twenty-four-year-old Alice rose to this challenge only to "learn nothing I didn't already know," she says. As her complaints imply, BPD cannot be presented accurately by those popular media lacking either the resources to make it clear to the public or the depth to enlighten borderlines. In fact, some psychiatric background and vocabulary are necessary really to understand BPD at all.

It is best, then, to clear a few more definitions out of the way.

The *personality* can be defined as an individual's adaptation to his world: the way in which he typically copes with and defends against feelings and impulses, sees himself and other people, responds to his environment, and finds meaning in his activities, relationships and values.

A *disorder* is an abnormal condition. It can be either

a *syndrome:* a group of symptoms indicating a particular abnormality without necessarily referring to its causes, or

an *illness:* an unhealthy condition that has both symptoms and some known or inferred cause or mechanism.

A *personality disorder* consists of inherent inappropriate patterns of perceiving, thinking and relating to others that cripple a person's functioning and can cause great suffering.

Borderline personality disorder is an illness that will require this entire book to define.

The complexity of BPD may be why I often had unusual difficulty enlisting the most highly respected specialists in the illness to contribute to my research for this book. This was the case even when I came recommended by colleagues. Letters and followup notes requesting interviews often were ignored; offprints had to be pried from their authors' grasps; voluntary responses ranged from guarded optimism to outright rudeness.* Many therapists expressed skepticism that a lay writer or audience could even begin to grasp the relevant issues.

This book nevertheless attempts not only to appreciate the complexity of BPD but also to explain it. Because the borderline concept is very diffuse, the explanation must unfold slowly in bits and pieces: symptoms of the illness here, specific possible causes there, *examples* that seem best to *represent* various aspects of the subject.

While such details are necessary to consider, it is likewise important to

---

*One noted psychiatrist troubled himself to write back, "I am really not enthusiastic . . . this kind of second order book doesn't turn me on." A few of the other experts who declined to be interviewed are identified where the context so demands.

present the entirety of the borderline experience, the somewhat arbitrary pattern that connects them. This entirety can be summarized in a single word: *difficulty*. Hallmarked by great intensity, instability, and immaturity, BPD creates unique difficulties for the sufferers and everyone involved with them.

This book features accounts by borderlines (some in the midst of hallucinations or fury), people close to them, and therapists who have worked with them. Readers in any of these groups can share as well as learn from the experiences with BPD that others have endured.

Therapists find borderline patients extremely frustrating to treat. Bombarded by the unique clinical difficulties created by BPD, therapists also face theoretical ones. The voluminous literature on the illness (4,000 books and articles to date, by one estimate[2]) is as chaotic as the patients' emotions. "The exponential rise in research and the literature defies any one expert's ability to comprehend or master," wrote John G. Gunderson, M.D.,* in 1989.[3]

More prosaically, "the further you move into the literature, the more of a swamp it is, and the more confused you get," says Craig Johnson, Ph.D., who has treated many eating-disordered patients who are borderline. One of the more difficult decisions involved in writing this book was that of where to show readers the depth of this swamp without drowning them in it. At least some of this confusion results from bickering. This book helps sort through the arguments. It also highlights the one guiding principle of treatment on which experienced therapists agree: never, *never* treat a borderline patient without consultation.

Families and friends of borderlines may suddenly have a suicidal person on their hands, throwing them into a foreign land populated by various therapists in both psychiatric hospitals and private practice. "People who hadn't believed in psychiatry or perhaps had never paid much attention to it find themselves in crises, their children poised between life and death," says the father of one borderline patient.

They have to ask themselves what is wrong with the child, to start with, and then answer other questions: should we commit her? Should we agree to pay hundreds of dollars a day for what might be long-term care? If we do, will she cooperate or just continue to bamboozle everyone?

"It has been pointed out, very importantly, that psychiatry is atypical in its treatment of the families of hospitalized patients," says Michael R. Liebowitz, M.D.

---

*The titles and affiliations of the therapists whose work is featured in this book are listed at the end.

We're not interested in them, or we don't relate to them well enough—or we view them as the source of the illness, which shifts the blame and causes real dangers for treatment as we conceptualize the problems. I advocate a much more medical model.[4]

Dr. Liebowitz's medical model is one of various theoretical orientations explained here that help determine attitudes toward the families of borderlines. This book will help concerned people come to terms with borderline feelings and behavior. And it will demonstrate that no one involved with a borderline is alone in feeling bewildered, anguished, furious, and helpless.

Borderlines themselves may have tried therapy that proved unsuccessful, or given up and quit after a brief time. Either possibility has reasonable explanations other than that the borderline is a bad patient or a hopeless case. This book examines and validates their experience. But it also indicates how much of their behavior is self-sabotage and explains what kinds of treatment might be appropriate.

It is not a self-help book. I hope simply to help readers de-personify BPD, to stop thinking of it as *me* or *her* or *them* and to substitute the pronoun *it*. BPD is never a person, even if it often seems to be.

The first section of this book describes the history of BPD and the theoretical implications of the concept. The history illustrates that the lamentable lack of knowledge about BPD does not imply either laziness or incompetence on the part of therapists, who have grappled with it for over a century.

The theory that appears here is not merely an exercise in abstract speculation inappropriate for a lay audience. Rather it is intended to serve some extremely practical functions. One is that of reassurance. The pain BPD causes everyone involved is often aggravated by bewilderment: Why can't these doctors explain what's wrong? Why isn't treatment helping? Do these therapists have any idea what they're doing? How can someone who seems so competent actually be so sick? Why doesn't anyone understand these raging emotions?

Another function is that of educating prospective patients as consumers. Many borderlines waste time and money on therapy that makes them worse. "I have a patient in treatment now who used to get into screaming matches with her therapist," says one psychiatrist. "She had no idea that therapy didn't have to be that way."

Such a situation does not necessarily mean that the therapist is incompetent. "Therapists who are ordinarily very good frequently end up doing ineffective therapy with borderline patients," says Marsha M. Linehan, Ph.D. Bad therapy occurs not only in private practice but also in hospitals. "You can find horror stories about any of the elite private psychiatric hospitals," says Judith L. Herman, M.D., "so it's not just a matter of state institution staffs not knowing any better."

Although the stereotype is that borderlines themselves "destroy" their therapy, many of them work hard at inappropriate treatment that they cannot recognize as such. While clarifying her own responsibility in therapy, education can help a borderline ask intelligent questions and perhaps avoid gross mismanagement of her case.

Appropriate therapy itself offers prospective patients a bewildering variety of alternatives. Therapists treating borderlines are implementing principles described by one or more of the experts who dominate the field. In psychoanalytic psychotherapy, for instance, a disciple of Otto F. Kernberg, M.D., will persistently confront a borderline patient because he views her primarily as aggressive. A disciple of Gerald Adler, M.D., and Dan H. Buie, Jr., M.D., will, with equal determination, constantly comfort her because he views her primarily as deprived. Both these disciples may or may not be highly suspicious of psychiatrists who prescribe medications for borderlines.

Because her treatment is likely to take years, the borderline patient in particular must educate herself about the methodologies available to her. As Dr. Gunderson emphasizes, she needs a therapist whose thinking and personality "fit." And any knowledge about her condition gained by the patient can provide the therapist with opportunities to understand her better. "The lack of knowledge about this disorder is something that works against us," says Joel Paris, M.D.

The early chapters focus heavily on diagnosis for three reasons, one being the unanimous complaint that people just don't understand *what borderline personality disorder* **is.** If this book is successful, readers will come away with a profound sense of what it *means* to be, to care about or to treat a borderline. They will understand that the appearance of BPD varies in any given patient at any given time. No more capable than anyone else of explaining concisely what the illness **is**, readers will nevertheless have learned about the issues it raises.

The second reason is that borderlines themselves are upset by being badly misunderstood. Paradoxically, some of the important symptoms of this most difficult of psychiatric illnesses often are not taken seriously. The third reason is that a patient's diagnosis shapes the entire course of her treatment and outcome. Misdiagnosis can have devastating results.

The first several chapters may seem to concentrate on psychiatry rather than on patients. I hope it will become clear why patients should know just how they fit into the profession's approach to their condition. BPD is not merely an illness; on several levels, it is also a metaphor for the field of psychiatry and the process of psychotherapy. For this and other reasons, I focus upon general theory and practice as opposed to family therapy, substance abuse, or other specific related areas.

I have structured the book to be read as a whole from start to finish. It will quickly become clear that like the theoretical stages of psychological birth, its chapters are interwoven and cumulative. Dipping into a chapter here or there will not only become confusing but also create misconceptions.

Everyone interested in borderlines either represents or shares in their experience to an extent unparalleled in other psychiatric illnesses. The shaky identities of borderlines are reflected in the many difficulties of correctly diagnosing them. The subject matter a therapist must master to treat BPD is as demanding as the patients themselves. The fear of engulfment that haunts borderlines is shared by those who venture into the theoretical "swamp." The rapid evolution of thinking about BPD makes the field as unstable as the patients' emotions, as confusing as their disturbances of thought. The splits in borderline perception occur likewise among the ideological divisions in the field.

Ultimately BPD is best defined not by what therapists think about it but rather by what borderlines themselves experience and how they behave. The case histories and descriptions included in this book therefore represent my attempts to transcend diagnostic criteria and capture something of their inner lives.

*I*deally the case histories illustrating any psychiatric illness would include patients of both sexes from a wide variety of locales and treatment backgrounds. Practically I was limited by the reluctance of many therapists to approach borderline patients about speaking to me and the overwhelming fear of the patients themselves they they would somehow be identified. Nevertheless, I did obtain interviews more than satisfactory for the purposes of this book.

I have interviewed adult borderline patients and their families from across the United States and Canada. The patients who appear here represent a reasonable cross-section of the widely varied people who are borderline; some of them have additional personality disorders or other conditions. Each fulfills the *DSM-III-R* requirements (these, the DIB, and other diagnostic tools will be explained later) *by the consensus of two or more therapists specializing in this field.* With some exceptions, these patients fall into three groups:

- *DSM-III-R* borderlines who have undergone psychiatric hospitalization for an average of 18 months. The goal of this treatment was to break down and restructure the personality. Like the outpatient therapy in which they are now involved, it was heavily confrontative and psychoanalytical. These patients are highly educated about their illness.
- *DSM-III-R* borderlines with various treatment backgrounds, some of whom are engaged in dialectical behavioral therapy for repeated self-mutilation and/or suicide attempts.
- DIB borderlines who have had only a few months' treatment each and are now participating in a research project. The therapists involved explain diagnoses only if asked and had told their patients that I was writing a book on "personality problems." I approached these patients only after the psychiatrist heading the project reassured me repeatedly, goodhumoredly, and correctly that they would not be distressed to learn their specific diagnosis from me.

I worry about the psychological realism of composite case histories and prefer instead to use first-person narratives in which, except for disguised details and speech patterns, the subjects use their own words. The names, ages, occupations, and other details that might identify these patients and their loved ones have all been changed to others selected at random. Each person who appears has read his or her writeup and quotations and confirmed that he or she is not recognizable. Although anxious to be fully disguised, a few patients expressed dismay that their presentations here do not show how dramatically they have improved.

I am grateful to the borderline patients who spoke with me, including those who put me in touch with other patients. Although no outsider can fully understand or communicate what it is like to be borderline, I hope that this book fulfills their expectations in other respects. I also thank the families of borderline patients who volunteered to help me try to spare others their anguish. Of course I would not have had access to any of these people without the help of the therapists who referred me to them and who would, I presume, likewise prefer to remain anonymous for their patients' further protection.

Having complained about the unusual lack of cooperation I encountered from many experts I approached while writing this book, I take equally unusual pleasure in acknowledging those who excelled in their contributions of time and interest.

Joel Paris, M.D., and Charles R. Swenson, M.D., were enthusiastic about this project from the beginning and generous with their time, assistance, and, in Dr. Paris's case, continued support. Among other favors, Dr. Swenson repeatedly loaned me his office and books; during a painfully refrigerated symposium at an APA convention, Dr. Paris loaned me his overcoat.

As part of the effort he volunteered to this project, Larry J. Siever, M.D., read most of the manuscript, made several suggestions, and reassured me that its errors at that stage were minor.

Each therapist whose work is featured was kind enough to check my writeups of his or her views. For reading entire chapters as well as their own quotations, I thank Paul S. Links, M.D., and Judith L. Herman, M.D. (who each read two), and Paul A. Andrulonis, M.D., Marsha F. Linehan, Ph.D., Dr. Paris, and Dr. Swenson. In *requesting* to read the relevant chapters, Thomas G. Gutheil, M.D., and Eric M. Plakun, M.D., set an admirable and most welcome precedent.

Alerted by John H. Greist, M.D., to my interest in his field, Charles Hodulik, M.D., called to offer assistance. In preliminary interviews, he and Robert J. Waldinger, M.D., supported my overall approach. I am also grateful to John G. Gunderson, M.D., Oren Kalus, M.D., and Otto F. Kernberg, M.D.

When circumstances required the work to be done in record time, Thomas H. McGlashan, M.D., gallantly paused in his administrative duties as Director of the Yale Psychiatric Institute to read the manuscript and write a preface. I am honored that this book bears the *imprimatur* of so outstanding a physician, scholar, and gentleman.

Frank Curtis, Esq., expertly and patiently handled contract negotiations, developed release forms, advised on issues regarding confidentiality, and (perhaps unknowingly) extended support from the real world. My editor, Susan Barrows, followed this project closely and graciously resigned herself to its length and complexity. Among other personalized services, she and her staff at Norton have sought to protect it from sensationalism by the media.

David Lane, M.L.S., and his staff at the library of the New York State Psychiatric Institute have been consistently helpful since B. Timothy Walsh, M.D., Director of the Eating Disorders Research and Treatment Program, made possible my use of these facilities.

Having wandered into the field of eating disorders a decade ago, I came upon Dr. Walsh and Jack L. Katz, M.D., Director of Psychiatry at North Shore University Hospital, the latter of whom introduced me to the personality disorders. Both of these psychiatrists have since contributed to my work as part of their respective medical ministries, for which they are renowned among their colleagues and recognized in the dedication of this book.

Notes

1. *Webster's Ninth New Collegiate Dictionary* (Springfield, Mass.: Merriam-Webster, 1989), p. 601.
2. Richard L. Munich, M.D., welcome address at the Psychodynamic Psychotherapy with Borderline Patients seminar, sponsored by The New York Hospital–Cornell Medical Center, Westchester Division, New York, 12 January 1991.
3. John G. Gunderson, M.D., *"Borderline Personality Disorder* Foreword," in *Review of Psychiatry,* Vol. 8, ed. Allan Tasman, M.D., Robert E. Hales, M.D., and Allen J. Frances, M.D. (Washington, D.C.: American Psychiatric Press, 1989), p. 5.
4. Michael R. Liebowitz, M.D., paper [affirmative] read at debate, "Resolved: The Etiology of Borderline Personality Disorder Is Predominantly Biological," 143rd annual meeting of the American Psychiatric Association, New York, 16 May 1990.

I

What Is Borderline Personality Disorder?

1

The Most "Difficult" Psychiatric Patients

"Are you going to explain in your book that we're not really the scourge of the earth, psychiatrically?"

"CARLA"

*F*ew happenings are as predictable as the media's discovery and sensationalism of another psychiatric disorder. Thus, if the average person were asked which psychiatric patients are the most difficult to treat, the answer might be a glamorous stereotype: the sociopaths guilty of cold-blooded murder, the psychotics who can exhibit superhuman strength, the multiple personalities capable of character transformation.

The current exploitation of BPD, however, merely magnifies a stigma carried by this illness within the psychiatric profession. Therapists would identify as most "difficult" their borderline patients, whom many of them view as the "scourge" referred to above.

Unfortunately I must illustrate how borderlines earned these labels before uncovering the reality behind them.

*T*he borderline "scourge" is a large and varied group of people. BPD is associated primarily with women, who are the majority of psychiatric patients and who seem to com-

prise at least two-thirds of borderline patients.* But it may afflict comparable numbers of men, who instead might break laws and be misdiagnosed as they proceed through the legal system.

The most reliable estimate of how many people in the general population have BPD was provided recently by Marvin Swartz, M.D., and his
colleagues. Based on data from 3,000 interviews originally conducted in
the Piedmont area of North Carolina by researchers at the National
Institute of Mental Health (NIMH), their study identified 1.8 percent of
that population as having BPD according to the most stringent diagnostic criteria.[1] If we round this conservative estimate to 2 percent and
assume that it holds true for the entire population, then roughly five
million Americans are borderline.

Within the psychiatric population, a reasonable current estimate based
on several studies is that borderlines amount to 11 percent of all outpatients and 19 percent of all inpatients (63 percent of inpatients with
personality disorders).[2]

This sizable number of patients is often treated by young therapists:
senior attending psychiatrists assign borderlines to residents as excellent
teaching cases, and new practitioners accept them because they need the
fees. Many older, more experienced therapists refuse to see them. "After
being hospitalized for two years, I moved back to my home town and
began interviewing therapists about outpatient treatment," says 24-year-
old "Hayley." "I'd call them up and say that I was diagnosed with
borderline personality disorder, and they would say, 'I don't work with
borderlines.' "

The stigma attached to BPD can be seen in the psychiatric literature,
where borderlines are described as experts in provocation and manipulation. Moderating a conference discussion later published in a professional book, Jonathan O. Cole, M.D., said that, "Even with John Gunderson's help at McLean, I end up feeling that borderlines are impossible
patients whom nobody likes."[3] One article notes that the term *borderline*
is often misused pejoratively for all kinds of reasons and that in many
psychiatric institutions it serves as "another colloquial expression of contempt, like 'gomer,' 'crock,' or 'turkey.' "[4]

Complaints about borderlines in the popular literature are even more
colorful. An article written by David Hellerstein, M.D., during his resi-
dency describes the borderline patient as one that "can glitter and strike
like a cobra" and summarizes the therapist's reaction:

---

*Borderlines are thus referred to throughout most of this book by feminine pronouns (and therapists
by masculine ones because of male dominance in psychiatry).

Forget the professional manner of the psychiatrist, forget the elegant and obscure theories of Otto Kernberg on borderline conditions and their relation to pathological narcissism. They give little protection; your knowledge entitles you to no mercy. People like this bring you close to murder.[5]

In his book *Love's Executioner,* Irvin D. Yalom, M.D., similarly exhibits the dismay and guilt he once felt at the prospect of treating a borderline. When the patient first consulted him, he writes,

> ... Everything ... about her ... shouted "borderline," the word that strikes terror in the heart of the middle-aged comfort-seeking psychiatrist. ...
> My first impulse was to get the hell away, far away—and not see her again. . . . But soon I heard my voice offering her another appointment. . . . more than anything, I believe it was shame, shame at choosing the easy life, shame at shunning the very patients who needed me the most.[6]

Other therapists who share Dr. Yalom's sense of humor likewise take borderlines seriously. A facetious article on single-session "thanato-therapy" (that is, psychotherapeutically induced suicide applied with borderlines in mind)* describes them as patients "notorious for late-night irrelevant 'emergency' phone calls, no common sense, no redeeming qualities, no income, and no health insurance."[7]

The patients mentioned here by Drs. Hellerstein and Yalom both made therapeutic progress during the limited time each psychiatrist saw them. So why do even successful therapists cringe at the prospect of treating borderlines?

*T*herapists describe borderline behavior ranging from seductive to catastrophic. Extremely dependent, borderline patients expect more than a therapist should reasonably provide. Rather than maintain personal responsibility, borderlines place therapists in the dilemma of having to take charge when they lose control, as one psychiatrist explains:

> Borderlines get intensely involved with therapists, and we get intensely involved with them, and then we find ourselves being thrown all over the map.
> A suicidal borderline is all over you: "I'm going to kill myself; you've got to call me," and this, and that. This emotionally charged person is calling you frantically, claiming, "You're the only person who can help me; you

---

**Thanatos was Freud's term for the death instinct.

must help me; you have to see me an extra time." You try to help, but you don't, and then she gets angry because you didn't help enough, you didn't say the right things.

The last statement highlights a salient feature of such interaction: the borderline patient's disappointment with or rejection of the therapist's efforts. A borderline often gets her way with her therapist only to decide that it is not, after all, what she wants. Describing a borderline patient he saw as a resident, a psychiatrist gives an example:

> A borderline was admitted to the inpatient psychiatric unit by an emergency room physician because of her suicidal tendencies. All she would say was, "I have to leave. I must leave. I won't commit suicide." She created a crisis: "I have to leave, or who will feed my kids?" This sort of thing can get you worried about her concerns. Usually we take a few days to know a new patient before arriving at such a decision, but she persuaded me that she had to leave and that she was okay. When I finally gave her permission to leave, she said, "I don't want to go," and refused to go.
>
> It's that sort of thing that can drive a therapist stark, raving mad. Borderlines put you in a position in which you feel a certain way and have been maneuvered into saying something or taking an action, and then they cream you for it. The patient flipflops on you: "How *dare* you do that sort of thing? How *COULD* you do that sort of thing? How could you have thought I could leave? I came in crazy! How could you just let me go?!" **UGH!**

Therapists who treat borderlines often note wryly that with these patients, no good deed goes unpunished.

Such retaliation is reported to occur dramatically as various forms of aggravation. Borderlines harass therapists with repeated phone calls (the later the hour, the better), sometimes phoning from hotel rooms in which they announce their intention to commit suicide. They pay unscheduled visits to therapists' offices, pleading for immediate attention and throwing violent tantrums when it is withheld. Some reprimand their therapists by wrecking their offices or attempting suicide right there. I have heard of one patient diagnosed as borderline who burned down her therapist's home.

Other patients express obsession with their therapists in quieter form. Recalling one period of her hospitalization, 30-year-old "Robin" says, "I was assigned to go out on passes with other patients from my unit, one of whom never wanted to go anywhere or do anything except sit in the parking lot next to her therapist's car." Such behavior can deteriorate into espionage on a therapist's private life. "My borderline patients patrol my street all the time," says Charles Hodulik, M.D. "They're constantly driving or walking back and forth in front of my house, but they're very much afraid to come any closer."

People skeptical about the value of psychotherapy would probably cheer for borderline patients: under their "training," many therapists have behaved equally outrageously. Some have come bounding out of the night with the police at their heels to break down the doors of suicidal patients. Other stay up until all hours trying to call patients they consider at high risk.

From his collection of legal cases involving borderline patients, Thomas G. Gutheil, M.D., draws several incredible examples of therapist behavior like this:

Case 3. In addition to doing therapy, a psychiatrist gave a patient with BPD hundreds of dollars; gave her medications from a supply he had prescribed to himself; and had her stay, at his invitation, in his own house—in a spare bedroom—during a housing "crisis." The psychiatrist slept on the floor in front of the spare bedroom door so that the patient could not leave without his knowing it. All of these actions were rationalized as being in response to the patient's needs.[8]

Borderlines admitted to hospitals find a larger professional audience for their expressions of rage, loneliness and despair. Sometimes they organize a patient revolution; otherwise they subdivide the hospital staff into "good" and "bad" people who then begin to alienate each other. Meanwhile, their outpatient therapists may be too pleased to have temporarily disposed of them to participate in such battles or advise on their care.

Capriciousness, undependability, impulsivity, selfishness, and plain nastiness: such qualities often result in borderlines' being rejected by those from whom they crave affection. Borderlines appear to exaggerate their misery; they mope; they fume silently to scare others with the prospect of an imminent explosion. Impatient, irritable, anxious, and volatile, they keep everyone around them on guard. If the attention of their audience drifts, they use ill temper and suicide threats as blackmail.

The borderline feels misunderstood and unappreciated. Idealistic and hypersensitive, she is appalled by the human frailties of those who fail to nurture her. Having implored others in vain to validate her anguish, the borderline uses her behavioral repertoire to express hostility, to get even with those who have failed her, and to frustrate their desire to help. When not condemning everyone else, she wonders whether her relationships fail because she herself is worthless and evil.[9] Yet the borderline remains unaware that others see her as an unattractive, self-pitying, obstinate, manipulative brat.

Such behavior is actually neither frivolous nor *manipulative* in the usual sense. Borderlines have no idea how to control their raging emotions, nor do they know how to elicit the expressions of caring that every person needs. They often misinterpret any attention as an expression of affection rather than common courtesy or the exercise of a legal or ethical obligation.

Inappropriate therapy exacerbates this situation. Without long-term, properly managed treatment, a borderline can't help sabotaging the good intentions of everyone around her. "It bothers me that there's such an awful stigma in the field, but I understand why it exists," says Hayley. "In the wrong treatment situation, it can be a mess. *I've* been a mess. I've been very difficult to work with."

But descriptions of *manipulation* (and many other terms used to describe borderline behavior) can actually reflect the feelings and inadequacies of the therapist involved as much as the actual reality. The experience of 34-year-old "Carla" helps explain why:

> I have to keep changing therapists because I burn them out. They keep getting too involved with me and can't take my self-destructiveness any more. I have deliberately tried to keep my distance from my present therapist, not calling her unless I absolutely have to, but still I found out after a recent overdose that I have the power to really hurt her. It's so scary not to know how or why this happens. Now I don't know what to do. Do other borderlines have this problem?

It's so scary not to know how or why this happens. Carla is not trying deliberately to seduce her therapists, and it is not *her* responsibility to maintain distance in the therapeutic relationship. Like many other borderlines, she is stuck having to "take care" of therapists who have been overcome by treatment difficulties.

In short, sometimes therapists are part of the borderline's problem rather than its solution.

Like Carla, "Ingrid" has learned to anticipate and try to minimize negative reactions to the symptoms of her illness. A 21-year-old borderline, Ingrid has emerged from a frenzy of chronic bulimia, heavy drinking, promiscuity, and suicidality; she works full time while attending school, playing several sports, and partying on weekends. While hospitalized on a borderline unit for 16 months, Ingrid began keeping a detailed journal of her feelings and observations.

One entry explains the dilemma of a motivated borderline patient trying to work with the staff of a prestigious hospital unit where rules are enforced with no reasoning allowed. Having been "blowing up all over the place," Ingrid wants to be honest with the staff about how she has been feeling. She knows, however, that they "want to hear some things, but they don't want to hear everything."

If Ingrid hides or lies about her feelings, she won't get well. But if while describing her fury she loses control, she will be locked in the "quiet room" (whose only furnishing is a mattress on the floor), and if she reports her obsession with eloping from the unit, she will be otherwise confined and lose privileges.

> I don't understand what being responsible means, or anything. Is being responsible telling them how I am feeling, or is it trying to sit with it? I feel like it is building even as I type, and I don't know what to do about it. I don't know who to talk to or anything. I can't go to staff, but I can't talk to patients because they won't know what to do. I don't feel safe around anything, and right now I want to be kept safe, but I don't want to be kept safe at the same time. Shit!!!!!!!!!!!!! I am incredibly tense right now and am thinking about going to the bathroom to throw up, but I can't do that because I know that [it would be] taking a major step backwards. There is nothing that anyone can say or do right now because if I say anything then they will say that I am being provocative. . . . I am so fucking confused. . . . I feel like everyone is sick of my shit. . . . I feel like crying, but I can't cry on the unit. But I can't go to my room because I know that I will throw or punch things. I am not angry, but I am. I just want to get rid of everything. . . . I can't lie, and I can't not lie. What the fuck am I supposed to do???????????? . . .

Although other psychiatric patients face them also, these conflicts are intensified for borderlines because hospital staffs expect them to provoke, manipulate, or act out bad feelings and are alert to squelch such behavior immediately.

But other borderlines run into trouble with therapists because they *don't* act this way. "It's almost impossible to explain BPD to anybody, even professionals," says 30-year-old "Melanie."

> While interviewing at one halfway house, I talked to a psychiatric social worker who had everything in front of her—all my records giving my diagnosis—but she looked at me and said, "I have absolutely no idea why you were hospitalized for two years. You look perfectly normal to me." What do we say to professionals who are so ignorant? For former inpatients in particular, this is probably one of the most frustrating problems.

As Dr. Gutheil has pointed out, attorneys are even more likely than outside therapists to be bewildered by the case histories of borderlines, whose treatment can create unique medicolegal difficulties.[10]

The therapeutic relationship is supposed to be paradigmatic of all of a patient's interactions with other people. But therapy is also only part of a patient's life compared to relationships with her family and friends.

And one clear similarity between "ignorant professionals" and families is their incomprehension of BPD. Many borderlines share the ability to "look perfectly normal" that Melanie describes here:

> My biggest dilemma with the borderline stigma is trying to get people to understand and accept any of it. It's very, very frustrating for me not to be believed or to be unable to communicate what I'm feeling. But it's frustrating for everyone else, too. They don't know what to do, and they don't understand why if I'm depressed, I just can't snap out of it. But what I have is more than just depression. There is no way to identify BPD—it's not nailed down anywhere, not even in *DSM-III*. There's no way to prove that something is terribly wrong with me.

Later we'll meet other borderlines who echo the frustration of having their inner torment invalidated in this way.

But as Melanie correctly notes, their frustration is shared by those who *want* desperately to understand them. The mother of a borderline who was treated for bulimia and alcoholism before being hospitalized for a year has been in this predicament. Since her discharge, the daughter has spent the past two years excelling in a satisfying job and is presently living with her fiancé. "But it isn't easy," her mother says.

> You don't always know when it's appropriate to say something or otherwise show your feelings and when it isn't. You can't be too sensitive because there are many times when you're dealing with a borderline patient that you feel squelched.
>
> We're all human, and sometimes the problems that you have to deal with . . . it seems that these patients want more than human expectations would allow, that they don't give you much room for mistakes. It's a difficult situation.
>
> There's no guarantee with anybody, and that is definitely proven with these patients. Three of the patients who were hospitalized with my daughter have since committed suicide. All you can do is work together with the therapist and the patient and hope for the best.

*A*s the mother's final comments suggest, the prognoses of borderline patient are as extreme as their behavior. Current estimates are that one out of ten treated borderlines will commit suicide, but two out of three who survive will improve, perhaps substantially. For now, we'll dwell on that good news. Amy Baker Dennis, Ph.D., who treats eating-disordered borderline patients, emphasizes what is all too often forgotten:

> *There is hope.* Borderlines *can* improve the quality of their lives. They need not feel like space invaders who have been dropped here out of sync with the rest of the world. They need not spend the rest of their lives fearing abandonment, aloneness, or becoming so attached to another person that separation will cause death. They can learn and practice the skills of developing appropriate, stable, healthy relationships, with all the resulting good and bad, in the context of therapy, where it's safe. Then they can go out and duplicate that relationship anywhere. But they must first exercise their right and responsibility to find the best therapists for them.

Repeating Dennis' implied reference to the strangeness of BPD but speaking more from the therapist's perspective, Dr. Paris agrees with this prognosis.

> This idea among therapists that they don't want these patients and that they're untreatable is really quite unjustified. Some of them *are* untreatable, but I've had fantastically positive experiences with many of them. Some of them were wonderful, extremely likeable people who did incredibly well. Even those patients who don't make gratifying recoveries can be managed with intermittent interventions over the years. Therapists don't have to carry them on their backs for their whole lives.
>
> People who say that they don't want to treat borderlines really don't want to get into all that emotional reaction and go to bed at night worrying that they will have a suicide on their hands in the morning. But the patients they treat with other personality disorders have results that are probably no better and no worse. It's just less of a hassle. It takes less out of the therapist.
>
> The crucial thing for your audience is to give a sense that BPD is not such an alien phenomenon. It's worse than what most people feel, but it's really something not that unusual or frightening. Certainly if patients are willing to follow through on treatment, a lot can be done for them.

In one sense, though, many borderlines have no choice but to get better. Long-term followup studies of borderline patients suggest that theirs may be a time-limited disorder. Some therapists may be unjustly taking credit for the fact that eventually symptoms subside: either life steps in to rescue borderlines or the illness just dies down. Such improvement seems to occur even without treatment.

But therapy is nevertheless recommended to try to prevent suicide, relieve pain, and improve the quality of life.

BPD is a fascinating psychiatric disorder because it is uniquely difficult to diagnose, understand, tolerate, treat, suffer from, recover from, and write about. That *difficult* does not mean *impossible* is a reason this book exists.

This chapter began by listing some complaints of therapists who dislike borderlines. We will learn that for every situation involving BPD, the opposite is also true: having recognized the reality beneath the stereotype, many other therapists specialize in treating borderline patients. (A number of borderlines—some of whom are, unfortunately, still disturbed—become therapists themselves.) Committed to years of work with each patient, these therapists are gamblers playing for the highest stakes—the enormous reward of guiding a severely ill patient to a fulfilling life.

The odds against a positive outcome make treatment success with a borderline patient all the more spectacular. It occurs each time the power of a disturbed survival instinct is overcome by the desire to help.

Notes

1. Marvin Swartz, M.D., Dan Blazer, M.D., Ph.D., Linda George, Ph.D., and Idee Winfield, Ph.D., "Estimating the Prevalence of Borderline Personality Disorder in the Community," *Journal of Personality Disorders*, Vol. 4, No. 3 (1990), pp. 257–72.
2. Thomas A. Widiger, Ph.D., and Allen J. Frances, M.D., "Epidemiology, Diagnosis, and Comorbidity of Borderline Personality Disorder," in *Review of Psychiatry*, Vol. 8, ed. Allan Tasman, M.D., Robert E. Hales, M.D., and Allen J. Frances, M.D. (Washington, D.C.: American Psychiatric Press, 1989), p. 9.
3. Jonathan O. Cole, "Chapter 5: General Discussion," in *Psychiatric Aspects of Minimal Brain Dysfunction in Adults*, ed. Leopold Bellak, M.D. (New York: Grune & Stratton, 1979), p. 62.
4. David E. Reiser, M.D., and Hanna Levenson, Ph.D., "Abuses of the Borderline Diagnosis: A Clinical Problem with Teaching Opportunities," *American Journal of Psychiatry*, Vol. 141, No. 12 (December 1984), p. 1529. Copyright © 1984, the American Psychiatric Association.
5. David Hellerstein, "Border Lines," first printed in *Esquire* (November 1982), p. 128. Reprinted courtesy of the Hearst Corporation and the author. Copyright © David Hellerstein.
6. Irvin D. Yalom, M.D., "Therapeutic Monogamy," in *Love's Executioner and Other Tales of Psychotherapy* (New York: Basic Books, 1989), pp. 213–14. Copyright © 1989 by Irvin D. Yalom. Reprinted by permission.
7. Kathleen M. Donald, Ph.D., and Bruce E. Wampold, Ph.D., "Thanatotherapy: A One-Session Approach to Brief Psychotherapy," *Oral Sadism and the Vegetarian Personality: Readings from the Journal of Polymorphous Perversity®*, ed. Glenn C. Ellenbogen, Ph.D. (© 1986; New York: Brunner Mazel, 1987), p. 45.

8. Thomas G. Gutheil, M.D., "Borderline Personality Disorder, Boundary Violations, and Patient-Therapist Sex: Medicolegal Pitfalls," *American Journal of Psychiatry*, Vol. 146, No. 5 (May 1989), p. 600. Copyright © 1989, The American Psychiatric Association. Reprinted by permission.
9. Theodore Millon, Ph.D., "On the Genesis and Prevalence of the Borderline Personality Disorder: A Social Learning Thesis," *Journal of Personality Disorders*, Vol. 1, No. 4 (1987), pp. 356–57.
10. Thomas G. Gutheil, M.D., "Medicolegal Pitfalls in the Treatment of Borderline Patients," *American Journal of Psychiatry*, Vol. 142, No. 1 (January 1985), pp. 9–14.

2

The Borderline
as Metaphor

. . . to grapple with the borderline concept is to wander onto a battlefield littered with the remains of earlier definitions, fought over by bitterly contending factions, and shelled by other factions who would obliterate the concept altogether in the conviction that it is the devil's handiwork or, at the least, a holdover from pagan times.

MARTIN LEICHTMAN, PH.D.[1]

As the most widespread personality disorder,* BPD is a common denominator of all the fashionable syndromes and traumata of the 1980s. The illness is associated with sexual abuse and can be the underlying cause of symptoms like eating disorders, other addictions, and self-mutilation. These conditions need to be treated differently in this case,[2] as Ingrid's description implies:

> It's difficult to understand the symptoms of a borderline. We can be borderline bulimics, or alcoholics, or drug addicts. It's not like common substance abuse. Regular alcoholics can never drink again, but borderlines can sometimes. We can have these symptoms because we needed them at the time, then just switch symptoms or get our acts together and not need them at all any more.

*In a debate with Dr. Gunderson at the 1990 convention of the American Psychiatric Association (APA), Hagop S. Akiskal, M.D., noted that "in Boston, borderlines are rumored to be endemic if not epidemic—they seem to flourish in the vicinity of psychoanalytical institutes."

Encompassing as it does all these potentially sensational areas, BPD has unfortunately been declared "the women's illness of the 90s." But it has been written about by psychiatrists for 100 years and observed by them in both women and men for twice that long. Why isn't it better known?

Having tried since 1987 to sell a book on BPD to puzzled editors, I can sympathize with the talk show hosts exhibiting carefully furrowed brows who are busily hawking this hot topic. Their audiences appear about to ask many editors' favorite question: "But just what **is** borderline personality disorder?" Presented with the usual bulleted lists of symptoms and vague advice about seeking psychotherapy, the public remains bewildered. How does borderline personality disorder differ from normal thoughts and feelings? they want to know. This question is difficult to answer.

*A*ppealing to common experience, the media describe borderline symptoms as different from wellness in *degree*. To do so can be unfair both to borderlines (the depth and quality of whose pain it seems to dismiss) and to well people (whose normal mood changes scare them into thinking that they may have BPD). Even the official diagnostic criteria describe the condition in terms with which most people can identify. "It's important to establish how the definition should be used," says Robert J. Waldinger, M.D. "A person who responds to a rough day by coming home and mixing a stiff drink is really different from a person who instead gets out a razor blade to slash herself."

Although some of its symptoms may seem common enough, borderline depression and anxiety are intangibly different from those seen both in well people and in other psychiatric disorders, possibly because of a different neuropathological basis.[3] Their overwhelming rage likewise appears unique. "Borderlines have a terrific anger," says one psychiatric resident during a class on personality disorders.

> It's not only that the anger is powerful, but there's a certain quality to it. It's not rage—it's very strong, but it's not just strong anger. I really don't have the words to describe it. . . . Maybe because I think of rage as being justified . . . It's not quite rage; it's not quite righteous indignation—there's something *disgusting* about the anger. It's an *unbearable* anger.

"Whitney," a 31-year-old borderline, tries to describe what makes the anger unbearable:

I just went through an angry period and feel as if I've emerged from a bubble I didn't know I was in. When I'm in it, I really believe that I'm angry at what I'm angry at, when in fact it's not just anger, it's extreme rage all out of proportion to whatever is going on. It makes me feel like a kid in a temper tantrum. I can't let go of it. It goes so deep down in my gut that it feels as if I'm never going to be able to reach down and get it out. There are no words to express it. It's so painful that I have to try to do something to make it go away.

While hospitalized, Ingrid became most angry whenever she lost privileges. Prevented from acting out, Ingrid had no choice but to try to relieve her feelings on paper. Except for disguising identities, I have transcribed this description from her journal exactly as it appears:

They just put me on fucking peer escorts gain. Tghey are a bunch of fucking assgholes. This doesn't help a fucjking thing. I am never telling them anyth again as long as I am in this shithole./sfuckllllllllllllll I hate when they move in. [Another patient] is a fucking asshole. She always says that I give fucking mixed messages. They can fuck themselves. If [one of the staff members] was here she would not have me on fucking peer escorts because she believe that I have to take some fucking responsibility for something every once in a while. Fuck them all to hell.!!!!!!!!!they can screw themselves. I hate them all. I don't see how this is going to do anything to help the situation. I hater them more than I can possibly say they are a bunch of assholes. She is a fucking asshole. I hope that they break a leg or some-

The intensity of such feelings underlines the borderline's sense of alienation.

An example of this detachment appears in Ingrid's journal in a passage describing hallucinations. Sharing a hospital room with another patient as she writes, Ingrid is nevertheless isolated in her terror and anguish. This description too is transcribed without correction:

It is only eight o'clock, usually this starts much later, what the fuck is going on with me. I can't believe this. I talked about all of this with a lot of people and I don't know why it is still bothering me. I am shaking again right now. Please God make it all stop. I can't go on like this. I should go talk to someone. I don't know why I am doing this. I am crying really hard now and I don't know why. I just want to die. Um, [another patient] is in my room right now but I can't describene what is going on because I can't handle fucking her up to. I was seeing bodies hanginger and I though really seriouslly about drinking bleach andthen going and hiding or something like that but I really don't want to die I just want everything to

I am seeing bodies bloated from drowning and arms with blood pouring out of the wrists and throats and this is really scary and I don't know what to do please make it all stop please stop the pictures I will do anything to stop all of the pictures this can't go on any more it is really fucked up maybe i should just do it and say forget about everything the only real way to do it in here is to hang yourself or use poison cutting might stop it obviously typing isn't except when I look at the words and the keyboard but as soon as I close my eyes it all comes back. I can't type forever.

Such experiences of hallucinating while maintaining a grasp on reality are common among borderlines and puzzling to therapists. "One of the problems with psychosis as a definition is that as with all of our definitions, the boundaries depend on who is talking," says Rex W. Cowdry, M.D.

I don't know exactly how to describe the psychotic experiences of borderlines. It's a very strange phenomenon that is qualitatively different from schizophrenia. Classical schizophrenic psychoses don't occur in BPD unless there is something else going on. Brief psychotic episodes that are quite dramatic, delusional and time-limited, with the borderline aware that she is hallucinating, those certainly do occur.

Schizophrenic psychosis typically consolidates several really bizarre ideas that maintain a life of their own over long periods of time. In contrast, borderline psychosis is a transient, often paranoid response to panic or other types of stress. Although like other symptoms it differs in kind from normal experience, borderline psychosis is less alien than the schizophrenic type and therefore easier for other people to imagine. And it is also easier to disbelieve. "The way borderlines become psychotic is so different from the way schizophrenics are psychotic that I keep feeling that they're faking," says another resident in the class, "that they're pretending to be paranoid or psychotic as part of their acting out."

Carla, however, did not fake a psychotic episode that was characterized by a life-threatening delusion:

One time I took out two quarts of blood because I believed that doing so would get the badness out of me. I was working in a lab where heparin was available, so I took syringes and heparin and went home and shot up 10 or 15 cc, waited about half an hour, then took a 16-gauge IV needle and drained my blood into four mayonnaise jars.

I talk a lot and tend to call people when I do self-destructive things. This particular night I called some friends on the staff of a psychiatric unit where I had been a patient a few times. While talking, I got involved with what I was doing and kept saying, "When is it enough? When do I know if I've got enough out?'' The person on the line asked me what I was doing, and they called the police.

I was convinced at the time that doing this would get the badness out of me and that it was the only thing that would help.

"This phenomenon has gone back and forth in discussions about what it should be called,'' says Dr. Gunderson, "parapsychosis, cognitive perceptual lapses, reality testing failures, minipsychosis.'' A suggestion for redefining borderline psychoses has been made by Kenneth R. Silk, M.D., and his colleagues. Borrowing from John Frosch's classic concept of the *psychotic character,* the group recommends describing such phenomena as *brief or prolonged altered experience of reality.*[4]

These struggles precisely to define borderline symptoms have characterized the professional literature for decades. Some therapists believe that borderlines act out rather than articulate their feelings because their illness originated during the preverbal stage of toddlerhood. In other words, people find BPD difficult to describe because of the limitations of language itself.

Another reason is the subject's size. Having opted to present BPD in some depth, I then had to select a limited number of topics that would best represent it. And no sooner would I try to clarify what seemed to be an isolated concept than I would need first to stop and explain something else.

Compared to other psychiatric disorders about which consensus has existed for 20 or 30 years, BPD is in flux. "The psychiatrist who leads our parents' support group talks about BPD completely differently from the way he did when we first started coming,'' says the mother of a borderline patient.

When he told us recently that borderlines do get better, I complained, "Why didn't you tell us that two years ago when our daughter was hospitalized and there seemed to be no hope?'' And he said, "Because we didn't know it then.''

"We're really just beginning to study these patients, and our knowledge base has doubled within the last year or two,'' says Dr. Liebowitz. "The next ten years will be very dramatic.''[5] Although encouraging, this situation also makes it difficult coherently to describe important advances in thought.

Many people don't understand BPD also because the psychiatric profession is far from sure how to define it. Part of the problem is what Thomas H. McGlashan, M.D., calls "the important thing about borderlines: they are more different than they are similar." The illness is often diagnosed by instinct when meeting a prospective patient has made a clinician's hair stand on end. The presence of a borderline electrifies the atmosphere, making others feel tense and self-conscious. "We know when we have borderline patients in front of us even though we don't know exactly what the illness is," says Dr. McGlashan.

For a long time, as we'll see, nobody knew what to call it either. And to this day, nobody is entirely sure whether it is one illness, a cluster of related syndromes, or a group of unrelated conditions coexisting at a certain level of pathology. Certain persistent questions of this sort likewise reflect a problem with communication.

In an episode from *I Love Lucy* titled "Paris at Last," Lucy Ricardo is arrested for passing counterfeit francs. She is unable to explain her innocence to the police, none of whom speak English. Summoned to the station, her husband Ricky arranges a line of communication: he translates Lucy's explanation to a German drunk who understands Spanish, who repeats it, in turn, to a *gendarme* who understands German, who relates it in French to his superior officers.

However comical this predicament may seem, it is not uncommon in science and medicine, including psychiatry. A metaphor seen in the psychiatric literature about borderlines is that of the *bucket brigade*. One of its references is to the transmission of ideas about BPD along a continuum connecting purely psychological to purely biological psychiatry. Unable to communicate directly, theorists at either extreme rely on relatively compatible colleagues to translate and otherwise act as intermediaries.*

This situation is not as passive as the metaphor would imply. Regardless of their theoretical inclinations, different generations of physicians and scientists have enthusiastically embraced concepts that they *wanted* to be valid. They have just as vigorously rejected that which they didn't want to hear, only to change their minds later.

This instability is exacerbated by the nature of psychiatry itself. The purpose of psychiatric diagnosis is to make descriptions of patients clearer and more precise, to identify additional patients with the same symptoms, and by studying them, to deepen understanding of the illness.

But psychiatry differs from other branches of medicine in that diagnosis results not from scientific tests but rather from conceptual consensus.

---

*The bucket brigade metaphor is applied also to the tendency of borderlines to see a series of therapists before finding the right match.

Having historically been an important focal point of such efforts, BPD has been, in a sense, a metaphor of the psychiatric profession.

The Parisian *gendarmes* showed considerably more good will toward their zany redheaded prisoner than often appears in communications about BPD. Even certain borderline specialists who work within the same realm theoretically "**hate** each other," says one therapist who is intrigued by the resulting fray.

Apparent in writings about the evolution of the borderline concept, another metaphor is that of war. The apt quotation by Leichtman that opens this chapter well describes the history of BPD. The present situation resembles that which existed in Central Europe after World War I, Leichtman writes, when different countries disputed the division of a broad geographical region and compromised in peace treaties that left much to be desired.[6] So too, special interest groups within psychiatry are still trying to shape the definition of BPD, meanwhile having settled for its current diagnostic criteria.

The geographical metaphor is well put. As each country has its own language, culture, religion, and customs, so do the factions in psychiatry have different diagnostic terms, theoretical orientations, cherished concepts, and habitual practices. All of them take an interest in BPD and observe it from many different angles. Although they cause profound theoretical and clinical difficulties, borderlines comprise one of the largest, most diversified groups of patients in psychiatry, and each bloc of therapists wants to claim this prize.

Another way to put this is to note that people afflicted with BPD tend to "measure" the stability of whatever social structure they occupy. Place a borderline within any group of people, and their relationships will split easily along existing fracture lines. Similarly, the borderline concept in psychiatry measures the distance between splintered ideologies as perhaps no other illness can.

Squabbling over BPD occurs within a context of larger factors that influenced its evolution as a psychiatric concept.

These factors can be visualized as a series of concentric circles, each influencing the circle just within it. The largest circle consists of the changes in American society that have occurred over the last few decades. These have altered social and economic factors in medicine and health care policy, which in turn have influenced theoretical issues in psychiatry. As Jerome Kroll, M.D., has explained, the large numbers of borderline patients and the implications of the concept itself have made it an important target of these changes and of broader philosophical, territorial and economic issues that helped form its current definition.[7]

Both the modern and the historical issues that have affected the borderline concept have involved all three of the major branches of psychiatry: the phenomenological, the biological and the psychoanalytical.* A borderline patient in particular should know which of these perspectives is being directed toward her illness and what that implies for her prognosis and treatment.

Notes

1. Martin Leichtman, Ph.D., "Evolving Concepts of Borderline Personality Disorders," *Bulletin of the Menninger Clinic,* Vol. 53 (1989), p. 229. Copyright © 1989 The Menninger Foundation.
2. See, for example, Amy Baker Dennis, Ph.D., and Randy A. Sansone, M.D., "Treating the Bulimic Patient with Borderline Personality Disorder," *Advances in Eating Disorders,* Vol. 2 (Greenwich, Conn.: JAI Press, 1989), pp. 237–65, and "The Clinical Stages of Treatment for the Eating Disorder Patient with Borderline Personality Disorder," in *Psychodynamic Treatment of Anorexia Nervosa and Bulimia,* ed. Craig Johnson, Ph.D. (New York: The Guilford Press, 1991), pp. 128–64.
3. Stanley P. Kutcher, M.D., "Borderline Personality Disorder Heterogeneity: Pharmacotherapy and Psychotherapy Implications," paper read at the 143rd annual meeting of the American Psychiatric Association, New York, 15 May 1990. See also David L. Gardner, M.D., and Rex William Cowdry, M.D., "Pharmacotherapy of Borderline Personality Disorder: A Review," *Psychopharmacology Bulletin,* Vol. 25, No. 4 (1989), p. 520.
4. Kenneth R. Silk, M.D., Naomi E. Lohr, Ph.D., Drew Westen, Ph.D., and Sonya Goodrich, Ph.D., "Psychosis in Borderline Patients with Depression," *Journal of Personality Disorders,* Vol. 3, No. 2 (1989), p. 99.
5. Michael R. Liebowitz, M.D., paper [affirmative] read at debate, "Resolved: The Etiology of Borderline Personality Disorder Is Predominantly Biological," 143rd annual meeting of the American Psychiatric Association, New York, 16 May 1990.
6. Leichtman, pp. 241–42.
7. Jerome Kroll, M.D., *The Challenge of the Borderline Patient: Competency in Diagnosis and Treatment* (New York: Norton, 1988), pp. 16–25 *passim.*

*A fourth branch, behavioral-rehabilitative psychiatry, may well take its place among the other three by the end of the decade; one such approach is the subject of Chapter 28.

3

Some Background

"I'm often told that my data are soft, but I'm not impressed that the biological data are that much more firm."

GERALD ADLER, M.D.[1]

Major discrepancies separate the explanations of BPD proposed by phenomenological, biological, and psychoanalytical psychiatrists. "BPD is a very controversial entity," says Paul H. Soloff, M.D. "We're arguing about what pieces are biologic and psychodynamic, and the backgrounds of the individuals investigating it pretty much determine their stand on what the entity is." Each branch of psychiatry heavily influences current conceptualizations of BPD. Because any given therapist practices within one or more of these frameworks, each of them needs therefore to be properly introduced.

Phenomenological Psychiatry

Phenomenological (also called *empirical* or *descriptive*) psychiatry is concerned with the directly observable mind and the study of behavior objectively rather than by inferred causes.

Phenomenological psychiatrists worry that varying descriptions of the same illnesses appear in the psychiatric literature. These investigators try to establish easily reproduced, reliable, explicit diagnostic criteria that will be used consistently in research. By reviewing psychiatric papers on a particular illness, studying large numbers of patients, and statistically analyzing the resulting data, they arrive at a list of symptoms that define it uniquely.

The best known example of descriptive psychiatry is the *Diagnostic and Statistical Manual of Mental Disorders,* the official diagnostic guide issued by the APA, of which the third revised edition published in 1987 *(DSM-III-R)* is now the standard. The presentation of diagnostic criteria for BPD in its predecessor, *DSM-III* (1980), triggered the explosion of new research in the field.

Classical phenomenological psychiatry follows principles associated with practitioners at Washington University in St. Louis. Many of these therapists are skeptical about BPD as a valid psychiatric illness, partly because it doesn't present the clean, unified diagnosis that is easiest to call valid.[2]

Psychoanalytical psychiatrists see phenomenological methods as exercises in creating meaningless categories—rather like distinguishing buffaloes from fish on the basis of size. Actually the phenomenological process starts with the simplest theory and builds upon it logically: when empirical investigation proves the theory inadequate to explain the observations, the phenomenologist adds another layer of complexity. The application of operational criteria, followed by that of the scientific method, provides a means of testing the validity of theories. But this process is not intended to substitute for deeper understanding.[3]

Biological Psychiatry

Biological psychiatry (also called the *medical model*) focuses on the underlying physical processes of the brain. Like phenomenological psychiatry, it describes and classifies behavior. Purely biological psychiatry does not, however, acknowledge that all kinds of factors influence the expression of mental disorders. Instead its practitioners assume that genetic and/or biochemical factors alone are the true causes of psychiatric illnesses and the bases by which to distinguish them.

Trying hardest to be scientific, biological psychiatrists tend most loudly to deplore the limitations of psychiatric research. But however imperfect they may be, the methods of biological psychiatry have revolutionized the treatment of organically based illnesses like schizophrenia and may eventually do so for other psychiatric disorders. Radical practitioners tend, however, to depreciate nonmedical forms of treatment, focusing narrowly on the findings of *pharmacotherapy* (drug treatment) as a major criterion by which to diagnose disorders and evaluate therapeutic outcomes.

Psychoanalytical Psychiatry

Although far less popular in today's psychiatric profession than the phenomenological or biological approaches, classical psychoanalysis figures importantly in the history of BPD. Theories grounded in modified psychoanalytical thinking are still enormously influential today.

Unlike the other two branches, *psychoanalytical* psychiatry bears little resemblance to a science. Psychoanalysis is based on a purely theoretical model of the structures of the mind and the motivation and meaning of behavior. It differs from phenomenological psychiatry by explaining as well as describing symptoms and from biological psychiatry by doing so in purely psychological terms. Although more liberal psychoanalysts allow for possible biological contributions to mental disorders, others are less concerned even with the causes of symptoms than they are with their deeper meanings.

Psychoanalysis originated as Sigmund Freud's method of investigating the minds of patients he saw in his office practice. As patients lay on a couch reporting whatever thoughts and feelings occurred to them, Freud would sit behind them silently devising interpretations of whatever they said. He thus established and affirmed his theories about the unconscious mind, the source of primitive, offensive thoughts hidden from awareness by the conscious mind. The conflict between the two, Freud thought, formed the basis of mental disorders.

Freud believed this conflict to be played out by the three parts of the psychic apparatus: the *ego,* the *id,* and the *superego.* The ego consists of both mental mechanisms (like perception and memory) and *defense mechanisms* (strategies for coping with unpleasant thoughts and feelings). It mediates between the primitive instinctual desires of the id, the social rules of conduct recorded in the superego, and the individual's perception of reality. Using skills like impulse and mood control, problem solving, and ability to relate to other people, the ego negotiates a compromise between the other forces. This compromise resolves conflict and enables a person to adapt to reality and function effectively. These *ego skills* or *functions* are often badly underdeveloped in borderlines.

Classical psychoanalysts see psychiatric disorders as fluctuating along a continuum extending from neurosis to psychosis. This conceptualization historically formed the basis of the borderline concept. *Psychosis* includes a wide range of major mental illnesses, either biologically or emotionally caused, that severely cripple a person's ability to think, feel, remember, communicate, and behave appropriately. Examples are schizophrenia and manic depression (now called *bipolar disorder*). *Neurosis* commonly refers to any emotional disorder, usually a maladaptive way of coping with anxiety or conflict, that is not psychosis.

A basic difference between the two is the ability accurately to perceive reality. Psychotics experience the long-term, hardcore hallucinations or delusions described earlier, while neurotics retain the ability to evaluate the world objectively and distinguish that which is external from themselves.

Freud developed psychoanalysis to treat neurotic disorders like hysteria (now called *histrionic personality disorder*). Patients with neuroses are able to experience *transference:* to view the analyst as they do significant people in their lives, to react to him unrealistically on this basis, and with his help, to recognize that they have done so. This reaction enables the analyst to delve into unconscious processes that affect the patient's relationships.

Psychotic patients cannot make such transferences. Borderlines can do so but have enormous difficulty recognizing and examining the process, even with the analyst's help. Thus the continuum of neurosis to psychosis is, so to speak, also one of mental disorders that are analyzable to those that are not.

In the psychoanalytical model, a patient's location on the neurotic-psychotic continuum is based neither on the severity of the symptoms nor on the prognosis. Rather it is determined by the unconscious conflicts and developmental arrest resulting from the childhood environment. In other words, the location indicates the state of the underlying personality structure. The analyst identifies the state—that is, diagnoses the patient's illness—simply by conducting therapy and observing its results. The emphasis is less on diagnosing the illness than on explaining it.

Classical psychoanalysis has fallen out of favor for many reasons. Some of Freud's theories have been discredited (and he himself was careful to emphasize that he was "not a Freudian"), but those analysts who disagree with him have no way to prove that their modified concepts are better. This problem is inherent in the entire analytical approach.

Other psychiatrists struggle to conduct valid, reliable, large-scale studies of carefully selected patients in comparison to normal control subjects. Psychoanalysts have traditionally offered unprovable theories based

on patients seen in their private practices. Focused on intuitive interpretations of unconscious processes often expressed in vague, ambiguous,
metaphorical terms, classical psychoanalysis is much like a philosophy or
a religion. Some psychiatrists believe that as an explanation for mental
disorders, psychoanalytic theory is about as legitimate as demonic posses-
sion.

Isolated and subjective, each analyst's observation is determined by his
theoretical assumptions, clinical experience, and individual idiosyncra-
cies. The analyst bases his therapy on hypotheses intended to prove their
own validity for diagnosis and treatment. (The latter is considered effective if a patient whose therapy has ended does not return for more.) If an
assumption needs refinement, the analyst collects no data—he merely
rethinks it. The results of such an approach can be self-serving reports of
success and reasoning that is at best circular.

An analyst might say, for instance, that because borderline patients see
others as totally good or bad, this symptom indicates that a patient is
borderline, when in fact patients with narcissistic personality disorder do
the same thing. And the concept of BPD is controversial within the
psychoanalytic community itself. Without the methodology of descriptive psychiatry to determine exactly who is borderline and who is not,
there is no way to tell whether different analytical models of BPD have
been based on the same types of patients.

The continuum concept of mental disorders has been proved an oversimplification. Biological and genetic studies show, for example, that
psychoses differ from neuroses in kind, not degree. Such findings are
ignored by pure psychoanalysts, who refuse to prescribe medications
even to patients afflicted with an additional biological disorder or two.
Purists also ignore or minimize innate features that may contribute to a
psychiatric disorder, focusing exclusively upon the childhood environment.

Psychoanalysis raises serious ethical questions for some psychiatrists.
"The controlled treatment data for psychoanalytic psychotherapy with
borderlines are virtually nonexistent," says Dr. Liebowitz. "When
you're considering years and years of therapy at a cost of thousands and
thousands of dollars, it's really incumbent to demonstrate its efficacy. It
must be justifiable."[4]

Yet as it taps the realm from which come philosophy, the arts, and
other attempts to communicate the unmeasurable, psychoanalysis offers
explanations for thoughts, feelings, and behavior that many people simply *know* to be true. Often enough, later empirical studies prove psychoanalytical theory correct. And at least some efforts are underway to
demonstrate in research studies, as clearly as possible, the efficacy of
psychoanalytical psychotherapy.

Diversity and Distrust

These three branches of psychiatry—the observable, the measurable, and the intuitive—are split between the primarily scientific and the *psychodynamic* approaches to mental disorders. As we'll see, each side is further subdivided into factions that also are mutually exclusive and apparently irreconcilable. The assumptions, procedures, and emphases of psychiatrists in each group are considerably different and the source of great mutual distrust.

These preoccupations are presented in their respective categories of professional literature (to which we should add papers by psychologists offering the results of controlled tests of mental structures and processes). As Dr. Gunderson and Margaret T. Singer, Ph.D., have pointed out, descriptions of borderlines—or any other psychiatric patients—are thus influenced by who is describing them, what methods were used, in what context they were observed, and how the patient sample was selected. Each group's methodologies influence its findings, the authors note, rather "like packing a suitcase and then being surprised later to find what is in it when it is opened."[5]

This diversity of approaches to the study of mental disorders is precisely what makes each so valuable. To paraphrase an example offered by Thomas A. Aronson, M.D.,[6] using the earlier descriptions by Ingrid and Carla: psychotic episodes in borderlines are observable symptoms (the domain of phenomenological psychiatry) caused by alterations in perceptual processes in response to stress (biological psychiatry) caused, in turn, by underlying psychological disturbance (psychoanalytical psychiatry). Like other psychiatric symptoms, these could be analyzed far more meaningfully through a combined approach that allows for and does justice to different levels of discourse.*

Approaches to Borderline Personality Disorder

Some of the most highly respected specialists in BPD have in fact blended the different approaches in various ways. "There is no contra-

---

*A recognition over the past several years that social and cultural factors contribute to the development of mental disorders has helped promote such a comprehensive approach indicated, unfortunately, by a new buzzword: *biopsychosocial*.

diction between an interest in empirical research and in psychoanalytic theory and technique," says Dr. Kernberg. "I had a background in psychoanalysis but was trained in descriptive phenomenological German psychiatry at a time when, in this country, everything was going dynamic and psychoanalytic."

A different mixture appears in the backgrounds of other experts. "This is a very incestuous field," says Dr. Soloff:

> I trained at the Massachusetts Mental Health Center two years ahead of Rex Cowdry and two years after John Gunderson and Thomas McGlashan. I inherited some of Dr. McGlashan's patients at Mass Mental Health. He is an analyst, a brilliant man who became Director of Research at Chestnut Lodge and is now at Yale. It's a whole crowd of nice guys.
>
> Basically the orientation in the training program was a psychodynamic, psychoanalytic understanding of the patient. But Mass Mental Health, which is Harvard's major training program, was also a major site for the development of psychopharmacology. I don't put labels on myself, but that's a very typical Boston model of being well trained in both psychopharmacology and psychodynamic psychotherapy.

Other noted alumni include Drs. Adler and Buie, who are primarily psychoanalytical, and Dr. Gutheil, who is articulate in forensic, psychodynamic, biological, and behavioral psychiatry. Drs. McGlashan and Gunderson are also empiricists; the latter has made the greatest phenomenological contribution to the current definition of BPD. His training inclines Dr. Gunderson to examine psychodynamic features as one way of understanding the illness and generating operational criteria, but his scientific approach is very compatible with that of the St. Louis school.

Another group of researchers who have studied borderline patients might be called "organic phenomenologists." Psychiatrists like Dr. Liebowitz, Dr. Akiskal, and Donald F. Klein, M.D., allow that BPD can be influenced by psychosocial factors because they interpret "medical model" quite broadly. These researchers look for biological determinants and evidence associating BPD with other psychiatric disorders known to be organically based.

Larry J. Siever, M.D. (who worked with Dr. Gunderson as a resident), Paul A. Andrulonis, M.D., and other researchers take a psychodynamic approach to therapy with patients while doing research in the biology of BPD. Yet another pattern appears in the work of Michael H. Stone, M.D., known as "the great integrator," who incorporates several possibilities into a basic theoretical stance. Both historically and currently, the literature on BPD in particular illustrates the need for such integration.

Movements in Psychiatry

The history of BPD also illustrates some major movements in psychiatry, as we'll see in detail in the next chapter.

One of these has been a movement from Europe to America. "It has been said that the borderline concept is the best and the worst that America has given to world psychiatry," says Dr. Akiskal.[7] Although their predecessors had originated the term *borderline,* modern European psychiatrists don't recognize the current definition of BPD. This is not to suggest that there are no borderlines overseas (they have been described in Iceland, England, Scotland, Switzerland, Germany, France, Norway, Denmark, and Japan[8]), or that European psychiatrists are not curious about the concept—simply that the diagnosis as such is not widely accepted.*

Another movement has been from phenomenological and biological to psychoanalytical psychiatry and back. Throughout the history of medicine and philosophy, theorists have used the principles of astrology, anatomy, and physiology to construct biological explanations of illnesses, including psychiatric disorders. From its beginnings, psychiatry has attempted to be a medical science focused on the diagnosis, the classification, and later the treatment of mental disorders thought to be physiologically caused.

As Dr. Kroll points out, our having been raised in a post-Freudian era leads us to assume that psychiatrists always offered psychological explanations for behavior. Actually the few generations during which psychoanalysis held sway were the exception rather than the rule.

Psychoanalysis flourished in America roughly from 1910 into the 1970s (especially in the 1940s and 1950s), during which time it divided into various theoretical factions, some of which contributed to the bor-

---

*Of course, cultures vary in their tolerance of certain behaviors and thus in their definitions of abnormality. Russians, for example, commonly envy each other with a bitterness that American psychiatry would pathologize as narcissistic. "In Beirut," says Dr. Akiskal of his birthplace, "dependence and dramatization are healthy, paranoia is appropriate, and obsessive-compulsion is useful if present in your personal physician. Obsessive-compulsion is of course a virtue everywhere, including America. Independence and individuation are so valued in the United States that people with other personality traits are somehow deemed undesirable, if not outright flawed in character" (Discussion of the symposium "Comorbidity in Personality Disorders" at the 143rd annual meeting of the American Psychiatric Association, New York, 17 May 1990).

derline concept. It later lost much influence as the scientific branches again muscled their way to the forefront. This time they came armed with sophisticated descriptions and medications for the treatment of genetically and biologically caused mental disorders that had traditionally been considered hopeless. Its biological and phenomenological branches are what justify psychiatry today to insurance companies and to critics who have increasingly questioned its legitimacy.

But psychoanalysis is far from forgotten, especially in borderline theory. A movement away from classical psychoanalysis has made modern psychodynamic psychotherapy into much more of a dialogue between patients and therapists, who sit facing each other. Borrowed in part from object relations theory, ego psychology, and other schools of thought, evaluated as scientifically as possible, such modified psychoanalytic treatment has revitalized the field while enormously increasing the understanding of BPD.

The focus has correspondingly changed from observation of asylum inmates to reports on private patients in psychoanalysts' offices and back to the high-quality controlled studies of psychiatric inpatients that are standard today. This is not entirely fortunate. Modern concepts of BPD remain grounded in analysts' observations of their patients during the 1940s and 1950s. Like present-day outpatients, these earlier borderlines differed from the much smaller numbers of inpatients who are studied intensively today.

The location and type of hospital determine specifically what kinds of borderlines it is likely to treat. One hospital's patients may not speak for all. And the atmospheres as well as the treatment programs differ even between hospitals renowned for their borderline units. Feminist researchers at one hospital, for example, are revising psychoanalytical formulations of BPD associated primarily with a second hospital; the policies of both hospitals contrast with the unrestricted, open environment featured at a third.

An Imbroglio

Consistent throughout the history of BPD is the confusion and exasperation it has caused. John E. Mack, M.D., has in fact wondered whether "there ever has been in psychiatry a syndrome about which so much has been written while so little agreement has existed in regard to its phenomenology."[9] Historically the literature has included both psychiatric and psychoanalytical papers whose concepts represent overlapping lines of development. Therapists whose papers review the themes and approaches described by their predecessors often disagree on what these are, how many can be isolated, or how important each is. Or they agree on a trend, then disagree on whose work represents it.

The term *borderline* itself still bothers many researchers. Dr. Stone has observed that the name of every other psychiatric illness in *DSM-III-R* includes a descriptive term providing some information about it. *Manic-depressive psychosis* or *attention-deficit disorder* creates some picture of the sufferer. But *borderline* is unique in offering no clue at all.[10] Borderline to what? An article by Dr. Akiskal and his colleagues (expressing his view that BPD is a "useless concept") has an often-mentioned title: "Borderline: An Adjective in Search of a Noun."[11] More than one therapist has noted that in the psychiatric literature, *borderline* can modify a condition, syndrome, personality, state, character, pattern, and personality organization as well as the names of psychoses like schizophrenia.* These usages, as well as many other names BPD has had (over 30 by Dr. Soloff's count),[12] represent the attempts of theorists to master its difficulties.

Let us see then where this notion of a borderline came from.

Notes

1. Gerald Adler, M.D., paper [negative] read at debate, "Resolved: The Etiology of Borderline Personality Disorder Is Predominantly Biological," 143rd annual meeting of the American Psychiatric Association, New York, 16 May 1990.
2. See, for example, Samuel B. Guze, "Differential Diagnosis of the Borderline Personality Syndrome," in *Borderline States in Psychiatry,* ed. John E. Mack, M.D. (New York: Grune & Stratton, 1975), pp. 69–74.
3. My thanks to Bruce M. Pfohl, M.D., for discussing this branch of psychiatry with me.
4. Michael R. Liebowitz, M.D., paper [affirmative] read at debate, "Resolved: The Etiology of Borderline Personality Disorder Is Predominantly Biological," 143rd annual meeting of the American Psychiatric Association, New York, 16 May 1990.
5. John G. Gunderson and Margaret T. Singer, "Defining Borderline Patients: An Overview," in *Essential Papers on Borderline Disorders: One Hundred Years at the Border,* ed. Michael H. Stone, M.D. (New York: New York University Press, 1986), p. 457.
6. Thomas A. Aronson, M.D., "Historical Perspectives on the Borderline Concept: A Review and Critique," *Psychiatry,* Vol. 48 (August 1985), p. 218.
7. Hagop S. Akiskal, M.D., paper [affirmative] read at debate, "Resolved: The Etiology of Borderline Personality Disorder Is Predominantly Biological," 143rd annual meeting of the American Psychiatric Association, New York, 16 May 1990.
8. Anthony W. Bateman, "Borderline Personality in Britain: A Preliminary Study," *Comprehensive Psychiatry,* Vol. 30, No. 5 (September-October 1989), pp. 385–90; Thuridur Jonsdottir-Baldursson and Peter Horvath, "Borderline Personality Disordered Alcoholics in Iceland: Descriptions on Demographic, Clinical, and MMPI Variables," *Journal of Consulting and Clinical Psychology,* Vol. 55, No. 5 (October 1987), pp. 738–41; Paul S. Links, M.D., Meir Steiner, M.D., David R. Offord,

*In this book it is likewise broadly used—or rather, abused—for conciseness.

M.D., and Alan Eppel, M.D., "Characteristics of Borderline Personality Disorder: A Canadian Study," *Canadian Journal of Psychiatry*, Vol. 33, No. 5 (June 1988), p. 336; O. Mors, "Increasing Incidence of Borderline States in Denmark from 1970–1985," *Acta Psychiatrica Scandinavica*, Vol. 77, No. 5 (May 1988), pp. 575–83.

9. John E. Mack, M.D., ed., *Borderline States in Psychiatry* (New York: Grune & Stratton, 1975), p. 69.

10. Michael H. Stone, M.D., "Personal Reflections: Borderline Personality Disorder—Contemporary Issues in Nosology, Etiology, and Treatment," *Psychiatric Annals*, Vol. 20, No. 1 (January 1990), p. 8.

11. Hagop S. Akiskal, M.D., Shen E. Chen, M.D., Glenn C. Davis, M.D., Vahe R. Puzantian, M.D., Mark Kashgarian, M.D., and John M. Bolinger, M.D., "Borderline: An Adjective in Search of a Noun," *Journal of Clinical Psychiatry*, Vol. 46, No. 2 (1985), pp. 41–48. Another critique of the borderline concept is Hagop S. Akiskal, M.D., Boghos I. Yerevanian, M.D., Glenn C. Davis, M.D., Doug King, M.D., and Helio Lemmi, M.D., "The Nosologic Status of Borderline Personality: Clinical and Polysomnographic Study," *American Journal of Psychiatry*, Vol. 142, No. 2 (February 1985), pp. 192–98.

12. Paul H. Soloff, "Borderline Disorders," in *Handbook of Outpatient Treatment of Adults*, ed. Michael E. Thase, Barry A. Edelstein, and Michel Hersen (New York: Plenum, 1990), p. 310.

4

The Borderland
Frontier

When we have portrayed the history of the usages of the term "borderline" in psychiatry, we will have simultaneously defined the term. Its history is its meaning.

MICHAEL H. STONE, M.D.[1]

*A*ttempts to diagnose mental illnesses date back to the writings of Hippocrates, Plato and Aristotle. Although the term *psychiatry* was not used until the early 19th century, by then various physicians had published treatises on what we would now call delusions, psychosomatic illnesses, pharmacotherapy, forensic psychiatry, and biological and genetic factors contributing to psychosis.

Description and Classification

For much of its early history, the practice of psychiatry was relatively simple. Psychiatrists determined whether people were sane or insane. Rational people were considered sane, even if disturbed; they moved freely through a society that tolerated their "eccentricities." Those unable to reason were insane: they lost their legal rights and were committed to asylums. There psychiatrists observed their behavior, attempting to diagnose and classify mental illnesses on the basis of what they saw.

The borderline concept originated with the refinement

of this practice. French psychiatrist Philippe Pinel was the first to recognize that some "mad" people could still reason; in a treatise published in 1801, he referred to their disturbed emotions and behavior as *mania sans délire*. The term *moral insanity*, introduced in 1835 by English psychiatrist James Cowles Prichard, similarly referred to the disordered personalities and lack of self-control he observed in patients whose intellectual faculties remained intact. Prichard's extremely broad category included what would today be called BPD but encompassed some neurotic and psychotic illnesses as well.

By the late 19th century, psychiatric classification had evolved to vague recognition of these three major categories of mental illness. Insanity, which was considered hereditary, was now called *psychosis*. *Neurosis* was a catchall term for milder illnesses that had been incorporated into psychiatric study. Situated somewhere between these indistinct categories was a large nebulous group of seriously disturbed, rather perplexing patients.

A primitive notion that persisted through these diagnostic refinements was that mental illness represented moral degeneration. The adjective having become depreciatory, *moral* insanity was increasingly associated with psychopathy* and was in fact renamed *psychopathic inferiority*. Like other illnesses, psychopathic inferiority was considered hereditary, a conclusion that was subjective rather than scientific. Sound moral judgment dictated that criminals, for instance, had to be psychopathically inferior. The first "borderlines," then, as Stone points out, were actually nondelusional sociopaths.

Although the term *borderline* was not yet in use, many case histories began to appear that closely resemble those of patients so diagnosed today. In 1890, French psychiatrist Jean Pierre Falret described the symptoms of what he called *folie hystérique*. These included impulsivity, identity disturbance, inconsistent ideas and feelings, an odd kind of artificiality, and *splitting:* arbitrarily seeing others or oneself as good one moment, bad the next. Falret's countryman Pierre Janet eventually provided more extensive descriptions of such patients.

If these French psychiatrists seemed unusually gifted at description of mental illnesses, the genius for classification belonged to their German contemporary Emil Kraepelin.† In his influential textbook *Psychiatrie,* successive editions of which appeared through the turn of the century, Kraepelin divided the major psychoses into *manic depression* and *dementia*

---

*Today *psychopathy* refers to antisocial behavior, but back then it included what we now call personality disorders in general.
†Descriptive empiricists are now often referred to as *neo-Kraepelinians*.

praecox (schizophrenia). The latter he characterized as a severe, chronic disease that offered little hope for remission.

Kraepelin was the first to regard the borderline condition as a milder form of psychosis. In later editions he applied the widespread term *constitutional psychopathic inferiority* to the amorphous, quasipsychotic illnesses he noted. He also referred to their various permutations as constituting a "borderline" or "borderland" between normal eccentricity and psychosis.*

Eventually the term *psychopath* (and within the next few decades, *sociopath*) became restricted to those psychiatric patients who showed antisocial tendencies. Thus freed from this stigma, the remaining personality disturbances began to attract more attention.

Traditionally grounded in physiology, psychiatry was closely related to neurology at the turn of the century. It evolved from a descriptive into a dynamic science (that is, one concerned with internal, unconscious motivation) partly as a result of this association. Freud was a neurophysiologist, and although he launched the psychological investigation of the motives of behavior, he believed that ultimately his theories would be proved by what he called "a scientific psychiatry of the future."

Description Becomes Dynamic

Although allegedly neurotic, some of the famous case histories Freud published are today suspected of having been borderline, and his theories have contributed greatly to the understanding of that condition.

The dynamic quality of Freud's approach made psychoanalysis very appealing to psychiatrists interested in the psychoses. Freud called the psychoses *narcissistic neuroses* and considered them beyond help by psychoanalysis. Inspired by Freud's formulations and the resulting treatment alternatives, not all analysts accepted such reservations. Enthusiastic work with patients who seemed borderline to dementia praecox was one reason the two illnesses became linked.

Another was a 1911 textbook by Swiss psychiatrist Eugen Bleuler, who renamed dementia praecox *schizophrenia*. Bleuler believed that there was a spectrum of schizophrenic disorders, all arising from underlying emotional conflicts, certain of which were treatable. Challenging

---

*The first psychoanalytical writers on the subject would later confuse matters by likewise referring to both a *borderline* (a point on a spectrum of mild to severe illness) and a *borderland* (a distinct illness).

Kraepelin's pessimism, Bleuler described several recovered patients, including contemporaries of some note. Bleuler's diagnostic criteria for schizophrenic conditions were vague enough to allow therapists to identify milder forms of this psychosis. American psychoanalysts in particular began to find more and more borderline patients.

Originally the area between sanity and insanity, then, the borderline became that between neurosis and psychosis, then edged further toward the latter as *borderline schizophrenia*.

Some of the borderline schizophrenics described at this time would today be diagnosed as having schizotypal personality disorder. Their most noticeable symptoms included odd speech, paranoia, hypersensitivity, recurrent illusions, magical thinking, and aloof isolation.

Other borderline schizophrenics were reclassified by later writers as having an *affective disorder,* one in which a primary disturbance of mood gives rise to related symptoms like dramatic emotional changes, substance abuse, unstable relationships, impulsivity, and difficulty being alone. One writer who appeared to recognize that a patient could border either schizophrenic or manic-depressive (affective) psychosis was Clarence P. Oberndorf, who presented a case of each type in a 1930 paper.

An entire group of "affectively" borderline patients was described in 1925 by the Austrian psychiatrist Wilhelm Reich. Like Freud, Reich discovered that symptoms of what are now called the various personality disorders would appear during psychoanalysis as the patient tried to protect distressing memories and instincts from therapeutic investigation. In the process of breaking through such defenses, Reich amassed much new and important information, some of which appeared in his long paper on the *impulse-ridden character.* The irrational, melodramatic patients that Reich described were skilled at splitting, a symptom that became central to later psychoanalytical theories about BPD.

Reich was among the few writers of the 1920s who stressed the importance of the impulsive condition and frequently referred to *borderline* patients. The Hungarian psychiatrist Franz Alexander studied a large group of patients similar to Reich's and called them *neurotic characters* in a 1927 report. Other popular labels for borderline patients were *pre-schizophrenic* and *schizotypal,* the latter used in other than its present meaning. In 1928, the Polish psychiatrist Gustav Bychowski encouraged the use of a modified style of psychoanalysis for mildly schizophrenic and manic-depressive patients whom he called *latent psychotics* and found difficult to treat.

Five years later, the Russian psychiatrist Jacob Kasanin coined the term *schizoaffective* in a paper on the successful treatment of schizophrenic patients. Although Kasanin thought of his patients as bordering neurosis and psychosis, some of them, as his neologism suggests, were also *between* the schizophrenic and manic-depressive psychoses. As Stone notes, they were thus "double borderlines."

The Movement to America

The psychiatric papers of the 1930s and 1940s on this subject are the first really to show the influence of Freudian theory: borderline disorders are viewed strictly in terms of what psychological factors caused them, what defense mechanisms resulted, and whether such patients could be analyzed.

The borderline condition aroused interest particularly in the United States, where psychoanalysis was thriving. As Stone explains, those American psychiatrists who had traveled to Vienna to be analyzed by Freud were joined back home by many early psychoanalysts who had fled Nazi Europe.

America maintained less of a split than in Europe between psychiatry and psychoanalysis, hospital-based and outpatient therapy. This meant that psychiatrists did not treat *either* psychotic inpatients *or* neurotic outpatients: many therapists were interested in tackling the "borderline" illness even though they disliked that term.

The more congenially psychoanalytical atmosphere helps explain why BPD has been described and studied almost exclusively in America. The rest of this discussion will focus on its continued evolution here.

The contemporary concept of *borderline* was introduced in a remarkably fresh, comprehensive, and prescient paper published in 1938 by Adolph Stern. Although he considered the symptoms he observed to be "rather obscure phenomena," Stern believed that they characterized a distinct illness that could be called "borderline." (Seven years later, however, he described it as *occult schizophrenia*.)

In 1941 Gregory Zilboorg identified a very broad category of patients ranging from sexual perverts and murderers to far more innocuous people whose emotions, especially hatred and inner rage, affected their perceptions of reality; he called them *ambulatory schizophrenics*. Although similarly large and diverse, the group of patients described in 1947 by Melitta Schmideberg were labeled "borderlines"; in 1959 Schmideberg refined her diagnosis and described the typical borderline in an often quoted phrase as being "stable in his instability."

In 1942, Helene Deutsch coined the term *"as-if" personalities* to describe patients who unconsciously presented a demeanor that other people perceived as vaguely "wrong." People noticed, Deutsch wrote, that "the individual's whole relationship to life has something about it which is lacking in genuineness and yet outwardly runs along 'as if' it were complete."[2] Such patients identified completely with those on whom they depended. Tepid, formal, superficial, and empty, as-if personalities formed immature attachments in which they parasitically adopted the qualities of others whose affection they wished to sustain. The poor sense of identity that gave rise to such a character disorder had been described over 50 years earlier by Falret.

Another well-remembered term for a borderline condition was introduced in 1949 by Paul Hoch and Philip Polatin. Hoch and Polatin described a group of patients who had a wide variety of symptoms and deeper, more pervasive anxiety than neurotics but whose disturbances of thought and feeling were more characteristic of schizophrenia. The authors called these patients, who resembled Kasanin's schizoaffectives, *pseudoneurotic schizophrenics,* and they found high numbers of them in their practices. (In a 1955 article coauthored with Samuel L. Dunaif, Hoch changed the term to *pseudopsychopathic schizophrenia.*)

Stone favorably cites Donald Klein's opinion that some of Hoch and Polatin's patients actually had *formes frustes* of manic depression. Hoch and Polatin believed, however, that they were describing a genuine variant of schizophrenia. In a letter written to Roy R. Grinker, Sr., dated 7 February 1963, Hoch in fact stated as much, adding, "I believe borderline should be dropped completely because I do not know what borders on what."[3]

These are just the best known of the many names that have been applied to the variety of patients lumped together in the borderline twilight zone. In 1968, Grinker and his colleagues would note that one contributor to a panel on BPD thought that there existed a *pseudo-as-if character.*[4]

The Height of Psychoanalysis

But these categories of patients offered clues that would later be used to assemble workable definitions of BPD. Unlike true neurotic patients, borderlines lacked a firm sense of identity, disintegrated psychologically when subjected to psychoanalysis, and regressed to infantile feelings and behavior when hospitalized. But unlike true schizophrenics, borderlines could perceive reality and recover abruptly and unpredictably. By the start of the 1950s, when ever larger numbers of borderline patients were being reported, however, their symptoms were still diverse and unclear.

One of the first writers to focus on the development and motivation of borderline behavior was Robert Knight, who published two papers on the subject in 1953. Knight's papers represent the next major attempt after Stern to champion the term *borderline* and try to define it systematically. Although he assumed that the disorder was based in schizophrenia and used the term *psychotic character* to describe it (as did John Frosch in an influential series of papers starting in 1960), his work was a major impetus for distinguishing the two illnesses.

Knight saw the borderline condition not as a single syndrome but as a level of pathology between neurosis and psychosis. As such it encompassed various illnesses and so could present widely ranging symptoms, including immature defense mechanisms and an unstable sense of reality. Rather than preconceived assumptions from either psychiatry or psychoanalysis, a complete inventory of these symptoms was, Knight felt, the proper basis for diagnosis. Knight noted that borderlines might require supportive therapy, firm limit setting, or other atypical approaches to their psychoanalytic treatment.

In May 1954 and December 1955, the American Psychoanalytical Association held all-day panels on "The Borderline Case." Although many noted therapists attended them, these meetings did little to clarify the borderline concept further.

One interesting idea introduced at the second panel was Jan Frank's suggestion that borderline patients had egos that were genetically atypical but not necessarily defective. Frank mentioned several persons of genius and talent who might plausibly be diagnosed as borderline, a notion that remains provocative to celebrity watchers today.

At this panel, concern was expressed that the treatment modifications recommended by Knight and others for borderline cases might compromise psychoanalysis or at least not fit into its framework.

Such variations on classical psychoanalytic theory were in fact being offered by psychiatrists belonging to "the British object relations school": W. Ronald D. Fairbairn, Michael Balint, Donald W. Winnicott, Harry Guntrip, and a separate group more closely influenced by Melanie Klein. These theorists seldom used the term *borderline*. But following Klein's groundbreaking analyses of children, they extended psychoanalytical theory past the Freudian structure into the preoedipal period (prior to age four), where issues apparently more relevant to borderline than to neurotic illnesses were played out.

As the borderline concept evolved through the 1950s, its definitions grew increasingly dynamic without any one becoming standard. During the auspicious decade to follow, subgroups of patients to whom these

various definitions applied helped determine who was and was not borderline.

The 1960s

An important category of borderlines emerged in 1965, for example,
with the speculations of Barbara Ruth Easser and Stanley R. Lesser
concerning hysteric personalities. Hysterics were supposedly the healthiest neurotic character type, but the authors had encountered at least
some patients who appeared quite ill in a particularly infantile way. They
explained these patients basically by reexamining Falret's notion of folie
hystérique (which that earlier physician had likewise distinguished from
hysteria) from a psychoanalytic point of view.

These sicker hysterics, whom Easser and Lesser called *hysteroids* and
Donald Klein later named *hysteroid dysphorics,* were paradigmatic of borderlines as they are defined today. Viewing their symptoms as biologically determined, Klein complemented the psychoanalytical descriptions
of Easser and Lesser with the notion of constitutional predisposition. In
the late 1970s, he and Michael Liebowitz began studying the responsiveness of hysteroid dysphorics to antidepressants, especially monoamine
oxidase inhibitors (MAOIs).

Klein applied his theories also to the findings of Grinker, Beatrice
Werble, and Robert C. Drye, whose work was the next major advance
in the borderline concept after Knight's papers. In 1968 these authors
published a book in cooperation with the Chicago Psychoanalytic Institute that was the first empirical study of a large group of "borderline"
patients.

The borderline diagnosis had by now become a wastebasket for
poorly understood or intractable patients. Grinker, Werble, and Drye
objected to its vagueness and to the psychoanalytical interpretations of
the illness (what Grinker called "the Freudian Grand Theory") that had
become popular.

Having selected a group of 51 hospitalized young men and women
who clearly were not schizophrenic, the researchers translated the ego
functions of these patients into observable, quantifiable behavior and
then had the hospital staffs describe them in those terms. Using the
resulting data, they isolated four subtypes, each of which was later to be
validated by other investigators.

- The first subtype was an angry, negative, hostile, severely disturbed
  group, two of whom had become schizophrenic at followup.

That there was indeed a borderline illness similar to schizophrenia was confirmed the same year in a book published by Seymour S. Kety, David Rosenthal, Paul H. Wender, and Fini Schulsinger. It reported the results of the Danish Adoption Study of Schizophrenia: certain adopted schizophrenics had several close relatives raised in different environments who were borderline. They resembled Hoch and Polantin's pseudoneurotic schizophrenics. The Danish study thus scientifically confirmed the observations of Bleuler and later psychoanalysts while suggesting that the borderline condition could be biologically based as well.

The other three subtypes found in the Grinker, Werble, and Drye study were:

- a "core borderline group" to whom the current borderline diagnosis could be applied because of their turbulent relationships, overt anger and depression, acting-out behavior, and poor self-identity,
- an "as-if" group who were withdrawn, intellectualizing, blandly adaptive, and unemotional, and
- a mildly disturbed neurotic group who lacked self-confidence and were disposed toward clinging depression and anxiety.

In a 1977 article, Klein noted that except for the as-if personalities, Grinker's categories corresponded to groups of his own patients who responded to particular drugs. He suggested that most borderlines had affective disorders and should be subdivided on the basis of their medication responses.

Grinker, Werble, and Drye concluded otherwise: that despite its range of characteristics, the borderline was a specific, consistent, stable syndrome, the essential quality of which was defective or distorted ego functions. Their study had several important effects:

- It changed the focus of study from individually described outpatients to large groups of inpatients.
- By separating schizophrenic from "core" borderlines, it weakened the notion of a neurotic-borderline-psychotic continuum that was central to classical psychoanalytic theory. As Kroll notes, psychoanalysts had a vested interest in maintaining the concept of borderline schizophrenia because it proved that such a continuum existed. But as American psychiatry shifted away from psychoanalytic thought, the link between the two illnesses was discredited outside that framework.
- It established the borderline illness as a distinct entity within an empirical and scientific context.

Both this scientific validity and its psychoanalytical tradition are reflected in the definition of BPD that is used today.

Modern Concepts of BPD

Scrambling to counteract their decreasing influence in the field, psychoanalysts interested in the borderline condition proceeded to revise classical theory and treatment methods into an approach more suitable for these difficult patients. They gave up the borderline schizophrenia concept but salvaged the continuum by more or less turning it sideways. Most people would visualize a smooth continuum with indistinct, fluctuating boundaries as horizontal; modern analysts instead locate mental illnesses on what might be viewed as vertical levels of personality organization or functioning.* Although a patient can move up or down this stack over time, each level itself is a stable gradation from mild to severe illness. Seen within this framework, the borderline has shifted slightly *away* from psychosis onto its own level.

Modified psychoanalytical theory and treatment have been greatly inspired by the work of Kernberg, who during the 1960s began to establish the borderline condition as a separate entity *within* this realm. Kernberg's theories remain central within psychodynamic thinking about borderline conditions. His comprehensive framework synthesized the reports in earlier psychoanalytic writings into a coherent, precise, and practical approach to the illness. By presenting it as a pathological personality organization distinguished from psychosis by reality perception, Kernberg further discredited the concept of borderline schizophrenia. Drawing upon his background in descriptive psychiatry, he defined the borderline condition in terms of what it is *not* as well as what it *is,* thus underlining its specificity and stability.

Kernberg is the single most influential modern psychoanalytic theorist studying the borderline condition. But his writings are, as Hellerstein's earlier quotation suggests, "elegant and obscure," characterized by complex terminology and sophisticated reasoning that place them beyond the full intellectual grasp of many other therapists. And his definition of what he calls *borderline personality organization* is the broadest ever created: it could be applied to about 30 percent of the general population. Kernberg's work therefore leaves room for modification by other therapists.

According to Gunderson, Kernberg has stimulated interest in the borderline concept, set high standards for other researchers, and influenced his own thinking. In a 1975 article considered to be a landmark in the literature of that decade, Gunderson and Singer continued the work of

---

*Some analysts imagine four levels: psychotic, borderline, narcissistic, and neurotic.

Grinker and his colleagues in proposing a new, precise, scientifically based definition of the borderline. This definition demystified the borderline concept and made it accessible to the majority of therapists who are not analysts. Having enabled the concept to flourish, Gunderson's work continues to inspire and facilitate research by other investigators who feel compelled to match its scientific precision and accuracy.

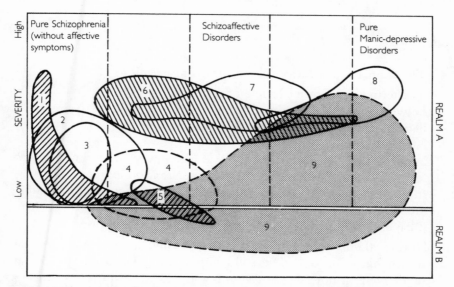

Michael H. Stone, M.D., "The Borderline Syndrome: Evolution of the Term, Genetic Aspects, and Prognosis," *American Journal of Psychotherapy*, Vol. 31 (1977), pp. 360–61. Reprinted with adapted caption by permission.

The figure above is one of several of Stone's different drawings (some three-dimensional) of concepts related to BPD. It shows the area between the schizophrenic and manic-depressive (affective) psychoses in which severe emotional disorders have been thought to exist.

The left vertical axis indicates the severity of the illness. On the right vertical axis, the illnesses located in Realm A are genetically related to either psychosis; those in Realm B are not.

The amoeba-like regions on the figure are some of the conceptualizations of BPD that have been summarized in this chapter:

1 *Ambulatory schizophrenia* of Zilboorg
2 *Borderline* of Schmideberg
3 *Borderline schizophrenia* of the Danish Adoption Study
4 *Borderline* of Knight
5 *As-if personality* of Deutsch
6 *Pseudoneurotic schizophrenia* of Hoch and Polatin
7 *Schizoaffective* of Kasanin
8 *Hysteroid dysphoria* of Donald Klein
9 *Borderline personality organization* of Kernberg

Each region represents *a group of patients*, some more ill than others, some showing genetic predisposition while others do not, and so forth.

The work of Kernberg, Gunderson and the authors of the Danish adoption study all contributed to the definition of BPD that appeared in *DSM-III* in 1980. By locating it once and for all in the general psychiatric community (who outnumber psychoanalysts by about ten to one), this official definition has greatly popularized the concept.

A Long Way to Go

To summarize the historical meanings of *borderline*:

- The term has referred to a line of demarcation
  between sanity and insanity (distinguished by the ability to reason),
  between neurosis and psychosis (distinguished by the ability accurately to perceive reality), and
  between analyzable and unanalyzable (distinguished by the ability to form and recognize transference and tolerate its interpretation).
- It has designated the milder end of a spectrum of schizophrenic disorders, and
- It has also been used as an adjective to modify various nouns.

Distinct theoretically as well as semantically, these usages are one reason the diagnosis of BPD is still being misused. David E. Reiser and Hanna Levenson note that *borderline* is abused by therapists to cover up diagnostic imprecision. BPD is still a wastebasket diagnosis, a label slapped on patients by therapists trying to pretend that their illness is understood.* It is used also to rationalize treatment mistakes or failures, to avoid prescribing drugs or other medical treatments, to defend against sexual issues that may have risen in therapy, to express hatred of patients, and to justify behavior resulting from such emotional reactions.[5]

Responses like these have been studied by Ruth Gallop, R.N., Ph.D., and her colleagues. Having asked psychiatric nurses how they would respond to hypothetical situations involving schizophrenic and borderline patients, the researchers found that the borderlines were less likely than the schizophrenics to receive empathy and caring from the nurses and more likely to be contradicted or belittled.[6]

One reason for this behavior is an interesting commentary on the history of the borderline concept. The nurses studied consider schizophrenics to be clearly ill, *biologically* disabled in their behavioral control. They are also more likely to respond positively to kind (as well as to

---

*In contrast, over the past several years George E. Vaillant, M.D., has given a talk entitled, "The Beginning of Wisdom Is Never Calling a Patient Borderline."

pharmacological) treatment. Borderlines, on the other hand, are supposedly "bad, not mad": they are viewed judgmentally because their undesirable behavior is considered more controllable and therefore deliberate.*

In this context, the term *borderline* thus connotes behavior in between the "fully controllable" (inexcusably bad) and "uncontrollable" (excusably mad).

The borderline concept has therefore come full circle also in terms of its pejorative connotations. A century ago, borderlines were considered examples of hereditary moral degeneration. More than other psychiatric patients, however, they are now belittled for *not* being biologically ill. Whether they actually are or are not "constitutionally inferior" is not especially relevant: borderlines have been condemned from their earliest history to the present day.

Yet its connotation does not entirely discredit the borderline concept. Dr. Adler explains:

> Labeling *borderline* pejoratively reflects the fact that like psychopaths or sociopaths, these patients elicit strong feelings from their therapists. But this doesn't take away from the usefulness of the concept, which depends on what you can do with it clinically. I find the borderline concept very useful even though these patients are obviously heterogeneous.[7]

The evolution of the borderline concept is often described by the metaphor of the blind men feeling the elephant, each describing a completely different animal. And this elephant runs in a herd, for the issues involved in defining BPD and diagnosing its sufferers encompass all of psychiatry, with no end in sight. As Patricia M. Chatham, Ph.D., writes, "The experts will continue to disagree over the precise etiologies and diagnostic criteria for a long time to come."[8]

Notes

1. Michael H. Stone, M.D., "The Borderline Syndrome: Evolution of the Term, Genetic Aspects, and Prognosis," *American Journal of Psychotherapy*, Vol. 31 (1977), p. 346. More detailed histories of the borderline concept can be found in the following sources, on which this discussion is based: Michael H. Stone, "1880s through 1920s" (pp. 5–13), "1930s and 1940s" (pp. 45–53), "1950s and 1960s" (pp. 149–58), "1970s and 1980s" (pp. 411–32), in *Essential Papers on Borderline Disorders: One Hundred Years at the Border*, ed. Michael H. Stone, M.D. (New York: New York University Press, 1986); "History

*This belief parallels the erroneous distinction in many people's minds between intense physical and emotional pain, the latter of which is considered less "legitimate."

of the Usage of the Term 'Borderline,' " in *The Borderline Syndromes: Constitution, Personality, and Adaptation* (New York: McGraw-Hill, 1980), pp. 5–33; John E. Mack, "Borderline States: An Historical Perspective," in *Borderline States in Psychiatry*, ed. John E. Mack, M.D. (New York: Grune & Stratton, 1975), pp. 1–27; Martin Leichtman, Ph.D., "Evolving Concepts of Borderline Personality Disorders," *Bulletin of the Menninger Clinic*, Vol. 53 (1989), pp. 229–49; Thomas A. Aronson, "Historical Perspectives on the Borderline Concept: A Review and Critique," *Psychiatry*, Vol. 48 (August 1985), pp. 209–22; Jerome Kroll, M.D., "Introduction" (pp. xi–xiii) and "The Politics and Economics of the Borderline Diagnosis" (pp. 3–25), in *The Challenge of the Borderline Patient: Competency in Diagnosis and Treatment* (New York: Norton, 1988); John G. Gunderson and Margaret T. Singer, "Defining Borderline Patients: An Overview," in Stone, ed., *Essential Papers*, pp. 453–74; William N. Goldstein, M.D., "Current Dynamic Thinking Regarding the Diagnosis of the Borderline Patient," *American Journal of Psychotherapy*, Vol. 41, No. 1 (January 1987), pp. 4–22; Roy R. Grinker, Sr., Beatrice Werble, and Robert C. Drye, "An Overview of the Literature," in *The Borderline Syndrome: A Behavioral Study of Ego-Functions* (New York: Basic Books, 1968), pp. 9–22.

2. Helene Deutsch, "Some Forms of Emotional Disturbance and Their Relationship to Schizophrenia," in Stone, ed., *Essential Papers*, p. 75.

3. Grinker, Werble, and Drye, p. 20.

4. Ibid., p. 21.

5. David E. Reiser, M.D., and Hanna Levenson, Ph.D., "Abuses of the Borderline Diagnosis: A Clinical Problem with Teaching Opportunities," *American Journal of Psychiatry*, Vol. 141, No. 12 (December 1984), pp. 1528–32.

6. Ruth Gallop, R.N., Ph.D., W. J. Lancee, M.Sc., and Paul Garfinkel, M.D., "How Nursing Staff Respond to the Label 'Borderline Personality Disorder,' " *Hospital and Community Psychiatry*, Vol. 40, No. 8 (August 1989), pp. 815–19.

7. Gerald Adler, M.D., paper [negative] read at debate: "Resolved: The Etiology of Borderline Personality Disorder Is Predominantly Biological," 143rd annual meeting of the American Psychiatric Association, New York, 16 May 1990.

8. Patricia M. Chatham, *Treatment of the Borderline Personality* (New York: Jason Aronson, 1985), p. 23.

5

The Official
Definition—and
What's Wrong
With It

Some believed that the borderline concept represents everything that is wrong with American psychiatry . . .

ROBERT L. SPITZER, M.D.[1]

The offical definition of BPD—that used in this book— was formulated in the late 1970s for inclusion in *DSM-III*. Although this edition was an enormous advance over the previous manual, many therapists believe that its diagnostic criteria for BPD leave much to be desired.

The History

The diagnostic manual was written by the Task Force on Nomenclature and Statistics of the APA under the direction of Robert L. Spitzer, M.D. Members of this committee at first hesitated even to include in *DSM-III* a paradigm of the borderline conditions described in the literature. The borderline concept had little scientific validity; it was steeped in unprovable theories, and its usage was confusing. Others felt, however, that the concept could be useful if defined by reliable criteria. All agreed that the patient population was large enough to merit an attempt to capture it.

It seemed to the committee that by this time the borderline concept was being used in two ways. One usage, found in the writings of Drs. Kernberg and Gunderson and Singer, referred to a collection of chronic personality features, especially instability and vulnerability, that profoundly influenced the patient's life and treatment prospects. The committee referred to this concept as *unstable personality*.

The second usage was a holdover from borderline schizophrenia represented in the Danish adoption study and in the committee members' consultations with its authors. Referring to a stable form of pathology that seemed genetically related to schizophrenia, this concept was named *schizotypal personality* by the committee.

Neither borderline concept had specific sets of criteria by which to define it. (A 1978 article by J. Christopher Perry, M.P.H., M.D., and Gerald Klerman, M.D., for instance, compared the criteria of Knight, Grinker, Kernberg, and Gunderson and found little similarity.[2]) Nor was it clear whether the two usages were distinct.

The committee therefore consulted with the various authors and with their help drew up tentative sets of criteria for each personality type. They then assembled these two sets of items (along with others not specific to borderlines) into a questionnaire sent to 4,000 members of the APA whose training and inclinations ranged from heavily psychoanalytical to primarily medical. They asked the psychiatrists to test the validity of the criteria by applying them to two patients, a borderline and a nonborderline. Of those mailed, 808 completed questionnaires were returned (along with some blank ones whose recipients had written, "I don't believe in this concept").

Having analyzed the results, the task force was satisfied that the unstable and schizotypal personalities were distinct and well defined by their suggested criteria (although half the borderline patients described had both diagnoses). They therefore split the borderline concept into two separate personality disorders.

The criteria for each disorder showed greater consensus than the names proposed for them. Proponents of the borderline schizophrenia concept accepted the term *schizotypal personality disorder*. Those who favored the other concept, however, argued that *unstable personality* was a misnomer, invoking Schmideberg's description of the borderline personality as "stably unstable." The name chosen instead was *borderline personality disorder*.

The Personality Clusters

During this process, schizotypal personality disorder was not only split off from BPD but also banished to another category of personality disorders. Referred to in *DSM-III* as "clusters," the three categories are

- Cluster A, the "odd, eccentric" group, which includes the schizotypal, paranoid, and schizoid personality disorders,
- Cluster B, the "dramatic, emotional, erratic" group, which includes the borderline, narcissistic, histrionic, and antisocial personality disorders, and
- Cluster C, the "anxious, fearful" group, which includes the avoidant, dependent, obsessive-compulsive, and passive-aggressive personality disorders.

Some therapists consider these categories arbitrary. For example, Theodore Millon, Ph.D., a member of the *DSM-III* Task Force and the Advisory Committee on Personality Disorders, claimed that he "never quite understood the importance of those dimensions that led us to cluster personality disorders in the manner described."[3]

Others see meaningful relationships between the illnesses within each cluster. Another way of viewing the clusters has been suggested by Dr. McGlashan, for instance, who notes that personality disorders, especially those in Cluster B, are essentially illnesses of interaction with others:

- People with Cluster A personality disorders withdraw: they do not want from others.
- Cluster B people exploit: they want from others without seeing or responding to what others want from them. They likewise give to others what they think others *should* want instead of what others *do* want, denying them distinct rights or feelings.
- Cluster C people comply: they want from others but accommodate to others' wants to avoid conflict.[4]

Another justification for the clusters is that the boundaries between all of the personality disorders are fuzzy at best, and BPD in particular tends to overlap with its neighbors in Cluster B. To compare it briefly to:

- *Antisocial personality disorder:* The borderline exploits people impulsively as an angry yet ambivalent response to disappointment and frustration. The antisocial more successfully does so as a coldly calculated means toward personal gain that seldom includes borderline self-destructiveness or desperation to be liked.
- *Narcissistic personality disorder:* In contrast to borderline dependence

and fear of solitude, narcissistic (and antisocial) personalities are more detached and self-centered. Narcissists are more stable and successful both socially and professionally, partly from having used others to boost and maintain their fragile self-esteem.

- *Histrionic personality disorder:** Similar to borderlines in their clinging dependence, manipulation, and desire for attention, histrionic personalities are less hostile and self-destructive, more stable, flamboyant, and likely to feel well in general. In contrast to the borderline's difficulties with sexuality, the histrionic has relationships, self-esteem issues, and pathology that are heavily sexualized and bound up with physical attractiveness.[5]

The relationship between the borderline and schizotypal personality disorders remains controversial. Distinctions between the two have been shown in an adoptive study,[6] in a twin study,[7] in drug studies,[8] and in clinical observations.[9] Yet the degree of overlap between the disorders reported in various groups of patients has ranged from 7 to 58 percent.[10] Stanley P. Kutcher, M.D., and his colleagues have found electrophysiological abnormalities unique to borderline and schizotypal patients; these data strongly suggest that the two illnesses are variants of a single disorder related to schizophrenia.[11]

The overlap between the borderline and other personality disorders is important because a patient's prognosis depends partly on which condition is dominant. A histrionic borderline, for instance, has a better prognosis than an antisocial one.

An estimated two-thirds of borderline patients have one other personality disorder, and one-third have at least two others. Researchers aren't sure whether the illnesses occur together, they have a common underlying cause, one personality disorder causes the other(s), or there is simply a resemblance between the diagnostic criteria.[12] They have enough to do for the time being to determine what there might be about BPD, other than its difficulty, that makes the illness unique.

The Definition

. The criteria for BPD listed in *DSM-III* and its revision, *DSM-III-R,* focus on pervasive instability of mood, behavior, relationships, and self-image.[13] This instability must appear by early adulthood in at least five of eight symptoms that are rearranged here under those focal points:

*Dr. Kernberg particularly dislikes the accepted definitions of histrionic and antisocial personality disorders, the latter of which, he says, is "hopelessly mixed up."

EMOTIONS

1. Emotional instability: shifts in mood lasting usually only a few hours.
2. Inappropriate, intense, or uncontrollable anger.
"Borderlines have floods of emotions, as if a dam breaks," says Melanie.

When I finally let out all my emotions in the hospital, I lost all maturity, all sense of being an adult. I just threw a major huge temper tantrum. It sounds weird, but it felt like a relief, a release, as if I had crossed the line and now was free to do whatever I wanted. And in a very primitive way, I did, through fighting, yelling, kicking people. . . .

When the emotions break loose, and they still do, it's like my total insides change. There's no way of stopping it. It's like a hemophiliac bleeding.

Melanie's description implies an important point: that some borderlines achieve excessive control over their anger.

BEHAVIOR

3. Specifically self-destructive acts like recurrent suicidal threats and gestures or self-mutilation.
Even a hospital setting cannot always protect a borderline from her terrible compulsion to hurt herself. Former inpatients describe vomiting, punching walls, drinking bleach, cutting themselves with broken light bulbs or wood chips, scalding themselves in the shower, and attempting to hang or electrocute themselves.

4. Potentially self-damaging impulsiveness (excluding that in #3) in at least two forms like substance abuse, compulsive spending, sexual promiscuity or per-version, eating disorders, shoplifting, reckless driving.*
A study by Rebecca A. Dulit, M.D., and her colleagues isolated a sub-group of patients who were no longer diagnosable as borderline when substance abuse was not used as a criterion. The researchers suggest that this group either has a milder form of BPD than the rest of the sample or shows borderline symptoms caused primarily by substance abuse.[14]

---

*In the psychiatric literature, terms like *promiscuity* and *perversion* are often misused in a moral and social sense to condemn certain behaviors, specifically those outside the common experience of nice middle-aged married white male psychiatrists. Actually, any form of sexual expression should be pathologized, or even criticized, only if it can harm oneself (as noted here) or others.

RELATIONSHIPS

5. Unstable, chaotic, intense relationships characterized by splitting.
"When I asked my therapist what my diagnosis was and he said borderline, I laughed, because I had conducted my life on the borders of
everything—never getting involved, never committing myself, going
from one boyfriend to the next," says 32-year-old "Sharon," who has
been beaten and raped by a series of violent men.

Borderlines describe their disturbed relationships as what Melanie
calls "the big number one topic with us." Some borderlines avoid people altogether; others constantly move in and out of abusive relationships; others earn affection as caretakers; all have difficulty getting close
to people physically, emotionally, or both.

One reason that borderlines can't maintain relationships is that many
of them are extremely mistrustful, even to the point of paranoia, without
knowing exactly why. Some spend years in psychiatric hospitals lying to
the staffs because of this fear or that of driving people away.

"Even if a borderline is doing well, a relationship with one can be
destructive," says Alice, who has had this experience with other former
patients.

Although focused on relationships in general, many borderlines are
unusually uncomfortable about their sexuality. Some are stereotypically
promiscuous; others are proceeding into their thirties with no loss of
virginity in sight, and still others try having sex a few times and then quit,
wondering what all the excitement is about. A considerable minority
appear to be homosexual, bisexual, or undecided.

*6. Frantic efforts (excluding those in #3) to avoid actual or anticipated aban-
donment.*
This criterion was changed from "intolerance of being alone" in *DSM-
III* to make it more behavioral and objectifiable for study. Many psychiatrists object to this change, which seems to me an improvement: comparatively few, if any, borderlines can tolerate a sense of abandonment,
but many choose to be solitary. Dr. Grinker and other researchers have
in fact described borderlines as "isolates" who use withdrawal as a defense.[15]

IDENTITY

7. Marked, persistent identity disturbance shown by uncertainty in at least two areas like self-image, sexuality, career choice or other long-term goals, friendships, values.

Many borderlines must struggle not to remain in or regress back into their illness because part of them wants to maintain that identity. Recovering borderlines themselves marvel at the tenacity of those they left behind. "I have no idea why anybody would want to hold onto this illness," says 23-year-old "Rebecca." "It is the worst experience anybody could go through." The reason is an identity crisis so severe that the choice is one of being borderline or being nothing.

8. Chronic feelings of emptiness or boredom.

To diagnose patients according to these criteria, therapists use the Structured Clinical Interview for *DSM-III-R* (called SCID-II), which was developed along with *DSM-III* to test for the presence of all 11 personality disorders.

DSM-III ended—well, almost ended*—the tradition of inventing names for the illness by officially calling it borderline personality disorder. Like other medical classifications, those in *DSM-III-R* are intended as starting points for further research.

The Criticisms

Their status as phenomenological diagnostic categories is one criticism of both *DSM-III* definitions of BPD: they reduce the illness to a set of symptoms without reference to underlying psychological structure. Here simplicity helps create confusion. The definition is a checklist of criteria, each of equal importance, that offers no means of understanding the illness. "It is of no help in treatment planning," says John F. Clarkin, Ph.D., "merely a hodgepodge of criteria by committee."

---

*Dr. Gunderson observes that a 1982 book by Donald B. Rinsley, M.D., is titled *Borderline and Other Self Disorders;* a 1984 book by William W. Meissner, M.D., is titled *The Borderline Spectrum.* He himself offers another meaning of *borderline:* the experience of uncertainty inherent in work with such patients "is a continuous reminder of the thin border of attachment and rationality within ourselves" (*Borderline Personality Disorder,* pp. 178–79).

Because *DSM-III-R* uses categories rather than measurements, a patient either has the illness or has not. Unlike the media stereotype of BPD as different in degree from wellness, the *DSM-III-R* definition is based on differences in kind. To psychoanalysts, who have traditionally located BPD on a continuum of severity, this creates particular difficulty.*

Another criticism is that any five of the eight criteria are required for diagnosis. This means that a patient could have every symptom *except* identity disturbance, impulsivity, and inappropriate anger and still be borderline according to *DSM-III-R* (although not according to either Dr. Kernberg or Dr. Gunderson). As Dr. Stone points out, the definition allows for 93 possible combinations of criteria (as opposed to 6 combinations in Dr. Gunderson's definition), so that some *DSM-III-R* borderlines hardly resemble others. And the existence or severity of each symptom can fluctuate in each borderline, making the diagnosis equally as unstable.

While to psychoanalysts the *DSM-III-R* definition of BPD is too narrow, to scientific psychiatrists, it's too broad. It is often applied to patients who seem nothing like the borderlines originally presented in the psychoanalytic literature. Although the Task Force sought to create a consensus of psychoanalytical and scientific thinking, the result pleases neither side.

The "Affectophiles"

One of the biggest criticisms of the *DSM-III-R* definition has been its highly controversial emphasis on the link between BPD and affective disorders. Modern borderlines are viewed primarily as very angry, depressed, unreasonable patients who may or may not be genetically prone toward a major or manic-depressive disorder.

The link between BPD and affective disorder does not necessarily imply a cause-and-effect relationship. It does, however, represent another general trend in psychiatry—that of today overdiagnosing affective disorders instead of schizophrenic ones. Affective illnesses are especially popular because their study attracts research funding and has been characterized by breakthroughs in antidepressant medication, cognitive therapy, and other tested forms of treatment.

*Some researchers are responding by scaling each of the criteria with cutoff points to identify their intensity. Clarkin and Stephen W. Hurt, Ph.D., for instance, are breaking down the criteria into related symptoms they call the Impulse, Affect, and Identity clusters (not to be confused with "clusters" of personality disorders).

While this characterization of BPD may result partly from the method used by the Task Force to define it, some researchers have suggested that more insidious reasons are involved. Notable among the hypotheses is that of Dr. Kroll, who believes that the borderline-affective link was made for political and economic rather than scientific reasons.[16]

Within the context of Dr. Kroll's argument, *borderline* acquires yet another meaning: between medical and psychodynamic treatment. Psychoanalytic psychiatrists want to maintain their hold on BPD, the one severe, long-term condition for which their treatment approaches still maintain credibility.

Some biologically and phenomenologically oriented psychiatrists meanwhile want BPD reclassified as an affective disorder for which the preferred treatment would be antidepressant medication. Insurance companies cover psychiatric care only for biological conditions like the psychoses. By presenting BPD to third-party payers as a medical condition, psychiatrists can attract the large borderline population away from nonmedical therapists like psychoanalysts, psychologists, and social workers.

Such maneuvers are the work of an outspoken and apparently powerful group of psychiatrists whom Dr. Kroll has dubbed the *affectophiles*. Their differences from their psychodynamic brethren seem to be as economic as they are theoretical.

Dr. Kroll likewise suggests that the reason the borderline, narcissistic, and histrionic personality disorders overlap so heavily is that "These three disorders in particular were teased apart in committee action to satisfy demands of different psychiatric constituencies."[17]

"I don't quite understand Dr. Kroll's logic," says Dr. Spitzer, who admires and likes him.

The definition wasn't that controversial. The *DSM-III* criteria were based on our empirical study, whose data speak for themselves. I don't know what this lobbying was or what the political considerations were. Nor do I consider the affective symptoms to be that prominent. Only one criterion refers to mood changes, and I doubt that anybody would disagree that mood changes are part of the borderline syndrome.

The Ninth Criterion

Although the situation has changed with the advent of *DSM-IV* (scheduled for publication in 1992), its political aspects apparently have not. The current issue is that of whether or not to add a cognition criterion to the BPD definition that would reinstate such symptoms. "It is a political reality," says Dr. Gunderson,

> that the reason this criterion did not get into *DSM-III* has to do less with any of the clinical literature or the input from advisors than with Dr. Spitzer's dominance. Psychotic–like states, paranoia, and failure of reality testing in response to stress have been central to the construct of the borderline personality and had been verified empirically by several groups as one of its most useful discriminating features.

As we'll see in the next chapter, these symptoms are stressed by Dr. Kernberg as well as considered fundamental by Dr. Gunderson. "I asked Dr. Gunderson while we were working on *DSM-III* and *DSM-III-R*— and I have asked him again during the *DSM-IV* debates—for case examples so that I could better understand what he was referring to," says Dr. Spitzer. "He never provided these cases.* He may be right, but I'm still unconvinced."

The controversy about the cognition criterion has created a delicate situation for Dr. Gunderson. As chairman of the Advisory Committee on Personality Disorders, he says that

> it's a strange position to be chairman of a committee and have an advocate role on a controversial issue. On the one hand, you might want to use that position to have things your way; on the other hand, I actually feel more inhibited in terms of taking any kind of advocacy role because I'm supposed to reflect the field. That's why the support from almost all of the advisors on this issue has been very important.

Of the 23 experts on BPD who have acted as advisors, 18 favor including a cognition criterion. The remaining 5 disagree for two reasons. One is their belief that research has provided insufficient empirical support for this change. "The studies Dr. Gunderson keeps mentioning as showing psychotic symptoms to be an essential part of BPD have included schizotypal patients," says Dr. Spitzer, a special advisor to the Task Force on *DSM-IV*.

The other is that adding a ninth criterion might unpredictably change certain patients' eligibility to be diagnosed as borderline, thus creating a discontinuity in the research literature. "I think another reason there has been such resistance to it is that everyone wants to believe that people

---

*A survey of vignettes illustrating such cognitive symptoms as suggested by Dr. Spitzer is being prepared for publication by Stephen Sternbach, M.D., and his colleagues.

either are psychotic or they're not, and the idea of somebody being a little psychotic or sometimes psychotic is threatening," says Dr. Gunderson. "It confounds a basic concept within psychiatry and maybe society at large."

Another major figure in the *DSM-IV* definition of BPD is Allen J. Frances, M.D., the present chairman of the Task Force, who has distanced himself from the issue but appears opposed to a ninth criterion. "Dr. Frances conducted one of the few research studies that did *not* show psychotic symptoms to be prominent in BPD," says Dr. Gunderson.

> Perhaps this reason or perhaps a desire to avoid all the controversy could explain his opposition.
>
> On the other hand, we have a number of research efforts ongoing that may help settle the issue one way or the other. I don't know that Dr. Frances would be strongly opposed to a recommendation that our committee felt confident about and is, I think, watching. I don't know what's going to happen with the cognitive criterion, but we'll probably reach some closure on it in the next year.*

In medical articles, *N* means number; it has been pointed out to me that the ninth criterion might appear not in *DSM-IV* but in *DSM-**N***.

A Life of Its Own

In the midst of all this lobbying, it's reasonable to pause and ask just where borderline patients themselves fit in. In one sense, they don't fit in very well, according to a recent study by Mary C. Zanarini, Ed.D., and her colleagues. These researchers found that the *DSM-III-R* criteria are too broad compared to the other means by which therapists diagnose borderlines: specialized semistructured interviews and the clinician's sense of how severly ill the patient is and how far the illness has progressed. "The *DSM* has taken on a life of its own politically, financially, and in many other ways," says Zanarini,

> It has become reified to the point at which trainees in particular take it as fact carved in stone rather than derived in a human way. We need to remember that these criteria are clinical concepts and that our research diagnoses need to match up well with the clinical standards from which they originally came.[18]

*Dr. Frances declined to be interviewed for this book or to add to the discussion here.

Therapists have tried to approximate such clinical standards by instead using some of the dozen or so other diagnostic tools developed over the past two decades. The best known of these is the Diagnostic Interview for Borderline Patients (DIB), created by Dr. Gunderson and his colleagues in 1981 and revised in 1989, and the Presumptive Diagnostic Elements (1967) and Structural Interview (1981) created by Dr. Kernberg. We should see, then, why the work of these two psychiatrists in particular has been so influential.

Notes

1. Robert L. Spitzer, M.D., Jean Endicott, Ph.D., and Miriam Gibbon, M.S.W., "Crossing the Border Into Borderline Personality and Borderline Schizophrenia," *Archives of General Psychiatry*, Vol. 36 (January 1979), p. 17. The development of the *DSM-III* definition of borderline personality disorder is fully described in this article, upon which my discussion is based.
2. J. Christopher Perry, M.P.H., M.D., and Gerald L. Klerman, M.D., "The Borderline Patient: A Comparative Analysis of Four Sets of Diagnostic Criteria," *Archives of General Psychiatry*, Vol. 35 (February 1978), pp. 141–50.
3. Theodore Millon, *Disorders of Personality: DSM-III: Axis II* (New York: Wiley, 1981), p. 63.
4. Thomas H. McGlashan, M.D., and Robert K. Heinssen, Ph.D., "Narcissistic, Antisocial, and Noncomorbid Subgroups of Borderline Disorder: Are They Distinct Entities by Long-Term Clinical Profile?" *Psychiatric Clinics of North America*, Vol. 12, No. 3 (September 1989), pp. 668–69.
5. Thomas A. Widiger, Ph.D., and Allen J. Frances, M.D., "Epidemiology, Diagnosis, and Comorbidity of Borderline Personality Disorder," in *Review of Psychiatry*, Vol. 8, ed. Allan Tasman, M.D., Robert E. Hales, M.D., and Allen J. Frances, M.D. (Washington, D.C.: American Psychiatric Press, 1989), p. 17.
6. Miron Baron, M.D., Rhoda Gruen, M.A., Lauren Asnis, M.S., and Sally Lord, M.S.W., "Familial Transmission of Schizotypal and Borderline Personality Disorders," *American Journal of Psychiatry*, Vol. 142, No. 8 (August 1985), pp. 927–34.
7. Svenn Torgersen, CandPsychol., "Genetic and Nosological Aspects of Schizotypal and Borderline Personality Disorders: A Twin Study," *Archives of General Psychiatry*, Vol. 41 (June 1984), p. 554.
8. Paul H. Soloff, M.D., "Borderline Disorders," in *Handbook of Outpatient Treatment of Adults*, ed. Michael E. Thase, Barry A. Edelstein, and Michel Hersen (New York: Plenum, 1990), p. 316.
9. Michael H. Stone, M.D., *The Fate of Borderline Patients: Successful Outcome and Psychiatric Practice* (New York: The Guilford Press, 1990), p. 152.
10. Richard J. Kavoussi, M.D., and Larry J. Siever, M.D., "Overlap Between Borderline and Schizotypal Personality Disorders," *Comprehensive Psychiatry*, in press.
11. S. P. Kutcher, D. H. R. Blackwood, D. F. Gaskell, W. J. Muir, and D. M. St. Clair, "Auditory P300 Does Not Differentiate Borderline Personality Disorder from Schizotypal Personality Disorder," *Biological Psychiatry*, Vol. 26 (1989), pp. 766–74.
12. Widiger and Frances, p. 16.
13. American Psychiatric Association, *DSM-III-R: Diagnostic and Statistical Manual of Mental Disorders*, 3rd ed., rev. (Washington, D.C.: American Psychiatric Association, 1987), pp. 346–47. Copyright © 1987, the American Psychiatric Association. Adapted with permission.
14. Rebecca A. Dulit, M.D., Minna R. Fyer, M.D., Gretchen L. Haas, Ph.D., Timothy Sullivan, M.D., and Allen J. Frances, M.D., "Substance Use in Borderline Personality Disorder," *American Journal of Psychiatry*, Vol. 147, No. 8 (August 1990), pp. 1002–7.
15. Susan N. Ogata, Ph.D., Kenneth R. Silk, M.D., and Sonya Goodrich, Ph.D., "The Childhood Experience of the Borderline Patient," in *Family Environment and Borderline Personality Disorder*, ed. Paul S. Links, M.D., M.Sc., F.R.C.P.(C) (Washington, D.C.: American Psychiatric Press, 1990), p. 99.

16. Jerome Kroll, M.D., *The Challenge of the Borderline Patient: Competency in Diagnosis and Treatment* (New York: Norton, 1988), pp. 3–10, 16–25.

17. Ibid., p. 6.

18. Zanarini's comment is from her presentation of a paper at the 143rd annual meeting of the American Psychiatric Association, New York, 16 May 1990. The revised paper is Mary C. Zanarini, Ed.D., John G. Gunderson, M.D., Frances R. Frankenburg, M.D., Deborah L. Chauncey, A.B., and Joan H. Glutting, B.A., "The Face Validity of the *DSM-III* and *DSM-III-R* Criteria Sets for Borderline Personality Disorder," *American Journal of Psychiatry*, Vol. 148, No. 7 (July 1991), pp. 870–74.

6

"Borderline by All Criteria"

"In the hospital, they tried to explain to us about borderline personality disorder and borderline personality organization, and I'm really glad you're writing a book so that I can finally understand all of it."

"ESTHER"

Melanie's observation that BPD is just "not nailed down" in *DSM-III* is shared by most therapists. One indication is that articles in the psychiatric literature describe patients who are "borderline by all criteria (Kernberg, Gunderson, *DSM-III*)."* Other psychiatrists attempt to compensate for the inadequacies of *DSM-III-R* by diagnosing borderline patients as would these two investigators.

Dr. Kernberg's Borderline Personality Organization

The renaissance of psychoanalytic theory in the 1960s is typified by Dr. Kernberg's highly influential concept of the borderline condition, which he has intended not to replace but to supplement the standard diagnosis with a deeper level of analysis.

Nevertheless, Dr. Kernberg's ideas not only differ from

---

*Because *DSM-III-R* made only minor revisions to the diagnostic criteria established by *DSM-III*, references to both versions are often to the latter.

classical psychoanalysis in theory but also improve upon it in practice. His work is psychoanalytical inquiry that offers a means to evaluate it empirically. As had Dr. Grinker and his colleages, Dr. Kernberg has described his propositions in observational terms that can be tested for reliability and validity.

Like Dr. Gunderson also, who tightened the borderline definition phenomenologically, Dr. Kernberg did so psychoanalytically. Dr. Kernberg's most recent book is, in fact, a handbook offering "a detailed and operational description of a therapy for borderline patients."[1] It presents the findings of the Borderline Psychotherapy Research Project underway in Dr. Kernberg's department.

When Dr. Kernberg first sought to integrate his interests in research, psychoanalysis, and descriptive psychiatry, however, the only such long-term project in existence was at the Menninger Foundation, where he began working in 1961. In the past, Robert Knight had been director of Adult Clinical Services, and his concept of borderline was used there. Dr. Kernberg disagreed, however, with the diagnoses of (and the treatment methods used for) many of the patients. In studying their cases, he found

> a mixture of clinical description and inferences. I had to sort out the descriptive part from the theory, which in turn made it necessary for me to define the terms that I was going to use. So I worked on the theory simultaneously with the clinical description.

Following the research subjects and treating his own patients, Dr. Kernberg developed a theoretical and therapeutic framework that integrates the thinking of the British object relations school with the ego psychology approaches developed at the Menninger Foundation.

Dr. Kernberg's concept is that of *borderline personality organization* (BPO). As Dr. Stone's amoeba map suggests, Dr. Kernberg's is an enormous category including patients with all kinds of emotional, behavioral and interpersonal problems as well as other personality disorders, phobias, addictions, sexual perversions, and hypochondria.* As such, it contrasts with the ongoing attempts by other investigators to subdivide *DSM-III-R* BPD into more specifically homogenous groups. One such subgroup of BPO that Dr. Kernberg calls *infantile personalities* corresponds to *DSM-III-R* borderlines.

We have seen that analysts divide psychostructural organization into levels of functioning. Each level indicates how the person consistently

*Broader still is the category of "the impossible patient" that has appeared in the psychiatric literature.

views himself, others, and the world, how he thinks about and interprets what he sees, and what problems are likely to result. Dr. Kernberg considers all of the above illnesses to be fluctuating symptoms of the borderline level: an underlying, specific, stable form of pathological ego structure. Or as Dr. Soloff puts it, "Borderline personality organization may be conceptualized as the steel infrastructure of a building over which can be built any of a variety of stylized facades representing the manifest character type."[2]

This pathological structure is the essence of the illness and the ultimate focus of Dr. Kernberg's form of psychotherapy. Its stability makes it likewise the source of the diagnosis. Its symptoms are transient—they can vary widely in type and number between patients and over time. Dr. Kernberg deemphasizes them as a means of distinguishing BPO from other illnesses. But to a lesser extent than Dr. Gunderson and *DSM-III-R,* Dr. Kernberg does observe particular signs and symptoms of BPO.

Dr. Kernberg bases his diagnosis of BPO on three categories of criteria:

1. *Specific signs.* This most important of the categories includes two features:
- Adequate capacity to perceive reality with respect to oneself, other people and the world. As we have seen, this distinguishes the borderline condition from psychosis. "The patient must be able to distinguish self from nonself and intrapsychic from external stimuli," says Dr. Kernberg, "and to empathize with ordinary social criteria of reality and explain any departures."
- Impaired ego integration. A person with a malfunctioning ego holds sharply contradictory and unassimilated attitudes about important aspects of the self. This fluctuating, amorphous *identity diffusion* permeates crucial areas of the personality and interferes with everyday life, especially relationships with others.

    "Borderlines can describe themselves for five hours without your getting a realistic picture of what they're like," says Dr. Kernberg. "They don't see their own contradictions."

2. *Nonspecific signs* include low tolerance of anxiety, poor impulse control, and undeveloped *sublimatory capacity* (the ability to enjoy meaningful work or hobbies).

3. *Primitive defenses* distinguish the borderline from the neurotic level. The most important of these is splitting, which appears as *primitive idealization* (the consistent view of a person as entirely good) and *devaluation*

(entirely bad), or as arbitrary switching from one to the other as circumstances dictate. To the borderline, oneself and others are defined by only the most recent feelings and behavior. "Borderlines read *each* action by other people because they have no sense of consistency and thus cannot predict behavior," says Dr. Kernberg.

This inability to reconcile contradictory perceptions into a realistic whole has enormous pathological consequences. To keep good and bad separate, the borderline must use various other primitive defense mechanisms. These include

- *Magical thinking,* in which the borderline conquers unconscious fears by indulging in superstitions, phobias, beliefs that thoughts can cause events, and obsessive-compulsive behavior.
- *Omnipotence,* the feeling of being all-powerful, totally successful, even eternal.
- *Projection,* denying one's unpleasant characteristics while instead seeing them in others.

Robin typically projects hostility; her defense backfires because the anger she is trying to disown is ultimately aimed at herself:

> When I was really stressed out in the hospital unit, I would think that people were trying to kill me. Sometimes when I'm really suicidal, I become a murder machine—I just can't see or think about anything else. I get really almost programmed to hurt myself, and I think that other people are trying to hurt me when it's actually me projecting the desire. I want the damage to be in my own hands rather than lose control to someone else, but I don't recognize this at the time.
>
> I used to walk around with razor blades in my wallet to protect me from others, but I would actually just whip out a blade and start cutting myself. The more suspicious, unsafe and afraid I felt, the more often I would cut.

- *Projective identification,* a more sophisticated form of projection in which the borderline perceives and identifies with the projected characteristics.

"Some of our crazy behavior results when we're trying to get another person to feel as we're feeling," says Whitney.

> At times this is much easier than trying to put the feeling into words. When I'm angry or humiliated, I try to do that to my therapist. For a long time I wasn't at all aware that I was doing it, and even now I'm not always aware of it until I think about it afterwards.

If Whitney perceives the anger she arouses in her therapist, for example, she will then try to manipulate him both to control his anger and to elicit

responses from him that repeatedly confirm its reality. But if her therapist catches on, he can instead process the anger by containing and
interpreting it, thereby making it "palatable" for Whitney to take back.

Other symptoms of BPO include:
- *Primary process thinking,* a type close to psychosis.
- *Object inconstancy,* an inability to see others consistently and thus
  maintain stable relationships. Borderlines have chaotic, extreme relationships in which they often have difficulty distinguishing themselves from others.
- *Evocative memory disturbance,* an inability to maintain the soothing
  memory of a beloved person or object that is absent.
- *Transient psychotic episodes,* which can result from severe stress, substance abuse, or lack of structure. In therapy, these can appear as a
  transference psychosis, in which the patient believes that the therapist
  actually *is* somebody else significant to her.
- *Denial,* which to most people is a refusal to perceive the truth about a
  particular situation. The term also refers to borderlines' tendency to
  experience emotional amnesia. "Borderline individuals are completely in each mood, so they have great difficulty conceptualizing,
  remembering what it's like to be in another mood," says Linehan.

At least some of these symptoms can result from other illnesses like
affective disorders. To help distinguish true BPO, Dr. Kernberg developed a structural interview designed specifically to define the patient's
psychostructural organization. It focuses precisely on the relationship
between the patient's interaction with the therapist, her ability to relate
to others in general, and her history of symptoms. As such, it is more
sophisticated, dynamic, and difficult to apply than the symptom checklist
approach to diagnosis.

But as Dr. Gunderson's work shows, there is far more to descriptive
diagnosis than mere checklists.

Dr. Gunderson's Borderline
Personality Disorder

Although trained as a psychoanalyst, Dr. Gunderson is widely regarded as the most scientific of the major theorists on BPD. Like Dr.
Stone, he is especially fluent in psychiatric Esperanto and enjoys the
respect of colleagues from several different factions.

Dr. Gunderson has focused upon discriminating BPD from psychoses and neuroses, from affective disorders, and, more recently, from other personality disorders. His criteria for defining BPD include the following, listed in order of importance:

1. *Intense unstable relationships* in which the borderline invariably is hurt. "This criterion is central such that while it's too general, I would hesitate to make the borderline diagnosis in its absence," says Dr. Gunderson. As we'll see in Chapter 16, he believes that these relationships occur on three levels of functioning.

2. *Repetitive self-destructive behavior,* often designed to make others rescue the borderline, particularly when she is threatened by loss.

3. *Chronic fears of abandonment* and panic when forced to be alone.

4. *Chronic unpleasant emotions* and the inability to enjoy satisfaction or well-being for any length of time.

5. *Distorted thoughts and perceptions,* often in response to lack of structure. Singer has shown that borderlines show intact reasoning and appropriate responses on structured psychological tests, but on unstructured tests their responses are more bizarre, unrealistic, illogical, or primitive than even those of schizophrenics.*

"Borderline distortions of interpersonal relationships and interactions cause a lot of trouble," says a psychiatric resident during the class on personality disorders.

In therapy sessions, when you try to sort these out, it is horrific because the distortion is so great. Either I hear the truth from the hospital staff, *or else I was THERE.* **Distortions** about how people feel about them, hate them, want them dead! . . . and I often feel unable to do anything about this in therapy.

Linehan points out that researchers increasingly have found emotions to cause corresponding distortions (and other problems) in people, rather than the other way around.

Less severe distortion can be caused by or mistaken for another borderline symptom, hypersensitivity. "One can postulate that borderlines are born with an unusual sensitivity to nonverbal communication," says Dr. Paris.

One of my colleagues did a study with the PONS [perception of nonverbal stimuli] test that showed that borderlines score extremely high. Whether their sensitivity is constitutional or environmental is another question. But it

---

*More recently (*American Journal of Psychiatry,* January 1991, p. 106), Kathleen M. O'Leary, M.S.W., and her colleagues have noted that literature reviews show "only limited evidence to support the validity of this pattern."

has raised the speculation that maybe borderlines notice more than the rest of us.

The line that divides distortion from hypersensitivity or accurate perceptions can be very difficult for the borderline to find. "My major fear is that my perceptions will be dismissed by other people if I'm showing another borderline symptom like rage," says Whitney.

People say I distort a lot, and one of my major problems is hypersensitivity. But I know that a lot of what I pick up on is true. My interpretation of it and reaction to it may be off, but my initial perception is accurate. I'm very, very perceptive and confident about that.

Now what I might do is to think that someone's anger, for instance, is caused by me. My perception of the anger is true, but my interpretation of it is a distortion. And sometimes people use my hypersensitivity against me. They defend themselves and write off my perceptions by saying, "Everybody knows that Whitney is hypersensitive." And that part's very frustrating.

Often borderlines become paranoid and have *dissociative experiences,* which can include feelings of unreality, strangeness, or detachment with respect to the environment or themselves. And as Dr. Kernberg also notes, they indulge in magical thinking.

6. *Impulsivity.* Researchers acknowledge that *impulsivity* is a misnomer for planned behaviors like binge-vomiting that are included in this category along with alcohol or drug abuse, promiscuity, fighting, or running away. Episodic and interchangeable, these behaviors often embarrass the borderline in retrospect.

7. *Poor social adaptation* that precludes significant academic or professional accomplishments even by intellectual or creative borderlines.[3]

"I speak on this subject quite often," says Dr. Gunderson,

and I'm often aware that I want to juggle the order of my criteria, which reflects uncertainty on my part about which of them ought to be given priority and for what reasons. Some criteria are more important than others. In a most general way, I think the critical thing is the borderline patient's capacity to change functional level in response to changes, most usually in interpersonal relationships.

To make BPD more systematic, reliable, and quantitative a diagnosis, Dr. Gunderson and Jonathan E. Kolb, M.D., created a semistructured Diagnostic Interview for Borderlines in 1976. The DIB examined borderline characteristics under five main headings: social adaptation, impulse-action patterns, affects, psychosis, and interpersonal relations. These correspond roughly to Dr. Kernberg's emphases on the sublimatory capacity, impulse control, anxiety tolerance, reality testing, and relationship issues explored in *his* structural interview.[4] The characteristics are scored, and when the total score exceeds the cutoff level, the patient is diagnosed as borderline.

In 1989, Zanarini, Dr. Gunderson, and their colleagues revised the DIB, the better to distinguish the borderline from other personality disorders. The DIB-R uses four headings:

Affects: Chronic (or major) depression (including a conviction of being bad), helplessness, hopelessness, worthlessness, guilt, anger (and frequent angry acts), anxiety, loneliness, boredom, and emptiness.

Cognition: Odd thinking, the experience of unusual perceptions, nondelusional paranoia, and quasipsychoses.

We have already seen examples of psychotic episodes in borderlines; Melanie tends to experience all the other cognitive symptoms:

At times my mind starts racing—part of it takes off, and the logical part doesn't know what to do about that. It's trying to catch up with the fear, the paranoia, the feeling that I've just got to get out of this, get rid of this pain, whatever it is I'm feeling. All that really snowballs and just keeps snowballing to the point that I become—not oblivious, but the concrete things around me change visually and perceptually. Colors fade to black and white. People I cared about five minutes ago, I just don't care about at all.

Everything becomes a total blur. The world seems to circle around, almost visibly. If you were talking to me from where you are, I might perceive you talking from behind me or on the other side of me. It's rather like an out-of-body experience except that I don't see myself having it. I can't get a grasp on what's going on, much less stop things. It's like a top spinning around that I want to get hold of but can't. It really is scary.

Impulse action patterns: Substance abuse or dependence, sexual deviance, self-mutilation, manipulative suicide efforts, and other impulsive behaviors.

Interpersonal relationships: Intolerance of aloneness; concerns about abandonment, engulfment or annihilation; counterdependency; serious conflict over help or care; stormy relationships, dependency, masochism, devaluation, manipulation, sadism, demandingness, and entitlement. This last section includes issues that arise in treatment: regressions, problems with *countertransference* (the therapist's emotional reactions to the patient), and "special" therapeutic relationships.[5]

The DIB is the best known, most widely used, and most influential of the diagnostic tools developed to supplement the *DSM-III-R* critera for BPD. Therapists use it either alone or with *DSM-III-R* to screen patients, and to date it has been the basis of over 70 research studies.[6] Having proved the *reliability* of the DIB (that is, its consistency and dependability), the investigators are now testing its *validity* (its ability to measure BPD and screen out related conditions).

A recent article by Zanarini and her colleagues compares borderline patients to a large sample of hospitalized and outpatients with other personality disorders. The study shows what features best distinguish BPD and in fact suggests how the view of personality disorders may evolve over the next decade.

In the past, Dr. Gunderson has emphasized the importance of anger as a feature defining BPD, but use of the Affect section of the DIB-R shows that no one emotion is specific to the condition. The authors note instead that "many borderline patients have a desperate need to convince others of the unique depth of their affective suffering" and that perhaps their need to confide in others about their pain, rather than its actual level, is what makes them unique.[7]

Borderlines would probably be outraged by this statement and dismiss it flat out. "Their sense that their pain is the worst—one could talk for an hour about that observation alone," says Dr. Cowdry.

It's colored by both the need to be special—in this case to be specially in pain, to achieve that distinction through suffering—and a sense I have that there's some truth to it. These dysphoric states that are triggered in borderlines are in fact exquisitely painful experiences. Just because we may not feel that the trigger justified the response, this doesn't mean that the response is not excruciating. The affective state is very primitive, that is, it's not nicely circumscribed depression about a particular job or marital situation to which you can apply all your thinking skills. It's a much more poorly differentiated reaction that mixes together depression, emptiness, anxiety, varying degrees of rage—it's sort of a tumultuous inner state that is intensely uncomfortable. And it persists partly because one aspect of the disorder is being unable to step back and put it into some perspective, that is to bind some of that dysphoria by thinking.

Use of the Cognition section has confirmed Dr. Gunderson's view that psychotic, regressive experiences are fundamental to BPD. Although several other personality disorders can cause psychotic experiences or cognitive problems, borderlines in particular have quasipsychotic experiences lasting two days or less.*

*Dr. McGlashan's research instead shows a high incidence of such transient psychotic episodes in schizotypal personality disorder as well. These brief psychoses are quite different in kind from those found in borderlines.

"Dr. Gunderson has previously not had control groups of patients with other personality disorders in his studies and has worked primarily in a hospital setting," says Dr. Spitzer.* "These new data are more convincing."

Applying the Impulse Action Patterns section of the DIB-R reveals that two forms of impulsivity are specific to borderlines: manipulative suicidal threats and, especially, deliberate physical self-destructive acts. The latter finding corroborates Dr. Gunderson's claim over the past decade that such acts are the "behavioral specialty" of BPD.

Their use of the Interpersonal Relationships section has helped the researchers isolate four patterns peculiar to borderlines: concerns with abandonment, engulfment, and annihilation; demandingness and entitlement; treatment regressions; and ability to arouse inappropriately close or hostile treatment relationships.

An empirical study by Dr. Kernberg and his colleagues found a 78 percent overlap between patients diagnosed as having BPO and those diagnosed with BPD using Dr. Gunderson's methods and criteria. Dr. Gunderson interprets this agreement to indicate that Dr. Kernberg's theories are based on the small subgroup of infantile personalities who are amenable to his type of treatment. His observation has led Dr. Gunderson to question whether Dr. Kernberg's theories and treatment principles apply to *all* patients with BPO (or even BPD).[8]

In fact, Dr. Gunderson sees potential problems with generalizations about diagnosis and treatment made from *any* reports by psychoanalysts, Dr. Kernberg included,[9] for the reasons outlined in an earlier chapter.

In Chapter 23 we'll learn the reasons Dr. Kernberg considers his theories to have been proven objectively in practice. In response to Dr. Gunderson's conclusion about the diagnostic consistency, he says,

> In our present research project, it is true that we are trying to select patients who fulfill the criteria of both BPO and BPD to get out of the semantic quagmire. But this was not true of the Psychotherapy Research Project of the Menninger Foundation, nor is it true of my clinical work with patients who have BPO but a very different constellation of characterological traits. I include in this category all the severe personality disorders, and Dr. Gunderson is not taking that into consideration.

"My general point is that Dr. Kernberg's larger conceptualization of BPO includes many subgroups, only some of whom would conform to what is now called BPD," says Dr. Gunderson. "The issue is that speak-

*This often repeated reservation about his earlier work singles out Dr. Gunderson unfairly but does not trouble him. "Despite the limitations in methods or samples," he says, "most of my original research has been replicated many times in other samples, so it has taken on more generalizability."

ing about BPO, Dr. Kernberg advocates in general an approach to treatment that leads to problems in dealing with patients having BPD."

We will examine the treatment approaches of both psychiatrists in Chapter 24.

The *DSM-III-R,* Kernberg, and Gunderson definitions of the borderline condition include elements of its earlier descriptions, especially those of Falret, Deutsch, Bychowski, and Hoch and Polatin. Of the three, Dr. Gunderson's is the most balanced definition, combining as it does the affective symptoms emphasized in *DSM-III-R* with the disturbed relationships and transient psychoses found in Dr. Kernberg's conceptualization.

Trying to define BPD is like staring into a lava lamp: what you see is constantly changing. This common observation adds another level to the metaphorical nature of BPD: the illness not only *causes* instability but also *symbolizes* it.

But however intangible, these definitions have immediate practical significance for the borderline patient, who must determine how a prospective therapist defines the illness and what he considers its causes and proper treatment.

Therapists agree that a distinct borderline disorder of some sort exists. It appears to be one of the most complicated forms of severe mental illness. This complexity, the relative lack of research, and the absence of a single effective treatment approach make it indeed difficult to "nail down."

But the confusion and jockeying among specialists in BPD prevent the illness from becoming a static concept. Rather, it continues to inspire more research, clarification, and compromise among proponents of opposing definitions, especially with the advent of *DSM-IV.* We are about to review an unofficial yet controversial definition of BPD that reflects just such efforts.

Notes

1. Otto F. Kernberg, M.D., Michael A. Selzer, M.D., Harold W. Koenigsberg, M.D., Arthur C. Carr, Ph.D., and Ann H. Appelbaum, M.D., *Psychodynamic Psychotherapy of Borderline Patients* (New York: Basic Books, 1989), p. vii.
2. Paul H. Soloff, "Borderline Disorders," in *Handbook of Outpatient Treatment of Adults,* ed. Michael E. Thase, Barry A. Edelstein, and Michel Hersen (New York: Plenum, 1990), p. 311.
3. John G. Gunderson, M.D., and Mary C. Zanarini, Ed.M., "Current Overview of the Borderline Diagnosis," *Journal of Clinical Psychiatry,* Vol. 48, No. 8, Supplement (August 1987), pp. 5–6.

4. Michael H. Stone, M.D., *The Borderline Syndromes: Constitution, Personality, and Adaptation* (New York: McGraw-Hill, 1980), p. 266.
5. Mary C. Zanarini, Ed.D., John G. Gunderson, M.D., Frances R. Frankenburg, M.D., and Deborah L. Chauncey, A.B., "The Revised Diagnostic Interview for Borderlines: Discriminating BPD from Other Axis II Disorders," *Journal of Personality Disorders*, Vol. 3, No. 1 (1989), p. 12. Copyright © 1989, The Guilford Press. Reprinted by permission.
6. Ibid., pp. 10–11.
7. Mary C. Zanarini, Ed.D., John G. Gunderson, M.D., Frances R. Frankenburg, M.D., and Deborah L. Chauncey, A.B., "Discriminating Borderline Personality Disorder from Other Axis II Disorders," *American Journal of Psychiatry*, Vol. 147, No. 2 (February 1990), p. 164. Copyright © 1990, the American Psychiatric Association.
8. John G. Gunderson, "Interfaces Between Psychoanalytic and Empirical Studies of Borderline Personality," *The Borderline Patient: Emerging Concepts in Diagnosis, Psychodynamics and Treatment*, ed. James S. Grotstein, Marion F. Solomon, and Joan A. Lang, Vol. 1 (Hillsdale, N.J.: The Analytic Press, 1987), p. 40.
9. Ibid., pp. 40–42.

7

The Maverick Definition, or Why Paige Says She Is Not Borderline

"I think BPD may turn out at a certain point to be an obsolete concept, but we're not there yet. Compared to many diagnostic entities it's comparatively well defined and well researched, and to call for its abandonment at this point is premature. But we do need to start reexamining and rethinking it."

JUDITH L. HERMAN, M.D.

*W*e'll see in Chapter 20 that a history of abuse (particularly incestuous sexual abuse) during childhood has been reported by high percentages of borderline patients. The symptoms of BPD overlap strikingly with those of other disorders produced by such experiences. Having wondered whether BPD is therefore a type of trauma disorder, some researchers are setting aside psychoanalytical theories about its origins to approach it primarily from this starting point. Some of them would like to see even its phenomenological definition acknowledge that many borderlines have been abused.

The Identical Cousin

If the other Cluster B illnesses are siblings of BPD, then *post-traumatic stress disorder* (PTSD) is its identical cousin. PTSD appears in a different section of *DSM-III-R,* classified as an anxiety disorder. Yet it so closely resembles BPD that researchers commonly look not only to borderline patients for histories of sexual abuse but also to known incest victims for evidence of BPD. "The association of BPD with PTSD is a much richer and more productive interface than that with depressive disorders," says Dr. Gunderson.

Like its cousin, PTSD has been long observed but poorly understood. Its victims are likewise stigmatized and pose credibility problems for those around them. The symptoms of PTSD found in *DSM-III-R* and observed clinically can be grouped under the four categories we used earlier for BPD:

- *Emotions:* intense, intolerable, poorly regulated emotions, especially anxiety, contrasting with inner deadness.
- *Behavior:* aggressive and/or self-destructive acting out.
- *Relationships:* difficulty functioning socially and professionally; sexual problems and inappropriate sexual behavior; alienation; lack of trust; avoiding and/or being victimized in relationships; evoking intensely negative reactions from others.

Andrea, a 28-year-old borderline, describes the self-mutilation and confusion that can result from previous abuse:

> I attack my vagina when I'm feeling sexual or feeling bad about myself sexually. Sex brings back the past. Trying to destroy the part of your body that is specifically for that purpose is like trying to protect yourself from harm. I would much rather be totally nonsexual. I hate these chemical changes that occur in me. And I really do not want to have children. But I'm feminine and do want to have children so I'm trying to destroy what's causing this personal conflict. I don't want to be denied children.
>
> I am sexually active with my boyfriend and feel inadequate when he doesn't respond to what I want. In order to have sex with him, I imagine that we've switched roles—that he is me and I am him. But he has the part and I don't. I get really confused and frequently masturbate but without touching myself internally. I've learned to stay away from my vagina as much as possible because all it does is cause trouble. I also feel upset when we have sex because he's going in there. I dissociate. But I want that part to be fulfilled. I have this instinctive programming from hormones that confuses

me. I really don't want to be sexually active, but I feel sexual. Constant confusion.

- *Identity:* difficulty maintaining a realistic view of the self; poor self-esteem; self-blame.

Although both borderlines and PTSD victims repress memories of their abuse, such symptoms are intensified when they are exposed to situations that resemble or symbolize it. Both groups also have difficulties with reality testing.

One possible relationship between the two illnesses has been suggested by Jean M. Goodwin, M.D., M.P.H., and her colleagues, who use acronyms to describe the adult symptoms of severe childhood sexual abuse. The post-traumatic symptoms seen in incest victims are represented by the acronym **FEARS**:

Fears and anxiety, including being easily startled

Ego constriction, especially sexually

Anger

Repetitions like flashbacks

Sadness and **S**leep disorders like recurrent nightmares.

A more disturbed response to extreme incestuous abuse indicated by multiple psychiatric hospitalizations is represented by **BAD FEARS**:

Borderline personality disorder

Affective disorder

Dissociation

Fears syndrome (that is, PTSD)

Eating disorders

Antisocial actions involving children or arrests and **A**lcohol or substance abuse

Reenactments like rape or battering

Suicidality or **S**omatization (recurrent complaints of physical symptoms that are not due to any illness).[1]

Dr. Herman and Bessel A. van der Kolk, M.D., have observed that the major difference between PTSD and BPD is simply that the criteria for the latter do not include a trauma history.[2]

The point is that PTSD looks similar enough to be mistaken for BPD. Such a diagnosis can do less than full justice to serious borderline symptoms. "Reducing BPD to a post-traumatic response to sexual abuse is simplistic and potentially ideological," says Dr. Paris. "You have to consider exactly what happened in detail to assess its impact."

According to Dr. Gunderson, the age at which a patient's abuse began suggests which illness might be the correct diagnosis:

It's very important to differentiate between traumas that help create or form a personality and those that give rise to PTSD. In that regard I think that it's very important not to try to diagnose PTSD in place of BPD, which it oversimplifies. PTSD is by definition and should remain by definition a diagnosis given to people who have had a radical change in their functioning, and perhaps in their already-formed personalities, as a result of trauma.

Yet informed survivors of abuse are rejecting a diagnosis of BPD in favor of PTSD. An example is apparent in the treatment history of 32-year-old "Paige."

Paige's Experience

I'm a recovered alcoholic and drug addict. When I started therapy I was 23 years old and 18 months sober, working and going to school full-time and living independently. I had just wanted some help while my mother was dying. By the time I left therapy five years later, I had been hospitalized eight times, had been given two courses of shock treatments, and was loaded up with neuroleptics and the maximum dose of a tranquilizer that just increased what was already terrible anxiety. I was on disability, I had to drop out of school, and they had a court order to send me to a state institution. But the paperwork got fouled up. I got an anonymous phone call from somebody on the staff who told me this and instructed me to request discharge, so I was able to leave against medical advice.

My hospital records have a primary diagnosis of "schizophrenia or schizo-affective," a secondary diagnosis of "borderline personality disorder," and comments that I'm "quiet," "cooperative," and "nondelusional."*

None of my records indicates that I was sexually abused by a neighbor from ages two to ten. There might have been someone else involved, but I don't remember. My sister was abused by a different neighbor and also witnessed some of my abuse. It was intercourse and oral sex and also—something I never will understand—inanimate objects stuck in me. I was hospitalized when I was eight for a really, really bad urinary tract infection and lacerations. The doctors didn't tell me anything about what was wrong; they just put me in stirrups and stuck more things inside me. That's when my parents found out about the abuse, but they never did anything about it because, they told me, the man's wife had a heart condition.

I was physically abused by my father, but what was really horrible was my mother's obsession with my body and its intake. When I was seven years old,

*By now readers are better educated than the hospital staff who wrote these notes and Paige's prescriptions, which I can confirm from having seen the records.

she brought me to Weight Watchers.* Every time I tried to eat on every single day of my entire childhood, she would ask, "Do you need that?" "Why are you having that?" Anything was more normal to me than eating. Between what was being poked into my body at one end and what I wasn't allowed to put into my mouth—and later, to be put on a drug that made me fat, so that the psychiatrist who kept increasing the dosage put me on a diet . . . to this day, if I could be anything, I would be a floating mind. Get rid of this package—that would be the ideal state for me.

If you look at the *DSM-III,* I guess I did have erratic moods, I did see things in black and white. Abuse makes it very difficult to trust your own judgments. You have to distort your own perceptions because bad things are being done by grownups who are supposed to be protecting you. Everything gets bent out of shape.

I did have suicidal gestures; at one point I did self-mutilate because it was one of the few things that alleviated this anxiety. But symptoms like these couldn't be worked with for five years, until I was taken off medication.

I have seen a social worker twice a week for five years since I left the hospital and haven't had any medication since. I'm in law school, on law review, and I have given lectures at a few organizations about the legal rights of psychiatric patients, which is my main interest.

Aside from the therapy, what helped me most was a support group for survivors of sexual abuse in which we had to give our names and those of our abusers and describe what had been done to us. I think that's probably the fastest way for anybody who has endured the experience to get through it and back on her feet.

I don't understand why they're labeling people borderline, since most borderlines have abuse backgrounds, a really large number of people. If people who have been abused as children are reacting in this particular manner with these particular symptoms, then it must be a natural reaction to some pretty horrendous stuff, not a mental illness. How are people suppose to adjust to life situations if everything is pathologized? It's hard for me to accept that kind of diagnosis. I don't understand the necessity of it sometimes, because what they're doing a lot of times is making victims of victims. At least therapists should ask whether patients were abused and make sure that they want to hear the answers. That could prevent a whole lot of misery.

My sister was convinced she was a borderline, or a bipolar borderline, but her psychiatrist keeps replying, "I'm sorry, but you're not—you have post-traumatic stress syndrome, and that's the way it is." I like this man very much. Surprisingly, my own therapist, who is very much within the psycho-analytic school, acknowledged that she did give me a diagnosis of borderline when I first started with her and later changed it to post-traumatic stress syndrome.

---

*Paige showed me a photograph of herself at this age: she was normal weight and muscular.

When Paige complains about "pathologizing" behavior into a "mental illness," what she really objects to are the possible *consequences* of being pathologized, which in her case were appalling. Yet such mismanagement of BPD is by no means rare.

PTSD is a mental illness, and Paige is committed to the psychotherapy she receives for it. The difference between her being diagnosed as a borderline or as a trauma survivor is primarily that now she has a good therapist who helps her deal with her past experiences and continue a productive life. Paige's problem was as much her initial treatment as her illness, and in this sense hers is an exceptional case. It nevertheless illustrates a major point: a trauma history must be addressed in treatment—appropriately—as an important dimension of BPD.

What Is Victimization?

Patients who were abused violently and/or while extremely young, for example, tend completely to repress those memories. Women abused during adolescence or less violently are more likely to use partial repression, dissociation, and intellectualization as defenses. Effective treatment of such patients includes carefully supervised recall; both groups face the task of integrating as adults the experiences that overwhelmed them as children.[3]

A crucial aspect of working with such memories is that of distinguishing them from current experience. Dr. Perry, Dr. Herman and their colleagues have found that the most powerful unconscious wish associated with BPD is one for reparation of past injuries. "One reason therapy with borderlines is often difficult is that they want somebody—a therapist, a lover, whoever—to make it all right," says Dr. Paris. "Life isn't like that." In what Freud called *repetition compulsion,* borderlines are drawn to the same situations and danger cues, hoping that events will come out differently.

Unfortunately, abused borderlines are relatively unskilled at recognizing dangers that other people would avoid. "Women with sexual abuse histories are at higher risk for repeated victimization inside and outside the treatment situation," says Dr. Herman. "The mechanisms are complex, but there's probably an adaptive failure in self-protection, side by side with this ragefulness which is not really protective at all."[4]

The risky behavior of borderlines raises the central issue of what constitutes true victimization (one that will be explored in later chapters).

Dr. Gunderson emphasizes that borderlines should not indulge their desire to be seen strictly as victims. "Experience is elaborated by subsequent experience," he says. "Borderlines are not the unwitting products of external circumstances." Dr. Kernberg shares this belief, partly because of the borderline's tendency to exchange her images of herself and other people. In sessions, for example, the patient often switches victim/ abuser roles with her therapist. She needs to recognize that during this process she identifies unconsciously and aggressively with her previous abuser(s), says Dr. Kernberg, or she cannot get well.

Some borderlines play the role of aggressor more consistently. "These women have often developed revenge motifs," says Dr. Stone.

> They know only sex as a way to relate and become seductive and provocative and bitchy. They are victims who now wish to victimize and get into positions where they provoke murder. Their habit memory systems have programmed them to repeat these situations.[5]

Attempting to cope with her trauma, the borderline becomes her own worst enemy, someone who repulses others while badly hurting herself. As a child, she was not responsible for her abuse, but as an adult, she is a survivor who must not perpetuate the past in the present. She must therefore be held responsible for the abuse of self and others, for learning to change this behavior, for making up for her past injuries herself, and for avoiding their repetition in the future.

Another Continuum

The centrality of the victim role in BPD makes clear to certain therapists that post-traumatic stress must be acknowledged. Suggesting that many borderlines would not have developed BPD had they not endured repeated sexual abuse during childhood, Dr. Kroll writes, "The pattern of self-destructive responses in the wake of the cognitive disturbances in a young adult with post-traumatic stress disorder is what makes some borderlines borderline."[6] One way to incorporate these elements would be to include a trauma history as one of the diagnostic criteria for BPD. But besides causing the same problems raised by the proposed cognitive criterion, a trauma history would intrude a causative factor into a symptom list.

An alternative is a reformulation of both the BPD and PTSD concepts. Dr. Herman and her colleagues have suggested that various adaptations to extreme stress might lie on a continuum. The most severe reaction would be multiple personality disorder, followed by BPD (again the "borderline" on the spectrum), with PTSD and panic-anxiety disorders at the milder extreme.[7]

BPD has certainly been associated with *multiple personality disorder* (a rare syndrome whose victims split psychologically into two or more personalities). In fact, in the next chapter we will meet Renée, who has both diagnoses.* Multiple personality disorder is classified elsewhere in *DSM-III-R* as a dissociative disorder, and *its* relationship to BPD is a whole other topic that won't be explored here.[8]

To incorporate all of these alternatives, Dr. Herman is recommending a new category for *DSM-IV*:

> I'm proposing an expansion of PTSD to a spectrum concept and the inclusion of an entity that I proposed to call *complex PTSD* and that has now been renamed *disorders of extreme stress not otherwise specified* or *DESNOS*. I wrote the concept paper for *DSM-IV*, for which there will be field trials. Once the concept gets out there and gains some wider recognition, we can go to the data and see what fits best.
>
> DESNOS tries to bring together descriptively the features of a complex syndrome seen in people who have been subjected to severe, repeated, prolonged abuse. So it covers traumata in adult life as well as the childhood abuse necessary for some of the features seen in borderline and multiple personality disorder.

The position of Dr. Herman and other feminists is dismissed by therapists who appear to have misunderstood it. These researchers propose not to eliminate the BPD definition (at least not until a better one has been formulated) but to consider alternative diagnoses for abused patients that will stimulate thought and add a new perspective to its already rich history. The importance of highlighting PTSD symptoms is that interventions aimed toward abuse might help resolve them while further clarifying how BPD actually develops.

The possibility that many patients may *look* without actually *being* borderline implies all kinds of problems for research studies. Followup studies are most likely to have had their results skewed by patient misdiagnosis of this sort. Likewise the possibility that BPD is, in some respects, a trauma disorder complicates its relationship with overlapping personality disorders. Might they *all* be, to varying degrees, trauma disorders? If so, why is this being recognized only now?

The intriguing answer to that question will appear in Chapter 20.

---

*Dr. Kernberg points out, however, that so-called multiple personalities are often induced by therapists who encourage patients to exaggerate what are actually symptoms of BPD.

Notes

1. Jean M. Goodwin, M.D., M.P.H., Katherine Cheeves, M.D., and Virginia Connell, R.N., M.S., "Borderline and Other Severe Symptoms in Adult Survivors of Incestuous Abuse," *Psychiatric Annals,* Vol. 20, No. 1 (January 1990), pp. 22–23. Copyright © 1990 by SLACK Incorporated. Used with permission.
2. Judith L. Herman, M.D., and Bessel A. van der Kolk, M.D., "Traumatic Antecedents of Borderline Personality Disorder," in *Psychological Trauma,* ed. Bessel A. van der Kolk (Washington, D.C.: American Psychiatric Press, 1987), p. 115.
3. Judith Lewis Herman, M.D., and Emily Schatzow, M.Ed., "Recovery and Verification of Memories of Childhood Sexual Trauma," *Psychoanalytic Psychology,* Vol. 4, No. 1 (1987), pp. 11–13.
4. Judith L. Herman, M.D., "Trauma and Neglect in Borderline Personality Disorder," paper read at the 143rd annual meeting of the American Psychiatric Association, New York, 17 May 1990.
5. Michael H. Stone, M.D., "An Integrated, Psychobiological Model of Borderline Personality Disorder," paper read at the 143rd annual meeting of the American Psychiatric Association, New York, 17 May 1990.
6. Jerome Kroll, M.D., *The Challenge of the Borderline Patient: Competency in Diagnosis and Treatment* (New York: Norton, 1988), p. 43.
7. Judith Lewis Herman, M.D., J. Christopher Perry, M.P.H., M.D., and Bessel A. van der Kolk, M.D., "Childhood Trauma in Borderline Personality Disorder," *American Journal of Psychiatry,* Vol. 146, No. 4 (April 1989), p. 494.
8. See Kristen Kemp, Ph.D., Alan D. Gilbertson, Ph.D., and Moshe Torem, M.D., "The Differential Diagnosis of Multiple Personality Disorder from Borderline Personality Disorder," *Dissociation,* Vol. 1, No. 4 (December 1988), pp. 41–46, for a discussion and a list of earlier references.

8

Renée: Things Can Be Different

Enough theory and criteria. In this chapter and the next, a borderline relates her psychiatric history.

I deliberately avoided asking the patients I interviewed how they fit diagnostic criteria: the focus here is not on BPD itself but on the experience of it. I therefore selected two high-functioning, contrasting patients capable of articulating that experience. In so doing, I run the risk of offending Alice and other readers with case histories that may seem *unborderline*. Unfortunately, however, more typically borderline stories might appear to be sensationalism.

Readers at a loss to identify meaningful commonalities between these two women can better appreciate therapists' struggles to identify and describe BPD.

My therapist has many times rubbed his head and asked, "Where did you get what you've got?" because there wasn't anything healthy at all in the home I grew up in, and yet I managed somehow to have a very strong sense of compassion and empathy and am very much able to love.

I was adopted as an infant, and I just made contact with

my birth family last year. The family history includes depression and alcoholism; a great-aunt had a lobotomy for severe bipolar disorder. My birth mother seems by all accounts to have been borderline. Two months after she was put in touch with me, she called to say, "I wish you had died at birth," and hung up.

A story that I laughed at along with my adopted family was that when I arrived in their home at the age of five days, I had scabs on my forehead and nose. I had been left crying for so long that I had turned my head from side to side and rubbed off the skin. When I had my first child, I recognized how long it would take a baby to do that. Things were no better in my new home. My adoptive father has said that I was never cared for at all at night and fed only according to my adopted mother's whims.

My birth siblings, who were raised by our real mother, say they can't believe that I got the same mother twice. My adoptive mother is very pathological, completely detached from any sense of what her feelings are. My adoptive father is very distant. His way of dealing with my mother has always been simply to not be there except when he unpredictably erupted in bitter anger and criticism.

They adopted three brothers from different families, all of whom are rather pathological. I think I'm the healthiest one in the bunch just because I recognized that there was a problem and did something about it.

I suffered some physical abuse, a tremendous amount of emotional abuse and neglect, and sexual abuse from an older brother for about seven years. Some of it was very violent. I was also violently raped by a stranger, as I have recently remembered. I had suppressed these experiences; my therapist and I are still putting pieces together.

My memory lapses extend back at least 14 years, as long as my husband has known me. My psychiatrist and I examined this situation and recognized that it had gone on this long when my group therapist suggested that I had multiple personality disorder. I think mental illnesses are on a continuum. Many borderlines swing between such extremes that we had assumed that my different personalities were just very different emotional states. I seem to cope very, very well most of the time and then go to pieces occasionally. But we couldn't explain my memory lapses and the blackouts I had begun having.

These symptoms resulted from my having started to remember the sexual abuse. A couple of weeks before that, I had my first experience of finding myself somewhere without knowing how I got there, wearing different clothes. That happened twice in a few weeks. Then a couple of days before the first memory came, I had an eerie sense of watching myself act like an uncontrollably furious person. I said to myself, "What is going on here—who is this person?" It was a rhetorical question, but the answer came right back, "This is Gina." I didn't know what to make of that, but my therapist became quite emphatic about the double diagnosis. Gina was one of my personalities.

It has become clear that Gina is entirely separate from Renée. There are six personalities altogether. Some apparently psychotic symptoms had originated with other personalities acting on their own or talking internally.

I recall pieces of the abuse. The memory I recalled two weeks ago was of oral sexual assault. My brother was very threatening and violent and had taken nude photos of me as one of his methods of coercion. He would leave sickening, violent pornography in my bed, describing mutilations and murders and rapes, and insist that I read it. He took my underclothes and damaged or wore them or left them stained with semen. He and another brother did sexual things with dogs. There was no one I could go to in the home.

It finally stopped when I was almost 17; he wanted intercourse and I said no, so he instead raped one of my girlfriends and left town. My mother blamed me for "letting it get out of the family." I didn't understand this until I was first hospitalized at age 31. At that point I confronted my mother and found out that she had known about it all along and had chosen not to do anything, which was pretty characteristic of her. My father was initially shocked. Over the course of about six months, he went from being deeply apologetic to telling me that it was all my fault anyway and that I deserved it. At that point they disowned me.

The situation was made more complex because the brother that was sexually abusing me was the one my parents were physically abusing the worst. That made it even harder because I ended up as his caretaker, the only one in the family who had any real emotional connection to him. I felt so bad for him. I must have hid in my closet a thousand times, praying that God would give me what my brother was feeling so that he could be relieved of it. It was more than I felt he could take. I remember them hitting him over the head with a big cast iron skillet, for example, because he wasn't learning his homework well enough in high school.

When they weren't after my older brother, they were after me. There were continual fights, screaming and yelling and hysterical crying daily. As I got older, my mother would impulsively slug one of us with a fist from time to time, or beat us with a wooden paddle.

But the emotional abuse was the worst. She was so berating. There were two of us she liked and two of us, including me, that she hated. It might have been a little easier to take if we had all been equally disliked, but we weren't. The comparisons were continual.

The striking thing as I look back on it is that I had every reason to have won her approval. I was the perfect student, a star athlete, a concert musician on several instruments, a community volunteer who got several awards. I was adored by my teachers, and I think that the good relationships I formed with them were what saved my life. But there was no way I could please my mother. She brainwashed me into believing that my birth family didn't want me because I was bad, and I was terrified that my adoptive family would also reject me.

The first time I had any counseling was just before I graduated from high school. I went to a psychologist who was active at a church I was attending. He did a battery of diagnostic tests that showed clearly that I had a lot wrong and was suicidal. He met with me three more times and then said, "Well, I think you're just fine," and wouldn't see me any more. I was horrified.

Shortly after that, we had a terrible, terrible fight at home. I almost killed myself then but decided instead that somehow I would live until I went away to college and to a better life that fall.

I had counted so much on college being an escape that it was horrible to find that all my unhappiness was still inside of me. I didn't know how to ask for help. I was so used to keeping up a successful front that I didn't know how to tell anybody what was wrong. But I did have some contact with the medical staff on the campus.

I think the staff must have realized that something was very much awry. In December, when I took 32 sleeping pills, the kneejerk response was that I would be sent home. I was the first suicide attempt on campus in 25 years, so it really hit the administration hard. The medical staff intervened and said, "That's where the problems spring from—if you send her home, you'll kill her." So the administration agreed that I could stay on condition that I see the school-affiliated psychiatrist as long as she deemed necessary and never make another suicide attempt. They effectively tied my hands with my fear of being sent home, or I would have tried again.

The psychiatrist put me on antidepressants, and seeing her was stabilizing, but we weren't really doing any discovery work. Therapy was kind of a day-to-day survival mechanism that didn't look at what was going on underneath. I saw the psychiatrist until the following year, when I left that school to get married. My husband was the first person whose love I didn't have to earn, and his affection made a tremendous difference in how I felt. We got married about six months after we met, almost exactly a year after the suicide attempt. I hadn't been home at all during this time.

We went to another school for a semester. Then I wanted to have children. So we left school, when I would have been a junior, and I had four babies, including twins, in the next six years. Each time I became pregnant, I got extremely depressed. The experience was like a continual five-year pregnancy with intensive depressive cycles.

It was really hard to cope when the children were small. The first one and the twins were only 16 months apart. There would have been another 16-month interval if I hadn't miscarried that fetus. The three toddlers and the miscarriage sent me into the deepest depression I had had.

Looking back, I see "borderline" stamped all over the experience, the way we look so much more functional than we are. Everybody who knew me thought I was just fine and patient and wonderful, and I just wanted to die. I would cope beautifully to a point and then just snap and be another person entirely. I would start screaming and was probably verbally abusive. It was very bewildering for the children, because everything would look just fine, and then all of a sudden I would be out of control with my anger. After I later ended up in the hospital, two of them started therapy.

I had determined not to be like my parents, and usually once it started I would get away from the kids. I would go into my room, close the door, and lie on the bed sobbing hysterically. Several times I felt so unworthy that I couldn't even lie on the bed: I would get down on the floor where I wouldn't be as close to God. I felt so bad because I had these feelings. When I miscarried, I felt it was a punishment for being an unworthy parent and really grappled with that.

But as the children got a little older, they were less demanding, behaved very well, and were very loving. It helped me feel less unworthy, that God would send me such wonderful children. Then with the next pregnancy, the depression hit again. It was a very difficult pregnancy physically and emotionally, and I was morbidly depressed by the time the baby was born. The birth caused all kinds of disasters. Both of us nearly died, and I hemorrhaged severely after the birth and apparently had a post-traumatic reaction to that. By the time the terrible physical experience was over, I didn't even feel that I was in my body. Emotionally I was completely numb for three months, even through the baby's pneumonia.

After about 15 weeks, the numbness suddenly shattered. It was as though everything that I should have felt a few months earlier when death was imminent had just hit me. The feeling went away after several hours but kept coming back out of the blue.

I mentioned some of these problems to a nurse I had hired occasionally to help out with the kids. She had a lot of psychiatric background.

She suggested that I get into long-term therapy and explained why that might help me feel better.

That was a key moment for me. It was the first time that I had the conception that things could be different.

So I started seeing an incredibly analytical psychiatrist with an excellent local reputation. It's only within the last couple of months that I've really looked hard at what went on there and decided that the problem wasn't me after all. I think this guy had some countertransference problems he had never worked out. We just stood still really. For the next three and a half years we had weekly sessions just looking at memories. It was good groundwork for what came later, because it gave me a pretty organized picture of what my childhood had been like other than what I had repressed.

But just before the three-year mark, things began to get really messy at home. I began to have odd symptoms that appeared pretty quickly to have to do with the sexual abuse.

I had intermittently experienced symptoms like these throughout our marriage. For the first two years my husband and I were married, about 75 percent of the times we had intercourse, I would black out. Everything would be fine, then I would black out, and the next thing I knew he would be there beside me, frequently crying, repeating, "Renée, come back." This just gradually decreased over the next few years and then things were pretty much all right. But now, although I wasn't having these blackouts, I would increasingly panic over any kind of intimacy. If my husband suddenly hugged or kissed me, the next thing I knew, he would be flattened against the opposite wall even though he weighs 250 pounds. Fortunately, he was patient.

I also couldn't bear to have anyone—not my husband or children, or anyone—hold onto my hands. I would panic and go nuts. And around this time a child abuse-homicide case was being very well publicized in the news. I couldn't handle any mention of child abuse or sexual abuse at all. I would just panic, throw down the paper or turn off the radio, and literally run.

My psychiatrist was not empathetic or directive; each session was straight free association with the last few minutes devoted to his analysis. There was no connection emotionally. So I had never been able really to talk to him about anything very personal. Week after week I would really struggle with myself, determined to talk about it that day, but I couldn't.

But I was afraid to leave him. I was really intimidated by the idea of trying to find another therapist. Trust was a really hard thing for me, and I really felt that I trusted him and couldn't bear the idea of starting over with somebody else just to deal with sexual issues.

I *had* been able to discuss these things with a male friend who had a master's degree in psychology and with whom we had a complicated relationship. He was my husband's immediate supervisor at work, my doctor's brother-in-law, and a lay minister in our church; his wife was a close friend of mine, and we did a lot of things socially. He decided that he should be a kind of secondary therapist who would help me work through the memories and the trauma.

This was a terrible mistake. The friend worked with me weekly for five months while I still saw the psychiatrist weekly as well. The psychiatrist knew about this arrangement and said as little about it as he did about anything else. So now I had one therapist who never asked about sexual abuse and a second one who focused on nothing else. If the friend had had the skills and we had developed the right relationship, we might have made headway. Instead we spent five months mucking around and not really getting anywhere other than traumatizing me worse.

Then one day when I called the friend after having an argument with my husband and becoming very upset, the first thing he said was, "I'm not going to be your therapist any more." At that point, he insisted that I leave my psychiatrist and instead see a social worker, another member of our church, who specialized in the treatment of sexual abuse. All his roles in my life gave him tremendous influence over me, so I consented.

After a few sessions, I began questioning the social worker's competence. I didn't hit it off with her anyway, partly because I have never been able to work well with a woman therapist.

So this was a disaster. I had left my previous therapist, who at least was there and whom I trusted, and now I felt very much adrift.

Around this time, the friend's wife took me out one morning and told me that someone had said that I was in love with her husband. It blew me away. My friendship with these people was my lifeline; this was the first time I had known wonderful people who really cared about me, and I about them. It was like having a family. I clung to things they would say, like, "Renée is one of the family." I was distraught over this and all its implications and because without recognizing it, I was starting to become seriously ill with encephalitis and was about to nearly die.

This threat to my friendship with these people was caused by the classic borderline reaction of panic and self-loathing. Although everybody else recognized that the story was gossip originating from a weird individual, I overreacted because I was already ill and thought I was being accused of adultery. I decided that I must be an awful person, or this would not be happening. I was devastated and felt like the world was ending. I didn't know what to make of it. And then I was hospitalized, nearly comatose, under the supervision of a physician whose presence kept reminding me of my recent conversation with his sister.

I developed an organic brain syndrome associated with the infection and was really, really sick. When I came out of that, I looked like a stroke victim, leaning on a cane with one side very weak. Even after I got out of the hospital, I had weird hallucinations and memory disruption.

Three weeks to the day after my discharge, I had an acute appendicitis attack and had to be readmitted for emergency surgery—again under the supervision of the friend's brother-in-law.

By then I had become bipolar, apparently from the damage caused by the encephalitis. I could cycle up and down from normal to manic five times in a half-hour; then about every three days, I'd cycle into the depression and become violently suicidal. It was like condensing six months of normal depression into an hour. One night my husband physically restrained me from killing myself.

At first everybody thought this would go away. The physician put me on lithium, which made me more normal, but I was still very depressed overall.

I had left the social worker and broken free of the friend's influence during the disruption, so I didn't care if he wanted me to go see her. So I had no therapist. I had to find one because I was falling apart. I couldn't sleep at night or stay awake during the day. I was enrolled as an engineering major at a local university with two quarters left to graduation. I had a 3.8 average and was applying to graduate school, but I couldn't study any more, so I left school on medical leave.

I interviewed three therapists. The first was lousy; the second I really liked; the third had me come back twice, then called the friend without my permission and told him to get out of my life. So he did. And so did my physician, very abruptly. I don't know whether he followed his brother-in-law's lead or whether he thought I had hurt his sister, but he called me into his office and said he would continue to treat my family but wouldn't be my doctor any more. In addition to the neurological trauma, I had a history of congenital heart problems, and here I was left with a lot of medical complications and no doctor. I felt so abandoned and distraught that I drove out into the country. Instead of committing suicide, as I planned, I eventually woke up in my car not knowing how long I had been there. In the middle of nowhere I had blacked out.

I called the third psychiatrist, furious that he had broken confidentiality. At that point the second psychiatrist that I liked called to ask if I had made a decision, but I couldn't do that because I couldn't think. And I wasn't ready to trust anybody. So I did nothing.

The next six weeks were probably the worst I have ever endured. I was obligated to play the harp and the oboe for a whole host of Christmas performances and couldn't leave anybody in the lurch. I wanted to die; I would go off and rehearse all morning and then come home and lie on my bed and try to talk myself out of suicide. Each day that was all I did. I had to stay out of my kitchen because I knew that I would pick up a knife and use it on myself.

It was an enormous, continual battle. Other than when I was engrossed in the music, there wasn't a minute that I was away from my suffering. My children became self-sufficient because I was in the bedroom trying not to die. I couldn't follow through on the therapy decision. What kept me alive was that I didn't want the concerts to be cancelled because I had let everybody down. What had kept me alive before this was always a sense of obligation to my children. But no depression had been as bad as this one: I was sure my family would be better off without me.

I reached the point of trying to call my former psychiatrist, who had been away for several weeks. I finished the last performance on Christmas night and finally got to see him two days after Christmas. I don't know where I got the strength to do this, but I sat down, looked him in the eye and said, "I have to be in a hospital, or I'll die." I didn't know what went on in a psychiatric unit, just that I wouldn't stay alive any longer with my obligations having ended. He agreed.

This psychiatrist did no inpatient work and had no hospital privileges. So we decided on the closest hospital with a decent reputation, and he called eight or ten psychiatrists who worked there and sketched out my case. Those who agreed to see me included the one I had interviewed and liked. So I saw him that night, was hospitalized immediately and stayed there for the next seven or eight weeks.

I was out for four weeks. I saw my psychiatrist twice a week and the medical director of the unit each day to try to work out medication. I couldn't take most of the tricyclics because of my heart condition; 800 milligrams of Desyrel had only a tiny effect, so he put me on Nardil, which had an impact within three weeks. On 75 milligrams, I felt considerably better. Then he tried to switch me to Parnate, and after just one dose, I ended up back on the unit for ten days with severe hypotension.

At that point the medical director decided to exit and let me work with my psychiatrist. So I had to separate from this man I had been seeing five days a week for six weeks. That was difficult, but I settled in well with my psychiatrist.

For about six months, I would spend one to three weeks in the hospital and then be out for a week or two, then back in and out. I had 17 hospitalizations within the year and ten the following year. Even when the depression was manageable from the Nardil, which was definitely the right drug for me, I would become acutely suicidal.

About four months into this, I had a psychotic episode and heard voices commanding me to kill myself. I knew that these were unreal; I never lapsed far enough into psychosis to buy it all, but it was happening, and that was a very bizarre episode. I remember my psychiatrist frowning over it a lot, and his admission note said that this was a very perplexing diagnostic situation because it just didn't fit one category or another. I think it was he who diagnosed me as borderline; it might have been the medical director, but I know they concurred on it. Along with depression, that was the primary diagnostic code on all the hospitalizations until the multiple personality disorder was discovered.

I finally got off lithium around this time and was no longer having bipolar symptoms, so we attributed that to the encephalitis and put it behind us. So I was on Nardil along with 13 other medications: cardiac drugs, psychiatric drugs, antipsychotic drugs, drugs to counteract the side effects of other drugs, too many drugs. It took me a year to get down to two or three.

After six months things improved, perhaps because it was then that I confronted my parents and we broke up, which was painful but caused more relief than sadness. It was the beginning of my understanding that I was not bad, but rather bad things had been done to me that weren't my fault. This was pivotal in my recovery.

I had been able to talk to this psychiatrist from the start about what sexual abuse I remembered. It was an excellent relationship. I felt comfortable and safe and could talk about everything and really felt close to him. I had never before encountered a therapist who felt what I was feeling along with me and helped me understand it. He's very analytical, but he connected emotionally too, with very powerful empathy. He has been very supportive as well.

My psychiatrist managed to have the same effect as the contract I had in college of binding up my suicidal urges until we could clarify them. I had become well acquainted with that particular inpatient unit and the staff there. We were very good friends, really, and I had a lot invested in being able to continue to go to that unit. So the psychiatrist wrote a no-harm contract into my discharge agreement with the hospital. This said that they would continue to accept me as long as my psychiatrist wanted me hospitalized and I had not harmed myself before I came in. It was a very fortuitous plan because it stayed what would otherwise have been a very destructive hand. I continued to struggle with my suicidal urges, able to control myself partly because I knew that if I did, I would be allowed back into the hospital.

This particular hospital hadn't been treating many borderlines who repeatedly hurt themselves. They simply didn't want such patients and arranged for them to go elsewhere. My case was the first they put into a special program they developed for personality-disordered patients who need repeated admissions. It helps the patients use their hospitalizations more effectively. The program is very structured, and at first I resented it because I was categorized and the plan was sometimes rigid and unreasonable. But overall it has been very useful and productive. The goal- and task-oriented approach, the staff's familiarity with me, and my own determination enable me to accomplish much more during my stays than most patients.

After about six months, the pattern settled into three or four days on the unit and then three weeks out. At one point I made it through an entire month without admission; this year I'm up to four months. Christmas is always really bad, though, because of lots of anniversary issues like the suicide attempt and my first being hospitalized. I had the only self-destructive episode that kept me from being admitted to the hospital on the one-year anniversary of my first admission there. I over-medicated, and a crisis line traced the call and sent paramedics who broke into the house. So I was refused admission for irresponsible behavior.

It's a paradoxical approach, and I can't explain it except to say that the staff felt it would work because they knew how much I depended on the unit and wanted to get better. And they knew that I had these drives to hurt myself despite my work in therapy. If their system hadn't been working, I would have damaged myself a lot. The two most borderline of my personalities, Gina and Beth, were chronically suicidal before being therapeutically merged with Renée.

I understand my symptoms and history much better now that we have identified the six personalities and their roles. The most flagrantly ill borderline, Beth, began the first self-mutilation I had ever done shortly before "committing suicide," as she saw it, by merging. Otherwise I had never done the cutting or burning or the other stuff I see among other borderlines. My harp playing has always been very important to me, so I didn't want to risk damaging my hands. And I've seen what their scars do to the lives of other borderlines. I don't have the physical brand on me that tells people there's something wrong. People generally don't even realize that I have any problems.

I know about other borderlines because of the group therapy I'm in. The medical director had looked for some kind of group support when I was first admitted to the unit and was having difficulty finding what he wanted because all the local groups seemed either too high- or too low-functioning for me. Finally he tried to get me into a group that was learning dialectical behavior therapy. I was put on a waiting list, then joined a group being run by a therapist involved in researching how well it works.

This group did badly for several reasons. Half the members dropped out quickly, so the group got very small and intense. There were two therapists observing the group leader, and four borderline patients. Two of the patients put tremendous pressure on the therapist leading the group to make it more supportive of their individual issues. So he tried having us spend half our time on dialectical behavior therapy and half our time sharing support, but we couldn't maintain that balance. And then some of the members got socially involved.

This created horrible havoc. I can't think of anything more nightmarish than a group of borderlines clashing with each other in a group whose therapist isn't in control. I would end up leaving the group each Monday night and heading straight for the hospital. In fact, it was this therapist who diagnosed me as having multiple personality disorder because I had begun dissociating and behaving strikingly differently from week to week, partly in reaction to the group. So I resigned, and the group broke up.

A few months later, I was invited to join a new group run by a more experienced therapist. This group has been very useful, especially as an adjunct to my psychodynamic therapy. I feel the two approaches complement each other when done skillfully and with really motivated patients.

The only bad thing about the group is that most of the members see themselves strictly as borderline—being sick, bad, and directionless is their entire identity. I refuse to see myself that way, or to believe that I will be ill permanently. Things can be different.

9

Esther: Feeling Like Nothing

I am manic–depressive as well as borderline* and was being given lithium while I was treated on a borderline unit. I really don't know which of my traits are caused by which illness.

I'm 23 now and have had something wrong with me since I was 12 or 13. Up until then my family had focused on my brother. He was really sick for several weeks when he was three and I was two. I remember how terrible it was. As a result he has learning disabilities. My father claims that he was always difficult, but after his illness he became really difficult. My mother was always coddling him and interested in him, and he was always pushing her away and causing trouble. He was always my parents' concern. I always got good grades and was what I thought the perfect child, so they didn't pay that much attention to me. . . .

My brother had to see a psychiatrist, and we had to have family therapy because of him. I resented this and did it as a

*Esther is a *DSM-III-R* borderline. The diagnosis of bipolar disorder in BPD is controversial. "Dr. Gunderson and I feel that manic depression so distorts the personality that you can't make an accurate diagnosis of BPD," says Dr. Paris, who uses DIB criteria. "Therapists are misdiagnosing the rapid mood swings of BPD as mild manic depression."

great favor. We would fight over my brother wanting the latest clothing fad. It was terrible. So we stopped going.

When my brother went away to school when I was 12, I was glad he was out of the house. But I had waited so long for my parents' attention that nothing would have been enough; it was disappointing. I hated when he came home from vacation. I love my brother, but he was always trouble. With him gone the rest of us got along much better.

I used to ask my best friend if she thought my parents loved me. They're pretty nice. My father has his own mental problems—he's so overreactive and overemotional. He's been in therapy. I always thought he loved me actually because he's warm and my mother is kind of coldish or something.

Around that time we had all kinds of changes. I was home alone with my parents for the first time. I started not wanting to go to school and having crying fits. I was really depressed and suicidal without knowing how serious that was. I had basically one friend with whom I would discuss my feelings, making her promise not to tell. I've always had lots of acquaintances and seemed popular but had only one or two real friends. Even now I have two really close friends whom I talk to every day. The others I don't care about or count on or talk to. It bothers me, but it's me, it has always been this way, maybe.

Then my family moved to another city. I made no friends in my new school and was really depressed and started bingeing a lot. I went from a public to a very competitive private school and was behind, so I felt insecure and inferior. Toward the end of my first year, I started to make friends but stayed chronically depressed and was out of school a lot.

That same year, my grandmother died. I would see my grandmother three weeks out of the year and talk to her each month on the phone. I loved her a lot because she was one of the few people who accepted me for being me. I had seen her two weeks before she died and wasn't very nice to her, so I felt guilty about it.

That year was the turning point; in my first case conference at the hospital, when they diagnosed me as borderline, they said that it was when everything started to unravel, or something.

The years that followed, everything got worse with depression and crying fits. I would always pick on my face; if I had a blemish I would pick at it until it looked terrible. So I looked bad and felt terrible . . . .

During my junior year, my father took me to the same psychiatrist my brother had seen because he didn't know what to do with me. I didn't like the psychiatrist for stupid reasons—like he would take out sucking candies and not offer me one. I would sit and count the books on his shelves. I didn't know what I was supposed to be doing there. But I did give him the journals I was writing for English class.

Then I got into a fight with my parents, and I ran to the window. I really don't think I was going to jump, but I was leaning out the window, just to get away from my parents. The psychiatrist said that if anything like that ever happened again, I should be hospitalized, and that I should think about that possibility anyway. I didn't like him, so I switched to a woman therapist.

The psychiatrist had insisted that I shouldn't go away to college because I would never make it away from my parents. That was really hard for me to hear. I didn't even know if I wanted to go, but everyone else was going, so I enrolled in a school for interior design.

Just before I started there, I went into a manic fit and was exercising constantly and felt really good and thought that the world was wonderful and that I wouldn't see my therapist any more. School turned out to be really good, and I became a totally different person or something. I even changed my name to Alyssa.

My roommate at school had been a good friend for many years. She was really bulimic and had a lot of problems, but I didn't know it. She acted really strange and ended up leaving after a month. I never really got another roommate. But I remember thinking, "God, my roommate's so sick," even though I myself would binge and then go to sleep. We would have starvation competitions. But when I was manic, I wasn't obsessed with food.

I started dating a guy named Ted who was captain of the football team at his college, really smart and nice, but he had a really severe drinking problem and had to have many women. I saw him on and off until I met Claude, who was totally the opposite, and for a while after I started to see Claude, I would see Ted occasionally or something.

But Claude was the first person I ever really loved, and he moved in with me. He was really bad. He was into crack and other drugs, and failing out of Ted's school, and not really all that nice, but I really loved him. He was in my room for about four months.

The first time I saw Claude, I was scared of him but intrigued too. He was a dark figure, always playing chess or drawing or smoking tiny cigars, and he seemed really deep. He didn't care about monetary things; he was kind of a free spirit but also really angry at everything. He was a petty thief and devious and mean sometimes. But he attracted people and was always respected. And just the fact that he would care about me so much, love me, made me feel that it was really amazing that somebody so awful could feel this way about me, that somebody who did such mean things or who could be such a terrible person to others could be nice to me. He never bought me presents or anything—he never did anything for me really. He meant well, I guess, maybe.

Ted and Claude had in common undependability. One was an alcoholic and the other a drug addict. I don't know what draws me to men like them, maybe that they must feel pretty bad about themselves too. I couldn't be with someone who had his life together. I once went out with a guy who seemed perfect, and I couldn't stand him because he made me feel so bad about myself. I was also bored when I was with him. I don't think I could be with anyone who was normal and had a nine-to-five job and was nice to me. I guess I would think I didn't deserve it. I have this ultimate feeling that I've been ruined in some way or cursed. And I'm so erratic, I don't feel I could ever, *ever* have a life that was Monday through Friday and weekends and stuff. . . .

When Claude and I broke up, I knew he cared, so it wasn't bitter. We both ended it. I didn't like the way that he was being unhappy. I said something about it, and he said we shouldn't be together any more. But I couldn't believe or understand it. It was really hard to see him around even though we said we'd be friends. I had even gone back to the woman psychiatrist because I had started to feel really bad. . . .

I had done cocaine before and had started to think about doing it on a regular basis because I didn't know what to do any more. Meanwhile my psychiatrist started giving me antidepressants.

Claude and I had broken up a few days before a friend's birthday. We gave her a lot of cocaine and did it all. I got really agitated and went off by myself to try to get rid of my extra energy and go to sleep.

But when I got back to my room, my head really started to hurt and I felt really bad. I decided to kill myself. I thought that God was telling me that this was the answer, this was what I should do, that everything would be okay. I thought I kind of saw him; I really felt his presence right there, reeling messages into my brain that I should do this. I had bottles and bottles of imipramine that my doctor kept giving me, so at 3 A.M. I went into the bathroom to take the pills.

But somebody stopped by my room, found me, took me to the hospital and made me sign into the psychiatric unit. When they were wheeling me up, I felt as if I had hit rock bottom. I was put on a geriatric ward because they thought it would scare me less.

I stayed there for 10 days and got really manicky. I was happy to be alive and learning all this stuff, and it was great. They didn't want me to leave, but I convinced them to let me go. At this time I knew something was wrong with me, but I was also in a lot of denial.

I went back to school, then a few weeks later got really depressed and wanted to quit. The new psychiatrist I had started working with after the hospital told my parents to make me move home. I didn't know anything about mental illness and thought there was nothing wrong with me. I thought everyone felt depressed just as I did, or something.

I moved home and became manicky, then got severe mono and was in the hospital, then got really depressed again, so I was up and down a lot. During this time I had moved into an apartment my parents owned and had roommates. I was doing all kinds of jobs and had no direction.

I had to have family therapy again after my suicide attempt even though I didn't want my parents to know anything. My parents were bothered and frustrated with me. We were trying to make changes in my life when I was really far down and it wouldn't have made a difference.

I didn't feel that my parents would understand the suicide attempt. They didn't like Claude, and they never valued my feelings and still don't. But I guess they had reason to feel this way. My parents really were overprotective after my suicide attempt. My mother would call me every day.

Meanwhile I also wanted to be independent. I don't know what I was thinking, just that somehow I could make my own living and support myself. I still think sometimes that I'll sell my car and buy a piece of junk and move into a hovel. I felt like that then. . . .

After working with me for a year, the psychiatrist said that he thought I was borderline and manic-depressive. During this time we had tried all different medications as well as the family therapy. The psychiatrist told me that he couldn't continue treating me in good conscience or something. He recommended long-term hospitalization. I really trusted him, so I agreed even though I wasn't really happy about it. I thought it would be three to six months, and if it was six, there was no way I was going.

When I went for my interview, I thought *I* was interviewing the *hospital* rather than they were interviewing me. I met with the medical director and hated him and was getting the flu and was really angry. There was no way I was going there. He told me that it was an all-female unit, and I remember screaming in the lobby that I wasn't going to any psychiatric charm school. I was outrageous. I had never been that outrageous before. And in the car, I was crying hysterically. But by the time my parents dropped me off at my apartment I had decided that I should go, maybe. I didn't see any alternatives. My life was going nowhere and I didn't know how to make it different. . . .

I was hospitalized for 18 months and now see a therapist who focuses more on my manic-depressive traits than he does on my borderline ones. I lived in a halfway house for the first five months after discharge and now have a two-bedroom apartment all to myself because a hospital friend couldn't move in.

The hospital was really good and bad. I made some really good friends that I still talk to, but it was very frustrating. I think I was acting a lot of the time, or something.

I went to school while I was in the hospital. I haven't been able to do that outside the hospital, but I did it then because I was afraid that if I didn't go to class or do my homework I would get in trouble with the unit. It was unusual—they let me out for school after I had been there only a few months because they saw it was a really big issue for me. But I have to say that I didn't always go to school when I said I did. I would do what they said while resenting it because ultimately I didn't see the point. I sort of believed in what they wanted but was very confused. It was a whole different society there, with nothing my choice any more. We had to follow the program, so I would avoid thinking about it. And now that I have my choice back, I choose not to do things.

I fit in at the hospital really well. I was on the patient activities committee most of the time I was on the unit. I was usually friendly to everyone. No one ever had a major beef with me, and I prided myself on being liked and not making trouble or something. I would just get really depressed or sort of manicky now and then.

It drove me crazy that the staff wanted me to be involved all the time, although I did give in. I can't believe how much the other patients affected me. I think I let myself feel things very much more when I was in the hospital. I was getting angry or hurt by other people. People outside don't act as outrageously, but in general I don't feel as much in the real world either. I just try to ignore things and feel that everything is okay. In the hospital everything gets discussed and examined and analyzed; outside you can just ignore things or just mention them or something. Things are much more matter-of-fact.

People on the unit were so different that sometimes it seemed as if *borderline* was just a name for people with problems. One patient would not want anyone to know anything about her; she would wear brown all the time and be quiet and thoughtful and good at crafts. Another patient would be really vocal and outrageous, throwing things when she was angry and grabbing the floor in group to talk about her problems. Totally different people with the same diagnosis. . . .

I don't really feel that great about my hospitalization. Things are a little bit different but not that much. My therapy has helped with my loneliness, but with concrete things like working or going to school, it's just the same. I seemed to make a lot of progress; after 18 months it was kind of time to leave. And I wanted to get out.

But I haven't done anything since then. Over the past two months I've been working at my parents' business a few days a week, but they just laid me off.

I don't think I could ever do anything consistently. I never have, because of my depressions. I think I've integrated into my personality a lot of things that I do when I get depressed that I also do even when I'm not. So even when I'm feeling okay, I end up ruining my jobs or something. I don't see how it's ever going to happen. I could see myself getting married to someone who would either take care of me completely or be as irresponsible and pathetic as I am. I just can't see having a happy life with someone else. I don't think it will ever happen, I really don't. . . .

I try to do something about it. I go to therapy and talk about it all the time and try to find things to do. I'm in a bad period now. My doctor thinks one of my biggest problems is this ultimate feeling of hopelessness. I guess that's what I'm upset about—I felt this way, and went into this hospital to do everything I could, and now ten months after discharge, two years later, I feel the same way and my life is very much the same.

I hadn't made a suicide attempt for a year before the hospital, so I didn't improve in that sense. I don't think that suicide attempts are my major problem. Right before the hospital, I was living rent-free in my parents' apartment, and I wasn't working or going to school, and I didn't know what I was going to do. And now my parents pay for my rent and a really expensive therapist, and I'm not doing anything. It's so strikingly similar. I always really sort of had friends; now I have friends who are almost as pathetic as I am—actually they're not, they just understand because they have the same problems. They're more accepting of what I am. All that's different is that I know what I should talk about in therapy.

While living at the halfway house I started taking three classes at a local university. After a few weeks I felt overwhelmed and really bored in one of the classes and thought, "Why am I doing this? I don't have to do this!" My big line to myself is "Why torture myself any more?" I really feel tortured. So I dropped that class.

I was really trying to stick with the other two classes. I did really poorly on the midterm in one of them, so I groveled to the teacher, and my father wrote half of my paper, and I got a B plus that I didn't deserve.

I was getting an A in the third class, but it was a lot of really boring reading in history and philosophy. Toward the end I couldn't concentrate to write the paper or read the stuff. I just buckled under and ended up failing that class. The semester ended with me saying, "I'm not going to school any more."

I'm not disappointed with my performance. I just don't feel that I can go on any more. During the semester, I felt like I was dying. Lately I've been so angry about how they make you stick with everything, even if there's no reason to do it. Just stick with it. Now if something's bothering me, I say, "Forget it." It's just my attitude. In high school if I was scared to go to school or didn't want to I would say, "Life is just for living—you don't have to do anything." That's how I live my life. In the short term I'm okay, but in the long term I end up with nothing. . . .

I often talk about living on a commune even though I don't know if I'd want to. If my parents wouldn't support me, I'd be in so much trouble. They would never do it; it will never happen. My parents have supported me for years. They're not overly permissive. I depend on them as my friends—not for emotional support, but I trust them. But before I went into the hospital, they said they would cut me off. That was one of the big issues for me, that I couldn't take it.

I really don't know what to do about myself. I'm waiting for some savior—no, really—God, or this rich man, or my doctor, to tell me what to do. I always had a problem even in school when we had to say what we wanted to be when we grew up. I would say that I wanted to be a comedian. I was so embarrassed because I had no clue—I have never had an idea of what I wanted to be. I said I wanted to be an interior designer because it seemed really cool, but I never knew why I wanted to do that.

I don't want to be so many things. I don't want to be a brain surgeon, or a cafeteria worker. All my jobs I didn't want to do.

I feel really awful when I see my friends who know what they want. I'm nothing. I can hang with these people or those people. I can never say, "I want to do this or be this," or something.

My parents were very involved with my treatment. They came to every family session and all the parents' sessions at the hospital, and they don't put any pressure on me any more. My mother says every so often, "Well, you might get a little job," and my father makes a noise when he hands me the checks, but they don't make me do anything. My therapist and I talk about how my parents should be sort of supportive but more boundaried in what they expect of me. Or they should just say "Here's all this money—do whatever you want." I'd probably be better off, maybe. I think they're resentful because they're getting older and want to live their own lives, but they can't help being really involved emotionally with me and wanting to see me okay. . . .

My parents used to talk all the time at the parents' sessions, and everyone thought that I had the greatest parents and that I was so lucky they were so involved. My parents seem terrific. They really are good. But something's wrong. I do fight with them. Lately we just take out our anger on each other whenever anything is wrong. My father might be pressured by his work, and if I don't lock the door, he'll go crazy on me and then apologize later. We don't stay mad about anything. My brother and I yell at each other and then forget about it.

I felt that my brother was my father's failure, and I was supposed to succeed and make my father feel that everything was great. So that's where I got the need to succeed. But my parents are realizing now that I'll never do that. I didn't even get anywhere beyond high school.

It doesn't make any sense at all to me . . . .

Basically I've decided that I'm never doing anything so that nobody ever expects anything ever. No, really. I told my therapist I can't stand another failure. I'm scared to take any kind of course, even if it's not for a grade.

I really love to take pictures, but I'm scared to pick up my camera. I'm paralyzed now. The pictures might not be as good as I want, or I might be frustrated. I took a photography course a few months ago and didn't even finish it, and I don't even know why. God, this is depressing.

The worst part about it is that I look like I'm competent, that I should be happy. I have concerned parents, a great apartment, money, friends; I'm not really ugly, but I'm so miserable. People don't ever see that. That's part of the whole borderline thing. So many people from the hospital were so nice and had so much to offer and were so wonderful, neater than anybody I've ever met, but they were so messed up. I still don't really understand that.

10

"A Very Borderline Thing to Do"

"Borderline personality disorder is simply the illness of not being taken seriously."
"ALISON"

We have thus far examined diagnostic theories about BPD from the viewpoint of professionals. What BPD **is**, and who has the illness, have different but equally crucial implications for borderlines and the people around them.

Borderlines worry about exposure not just for the obvious reasons but because they know that *other people can't understand their illness.* While the stereotype of BPD tends to be taken very seriously, its reality often is not. The whole situation is incomprehensible.

And yet the illness is an issue that cannot be avoided in relationships. "One of the biggest dilemmas you'll find is who to tell and how, when and where to tell them," says Ingrid.

> When you're dating someone, he has to know a little bit, but how much? It gets crazy and very complicated. When are you going to be aware that you're borderline, as opposed to just having a good time?

Even though effective therapy teaches the borderline patient to be honest about herself, this practice might backfire because all conflicts in a relationship can then be blamed on her. Or the borderline can be comfortably stereotyped by others as someone who *always* distorts things, who just wants sympathy, who is determined to have her way, or whatever else the observer chooses to believe.

Such invalidation of their experience on so many levels is torture to borderlines. It is impossible to overemphasize how serious this illness is and how much pain it causes. This chapter will therefore highlight some of its features that exacerbate BPD because they are so poorly understood.

Borderlines are incomprehensible partly because each is a bundle of contradictions. Able to "read" other people with remarkable intuition, borderlines are unaware of how their behavior affects them and likely to be victimized by the most obviously threatening of potential abusers. Emotionally intense and heavy-handed, borderlines are nevertheless extraordinarily hypersensitive. They complain that their suffering greatly exceeds that of normal experience, yet they also self-mutilate and flirt with suicide. They are desperate to avoid abandonment yet capable of withdrawing from society or treating others with chilling indifference or disdain. Their submissiveness and defensiveness alternate with sheer contempt.

Viewed by others as incredibly manipulative, borderlines themselves feel powerless. They act completely entitled yet have very little self-esteem, expressions of which others often misinterpret as attacks.* One minute borderlines can be in a suicidal crisis; the next they can behave cheerfully. The same people at whom they rage one day can terrify them the next. The directness of their behavior belies the ambiguity of their language and their ultimate elusiveness.

Inside each borderline appears to be a miserable, frustrated two year old screaming to get out. Their immaturity is one reason they are patronized like children.

Other people can be seduced into borderline behavior, catching the emotional charge as if it were contagious. Anyone who is violently upset can distort what he sees, behave inconsistently, or show other symptoms of the illness while projecting them onto the borderline who is the source of the excitement. This denial frightens and enrages the real borderline by discrediting her perceptions of that person.

What then is the difference between normal emotional range and

---

*An example would be, "You don't care about me," which might actually mean, "I'm not worth anyone's caring about."

borderline behavior? And what about BPD is hardest for other people to understand?

Depth of Feeling

In Chapter 6 we noted Zanarini's suggestion that borderlines are perhaps distinguishable less by the depth of their suffering than by their need to communicate it to others. Robin both echoes and disputes this notion:

> That's a very borderline thing to do, to want to make everybody understand. But I don't know how much understanding you can get from reading a book or listening to patients and not actually feeling something. That's my basic gripe, that you can't make people understand feelings that they've never experienced.
>
> Last week on the phone you said you thought you were beginning to understand how we feel. When people say things like that to me, it really pisses me off. Right, you know how it feels—*you don't know shit!*

The insistence that borderline feelings are uniquely intense is shared by all the patients I have talked to except Ingrid. "I don't know necessarily that borderline pain is that much worse than other people's," she says. "The way we *respond* to pain is different. Borderlines *want* to believe that their pain is worse."

Yet the responses are so outrageously "different" as to make Ingrid's distinction questionable. "Other people don't cut themselves when they feel bad," says Robin.

> If others could feel things as intensely, they couldn't cope with those feelings in a healthy way. When I'm depressed, I can't regulate it; I can't work; I can't function; it's out of control. Other people feel crummy and still go to work. . . .

Combined with the intensity itself is the borderline's lack of coping skills that other people take for granted. Whitney explains that

> we don't understand what these very intense feelings are about or where they're coming from, and so we can't even begin to deal with them. So we develop different ways of coping, whether pushing them down, denying them, mutilating ourselves, becoming addicts, or whatever. Until somebody points out that there's a different way of processing and handling them, we just don't know any better.

Even when borderlines succeed in communicating their distress, it can be misinterpreted as the product of their own exaggeration or other distortion. This is especially true of the depression Robin describes that precludes her being able to function.

Many people believe that borderlines often can't see past their illness to their better qualities. Rather than recognizing their obvious talent and their capacity for understanding and exercising good judgment, people think, borderlines instead distort themselves to look their worst.

Therapists who observe this behavior explain it as the desire of borderlines for validation and their idealistic belief that saviors will rescue and transform them—a belief that when disproven causes very destructive rage. Another suggestion is that borderlines fail to fulfill their academic and professional potential not because of impairments like disorganized thinking or emotional instability but rather because of impulsive behavior or other practical consequences of these symptoms.

Of course borderlines do have distorted perspectives; Ingrid says that "until you can feel what it's like to think distorted, you can't understand what borderline is all about." And the tendency to feel helpless and desire to be rescued are so common among borderlines that Linehan has labeled these symptoms *active passivity syndrome*.[1]

The implication is that borderlines could certainly function capably if they would just get their acts together. Borderlines *think* that they can't function, many people insist, just as they *think* that their feelings are uniquely intense.

But such assumptions about borderline competence are overgeneralizations. Borderlines actually have varying levels of personal, social, and professional functioning, from low to high, for several different reasons, and they can function inconsistently at whatever level they happen to occupy. To expect consistent competence from them too early in therapy is absolutely to court disaster.

The misconception that borderlines underestimate their capability disregards an extremely important feature of their illness that has been best described by Linehan as *apparently competent person syndrome*.

Apparently Competent Person Syndrome

The psychiatric profession itself is partly responsible for the fact that apparently competent person syndrome is not widely enough recognized. One reason is the standard view of psychological development, which holds that people progress chronologically toward maturity. Borderlines are an exception to this rule; their instability affects their competence as profoundly as it does every other aspect of their lives.

Another reason is the traditional assumption that a treatment setting is like a laboratory in which a therapist can study how the borderline behaves in the real world. Thoughtful therapists have recognized that this is not necessarily true. "Not enough attention has been paid to the actual disabilities or dysfunctions shown by borderlines out in the community," says Paul S. Links, M.D.

> The profession has instead focused on their interactions with the health care system, where they may show more problems than they do elsewhere. They are less successful in work and in relationships than we or they might wish but seem capable of handling the tasks of daily independent living quite well. If we better understood what dysfunctions they actually have, we could perhaps intervene more effectively.

Even Dr. Links' suggestion that borderlines are capable of living independently may be too broad a generalization. But the point is to determine *accurately* where their competence lies. Linehan's concept helps define borderline disabilities more precisely.

One pattern of apparent competence is that the borderline appears always to function well, especially in professional or academic situations that are structured, supportive, or both. Meanwhile she is binding her interior fragmentation with shoestrings, perhaps spending many, many hours crying hysterically or using self-destructive behaviors to cope. This type of borderline believes that nobody ever sees her true incompetence and in fact wishes that she performed less well so that people *could* see. Thus we have heard Renée complain about being misperceived as the perfect mother.

A second pattern is for capability not to carry over into what most people, including borderlines themselves, see as closely related areas. "I was an underachiever because I had so much static in my head from anxiety that I couldn't hear what was going on in class," says Paige.

> Nothing made sense. Yet I won the poetry contest at school and was having letters published in *Time, The Washington Post,* and the local paper from the time I was 13. So I wasn't stupid, but nobody ever said, "Look, she's getting a 62 in English but winning this award."

"I can make a speech to 500 people easily," says Ingrid, "but walking into a room with 10 people having coffee is horrendous to me."

Yet another pattern is that of functioning inconsistently over time. A borderline can be competent one day and incompetent the next. She doesn't merely have "off days," nor does she necessarily fake incompetence to avoid consistent responsibility. Rather, her competence unpredictably short-circuits. Just as a blown fuse might as well not be wired, so too the borderline who has short-circuited might as well never have demonstrated competence at all.

"I pride myself on holding down a highly technical job, but at times I have had to be taken to the hospital in mid-shift," says Carla. "The bad spells can come on literally within a matter of hours."

As Linehan notes, their incompetence is extremely difficult for borderlines to explain, partly because they appear so capable to others. As a result, those around her discredit the borderline's incompetence and infuriate her by their misunderstanding and expectations. Or the borderline buys into the general consensus and becomes convinced that she should be living up to the reasonable standards of others. Whenever she fails, she then feels guilty about her presumed lack of motivation and concludes that she is bad. Like her anger, her guilt can provoke self-destructive acting out, including suicide.[2]

Unstable and patchy in her competence, the borderline may attempt to cope with her predicament by overextending or crippling herself to preclude accusations that she is going back and forth.

This terrible situation becomes even worse if the borderline's therapist is not alert to it. Therapists see their job in part as helping their patients function as well and as happily as possible. But it does not further this goal to emphasize their positive performance histories to borderline patients and assume that these can continue.

The worst mistake in this situation is to misinterpret the borderline's incompetence as deliberate avoidance of responsibility or some kind of defense. "The tendency to overattribute lack of progress to resistance rather than to inability is especially dangerous," writes Linehan.[3] In the borderline's world, a fine line separates support of her strength from invalidation of her suffering and incompetence. Pressure from those around her consistently to maintain and increase her functioning is a good intention that leads straight to hell.

As more comes to be known about BPD, perhaps more people will recognize that their expectations about borderline competence are often unreasonable. People make what Linehan calls "rather predictable cognitive errors in evaluating other people," one of which is an assumption that behavior generalizes across dissimilar conditions or contexts. For a borderline, the context is often her mood; thus an observer unaware of what is going on inside her really should have no idea what to expect.

"The only way you can recognize how sick they really are is to go through the experience with the patient yourself and learn that she is telling you the truth," says the father of one borderline patient. "You can't understand it otherwise."

Of course, many borderlines *can* function. Merely to continue *living* with BPD, let alone to endure treatment for it, requires enormous strength. But this capability is full of holes whose locations are known only to the borderline, and often not even to her.

Apparently competent person syndrome illustrates one of the most important principles of therapy with borderlines: not to entertain preconceived assumptions about any particular symptom at any given time. The therapist and patient must work together to uncover her dynamics, in this case to tease apart self-generated helplessness from genuine incompetence. "I believe very firmly that you should rarely do something for a borderline individual that she can do for herself, and you should never require her to do something she can't do," says Linehan.

> I do very little for these patients on the one hand, and on the other, I do much more than most therapists. I believe that in effect, you must push borderline individuals with one hand and simultaneously hold them up with the other. Using the principles of shaping, you must figure out where they are and then demand that they go an inch further, stretching themselves without breaking.

Maintaining a delicate balance, the therapist supports and strengthens the borderline's active use of her capacities while at the same time recognizing, validating, and allowing for her genuine limitations. Within this context, the limitations themselves can begin to be therapeutically addressed.

''Manipulation''

Another aspect of borderline capability that is frequently overestimated, as it were, is their power to manipulate. What appears to other people as an arbitrary exercise of influence is to the borderline a means of actual survival. Borderlines just don't know how else to relate to other people. "What isn't manipulative in a child can be very manipulative in an adult," says Dr. Siever.

> Although they can be apparently manipulative, primitive personalities don't think about their behavior as such. They're trying to meet their needs in the

only way they know how. Somebody has to relieve their anger or anxiety or distress or sense of impending annihilation *right now*. They are trying to enable a response to soothe them, to help them feel better.

What is implied by Dr. Siever's remarks is here articulated by Whitney:

> To the rest of the world, we may seem very manipulative, angry bitches who do bad things. But the reason behind it is that we're trying to avoid a lot of hurt. What my borderline friends want is a close relationship, but they don't know how to get from point A to point B because nobody ever taught them. They may use the mechanisms that they've learned, like manipulation, to feel close to somebody.
> I don't manipulate for the sake of doing it but because I feel abandoned and rejected. I'll throw a temper tantrum and storm out of a group, for instance, when all I want is some attention and caring.

Often the manipulation is not even conscious, much less deliberate. "It's an interesting sickness because I think they come actually to believe what they're thinking, so that they're no longer lying," says another father.

> Time after time our daughter would look us straight in the eye and say that everything was fine, and she believed that herself until the minute she had to purge. After she purged she believed, like an alcoholic, that she wasn't ever going to do it again.

More deliberate manipulation is often an act of desperation: the borderline attempts suicide, for instance, to make people take her illness seriously. Probably the most exasperating type of behavior, these *manipulative suicidal gestures* can say as much about the boneheadedness of people around them as they do about borderlines. "To say that we're grabbing for attention doesn't feel the pain," says Ingrid.

> These suicide attempts are not saying, "Put me in the spotlight"; they're saying, "This is the only way to show how bad I'm feeling and get help." They are just as painful as the more serious suicide attempts, and although it's hard to take them seriously, a lot of them succeed.

As more than one followup study of borderline patients has shown, attempts that fail accurately predict later completed suicide. Repeated suicide attempts "must be taken seriously," writes Dr. Paris, "even if they appear to be 'manipulative.' "[4]

Suicide

Yet the borderline herself often shows an extremely casual attitude and openness about suicide that bewilder and upset others. One reason is that apparently suicidal behavior may actually be a form of self-mutilation, the subject of the next chapter. "Clearly a large number of suicide attempts by borderlines aren't suicide attempts at all," says Dr. Cowdry.

> Like self-mutilation, they are attempts to relieve, at least transiently, their distress. Relatively commonly, a borderline will become intensely dysphoric, take an overdose of Valium, and be discharged from the hospital the next day. She felt guilty or distressed, punished herself by overdosing, and felt relieved enough to move forward to the next peak of guilt. This tactic may work in part because borderlines tend to take benzodiazepines, which are anticonvulsants that calm overactive sites in the brain.

What makes even such "self-medication" dangerous is that many borderlines are unable accurately to assess the risk posed by their destructive behaviors. As we'll see in Chapter 20, high percentages of these patients report histories of childhood abuse. Preliminary findings suggest that particularly sadistic, violent abuse increases the victim's risk of suicide. Eleanor Saunders, Ph.D., and Frances Arnold, Ph.D., point out that perhaps the abused child initially views suicide as a potential escape from her trap and later sees it as a real way to avoid further suffering, fear, rage, or abandonment. The abused child who has become borderline can't perceive danger, mistrusts her own perceptions, and may dissociate under stress, which further weakens her ability to protect herself.[5]

Another reason that borderlines view suicide casually is their conviction that they are evil. The borderline believes that she deserves to die and that her suicide will hurt no one else. "I took a large supply of pills with me on a wilderness vacation so nobody could find and save me before I died of the overdose," says Carla. "But when I got to my campsite, it was so beautiful that I couldn't justify leaving my rotting body there to spoil nature."

Similarly, for every borderline who calls people from a motel room threatening to hang herself or overdose, another would never dream of doing such a thing. These borderlines would sooner die than bother someone else with their suicidal feelings. And because of this reticence, some of them do.

Like other suicidal people, borderlines can become so lost in pain and despair that they don't consider the potential repercussions of their deaths. Alice has seen reactions to the suicides of several other patients from her hospital unit and declares that she will never put her family and friends through such an ordeal.

> If anything, I go out of my way to please people, not hurt them. Whenever I've tried to kill myself, I wasn't thinking of my family, but I also never made a long-range plan for suicide. I couldn't think of anyone or anything else. I was so gone that I really, truly believed that this was what I had to do.

Chronic denial strips suicide of all emotional resonance; thus borderlines discuss the subject matter-of-factly as a reasonable option. "Ingrid really believed that all people think of suicide as a viable alternative to coping with life," says her mother.

> She has said to us, "Everybody thinks about suicide when they're having problems, don't they?" It blows your mind. And you hear that from your own child, who you thought you brought up to be this nice, adjusted, happy little girl. It's very, very difficult.

Ingrid's journal describes a therapy session in the hospital that addresses this attitude:

> [My therapist] said that she had heard that I was trying to teach [my roommate] how to tie a noose and teach her how to kill herself. I don't know; I don't feel like I was doing anything malicious. . . . [My roommate] was just as responsible as I was because she asked about it, I didn't just volunteer the information to her. . . . [My therapist] said that it used really poor judgment, and in a way I don't even see that at all. It doesn't occur to me that [my roommate] wouldn't have thought up a plan by herself if she was thinking about suicide. I don't feel like I could have caused her such an intense nosedive. I am sorry if I did cause her so much trouble and I feel guilty about it and kind of want to stop talking to anyone so that I don't hurt anyone else the way that I hurt her, but I don't think that would be productive.

The nonchalance Ingrid shows here is for other borderlines part of a larger picture. As we'll see in Chapter 19, many families in which borderlines grew up are so pathological, and so isolated, that the child learns no standard of normal thinking and behavior.

The point is that when a borderline tries to talk about suicide, in therapy or anywhere else, she is not necessarily toying with her listener or trying to be rescued. "There is a very sadistic way to talk about suicide," says Whitney, "and there's a nonthreatening way to do it that tells people that you're not in danger and just need to express the feeling." After all, talking is always better for a borderline than acting out.

The Fatal Attraction Stereotype

Like the borderlines who would never disturb anyone else with their suicidal feelings, Alice and Ingrid have expressed concerns about hurting others that contradict another common stereotype about their illness. We have seen the stigma about BPD that permeates the psychiatric profession. The corresponding stereotype among the public is that of "the *Fatal Attraction* illness."*

Like its thematic predecessor, *Play Misty for Me,* the film *Fatal Attraction* presents examples of borderline behavior that are accurate only up to a point. The inaccuracy is that both films show the borderline character from her male lover's point of view, acting out the fury of the "woman scorned." The thoughts and feelings that this chapter attempts to explain are not revealed. "The film makes us seem like totally screwed-up people, with nothing that others can relate to, totally out there, too extreme," says Robin.

Some borderlines do act out destructively toward others. Andrea, for example, worked as a cook in order to poison other people's food with cleaning chemicals. Other borderlines, however, express horror at the thought of doing any harm. Distinguishing borderline from normal behavior, for instance, Robin says, "I don't think that the average person believes that doing something wrong makes you so horrendous a person that you must be made to suffer." Asked to define "something wrong," Robin replies immediately, "Something wrong is something that hurts somebody else."

Although Rebecca worries about losing control of what she calls her "explosive" anger, she emphasizes that it is directed toward no one but herself. When she was 17, Rebecca tried to shoot herself through the heart with one of her father's target practice rifles. Having missed death by a few inches, Rebecca instead found herself in a long-term hospital unit attending her case conference:

> They asked incredibly stupid questions like, "After your attempt, why didn't you go after the rest of the family?" That was a bizarre question that made

---

*A recent article in the *New York Times* may unfortunately have created another: "the Jeffrey Dahmer illness" (Daniel Goleman, "Clues to a Dark Nurturing Ground for One Serial Killer," 7 August 1991).

me so angry that I couldn't talk to them about it. I was furious that they would even *think* that I would hurt somebody else. Hurting one of my family members was just *beyond* me. I couldn't understand the question, and I'm still angry about it.

Rebecca likewise characterizes *Fatal Attraction* as "unrealistic . . . bizarre . . . totally strange."

It helps to keep in mind that no matter how outrageous or upsetting borderline behavior can be, it may well be *intended* either as self-punishment or as an expression of frustration and despair. The need for understanding, for validation, to be taken seriously, along with the anger at oneself for not deserving to have such needs met, can hardly be more dramatically expressed. But this doesn't mean that observers should take the expression personally.

A Two-Way Street

Borderlines may help ease their frustration about being misunderstood by keeping in mind that they themselves sometimes can't make sense of each other. Melanie explains her difficulty understanding the behavior of other borderlines in the hospital:

> I used to rip my nails apart and eat away at my own skin. But I had never heard of nor had any desire to cut myself with a razor blade; the idea nauseated me. That was one of the big culture shocks about the unit. Also eating disorders—I couldn't imagine eating and then wanting to get sick. I didn't understand bulimia at all. But at the same time I was doing my own little self-destructive things. If I did them, they weren't disgusting; if someone else did them, they were.

Most borderlines who cut themselves probably came up with that idea on their own and, for their part, would not understand why it disturbs Melanie.

Borderlines therefore might try to anticipate how their words or behavior can affect people. They can accept the likelihood that whatever understanding they do receive from "outside" will be intellectual rather than emotional. That's better than nothing.

Appreciating Instability

To help both borderlines and those around them, such understanding must include recognition that the only trait consistent to these patients is change. To interact with a borderline is constantly to resist identifying the patterns of consistency in most people that we take for granted. The observer must continually relocate the borderline emotionally, cognitively, behaviorally, and functionally *in the present,* disregarding the state she was in five minutes, three hours, or two weeks ago. The effort involved can be both discomforting and exhausting.

These remarks apply fully to the contents of this chapter, which merely presents some accurate ways in which to view borderline behavior. It does *not* suggest that any one of these interpretations is always valid. No one can ever presume to know in advance why a borderline is behaving in a particular way at any given time.

Notes

1. Marsha M. Linehan, Ph.D., "Dialectical Behavior Therapy for Borderline Personality Disorder: Theory and Method," *Bulletin of the Menninger Clinic,* Vol. 51, No. 3 (1987), pp. 266–68.
2. Ibid., p. 268.
3. Ibid.
4. Joel Paris, M.D., "Completed Suicide in Borderline Personality Disorder," *Psychiatric Annals,* Vol. 20, No. 1 (January 1990), p. 20. See also Joel Paris, M.D., David Nowlis, Ph.D., and Ronald Brown, M.D., "Predictors of Suicide in Borderline Personality Disorder," *Canadian Journal of Psychiatry,* Vol. 34 (February 1989), pp. 8–9; and for a different patient sample, C. Wesley Dingman, M.D., and Thomas H. McGlashan, M.D., "Characteristics of Patients with Serious Suicidal Intentions Who Ultimately Commit Suicide," *Hospital and Community Psychiatry,* Vol. 39, No. 3 (March 1988), pp. 295–99.
5. Eleanor Saunders, Ph.D., and Frances Arnold, Ph.D., "Borderline Personality Disorder and Childhood Abuse: Revisions in Clinical Thinking and Treatment Approach," Work in Progress, Working Paper Series, No. 51 (Wellesley, Mass.: The Stone Center for Developmental Services and Studies, Wellesley College). I am grateful to Catherine Steiner-Adair, Ed.D., for alerting me to this paper.

1 1

The "Behavioral Specialty"

"People don't understand hurting yourself at all."

"INGRID"

Of all the symptoms of BPD, the one that makes the least sense to observers is self-mutilation.* Other people can imagine uncontrollable emotions and confused thoughts; they can relate to the use of addictive substances; even suicide attempts make theoretical sense. But what Dr. Gunderson calls the "behavioral specialty" of borderlines is beyond the realm of most people's understanding and sympathy. We have just seen that even borderlines who mutilate themselves find methods they don't use both alien and disturbing.

Yet many borderlines hurt themselves, with cutting or burning the most frequently seen method of choice. Self-mutilation seems to these borderlines an obvious alternative to emotional pain. "I have done it since age nine or ten, for different reasons at different times, but it was always something natural that I just had to do," says Robin. "Sometimes it will be on my mind and I'll keep putting it off and putting it off until I can't wait any more."

*Defined by psychiatrists as the deliberate alteration or destruction of body tissue with no lethal intent, self-mutilation is also referred to by terms like *deliberate self-harm syndrome* and *parasuicide*.

Like other symptoms of BPD, self-mutilation is subject to misconceptions. Although Robin's words imply that each act of self-mutilation can serve a particular (even urgent) purpose, many therapists automatically assume that such flamboyant behavior is *always* hostile, manipulative, or otherwise outwardly directed.

More ''Manipulation''

Dr. Kernberg, for example, sees self-mutilation primarily as a means of acting out a desire for revenge.* Ellen Leibenluft, M.D., and her colleagues have in fact described cases of patients who self-mutilated in response to perceived separation, loss, or failure; one patient, Mr. D., wrote that burning himself with a cigarette seemed "a way of getting revenge with my psychiatrist."[1] This motive makes sense in terms of the tendency among women (and male homosexuals like Mr. D.) to direct their anger toward themselves.

Frustrated by "not being taken seriously," Alison would cut herself and use a toothpick to write notes in blood describing her misery. The effects of such self-mutilation on the targeted person can be used to make the point or to persuade him or her to do what the borderline wants.

A victim of childhood abuse feels an overwhelming loss of control to and sense of rage at the perpetrator(s). Saunders and Arnold suggest that having since developed BPD, such a victim may compulsively use self-mutilation to control her experience or to manage anger, abandonment, and loss of control when faced with similar adult situations.[2]

Not only acts of self-mutilation but also their consequences can be applied to this purpose. Some borderlines cut or burn themselves badly enough to scar. As Renée has noted, many of them end up with arms and legs covered with scars and take a perverse pride in this scorecard of painful experiences. Those borderlines who exhibit their scars are gratified by the reactions of others, as Carla explains:

My legs are just as bad, but people ask me about my arms. I have 32 burns, one of which has had to be excised, skin grafts, and lots of cut scars. People ask me if I have had tattoos removed or things like that.

I'm very perceptive about how people might react. I tell them that I have

*Dr. Kernberg believes also that one subgroup of patients with BPO whom he calls *malignant narcissists* self-mutilate to demonstrate a sense of triumph, independence, and power over pain and death.

difficulties and take out anger on myself or that I perceive myself as bad and punish myself.

If I'm angry, or having a bad day, I tell them that I was gang raped and mutilated, which makes them feel bad for asking.

It doesn't occur or matter to borderlines who use their self-mutilation against others that they are hurting themselves even worse.

The Inner Drama of Pain

A misnomer frequently applied to self-mutilation is the adjective *impulsive,* possibly because to most people, such behavior is by definition out of control. Actually, even self-mutilation that is not deliberately manipulative is often highly controlled. Many borderlines carefully cut only areas of the skin that are hidden under clothing; or they avoid cutting deeply enough to require stitches because they do not want to reveal their behavior to emergency room personnel. Some use self-mutilation to control other undesirable behavior. A borderline might mutilate her genitals, for example, to prevent herself from masturbating or to resolve some sexual conflict. For others, the self-mutilation itself is an equivalent of masturbation or intercourse that is performed as a highly controlled ritual. "Hurting myself is a sexual thing, a turn-on," says Robin. "Painful or life-threatening acts are as close as I've come to having a sexual feeling."

Actually, *all* self-mutilation is to some extent a pathetic attempt to control somebody or something. For most borderlines most of the time, the target is not other people but their *dysphoria,* an intensely uncomfortable mélange of depression, anxiety, rage, and despair. "This distress can be measured by the lengths they go to in an attempt to get rid of it," says Dr. Cowdry. Borderlines are driven to self-mutilation because they know of no better way to cope.

Self-mutilation can, for instance, define a way out of the misery once and for all. Alison began cutting her wrists simply to prove to herself that she was capable of committing suicide.

As Dr. Cowdry described in the preceding chapter, many borderlines self-mutilate as a form of punishment to relieve their guilt about being "bad" or symbolically to destroy parts of themselves that they hate. When angry with herself, Ingrid would secretly scratch *bitch* or *fat* on unobtrusive areas of her skin. Robin would cut her arms or legs, punch walls, or mix and abuse drugs:

> I would take enough drugs to think that I wouldn't kill myself but would get really sick. I needed to make myself sick the same way as to cut myself. Drugs turned out to be more dangerous. I used marijuana just to numb my head, but mixing pills was different.

This is an important distinction. A borderline who abuses drugs as her preferred method of self-punishment might easily be mistaken for an addict. Robin first tried drinking and drugs to be social, then used a variety of chemicals more successfully to hurt herself. The only drug on which she became briefly dependent was a tranquilizer prescribed for her in a day hospital.

Borderlines insist that self-mutilation relieves anxiety and other unpleasant feelings. This is true especially when the borderline has been hiding her inner self behind a socially acceptable facade, as Melanie mentioned in Chapter I. The relief varies from a pronounced physical and emotional change to simple distraction. "Hurting myself was a way to take the pain inside and put it outside so I could see it for a couple of hours, or a couple of days sometimes," says Alice. "I could concentrate on what I did to hurt myself instead of what was going on in my head, and it worked." As her explanation implies, improvement could result partly from the borderline's having administered some of the pain herself so that she need not feel completely helpless.

Following the rule that for every statement made about BPD, the opposite is also true, some borderlines use self-mutilation to *escape* from distraction or numbness. We have seen that borderlines are plagued by dissociative experiences. Melanie's description in Chapter 6 of her cognitive symptoms is one example; other borderlines describe dissociation as a fog or a glass bubble and mutilate to bring themselves out of this state. As Robin says, "There have been one or two times that I don't remember self-mutilating, but I woke up the next morning with blood around me." Other borderlines are distressed because they feel completely numb; they mutilate themselves to prove, by pain or blood flow, that they are still alive.

Dissociative symptoms can of course result from previous trauma. "We have the data now showing that the correlation between self-mutilation and abuse, especially early childhood and sexual abuse, is extraordinarily powerful," says Dr. Herman. Dissociation may be an intermediary connecting the two. Or the self-mutilation can replay the abuse itself, with the borderline identifying with the perpetrator(s).

Such reenactment is part of Andrea's compulsion to cause herself pain. Andrea's mother used to pour bleach into her bath water and her vagina, beat her, and burn her fingers; she was also beaten, burned, and stabbed by her father and brothers. The result is Andrea's preoccupation with what she calls "toxic wastes":

> By toxic wastes, I mean that I consume household chemicals, mothballs, silicone packets that you find in shoes, formaldehyde, lawn and garden chemicals, plastic, soap, medications, and bleach. Besides eating chemicals, I put them up my vagina, in my eyes, and frequently in my eardrums. Try to explain that to a doctor. By the time I see a doctor, I want to get rid of the pain, and the doctor won't help me. So I deal with pain by trying to kill myself little bits at the time by giving myself cancer. But who can deal with cancer if she can't even deal with pain?
>
> I won't take pain pills because I get reactions. And anyway, my family ethic was that I was expected to tolerate pain, or else I would get beaten up more.
>
> I ingest chemicals also because I don't feel adequate; I should be killing myself; I don't deserve to be here; everyone else has achieved.
>
> I don't even act like any borderline I know of. Most of them cut or burn, and I'd never do that.

Andrea's confused obsession with pain was evident during her interview, which took place while she was recovering from major surgery without the use of analgesics.

Self-Medication

That self-mutilation is not necessarily directed at others is shown by these testimonies from borderlines themselves. That it is a form of self-medication is suggested also by more objective evidence.

Dr. Cowdry distinguishes between two forms of self-mutilation. That revealed to others may be manipulative and is best addressed by psychotherapy, while that performed privately to manage dysphoria may respond to appropriate pharmacotherapy. To distinguish the two, says Dr. Cowdry,

> you need to set aside your initial reaction, "This is manipulative because it stirs up a lot of feelings in me," and look at the actual circumstances. You assess the nature of the episodes. To the extent that the episodes are not clearly communicative—especially if they are private—pharmacotherapy might be indicated.

It is important to emphasize that a communicative act is not necessarily a manipulative one.

A notable case in which pharmacotherapy "cured" a borderline of excessive self-mutilation is that of a 26-year-old patient of Dr. Kroll's referred to in his book as Case 25. Some of this woman's self-mutilation reenacted sexual abuse she endured as a child and later as a prostitute trying to support her bulimia nervosa* and drug addiction. After each of several rapes, for example, she would rupture herself with a coat hanger (and ruptured her cervix and rectum at other times); she also trimmed her labia with sewing scissors four times to "look normal and not like a whore."

The patient recovered dramatically on a regimen of Parnate (an MAOI antidepressant) and lithium. One year later she was attending college, dating seriously, and not self-mutilating at all.[3] Dr. Kroll notes that she did not appear overtly depressed or suffer mood swings. Instead her self-mutilation seemed to have a life of its own whose purpose was to cause her constant pain. (Although the symptom responded to drug treatment, it apparently was not intended to manage dysphoria and therefore does not fit Dr. Cowdry's second category.)

The Biology of Self-Mutilation

A related line of evidence that self-mutilation is focused within consists of other biological findings that are not yet generally accepted. As we'll see in Chapter 18, studies show that "impulsive" self-destructive behaviors, including self-mutilation, can be correlated to certain aspects of brain metabolism. Either constitutional or acquired differences in the brain function of borderlines could make them hypersensitive, especially to infantile feelings like Whitney's earlier description of her rage. Most adults have thought processes and defenses that automatically regulate their feelings and can't even imagine what the absence of this emotional thermostat would be like. But borderlines either have not developed this capacity to begin with or lose it under stress. They compensate for this deficiency with self-mutilation.

Some borderlines are fascinated to learn that approximately half of those who self-mutilate feel no pain. A logical hypothesis to explain this self-induced analgesia is that the mutilation releases *neuropeptides* (naturally occurring substances that dull the senses and relieve pain). Years ago, Jeremy Coid, M.R.C. Psych., and his colleagues found plasma levels of metenkephalin (one type of neuropeptide) to be raised in a

*DSM-III-R slightly revised the definition of bulimia and renamed it *bulimia nervosa*.

group of borderlines whose self-mutilation did not hurt them but did relieve their dysphoria or dissociation. The level of metenkephalin depended on how severely and recently the patients had mutilated themselves.[4]

Those borderlines who feel pain and those who don't are nicely represented by two patients in a group that has been studied by Mark J. Russ, M.D., and his colleagues. They are identical twin borderlines: one feels no pain when she self-mutilates; the other doesn't self-mutilate and has felt pain during a cold pressor test.*

To study this phenomenon, Dr. Russ's group conducted cold pressor tests on three groups of age-matched women: borderlines who feel pain while self-mutilating, borderlines who don't feel pain, and normal controls.[5]

The borderlines who feel no self-inflicted pain gave pain ratings during the cold pressor test that were significantly lower than those of the controls, while the borderlines who do feel pain gave ratings slightly higher than those of the controls. Both groups of self-mutilating borderlines, then, had abnormal perception of pain.

The subjects also completed two standard mood inventories, one measuring their emotional states at that moment, the other their level of depression for that day. Both groups of borderlines had anxiety ratings higher than those of the controls. The pain-free borderlines were more depressed than those who felt pain; they in turn were more depressed than the controls. After the cold pressor test, the levels of depression, anxiety and confusion were significantly lower in both groups of borderlines but not significantly different in the control group.

"While differences in pain ratings among the groups may represent differences in neurophysiological mechanisms, other explanations are possible," says Dr. Russ, "including differences in levels of depression and/or dissociation, as well as various psychological factors."

Dr. Coid's group had themselves suggested that self-mutilation must involve more than the release of metenkephalin they had noticed. Another research approach is to use the opiate antagonists naloxone (which is given intravenously) or naltrexone (which is effective orally and for a longer period of time) to try to determine whether *endorphins* (another type of neuropeptide) are involved in borderlines' reactions to self-mutilation. Dr. Russ's group is taking this approach with larger samples of borderline patients. "Because we can't directly measure endogenous opiates in specifically relevant areas of the brain, we instead measure

---

*A standard laboratory test in which subjects immerse one hand in painfully cold water and record their responses.

different aspects of the endorphin system looking for peripheral handles," says Dr. Cowdry.

> We then make indirect inferences about what is ultimately a process deep
> within the brain. If naloxone and naltrexone help self-injury, it must be
> because they're blocking some endogenous site, whatever it might be.
>
> There are a whole set of classes of endogenous opiates that probably serve
> very different functions in different regions of the brain. There has been a lot
> of loose speculation about their meaning. For example, we found signifi-
> cantly elevated levels of beta endorphin in the resting blood samples of
> individuals with distant histories—at least two weeks, but often longer
> back—of self-mutilation. It was higher in the borderline group as a whole
> but specifically elevated in those with a history of self-mutilation.
>
> Do the high endorphin levels interfere with the self-regulatory process in
> terms of whatever role they may have in reward and drive regulation? Or are
> the levels high simply because these individuals chronically release excessive
> amounts of beta endorphin from pituitary stores purely as a secondary phe-
> nomenon, a measure of their chronic high stress levels?

We will see in Chapter 18 that biological approaches to BPD are all
based on such inferences at this point. Another such theory suggested by
Saunders and Arnold is that early repeated traumata might code self-
mutilation and other physiological patterns into the sensory motor system instead of the regions of the brain that produce language. Rather
than describe her previous abuse, then, the borderline must literally or
symbolically act it out.[6]

Borderline Bulimia Nervosa

Yet another indication that self-mutilation has an inherent purpose
relates to indirect methods of harming oneself. Robin has explained that
she mixed drugs; another example is borderlines who have bulimia nervosa, the binge-purge syndrome.

Researchers tend to measure the incidence of BPD among bulimics
rather than that of bulimia nervosa in borderlines. Various studies show
that from 2 to 44 percent of bulimics may be borderline (the range is
attributable to the studies' using different diagnostic criteria and having
other methodological problems).[7] Self-mutilators in particular appear to
have a high risk for an eating disorder, especially bulimia nervosa (and
vice versa). Armando R. Favazza, M.D., and his colleagues have therefore proposed that *deliberate self-harm syndrome* be made a new diagnostic

category in *DSM-IV*. It would be defined as an impulse control disorder, distinct from the personality disorders, that incorporates all such behaviors into a specific group.[8]

A person who is not borderline can start vomiting as a weight control method, then become addicted to binge-vomiting. For borderlines, that behavior can serve another purpose, as indicated by the different treatment approaches commonly used for borderline and nonborderline bulimics.

Bulimia nervosa the *illness* is like alcoholism or drug addiction in that the patient must stop binge-vomiting in order to engage fully in psychotherapy. Strange as it may sound, bulimia nervosa the *symptom* of underlying BPD is instead tolerable in treatment as a medicative adjunct to psychotherapy; its elimination is a secondary goal at best. A widely accepted psychodynamic treatment approach allows the borderline bulimic to continue binge-vomiting indefinitely because doing so helps stabilize her enough to benefit from psychotherapy.[9] If the therapist forces the borderline prematurely to stop binge-vomiting, she may switch to another self-destructive symptom.*

Laxative abuse adds another dimension to borderline bulimia nervosa. According to Johnson, borderline bulimics are three times more likely than nonborderline bulimics to abuse laxatives. "This makes so much clinical sense," he says. "Laxative abuse can be a kind of self-mutilatory equivalent; for many of these patients, the function it serves is quite different from simply protecting them against weight gain."

Surgery as Self-Mutilation

Finally, we should note that attacking other people through self-mutilation has an opposite extreme—persuading others to "attack" the self. Some borderlines enlist surgeons to hurt them, as Johnson explains:

> Borderlines work their way through the medical profession, angering physicians along the way, and often wind up with surgeons who finally operate on them. Many of them have had multiple surgeries: gall bladder, hysterectomy, laparoscopy, a lot of elective or exploratory surgery looking for something wrong. In part this is to make another person injure them, so that they need not do it to themselves, and in part they are attracted to anything that offers

*Cognitive-behavioral therapists find, however, that borderlines in general tend not to substitute symptoms in this way. Dr. Kernberg permits no life-threatening or clearly manipulative behavior by his patients, and some of his followers tolerate no self-damaging symptoms at all.

some potential explanation or faint hope of relief from their condition—
health foods, allergy shots, or whatever. The medical community may not
be alert to this group.

But although their means of self-mutilation are certainly manipulative,
the ultimate goal of the borderlines is still their own relief.

A Different Meaning Each Time

Self-mutilation by borderlines resembles repeated suicide attempts in
several respects. Both behaviors should always be taken seriously: a suicide attempt may succeed, and self-mutilation is difficult to treat and
may become addictive.

Both behaviors can occur for different reasons at different times. The
motives for self-mutilation are as diverse as borderlines themselves. It is
therefore very important not to have preconceived assumptions about
the cause(s) of any single act of self-mutilation, let alone about this
symptom in general.

Neither suicide attempts nor self-mutilation should be taken personally. (A therapist who believes such behavior to be directed toward him
might interpret it as a result of the patient's transference but still not take
it *personally*.) Even as a clearly manipulative or hostile act, self-mutilation
represents the borderline's pathetic attempt to communicate in the only
way she knows how. At least she is still trying to interact.

And like suicide attempts, self-mutilation often doesn't involve other
people at all. However sick or disgusting it seems, self-mutilation performs the postive—if poorly chosen—purpose of helping the borderline
cope. The borderline's serendipitous discovery that causing pain relieves
it is increasingly being supported by hard data.

In one respect, however, self-mutilation and suicide attempts are
exact opposites. A genuine suicide attempt is the ultimate act of hopelessness. Self-mutilation, on the other hand, clearly indicates that the
borderline has *not* given up. Therapists in particular should keep in mind
that the borderline's desire to feel better is, at least, a sign that she may
eventually renounce her self-mutilation with professional help. "Ultimately, the therapist may have to accept the limitations of the treatment," writes Lawrence H. Rockland, M.D., "remind him/herself that
mutilation, however flamboyant, is preferable to death, and consider the
possibility that perhaps the patient really is doing the very best she
can."[10]

Notes

1. Ellen Leibenluft, M.D., David L. Gardner, M.D., and Rex W. Cowdry, M.D., "Special Feature: The Inner Experience of the Borderline Self-Mutilator," *Journal of Personality Disorders,* Vol. 1, No. 4 (1987), p. 321.
2. Eleanor Saunders, Ph.D., and Frances Arnold, Ph.D., "Borderline Personality Disorder and Childhood Abuse: Revisions in Clinical Thinking and Treatment Approach," Work in Progress, Working Paper Series, No. 51 (Wellesley, Mass.: The Stone Center for Developmental Services and Studies, Wellesley College).
3. Jerome Kroll, M.D., *The Challenge of the Borderline Patient: Competency in Diagnosis and Treatment* (New York: Norton, 1988), pp. 170–72.
4. Jeremy Coid, Bruno Allolio, and L. H. Rees, "Raised Plasma Metenkephalin in Patients Who Habitually Mutilate Themselves," *The Lancet,* Vol. 2 (September 3, 1983), pp. 545–46.
5. Mark J. Russ, M.D., Steven D. Roth, M.D., Alexander Lerman, M.D., Richard D. Shindledecker, M.A., Steven Mattis, Ph.D., "Pain Perception in Borderline Patients," paper read at the 144th annual meeting of the American Psychiatric Association, New Orleans, 13 May 1991.
6. Saunders and Arnold cite papers published by Janet (in 1889) and Freud (in 1896 and 1920) and Bessel A. van der Kolk, M.D., "The Compulsion to Repeat the Trauma: Re-enactment, Revictimization, and Masochism," *Psychiatric Clinics of North America,* Vol. 12, No. 2 (June 1989), pp. 389–411.
7. Amy Baker Dennis and Randy A. Sansone, "Treating the Bulimic Patient with Borderline Personality Disorder," *Advances in Eating Disorders,* Vol. II (Greenwich, Conn.: JAI Press, 1989), pp. 237–38; Harrison G. Pope, Jr., M.D., Frances R. Frankenburg, M.D., James I. Hudson, M.D., Jeffrey M. Jonas, M.D., and Deborah Yurgelun-Todd, M.A., "Is Bulimia Associated with Borderline Personality Disorder? A Controlled Study," *Journal of Clinical Psychiatry,* Vol. 48, No. 5 (May 1987), pp. 181–84.
8. Armando R. Favazza, M.D., Lori DeRosear, D.O., and Karen Conterio, "Self-Mutilation and Eating Disorders," *Suicide and Life-Threatening Behavior,* Vol. 19, No. 4 (Winter 1989), pp. 352–61.
9. Dennis and Sansone, "Treating the Bulimic Patient," pp. 237–65; and "The Clinical Stages of Treatment for the Eating Disorder Patient with Borderline Personality Disorder," in *Psychodynamic Treatment of Anorexia Nervosa and Bulimia,* ed. Craig Johnson, Ph.D. (New York: The Guilford Press, 1991), pp. 128–64.
10. Lawrence H. Rockland, M.D., "A Supportive Approach: Psychodynamically Oriented Supportive Therapy—Treatment of Borderline Patients Who Self-Mutilate," *Journal of Personality Disorders,* Vol. 1, No. 4 (1987), pp. 350–53. Copyright © 1987 The Guilford Press.

12

The Heirs of Ismael

"When I go through the residential centers, some of these borderline children literally run up to me and grab onto my leg, so that I'm dragging them down the hall. They have such enormous, enormous needs. I get calls as one would with borderline adults that a child has overdosed, has been self-mutilating, is running away, is showing an extreme degree of impulsivity."

PAUL A. ANDRULONIS, M.D.

*I*t's a heartbreaking image—that of a sick child whose very illness makes it so desperate for love.

The children described by Dr. Andrulonis are surprising in two respects. One is that despite having become ill so early, these children are fortunate compared to many others like them. They will receive therapy that may help them avoid a lifetime of cumulative disasters.

The other surprise is that the majority of children from whom Dr. Andrulonis must gently dislodge himself to continue down the hallway are not, as one would expect, little girls. They are little boys.

We have seen that women diagnosed as borderline are misunderstood, scorned, and shunned by many members of the psychiatric profession. Dr. Andrulonis believes that male borderlines are likewise avoided, but for the opposite reason—therapists don't recognize that they *are* borderline. Their symptoms are expressed differently enough for males to be misdiagnosed as sociopaths, in comparison to whom even borderlines look good. Because the few men who are correctly diagnosed so closely resemble borderline women, most researchers don't focus on gender distinctions.

Skilled at finding erudite quotations with which to introduce his papers, Dr. Andrulonis cites as a prototype of the borderline male the outcast Ismael, the "wild ass of a man" described in the Book of Genesis. Borderline males fall ill very early in childhood; unless such boys are correctly identified and properly treated while still grabbing their therapists' pants legs, their prospects for recovery may be slim.

Are There Borderline Children?

Estimates of how many adult borderlines are female vary from about 65 to 80 percent, depending on the criteria being used and the ages of the patients studied (women predominate particularly between ages 16 and 35).[1] A reverse ratio may exist in childhood: Dr. Andrulonis believes that 70 percent of borderline children are male. He describes them as "controlling, anxious, clinging and poorly school-adjusted male [children] filled with anger and hatred."[2]

The diagnosis of BPD in children is controversial, partly because some researchers consider the adult criteria inapplicable.[3] Paulina F. Kernberg, M.D., and Dr. Andrulonis are among those experts who insist that just as children have personalities, they can have personality disorders. "I really think that this is the majority view at present," says Dr. Andrulonis.

> I think more and more child psychiatrists are diagnosing children as border-line, and many of them use the adult criteria. You can see borderline pathology very early on, by age five or six, that is just about identical to what appears in adults.

Research on disturbed children and adolescents by Anna Freud, Melanie Klein, Margaret Mahler, James F. Masterson, M.D., and other investigators has illuminated the adult borderline condition. Clearly identified borderline children[4] would make possible long-term prospective studies of how the illness develops. But they would also be the subject of another book.

Dr. Andrulonis emphasizes the childhood disorder because although his research has been biologically oriented, he believes that early environmental factors contribute equally or more to the development of BPD. Many borderline children have family histories of depression, addictions, and divorce; some are adopted, and many have also suffered ongoing abuse. "I'm becoming even more impressed with how characterologically impaired little children can be and how damaged by the

ages of six through eight," says Dr. Andrulonis. This environmentally
afflicted group is one of three into which Dr. Andrulonis' research has
led him to divide borderlines.

A second group consists of borderlines whose personality disorder
appears to overlap with constitutional or genetic depressive illness. (To
varying degrees the findings of Harrison G. Pope, Jr., M.D., and Drs.
Akiskal, Links, Stone, Liebowitz, and Donald Klein agree with Dr. Andrulonis' descriptions of these patients.) Like those in the first group,
these borderlines are mostly females whose illness resulted primarily
from environmental factors.

Organic BPD

A third group of borderlines have greater vulnerability even to less
pathological environments that results from organic brain dysfunction.
Some have significant brain pathology resulting from insults like encephalitis, seizures, or head trauma. The majority, and the main subject
of Dr. Andrulonis' attention, are those with attention-deficit/hyperac-
tivity disorder and learning disabilities (ADHD-LD). Most of these borderlines are male.

In the early 1970s, when BPD was just starting to be evaluated systematically, Dr. Andrulonis was studying hyperactive children. Following the children into adolescence, Dr. Andrulonis and his colleagues saw
them develop distractibility, learning disabilities, and symptoms of episodic dyscontrol syndrome, minimal brain dysfunction, and BPD.

The symptoms of episodic dyscontrol syndrome and minimal brain
dysfunction in adults have been articulated by Leopold Bellak, M.D.,
who sees a frequent overlap between the two. *Episodic dyscontrol syndrome*
(EDS) can cause violent, impulsive behavior; diffuse anxiety, depression,
or inability to experience pleasure; low frustration tolerance; rage; and
quasipsychotic episodes.

Minimal brain dysfunction (MBD) can cause sociopathic, assaultive, and
restless behavior in men and promiscuity, depression, and suicidal gestures in women. Dr. Bellak believes that this disorder specifically causes
many of the symptoms of borderline men: those of EDS along with
emotional lability, distractibility, hyperactivity, addictions, and suicidal
gestures. Men with minimal brain dysfunction crave but can't maintain
intimate relationships, nor can they generally hold down jobs. They
require constant stimulation to ward off the emptiness they feel when
isolated.[5]

Under stress, adults with ADHD can regress into impulsive behavior strikingly similar to that of borderline patients. Dr. Andrulonis' research shows that starting from childhood, male borderlines with ADHD-LD are out of control emotionally, socially, behaviorally, and academically; they are needy, clinging, and plagued by a poor sense of identity and self-esteem.[6]

Dr. Andrulonis believes that both EDS and MBD reflect abnormality in the brain's limbic system, about which we will learn more in Chapter 18. Ironically enough in this context, *limbus* is Latin for *border*. When electrical discharges moving across this border are balanced or synchronized, the person responds to environmental stimuli with appropriate levels of emotion.[7] Excessive or haphazard discharges produce emotional overload and impulsive thoughts. If not checked by the brain's control mechanisms, these thoughts and feelings are acted out destructively.

Borderline men are more likely than borderline women to have EDS and MBD because the brains of males are more vulnerable than those of females during pregnancy and delivery. And in terms of the amount and types of abuse, likelihood of separation, and foster placement difficulties or failures they may suffer, boys may be worse off than girls. It is hardly surprising that they trip over into BPD.

A Relevant Digression

In the course of discussing male borderlines with several therapists, I came across some reservations about Dr. Andrulonis' findings well representing the divergent opinions that surround any aspect of BPD. To illustrate the difficulties of generalizing about the illness, I have assembled separate observations on this topic into a logical progression intended to be humorously exasperating. All the participants quoted have read and approved this arrangement of their observations, which follows:

Jack R. Cornelius, M.D., Dr. Soloff, and their colleagues publish a study showing that neuropsychiatric abnormalities are uncommon in borderlines. The group seriously questions the methodology and patient samples represented in Dr. Andrulonis' work, including his not having compared his borderline patients to normal control subjects. (The researchers do not, however, address the gender differences between the patients used in each study.)[8]

Along come O'Leary, Dr. Cowdry, and their colleagues to point out that Dr. Cornelius' group did not use controls *either,* a deficit that they declare "clouds the interpretation of that study."[9] "I'm sure that Dr. Cornelius intended his observations as constructive criticism, just as we did ours," says Dr. Cowdry.

> I tend to believe Dr. Andrulonis' findings of an elevated ADHD-LD incidence in males. I can't say much more about that because we've studied almost exclusively women, and Dr. Andrulonis didn't make any claims about females. But our study shows cognitive neuropsychological testing abnormalities in BPD in females, and I know of at least one other study whose findings are very similar to ours.

We'll examine the results of the O'Leary study in Chapter 18.

Dr. Links, who practices in Canada, likewise reports that his colleague Robert van Reekum, M.D., has studied a group of mostly male patients from a VA hospital in the United States. Dr. van Reekum found much higher rates of histories of traumatic brain injury and acquired and developmental brain dysfunction in the borderlines than he did in other psychiatric patients. These histories were highly correlated with the frequency of borderline symptoms. Dr. van Reekum is now doing a prospective study of male and female borderlines in a general psychiatric unit. "There is a great need for further neuropsychological testing," says Dr. Links, "to try to document what difficulties these patients have that ultimately lead to impaired functioning."

Is there a great need? Dr. Soloff declares that patients who have neuropsychiatric abnormalities are not borderlines anyway. Psychiatrists diagnose patients phenomenologically but think of them *etiologically* (in terms of the disorder's *causes*). "If you look at the borderline as a syndrome defined by signs and symptoms and for which we have no etiology, then if you apply Dr. Spitzer's rigid rules, you can say that these people have BPD," he says.

> But most of us don't believe that concept. Most of us believe that there are biologic elements and childhood experiences that produce a condition in the sense of character type that is stably unstable but consistent over time. Although their behavior looks borderline, it's really unreasonable to call people with neuropsychiatric abnormalities by the same label that you call people with identical signs and symptoms but no brain damage.

These comments recall the controversy about whether BPD in female borderlines is a trauma disorder. Let's say that three people each fulfill the criteria for BPD: one has brain damage, one has a history of severe abuse, and the third has neither. Are all three of them truly borderline?

What determines the legitimacy or illegitimacy of any one cause of borderline symptoms?

Not ruling out the possibility that neuropsychological impairment might be present, Dr. Siever confesses that he has not seen much obvious MBD in adult male borderlines at the VA medical center with which *he* is affiliated. "While I was at McLean Hospital, however," he says, "a number of male adolescents did have MBD or some subclinical seizure disorder."

Dr. Siever does not fully agree with the widely acknowledged possibility that borderline males are misdiagnosed as antisocial. "I think that antisocial personality disorder is not the same as BPD because it's missing the affective component," he says.

Most borderline patients seek clinical treatment because they are depressed. I think that much of the male equivalent of borderlines may be as close—or closer—to narcissistic as to antisocial personality disorder.

But Dr. Paris, who is writing a grant proposal to study male borderlines, believes otherwise. "BPD and antisocial personality disorder are possibly two versions of the same thing—the relationship between them is interesting," he says.

While some male borderlines are antisocial, some are not. It has been shown that a larger percentage of male borderlines than we would expect are homosexual, and that's interesting. And as Dr. Kroll points out, the syndrome has been defined in such a way as to emphasize symptoms more common in females. It's as if whoever wrote the definition had females in mind.

But I think that Dr. Andrulonis, like others researching biological factors, hasn't really proved his point.

Well, at least we have ended up back where we started.

In light of Dr. Paris' comments, we can note that the definition of BPO is less sexist, so to speak, than that of BPD. "There are as many males as females with BPO, and they are moved into one or another personality constellation by the cultural expression of their symptoms," says Dr. Kernberg. "BPD was described [by Dr. Gunderson] primarily in women hospitalized at McLean, so it picked up one dominant manifestation of severe pathology."

And here we had just heard about male adolescent borderlines with MBD who could be found in this very same hospital.

Actually some of this skepticism about Dr. Andrulonis' work represents a misunderstanding of his position. His publications have discussed organic brain damage, but his most convincing clinical descriptions of the borderline male's illness course have not yet appeared in print. "Lectures are open to subjective interpretation," says Dr. Andrulonis. "Having changed affiliations, I will now have more time to publish material that emphasizes the importance I attach to environmental factors." Meanwhile the percentage of borderlines who are male and the exact nature of their illness remains to be proven.

BPD in Boys and Girls

The organic component of their illness is one reason that the development of BPD in boys described by Dr. Andrulonis is different from that of girls.

Dr. Andrulonis' female borderline patients are more likely than males to come from families with histories of affective illness. If deprived or abused, these girls react more resiliently than boys until adolescence breaks them down. Through grades seven to nine, a borderline girl will start to show depression, eating disorders, acting out, or other symptoms of her personality disorder. She then enters the mental health system, where she will be hospitalized more often than a male borderline and may receive antidepressants or lithium.

Borderline boys come from families more likely than those of girls to have histories of alcohol or drug abuse. The boys do not share the quiet, asymptomatic period of childhood during which borderline girls stay in one piece. Rather than "acting in," the boy acts out his depression and impulsivity aggressively and antisocially.* By about fifth grade, his hyperactivity, behavior problems, and learning disabilities have caused family, academic, and social difficulties. His impulsivity starts him early on a career of drug and alcohol abuse, stealing, traffic violations, and violence. Instead of receiving psychiatric care, however, males are dealt with by their schools and often end up in the legal system.[10]

Despite their head start on symptomatology, borderline boys are hit by adolescence just as hard as borderline girls. In fact, adolescence is just as difficult for *all* boys as it is for girls. Suicide in adolescence is primarily a male phenomenon, but until recently, the implications of this finding weren't clear. "The suicide statistics are shaking up researchers with

*Zanarini's research on borderline impulsivity has shown that the incidence of antisocial personality disorder and substance abuse in males is paralleled by that of eating disorders in females ("Impulsive Phenomenology of Borderline Personality," paper read at the 143rd annual meeting of the American Psychiatric Association, New York, 16 May 1990).

evidence that adolescent boys can be depressed too," says Dr. Andrulonis.

> Maybe the girls suffer milder depression that results in suicidal gestures, while boys more commonly become so profoundly depressed that they kill themselves.
>
> I feel that depression is very common in BPD. These suicide studies may indicate that the borderline diagnosis is likewise more common among males than researchers have seen up to now.

Dr. Andrulonis believes that adolescent boys as well as girls seek to define their uniqueness within the context of ongoing relationships; for them a loss of a parent, a girlfriend, a sibling, or a friend is devastating. Adolescent and adult borderline males tend to have unstable, intense, narcissistic, highly dependent romantic relationships just like females. Their despair over actual or prospective loss is equally dramatic, profound, and likely to result in suicide attempts, particularly when they have tried to soothe themselves with alcohol or drugs.

Dr. Kernberg agrees that males and females are more alike emotionally than their social stereotypes would imply. "Freud's theory of the different development of little boys and little girls requires significant revisions," he says.

> The important differences between the sexes cut across ideological simplifications. It is a cliché that women are more involved in relationships, warmer, and more dependent and men are more differentiated, sharper, more independent. In other cultures and in history, manliness has been associated with impulsivity, with strong emotions, with exuberance, what now would be considered female traits. Clinically men are every bit as dependent and needing of contact as women, and women are every bit as aggressive and hostile as men.

We must keep in mind, though, that to some extent this similarity between patients of the opposite sex could reflect their sharing the same psychiatric illness.

Dr. Andrulonis finds that as they approach and proceed through adulthood, borderline males become associated with severe conduct disorders. Their attempts to relieve their emotional instability, emptiness, and irritability lead them into alcoholism and drug abuse. Their low tolerance for frustration makes it difficult for them to stay in school; they likewise wander between jobs and residences. Although they crave attention, borderline men remain isolated and lonely because they are socially inept.

These men seldom seek psychotherapy. Those who do happen into hospitals show fewer quasipsychotic episodes than do borderline women. Their medications, however, are usually limited to antipsychotic drugs to curb their aggressive outbursts or general agitation. Dr. Andrulonis feels that like borderline women, they should have the opportunity to try antidepressants as well.

Had their illness been correctly diagnosed when the symptoms began to appear, borderline males could be spared much suffering. "I'm making a plea to see the borderline dynamics earlier on and try to intervene with psychotherapy sooner rather than later," says Dr. Andrulonis.

> As a child and adolescent psychiatrist, I've seen many tragedies that occur because little boys' emotional difficulties were not taken seriously. We should not just put them on Ritalin and forget about them.
>
> When you see a little boy with a label of ADHD, for example, ask also how impulsive is that child? How depressed? What are his self-esteem issues? What are the dynamics of his problems and misbehavior? Perhaps this little boy needs a mental health professional to work comprehensively with him, his family and his school. People need to start appreciating the complexity of ADHD, even conduct disorders, and not just take a simplistic special education, behavior modification, or medication approach to these problems.
>
> If these boys are treated simplistically, they are eventually labeled troublemakers and underachievers and proceed to deteriorate. I see them here in the hospital as adolescents and think, my God, something could have been done if people had just understood a little bit more and intervened psychotherapeutically as well.

Meanwhile, borderline males whose illness has progressed into adulthood can nevertheless be helped. Dr. Andrulonis finds that particularly during adolescence, borderline males respond especially well to cognitive therapy approaches. Because boys have had difficulties as long as they can remember, it helps them to list their strengths and accomplishments and to have guidance in approaching and solving their problems. "Sometimes the men appreciate that concreteness," says Dr. Andrulonis.

> We still do some psychodynamic work, but there's often so little to their egos that it helps for them to develop an intellectual understanding that they're not total failures and to find positive aspects about themselves. Then we can take a problem-solving approach, not unlike some of what Dr. Kernberg does, particularly with hospitalized patients.

The males tend, however, to be more sensitive than women to therapeutic limitations such as being forbidden to act out.

The key to a borderline male's recovery appears to be the very thing it is hardest for him to find. Borderline males scare therapists away even faster than females do, for two reasons. One is that although bad enough, a history of self-mutilation and suicide attempts is less frightening than one of violence and property destruction. The potential for complications in the treatment of a male borderline is considerable.

Another is that their illness causes male borderlines all kinds of real-life difficulties. Many female borderlines are on disability or welfare, but males are often in real financial and legal trouble complicated by serious substance abuse. Such practical problems overwhelm therapists, who often quit or refer the patients elsewhere.

In doing so, they remove the essential component of the borderline male patient's care. "It makes an enormous difference to these men if they find mental health professionals who will stick with them," says Dr. Andrulonis.

> The men who have support through their dealings with the drug and alcohol programs, the courts, the creditors, will keep coming back to therapy. If therapists would just give them a chance, I think they would find them good psychotherapy cases and as responsive as women to aggressive application of the proper techniques.

Perhaps disabled neurologically as well as psychologically, borderline men need a complex system of structure and control provided by special education, rehabilitation, and job training as well as supportive, relationship, and cognitive therapy from a mental health professional. It is important that the family as well as the patient be educated about his illness and that they participate in family therapy. With all these aides in place, the prognosis for borderline males as described by Dr. Andrulonis is guarded but hopeful.

The Course of the Borderline Male

A similar sense of qualified optimism emerges from two long-term followup studies of borderline patients. A paper by Karen K. Bardenstein, Ph.D., and Dr. McGlashan, the author of one study, compares gender differences between the patients' lives since their treatment. The findings are that although male borderline patients tended to leave the hospital against medical advice and drift out of the mental health system, they were more likely than female patients to be functioning well at followup.

These researchers describe the chaotic, solitary life style outlined by
Dr. Andrulonis, which mellows as the borderline male grows older.
Having defined himself occupationally, the borderline male actively in-
vests himself in his career, becomes more productive, and feels more
competent. He improves his ability to maintain relationships and may
consider marriage. In any case, he often supplements the structure and
companionship provided by his work with that found in other institutions like Alcoholics Anonymous or religious organizations.[11]

Dr. Stone's long-term followup study of borderline patients likewise
shows that males marry less often than females, find structure and solace
in work or hobbies, and use obsessive defenses to cope with solitude.[12]
But Dr. Stone did not find the same pattern of overall improvement in
male borderline patients shown in Dr. McGlashan's study.

The discrepancy could reflect not just a difference between the patient populations but also self-selection among those admitted to each
hospital. Psychiatric hospitals in general are, of course, likely to treat the
sickest female and the healthiest male borderlines. Dr. McGlashan believes that this selection factor may have skewed his findings. "I'm not
really sure that male borderlines do better overall than female borderlines, although that was true of our sample," he says.

For his part, Dr. Andrulonis isn't sure which gender eventually makes
better recoveries. He points out that male borderlines have more difficulties than females to look back on but agrees with my observation that
women are less likely than men to cope well with aging.

In a later discussion of followup studies, we will see that female borderlines in general have good prognoses. That their prognosis is unclear
compared to that of males suggests that the latter are much better candidates
for effective treatment than many therapists might think. And therapists
may underestimate how many male borderlines exist. "I feel that BPD is
probably just as common in men as in women and is just misdiagnosed,"
says Dr. Andrulonis.

The borderline diagnosis is made five times more often in women—that
doesn't mean the clinicians are right—but the men fulfill all the criteria that
women do. It's very important for forensic psychiatrists to recognize that
these men are core Gundersonian borderlines. They form very close relationships; they are extremely depressed, and these two characteristics make
them very treatable.

These comments may arouse considerable skepticism. Today, few
therapists would want to sort through the violent, chemically dependent
criminals clogging the courts and prisons to find the depressed, lonely

borderline males hiding beneath sociopathic facades. But Drs. Andrulonis, Gunderson, McGlashan, Stone, Siever, and other therapists have worked effectively with male borderlines for years. Apparently no patient frustrated by the challenges of psychotherapy has pulled out an Uzi yet.

Notes

1. Michael H. Stone, M.D., *The Borderline Syndromes: Constitution, Personality, and Adaptation* (New York: McGraw-Hill, 1980), p. 291.
2. Paul A. Andrulonis, M.D., and Lawrence V. Silvia, A.C.S.W., "Borderline Personality Disorder in Children and Their Parents," paper read at the 139th annual meeting of the American Psychiatric Association, Washington, D.C., 12 May 1986.
3. See, for example, Theodore A. Petti, M.D., M.P.H., and Ricardo M. Vela, M.D., "Borderline Disorders of Childhood: An Overview," *Journal of the American Academy of Child and Adolescent Psychiatry*, Vol. 29, No. 3 (May 1990), pp. 327–37.
4. Arguments for and against the existence of BPD in children can be found in Paulina F. Kernberg, M.D., and Theodore Shapiro, M.D., "Resolved: Borderline Personality Exists in Children Under Twelve," *Journal of the American Academy of Child and Adolescent Psychiatry*, Vol. 29, No. 3 (May 1990), pp. 478–83.
5. Paul A. Andrulonis, M.D., "The Borderline Male," paper read at the 143rd annual meeting of the American Psychiatric Association, New York, 17 May 1990.
6. Ibid.
7. Paul A. Andrulonis, M.D., Bernard C. Glueck, M.D., Charles F. Stroebel, Ph.D., M.D., Naomi C. Vogel, M.A., Anne L. Shapiro, and Dorothy M. Aldridge, "Organic Brain Dysfunction and the Borderline Syndrome," *Psychiatric Clinics of North America*, Vol. 4, No. 1 (April 1980), p. 51.
8. Jack R. Cornelius, M.D., Paul H. Soloff, M.D., Anselm W. A. George, M.D., S. Charles Schulz, M.D., Ralph Tarter, Ph.D., Richard P. Brenner, M.D., and Patricia M. Schulz, M.S.W., "An Evaluation of the Significance of Selected Neuropsychiatric Abnormalities in the Etiology of Borderline Personality Disorder," *Journal of Personality Disorders*, Vol. 3, No. 1 (1989), pp. 19–25.
9. Kathleen M. O'Leary, M.S.W., Pim Brouwers, Ph.D., David L. Gardner, M.D., and Rex W. Cowdry, M.D., "Neuropsychological Testing of Patients with Borderline Personality Disorder," *American Journal of Psychiatry*, Vol. 148, No. 1 (January 1991), p. 106.
10. Andrulonis, "The Borderline Male."
11. Karen K. Bardenstein, Ph.D., and Thomas H. McGlashan, M.D., "The Natural History of a Residentially Treated Borderline Sample: Gender Differences," *Journal of Personality Disorders*, Vol. 2, No. 1 (1988), pp. 69–83.
12. Michael H. Stone, M.D., *The Fate of Borderline Patients: Successful Outcome and Psychiatric Practice* (New York: The Guilford Press, 1990), pp. 138–39.

13

Gerry: Being Very Lucky

I come from a family that has a lot of accomplishments, except for my father. But my parents used to fight continuously. My father is an alcoholic, and I imagine my mother is too. After they split up, my father stole me out of the house a few times. I always used to back him up while my brothers always stuck with my mother. So she's always had it out for me on that.

My cousin is a homosexual, so my father always embedded in us that we'd better be macho men. The way he always beat the shit out of me, wanting me to be a man, was a big factor in how I am. He would work very hard, then on Friday he would come home, shower, give my mother whatever money she needed and take off until Sunday morning. Then we would all go to 10:00 mass and have brunch at home. It was very weird and hypocritical.

My mother doesn't know what she wants. She sees things in black and white and is constantly changing from minute to minute. She has a second-grade education and believes everything on TV.

I always tell her that she loves my brothers more than me. And she does. My mother never hugged me and doesn't like to be kissed, even now. She fed and clothed us, and that was all she has to do. She once stabbed one of my sisters with a kitchen knife for not listening to her.

My father is a very tender, kind person who loves me. He has been divorced from my mother a long time and lives in the Virgin Islands now. I call him up and he offers anything I need within reason, and I get it. As a kid I used to go out to shine shoes and run errands, but my father didn't want me to do any of this. I was supposed to ask him for money. Even today.

A stable family, no knives and fighting, would have made a big difference. It was a very crazy situation. I have gone through some very bad experiences with my parents, and they had a lot to do with my anger.

One Christmas I went and shined shoes, starting with a nickel and ending up with 95 cents. I went to buy a doctor's set, but it was a dollar, so instead I bought some cards and two records. I didn't know how to tell my mother I had earned the money, and as soon as I came home, the first thing she said was, "You stole these things." By then it was dark, so she made me take off everything except my underwear and stand outside in the snow until I had said the entire rosary. When my father came home, she told him, "He stole these things." My father came outside, picked me up and started beating me with his belt and drew blood, and that wasn't the first time.

My father doesn't know how to say no. If I had known how to do it from the beginning, that would have helped me a lot too. I would be less angry.

In our culture, the man is the dominant figure, and what he says goes. I've been brought up to see my father going to bed with a woman and drinking two or three bottles of liquor. That was being a man, not how intelligent you were. If you didn't fight, you were a pussy. I resolved that, but I have it systematically inside me. I'm scared of getting married again or living with a woman because I don't know if that feeling is going to come back. So I'm a little afraid of a relationship with a woman because I don't want to go where I went with my second wife. I really loved her a great deal. I don't want to go through a relationship and do my bit and break up and go to court again. I'm not into that and I hope . . . so far I'm not that way.

When I was a kid, the school wanted me to see a psychiatrist, but my parents wouldn't allow it. I was very disruptive in school, got into fights and things. I hit a kid over the head with a chair and fought with my brothers.

I just had a history of being very violent. I grew up in the ghetto, where you had to fight to make it. I shot a kid in another city who was trying to rob me. I worked as a security guard for a while when I lived there and was licensed to carry a gun. I never had a record for them to check, and they didn't look at a psychological profile when they hired me. I also knew a lot of police officers, so they didn't keep too close an eye on me.

I got my way, and to this day people are afraid of me. I've changed, but they see me the old violent way. I like to fight even though I get hurt. I look forward to getting hurt. It makes me feel better. I don't know what it is, but I get to the point where like a child, I'm looking for attention. I didn't know how to get that attention and love or whatever you want to call it except by being bad.

Basically my sickness has been that I strike.* I was very hostile, very dominating about women and wanting things done my way. In my home it was always physical force. I knew nothing else and didn't know how to communicate or compromise or whatever—it was just my way. I did a lot of drinking, which didn't help.

After my father left my mother, we lived in a house where a man abused me sexually. I would masturbate him, and he would buy me things. I didn't get hung up on it, maybe because of the kindness I got out of it, compared to my father leaving. I don't have any hangups with homosexuality. I don't do that—I love women a great deal. I was a young kid, and it was something to try and a way to get things. I don't think anything of it.

It was that way with the daughter of one of my cousins. He had sex with her for five years because she used it to get things. See what happens? I felt really bad because I didn't know whether to love or hate my cousin. I would never do that to my children. I would beat them up, but not molest them.

In Catholic school when I was an altar boy, I was touched by a priest. He would tap me in the ass, little games. I had homosexual acts with some people in Catholic school also. I don't say this to everybody. I had a very mixed-up bag.

When I was 19, I joined the service and was stationed in another city. Three years later, I met my first wife in a bar off the base. I knew her only about two months before marrying her, and right away she got pregnant and we lived in her father's house for a while.

What bothered me drastically was that I couldn't be a man there. If anything went wrong and needed to be fixed, she would always go to her father. We never worked anything out ourselves. I would get very angry. Her father was a very narrow, unsophisticated, illiterate man, but he was a good mechanic who taught me to cut up cars.

---

*Gerry's hospital records describe him as paranoid, histrionic, and borderline, with major depressive disorder and alcohol dependency.

My first wife was very rough and thinks in black and white the way I used to do. She loved me a great deal even though we had a history of fighting. I beat her and my first son a lot. One time I threw the TV through the window. I would hit my wife, then we would go to court and get back together.

She put up with a lot. I like living and used to go out and party, have sex, and get drunk almost every night with four to six hundred dollars in my pocket.

I earned all this money. I worked for a big social services agency. I got a law student to help me put together a grant proposal for a new program, sent it off, and got a six million dollar grant. In ten years' time I put together about eight or nine million dollars for them. I got very close to several philanthropists, clergymen, politicians, and lawyers. I was paid very well and did consulting and made connections with banks to get loans.

I took the mother agency to court with a big law firm because they were taking funds and the program was not being administered properly. It was a really big case that backfired because I didn't keep very good records. I had a John Doe indictment, but I beat that.

Then I left the agency. I'm a fighter. To help it grow, my program needed somebody more sophisticated than I was and also more lenient and tolerant. I used to fly off the handle and thought I knew it all. And I did. I was very successful, so I must have been doing something right. Besides, if you carry a .38 Smith Weston and have lots of money and know the right people, you get away with a lot.

My new business was used and scrap cars. It was a legitimate business that did really well with my wife managing it. But a lot of cars also came through out of nowhere with parts they didn't need. My wife didn't know about it. But I ended up going to court for moving stolen cars.

That was the second time I cut my wrists. I had done it in the service too. I always make situations worse in my mind. I torture myself in a certain way, that the worst is going to happen, and it doesn't. The court hearings just continued and continued for four years, so one day—I don't know how it was. I took it to superior court, and it just dragged on, so I thought I was going to jail and cut my wrists. I felt really depressed. But I ended up beating the rap. I was about 33 then.

While this was happening I was getting divorced from my first wife to marry my second. This worked out pretty well for a while. But I had a tendency to think that I wasn't worthy of the wife or money that I had. I accomplished a lot and helped a lot of people, but still I was hostile and had a low opinion of myself. I would say that all I did was really nothing.

I was with my second wife for seven years. She has degrees in nursing and public health. I liked to stay home and watch TV, and she liked to entertain and bring all kinds of people home and go out, and I didn't enjoy those things after a while.

I thought I was losing her because she stopped doing things she had done before. One of the things that got me really upset was that she didn't want to have sex with me any more. She said she'd give me money if I wanted to have a woman outside. But I really loved my wife a great deal and wanted her sexually.

I came home one day, and my wife was cooking and I was sitting down, and all of a sudden I flew off the handle and started hitting her. It happened just right off the spot. Then another time she had some very respectable people over and I took her into another room and hit her again for no reason at all.

Things had changed when my son was born. I got very close to him because I had never seen a child being born. But my wife changed her love and kindness from me to the child. She would kill for him. I got jealous and would hit him. If he did something, my wife would talk psychologically about Dr. What's-his-name, Spock? I would say, "You do it my way, or I'm going to kick your ass." So she shut up.

But I learned that for that moment, physical force might win, but eventually people get to resent and fear you. My wife really feared me because I got drunk one night and when my next door neighbor messed with me, I got my shotgun and went to his door to shoot him. But I was lucky, very lucky, and I didn't. He went out his fire escape and got the cops, who took me to the hospital. I was really lucky because my wife was an emergency room nurse and knew the cops. And the neighbor didn't press charges, so I was really lucky on that.

I ended up in the hospital here because I was drugging and drinking and really depressed because I had been thrown out of my house. I came home and two police officers and the manager of the apartment came in and told me they had a restraining order and I had to leave. So I did.

When I cut my wrists I had started going to a community health center where they gave me Mellaril, Tegretol and lithium. When I moved back home here, I used up this medication and couldn't sleep. So I came to the VA Hospital and got more Mellaril and Tegretol to calm me down.

But I had a lot of hate and really wanted to kill my wife. After watching me here for three or four weeks, they took me into the psych ward, and all I could talk about was killing her. I had a nervous breakdown and was really depressed. I spent about two months in the psych ward. They took the other meds away and gave me Navane.

I had it out with the doctor because I didn't know that by law your confidentiality must be broken if you threaten somebody. I didn't want to upset my wife at the time, but when I was leaving, he had to call to tell her. My brother had brought in a bottle of soda, and I broke it to cut my wrists again. But the doctor made the call anyway. Then we had to talk it all through.

After that I was let out and lived with my one sister. Once I divorced my second wife, my first wife became very close to me. She came twice to see me and spent about $1500 on me each time. I would go to see my kids and she would let me stay in the house, eat, have sex, do whatever I wanted. This lasted until one day she told me that she hated my guts and everything I stand for. I told her I was sorry about the women in my life and apologized for hurting her, but there was nothing I could do to stop her hurting, and that was it. I've changed and I don't go after women like I used to.

She didn't talk to me for a while. Then I happened to be in town and she came by to show me how well she was doing as manager of the used car business. We talked, and she left, and that was it.

Next month my older daughter is getting married and I have to sit at the head table with my wife. Plus my daughter by my second wife is going to be flower girl. So all my children, my two ex-wives, and 200 people—it's going to be interesting. My second wife says, "If there's any problems, I'm leaving," and I say, "I'm not drinking or anything, not looking for any problems, so there won't be any."

Anyway, I kept coming to the VA and talking to my therapist, who had a great interest in me. She was the greatest help I had.

I miss my therapist a great deal since she left the hospital. She cared enough not just to see me at scheduled times—her door was always open to me. I was supposed to see her once or twice a week, then every two weeks, but any time I needed help, she was there. She was firm when she had to be and a friend when she wanted to be. Her ethnic background helped her understand the problems I was going through.

I would get headaches, and my body and spirit were being separated and I would have no control over myself. I would take aspirin and eat and sometimes it would go away. I don't know whether it was the drugs or the alcohol or the combination or what, but I would get sick, and I would go to her. They were not supposed to give out medications, but she would give me aspirins and stuff and help me out and talk to me and say, "Don't leave the hospital until you feel better."

Whatever problems I had we worked out together. I had been masturbating but then I met a girl and went to bed with her, and it felt good. But I was looking for a girlfriend to go out with and this girl was very—not cold, but she would go to bed and then say, "See you later," and that was it. My therapist and I worked through that. She would say,

"Doesn't it feel good to be with a woman and work things out?" and I would agree. I really enjoy that.

I lied to her sometimes, and she would know it. I don't know how to lie with a straight face. I can tell you not all the truth and get away with it, but to lie is a different thing. She was very clever. She knew I was doing drugs too, and she let it go for a while.

When I first moved back home, I didn't know anybody any more and made friends with a woman who sold drugs and drank a lot. She was my best friend, and I wanted to go to bed with her. But she likes to use people, and when she doesn't need you, forget it. She would punish me by not talking to me, acting like a little kid.

My therapist said, "Look, you can go to jail if you hang around with her. You're losing your health—you don't know what they're putting in that powder." Finally I came to a group meeting and got an ultimatum: "Either stop doing drugs and drinking, or we'll let you go."

And the idea of losing my therapist meant so much to me that I stopped. I stopped drinking and doing drugs and got more into myself. I stopped being violent. I just stopped.

The drugs had a lot to do with the violence. I used to smoke marijuana to calm me down, and it does help a great deal. I would go out drinking and put away a fifth easily and become very violent. I started coke in the service and did a lot of drinking and became Dr. Jekyll and Mr. Hyde. I didn't do that much coke after that until I moved back home. But I stopped. I was very lucky.

I signed a contract with my therapist. And I would go to AA meetings and started going to Narcotics Anonymous until they stopped having the groups nearby. I might start up again tomorrow, you can never tell, but I haven't touched coke in three years. And I haven't the stomach for drinking any more.

I had three or four therapists after mine left. I got close to one of them, I forget his name, but his schedule was changed. I used to stay away too, or not come sometimes and make excuses. I just didn't feel like coming. I played a game, that was it. I didn't have a therapist for a while. I don't have one right now, and I'm not on medication. I've been off the Navane for a month. They cut the dosage from five milligrams to two, then stopped it because I wasn't depressed.*

I had been required to come once a month to check in because I was on medication. I had a monthly meeting this morning that I didn't attend because I had to work. Group therapy was a waste for me.

---

*Navane is an antipsychotic drug; we will see in Chapter 27 that such medications may have an antidepressant effect in some borderline patients.

I didn't have the patience to listen to other people's problems, and I just didn't care. It's not that I know it all, but I've gone through prisons, I've helped prisoners and drug addicts, and most of the time they go back to drugging and drinking and crimes and stuff. Some people get a thrill out of doing that. I got a thrill out of breaking the law and seeing how far I got away with it. And I happened to be lucky to have the money and the resources to beat the raps.

I've been very clever. But I don't need those things any more.

But this whole program meant a lot to me. I just like the hospital. My life is here; I work here now. I'm not cured, but the five years of being here mean a great deal to me. I'm a good worker; I have certificates for my work, and I just got promoted, so I have more money and responsibility.

Work has helped me tremendously also, no matter what kind it was. I've had the best jobs and the worst ones. Being given a job really helped me in my therapy here. When I came in, I was cleaning toilet bowls and mopping. I never gave up. I've always had the ambition that something better would come along and I was capable of doing it.

I have to work, physically or mentally. And I don't know how to do it in an atmosphere without having a challenge. When things come too easy, that gets me into trouble. I have to be channelling my energy into a challenge. I like to do the impossible.

Believe me when I tell you this, I am very lucky, very lucky, and God must be . . . No matter what kind of shit I get into, I come out smelling like roses.

Some people work all their lives without getting grant money, and I got six million dollars the first time I tried. I had the indictment, and I beat that. I was brought in for stolen cars, and I beat that. I've been very lucky that I'm not in jail right now. Hitting my wives, my children, whatever. I've been very lucky.

I made a lot of my problems myself because I have a mechanism, and I hope it doesn't come back, that I'm doing very well and then I destroy things.

I've been very lucky. When I moved back here, I befriended an old Irish man in the nursing home. I took him out of the home and have him living with my aunt. He took me to northern Ireland and paid for everything. He took $4,000 and told me to spend it however I wanted to. We came back and he bought me a new car. I take him to services on Sunday and we have supper at the church every Wednesday night.

I had always been interested in Irish history and politics. In our ghetto there was an Irish section, with Catholics and Protestants just like over in Belfast, fighting with each other all the time. The civil strife in Ireland got really bad just as I left to join the service, and I sometimes wondered how people in that neighborhood coped with it. I have felt very close to those people and Protestant Unionism for a long time, not just because it was good but because the Catholics were fighting with them about it.

I registered in the service as a Protestant but never knew how to go about converting. In the hospital I started going to services. The chaplain here helped me convert. My father understands and has known about it through the years. My mother does not understand. She is very narrow-minded, very ignorant, and won't have a Protestant in the house. I went to Catholic school. She has no son who is not a Catholic.

I feel close to the Protestants in northern Ireland. Practicing the religion has given me a new set of values. The people in my church live Christianity every day of their lives. Last month we launched a fundraising campaign to bring children from Belfast over here to visit, and I've been really busy with that. And I'm studying really hard so I can start teaching Sunday school classes and night classes in northern Irish history and current affairs.

I've always done stuff like this, service work with different churches. I've gone to work camps and painted houses and done construction. One summer I helped rebuild a school for the blind and a place for crippled children, and I've enjoyed that. But Irish Protestantism has always been with me since childhood.

I changed because I wanted to be liked for me. I'm getting older and wiser, I hope. Through the therapy and talking and working at the VA hospital and being in this city with the violence—always somebody is more crazy and violent—I've calmed down a little bit. I changed because I wanted to live a little longer. And I'm busy with the church. I just don't have time to do things any more.

My mother still gets me very upset. She's ignorant, and I don't have the patience to sit and explain to her. I don't want to hit her, but I argue, and I don't want to go back to where I was before, argue and hit.

Two of my children will soon be going to college. It all comes down to money. I want to be a millionaire, and I will accomplish that because I want them to have an education. It's very important. The beginning of knowledge is awareness of ignorance. The world and people and sickness would be helped more if people were more educated, and everybody would be a lot closer. Ignorance has a lot to do with people's anger.

I will become a millionaire by working hard. I have known since childhood that I was destined for something great. People keep telling me I'm blessed. And I helped a lot of people, but you can't do that without helping yourself. Now I'm learning how to channel this anger into doing that. I have to accomplish more than I have, learn to read more, to write, to channel my energy.

I want to help my children and others. I have always been able to help others, but I didn't know how to help myself. I've been very lucky. Lucky I'm not in jail. And very lucky that I went into the service, because all this therapy would have cost me a great deal of money. I couldn't have paid for all this.

To a young man in a ghetto, I'd say, "Don't give up. There's always a light in the tunnel." It's very hard to live with drugs and alcohol and poverty. In our neighborhood, people were on welfare, parents had babies with no milk, no diapers. I've been very lucky because I have never known starvation.

I would say to that person, "Don't give up. And find somebody who cares enough for you to help."

14

A Family Illness

"It has been the most difficult thing in our lives. For two years we couldn't think about it without crying. And it continues to be very demoralizing that our daughter seems fine but claims to cry herself to sleep each night. It's very difficult to understand."

"INGRID'S" FATHER

BPD exists not in a vacuum but in the relationships stirred up around the borderline. "What borderlines want often seems so reasonable and what they're unhappy about often seems so justifiable that people easily lose objectivity," says Dr. Hodulik. "Any well-meaning person around the borderline can become a co-character or dance partner who is manipulated and turned upside down and gets lost, not really knowing how to respond." Although they can be friends, lovers, or spouses, the dance partners with whom borderlines have the most significant relationships are their families of origin.

The families of borderlines are often the targets of the "manipulation" described earlier. In this case, the borderline's behavior may be intended to demonstrate the depth of her pain and to maintain a strong connection. "Our daughter spent months trying to convince us that we needed marriage counseling instead of what we really needed, which was to get her fixed up," says one mother. "But they want you to get involved in the same kinds of things they are."

While being drawn into the child's illness, the families of borderlines may find themselves being distanced from everybody else. Any type of psychiatric illness carries a stigma in the minds of many people. Close relatives and friends may never even mention the illness, let alone visit a patient who has been hospitalized for months. Suddenly families are ostracized from the social circles upon which they had depended for support.

In this and other respects, the experience of people close to her as well as that of the borderline herself is part of what defines BPD.

Although BPD is a "family illness" in several senses, the voluminous literature on borderline patients all but excludes their families. "I'm really pleased to see your book include chapters on families because there is not much written or even known about them," says Dr. Links, the editor of a new professional book on family environment and BPD that has started to fill this gap.[1] Like the borderlines, their families are what Dr. Links calls "very variable." No one would characterize the family life of any borderline as optimal, and often recovery requires the patient first to separate from her family, but other generalizations are at best tentative.

One is that many borderlines grew up in families who subjected them to the worst abuse imaginable. "These severely dysfunctional families would be toxic for any child," says Dr. Links. Their definition of the borderline child's illness would probably range from a source of entertainment to a threat to their continuation of abuse. And in this context in particular, my descriptions of the families of borderlines unfortunately represent a selection bias. "You have a real problem," says Dr. Gunderson, "in that the more prototypic parents of borderlines are the least likely to give you material."

It is difficult to determine how even less prototypic families view BPD because the stress of the illness creates amnesia. Like borderlines themselves, their families complain that they can't remember the chronology of events during the illness crisis. As the family suffers along with the borderline child, years of constant heartache become merged. "My daughter has been out of the hospital for almost a year," says one mother, "and now it's finally getting to the point where the phone can ring without my worrying that it's her."

These families may function so well socially that they appear to be healthy and loving. They aggravate the hospitalized borderline by visiting her each week, bringing care packages and charming even the other patients, who really ought, she thinks, to know better. This expressed interest in the patient's treatment can be a source of great stress for the family.

Wanting to Know

While recognizing that confidentiality must be respected, families can find practical problems compounded by their being left in the dark about what therapy entails. "There is a very big inconsistency," says one father.

> Mental health professionals considered us a very important part of our daughter's treatment yet made no effort to give us any direction or knowledge about it, let alone any peace of mind. We felt almost that they interacted with us only to see how it affected her. They never explained what our role should or would be.

"We had no guidelines," says the patient's mother.

> We would come away from meetings and sessions with them and say, "Well, what are we supposed to do now? How are we supposed to feel about this?" They don't really know what to do with families. Maybe that's because they open up a Pandora's box in approaching families, because they never know what they're going to find.

Some families find that having to deal with psychiatric bureaucracies is a nightmare in and of itself. Because borderlines often require years of psychotherapy and/or long-term hospitalizations, decisions about their care can make tremendous differences in a family's financial status. Such decisions may be required suddenly in times of great crisis, sometimes under pressure from a hospital seeking to fill beds or transitional care facilities.

Confusion about treatment can cause fights over how the borderline's illness should be handled. As noted in Chapter 2, their responses to borderlines can weaken the fracture lines of any group, including their families. Because fathers and mothers play different roles in the child's life, they may take opposite stands. "My wife and I would leave family meetings and be fighting furiously by the time we got home," says one father. "I would be exasperated, asking, 'How can you not see this? How can you do that?' and she would be insisting, 'I'm the mother, and I have to do it that way.' " Unless such conflicts are resolved, the child's illness may result in the parents' divorce.

Refusing To Know

Families educated by their experience with BPD speak of "the denial stage," a kneejerk refusal to accept responsibility for contributing to the patient's illness. Some get past this stage and develop an uneasy truce with the borderline, an ability at least to listen and to recognize the truth. Others refuse even to admit that the illness is serious and the child not yet cured.

"Most borderlines arise in families where all the siblings have serious problems too," says Dr. Gunderson. But if the siblings appear well-adjusted or if the borderline is adopted, one form of denial is to single her out from the rest of the family. Parents who have always assumed that everything was fine suddenly learn that one of their children has been miserable. Their tendency is to claim that the family is healthy except for the sick child, who had different needs they didn't know about. The borderline is seen as the child who just doesn't fit in or who felt compelled to rebel against the family status quo.

"My father often says that all of his other children turned out fine," says 23-year-old "Emily," whose siblings are much older. "But he forgets that they were close enough in age to support each other and he was younger and too busy to focus on abusing them as he did me."

Not Knowing

Other parents refuse to accept responsibility because the early symptoms of BPD were expressed in ways they would have addressed but could not recognize. For them, the experience of BPD can include the shock of disclosure.

It can be difficult to know when a child's withdrawal, frenetic activity, fear of physical contact, or resentment of a favored or learning-disabled sibling masks deeper problems. "This is the failing, the not recognizing," says Emily's father.

> Almost every other parent I meet says, "I'm not to blame for this." But it's not a question of blame but rather one of not being aware of all the facets involved in the development of a child and of trying to generalize from one child to another. It's not a failure with malicious intent—we have done everything in the name of love for the child.

Emily's father learned that his expressions of love for his daughter were, in fact, abusive:

> When Emily was about six, we put her in a school that offered some classes conducted in a foreign language of our choice. I signed her up and tried to force down that education. Emily was a slow learner, as I am myself. I was willing to compensate by spending more time learning what I had to, and I became a tax attorney by studying especially hard. I tried to tutor Emily. In the process I would scream and holler at her if in spite of many repetitions of the material at hand, I didn't see improvement in her comprehension.
>
> Emily mentioned several times during family support meetings that I abused her. My verbally expressed displeasure scared her to the point where she would wet her pants. Some parents agreed with her that I was abusive.

"I would wet my chair when he hit me," says Emily. "This happened many times."

Parents who don't learn unpleasant facts about themselves when a child becomes borderline may instead hear shocking disclosures about other family members. One mother of five explains how her husband sexually abused their daughters, including one who became borderline, without her knowledge:

> Incest was so far removed from anything I had ever known, growing up in my big loving family. I think the things around me are normal, and I don't look for quirks. I trust people. This is why I handled things as I did. I thought my guidelines were sufficient. I demanded decent behavior; I was here all day; I love children and now teach school.
>
> With five children, I couldn't move back and forth, and my husband completely shut me off from my family, as if they might figure out what he was doing. People in his office, at church, thought he was wonderful. I seemed to be the only one having any difficulty with him. It made me doubt my own judgment.
>
> All the children have told me that they knew I was there for them. I tried so hard to establish an atmosphere in which any of them could come and talk things over with me. I worked so hard at my marriage.
>
> I don't know why they couldn't tell me. I adore my children—my whole life was for them.

Victimization and Blame

Such denial and explanations are reactions to an experience common to families: that of being blamed for the borderline's illness. The tendency of therapists to blame them is rooted not only in psychoanalytic tradition but also in empirical studies whose results were misinterpreted. Twenty years ago, for instance, therapists believed that families contributed to the development of schizophrenia because they studied the parents of schizophrenic patients with no normal families used as controls. "Without good controlled studies in which the families are observed by researchers who don't know the diagnoses of the children, we'll make all kinds of unwarranted inferences," says Dr. Liebowitz. "Schizophrenic and borderline families may have conditions common to all families."[2] "I hope we've learned from this example, where we've called mothers schizophrenogenic and then really didn't have any way of helping them," says Dr. Links.

We will see in Chapter 19 that families do, in fact, contribute to the development of BPD. This does not, however, mean that they should be *blamed* for causing the illness. Should Renée be blamed because two of her children have needed psychotherapy?

Misdirected blame appears particularly in the context of abuse. The mother's description above suggests one reason that it might be unwarranted. Another is what Dr. Herman calls one of the most consistent findings in abuse studies: an unusually high rate of serious illness or disability (schizophrenia, depression, or alcoholism, for instance) in mothers of sexually abused daughters.[3] These mothers are entitled to compassion. "There is a power imbalance in which the mother really must hold on to the marriage at all costs," says Dr. Herman.

She can't protect herself, let alone the children. Some psychoanalysts got into raving mother blaming without any understanding of the power relationships within these families.

Along with denial and explanations, the automatic response of families who feel blamed is to echo their daughters' complaints of misery. "I still attend family support groups because I learn a lot," says one father.

All the parents, including me, deeply resent feeling put upon by the stress of having a child like this. We all seem more concerned with what it's doing to

us than we are with the patients. I hear it all the time: "Look what it's doing
to me."

When Ingrid's parents complained about their anguish, she responded
with what she herself was learning:

> All my father would ever say was, "Tell me the facts. The facts are that we do
> this for you and your brothers." It was always facts instead of feelings. He
> would say things like, "We're miserable because of you." I would say,
> "Then go get help. You can't blame the misery in your life on me unless
> you're willing to seek treatment and learn how to deal with it." But my
> parents wouldn't accept their responsibility until the social worker told my
> father that if he didn't change his attitude, I would die.

Such mutual blame and refusal to accept responsibility is completely
unproductive and makes everyone in the family feel worse.

"This is a difficult, sensitive problem," says Dr. Gunderson.

> One important thing to note is that the parents of borderlines are themselves
> often the products of very troubled family backgrounds. Certainly it softens
> the implied criticisms of them to see them with the same kind of compassion
> that should be directed toward borderlines. It's not easy if you simply talk to
> borderline patients because they often feel so enraged about how their par-
> ents failed them that it is hard for them—and sometimes for clinicians as
> well—to see their parents as victims of the same problems from their own
> pasts. We see multigenerational transmission. The parents' own difficulty in
> managing angry feelings is manifest in their either being too punitive or
> withdrawing from their children when such feelings arise.

"My father used to see himself as a provider," says Emily.

> He thought that by giving us a nice home and food on the table, he was
> doing his job. I guess he never really had much of an emotional life—he left
> that for my mother to handle. The way he was brought up was abusive too,
> but he didn't see it that way. At least that's what he would say—"That's the
> way things used to be done."

"I'm beginning to forgive my mother, but it's a very slow process,"
says Sharon, the abused borderline daughter of an abused borderline. "I
know she did the best she could, but she still has many of the same
problems. I feel very lonely facing the fact that I'm never going to have
the mother I wanted." I asked Sharon whether she would feel better if
she had legitimate reasons to be less angry with her mother. "I don't

know," she replied. "The child inside me is still crying and can't let go of what happened." This is an important point for borderlines to consider: that the *adults* inside them nevertheless have the right to get past the pain and be free.

But a call for understanding and compassion does not imply that families get to wriggle off the hook. The same principle that borderlines must learn applies also to their parents. "It's not inconsistent to see parents as very troubled people, without blaming them," says Dr. Gunderson, "while also not flinching from holding them responsible for the inadequacies that damaged their children."

A concept that Stephen A. Mitchell, Ph.D., has applied to neuroses, one that holds true also for borderlines and their families, is *accountability without blame*.[4] Borderlines need to blame others and feel compelled to have what was denied made up to them, refusing to accept that this is impossible. Parents feel the need to redirect blame away from themselves. In so doing, both forget that being held accountable means having the power to change. "Definitely cite the fact that parental patterns that can both cause and perpetuate the borderline's problems can be changed," says Dr. Gunderson. Family members coping with BPD might help both the patient and themselves through therapy, intervention, and/or support.

Family Therapy

The issue of family therapy often does not arise until a borderline is hospitalized for long-term treatment, making her illness undeniable. In this case, family therapy is one aspect of the patient's own treatment.

Hospital policies vary concerning family therapy for borderlines. The inpatient units in Dr. Kernberg's department admit only those patients whose first-degree relatives agree to attend family sessions. As part of their earlier work with inpatients, Drs. Masterson and Rinsley recommended that borderlines be separated from severely ill families by whatever means were necessary. One rationale for such an approach is to disrupt the family's pathology and enable the patient to interact with the hospital staff as a new and healthier "family."

Noting that Chestnut Lodge does not require family therapy, partly because patients come from across the country, Dr. McGlashan says that

I can't generalize about how helpful it is. Many of the borderlines in our followup study were estranged from their families and most comfortable away from them. Yours is an interesting question because I've seen very little in the treatment literature about family therapy.

One reason the topic is neglected could be that hospital units have been less influenced than outpatient therapists by psychoanalytical theory, in which the family would, of course, be implicated.

Other therapists believe that whether or not family therapy is appropriate depends upon the individual family itself. Dr. Gunderson recommends that family members always be informed about the borderline patient's treatment progress; the hospital staff also needs to decide, however, whether the family is primarily overinvolved with or neglectful of the patient. Overinvolved families become anxious when separated from the borderline; if not allowed to participate in her treatment, they will withdraw their support and become actively hostile. Family therapy is probably not appropriate, however, for neglectful families, who resent the borderline's neediness. Such families of Dr. Gunderson's patients meet separately in a more supportive, less exploratory context that educates them about BPD and makes clear the goal of helping the patient achieve independence.[5]

Too many types of family therapy exist, too little of which is applied to borderline patients, to make other than the vaguest generalizations about its efficacy. Saul L. Brown believes that "preliminary, and, often, concomitant work with the patient's family is of equal importance" as the borderline's own individual psychotherapy.[6] Certainly family sessions enable a therapist to direct a patient's own treatment more precisely. Family therapy can reveal which relatives are most and least supportive, whether family difficulties are unresolved from the past or ongoing, and how the family's interactions play into the borderline symptoms. The sessions are a safe place in which the patient can get feedback and, in some cases, disclose incest or other forms of abuse. Ultimately the patient may see her family more realistically and learn better management of the symptoms they aggravate. "I do a healthier kind of distancing from my parents now," says one patient, "instead of being drawn right into the same old back-and-forth with them."

Unfortunately, such treatment does not always help the *family*. The approach(es) taken with the families I interviewed was often seen as a waste of time that alienated relatives and patient alike. All participants hated the therapy except for one family that switched gears and now describes it with the zeal of the converted. This family has continued therapy since the borderline child's release from a hospital because it frees them at other times *not* to fight with her.

Expressed Emotion

An alternative to therapy through which her family might help the borderline patient has been proposed by Dr. Links and his colleagues. The group plans to study a factor borrowed from work with families of schizophrenic patients. Research has shown that certain family attitudes toward or interactions with schizophrenics seem to play important roles in the illness course.

The overall index of a relative's emotional relationship with a patient is termed *expressed emotion*. It is based on the number of critical comments made about the patient and the amount of hostility and emotional involvement shown, determined by both the content of the statements and the relative's tone of voice.[7] High levels of expressed emotion in the family lives of schizophrenics have been shown to increase rates of recurrence, while low levels improve the prognosis.*

"Our thought has been to explore this concept in patients with BPD," says Dr. Links.

We want to see if there are particular interactions with their family members that perpetuate the problems. There's no reason to believe that whatever causes the problem also keeps it going. If expressed emotion is a useful concept, if it keeps difficulties going, then that will be a focus of attention directed toward ways in which we can help families change.

Researchers in schizophrenia have established groups that effectively educate families about the illness and the kinds of impairments that result. Applied to BPD, such an educational program might stress mood instability, rage, inconsistent competence, self-mutilation, and suicide threats. "The family might learn, for instance, the difference between suicidal threats that really mean 'Pay attention to me; I need something from you' and those that represent true risk," says Dr. Links. "Education can help the families respond appropriately to the expression of suicidal thoughts rather than either reject or overrespond to them." It can also empower the family and ease their minds.

Once educated about BPD, families would then be helped to change the quality of their interactions. When a member is ill, for instance, a family normally tends to become overinvolved. But if a borderline pa-

*The same holds true for cases of depression and attempts to maintain weight loss.

tient can function well in everyday life, such attention is really not necessary. "If their families can give borderlines some autonomy, often they can rise to the occasion," says Dr. Links.

Dr. Gunderson cautions against too literal an application of the expressed emotion construct to borderlines:

> The problem is that expressed emotion was built on the idea of telling the parents that they have a diseased child and that they need to recognize that the child is not responsible for its behavior. That's a hard one to apply too literally to borderlines.
>
> The part that does apply very nicely is that the parents' angry expressions of criticism toward the child will be harmful, not helpful. The directive to stop it, and supports and instruction on how to deflect those angry criticisms, might be more broadly useful.

Thus BPD might also be an illness susceptible to family cooperation. Undoubtedly the families of many borderlines are too dysfunctional to be interested in such education. In the next chapter, however, a borderline's father demonstrates just how much potential motivation a program like this could tap.

Healing Battle Scars

Therapy and intervention that help the borderline child are indirect means by which her family members can help themselves. More direct sources of assistance are supervised support groups for relatives of borderline patients. Bombarded by complaints about how horribly the child has been treated, parents rejoice to meet others who endured such attacks months earlier and can inform them of what to expect. Parents can also see that borderlines come from all different kinds of family backgrounds and so put their own situation into better perspective. It is also useful for parents to learn about the course of recovery—that the child will have relapses, for instance, and that even a few years of hospitalization do not "cure" BPD.

Battle-scarred families encourage each other to ignore certain upsets and otherwise maintain some perspective on the borderline's illness. "It's very common for therapists, family, and friends to get caught up in trying to meet demands that become increasingly unreasonable," says Dr. Waldinger.

One of the most difficult yet most helpful things is to pay close attention to what you can and cannot reasonably do and stick with that. It is no service to the borderline to bend over backwards and do increasingly more, because eventually you'll fail, and learning to cope with disappointment is an important developmental task. More isn't necessarily better.

The trick is to be there for the borderline without getting caught up in her pathology, to draw a line between providing support and feeding into the illness. "A part of our daughter still says that if we get too comfortable, she has to stir things up," says one father. "With the help of our family therapist, we had to set up very clear guidelines on how our relationship with her can go, because if we don't follow those rules, we become enablers."

Although a borderline desperately seeks proof that she matters and believes that if abandoned she will die, her family doesn't help by allowing her illness to ruin their own lives. If a borderline is hospitalized, for instance, the family might have to proceed with gatherings or vacations despite the patient's complaints about their callousness. Sometimes parents must issue an ultimatum that the borderline in treatment *cannot* behave in certain ways without being disowned. "For the first time in three years, our daughter admitted not only that her illness wasn't our fault, but that our guidelines about discipline had helped prevent her from getting even deeper into trouble," says a father. "And this was the approach we took when she was hospitalized—that if she ever tried to elope, we would no longer be there for her."

The possible causes of BPD include both biological and environmental factors. Every family must wonder whether a healthy home life can prevent the illness from developing. "The borderline's biological vulnerability requires stress to warp it into a disorder," says Dr. McGlashan. "A decent family keeps the vulnerability potential rather than actual." Obviously an honest self-appraisal by *any* family can't hurt.

A family might consider, for example, the earlier observations that sometimes the borderline doesn't fit in but more often the other siblings are also disturbed—and may need attention. "Don't apply general rules to every member of the family," says a father. "Be observant of and flexible about what each child needs and take the time to listen, because a child may be crying out with no one to hear."

Other coping techniques that parents of recovering borderlines report having learned are to:

- "Understand how serious the illness is, and don't expect recovery to be easy for either you or the patient."
- "Find a treatment program that you believe in, and leave the border-

line's recovery to that. Don't interfere with treatment, or you'll just prolong it."

- "Recognize that your behavior patterns, as well as your child's, are going to have to change."
- "Be honest yourselves and demand honesty from your child."

It helps also to understand that like any other crisis, BPD is also an opportunity for a family to learn and to grow. The life-or-death situation that often results can force a family to recognize its problems. As Emily says, her illness was her father's "back door way of getting into himself instead of right on."

Faced with having to wonder whether a borderline can ever have a normal life, some families have benefited from contributing to the ongoing research into BPD. "I really believe that there are many, many undiagnosed borderlines who could be helped and aren't because nobody pinpoints the illness and sends them to the right place," says one mother. "We stay involved hoping to help," says her husband. "It hurts to spend an evening sitting and talking to you; it really hurts. But we have to do anything we can."

Notes

1. Paul S. Links, M.D., M.Sc., F.R.C.P.(C), ed., *Family Environment and Borderline Personality Disorder* (Washington, D.C.: American Psychiatric Press, 1990).
2. Michael R. Liebowitz, M.D., paper [affirmative] read at debate, "Resolved: The Etiology of Borderline Personality Disorder Is Predominantly Biological," 143rd annual meeting of the American Psychiatric Association, New York, 16 May 1990.
3. Judith Herman, "Recognition and Treatment of Incestuous Families," *International Journal of Family Therapy*, Vol. 5, No. 2 (Summer 1983), pp. 83–84.
4. Stephen A. Mitchell, Ph.D., "The Origin and Nature of the 'Object' in the Theories of Klein and Fairbairn," *Contemporary Psychoanalysis*, Vol. 17, No. 3 (July 1981), p. 396.
5. John G. Gunderson, M.D., *Borderline Personality Disorder* (Washington, D.C.: American Psychiatric Press, 1984), pp. 155–58.
6. Saul L. Brown, "Family Therapy and the Borderline Patient," in *The Borderline Patient: Emerging Concepts in Diagnosis, Psychodynamics and Treatment*, ed. James S. Grotstein, Marion F. Solomon, and Joan A. Lang, Vol. 2 (Hillsdale, N.J.: The Analytic Press, 1987), p. 209.
7. Paul S. Links, M.D., M.Sc., F.R.C.P.(C), and Heather Monroe Blum, Ph.D., "Family Environment and Borderline Personality Disorder: Development of Etiologic Models," in Links, ed., *Family Environment*, p. 19.

15

Sandra and Martin: One Family's Experience

Many of the issues raised in previous chapters can be seen in the following description by "Martin" and "Sandra" of their borderline daughter Hayley (whom we met in Chapter 1) and how her illness affected the family.

I interviewed Hayley, her parents, and her brother and sister (who were much less involved with the illness and so are not included here). Hayley's case history, which is summarized quite thoroughly in this conversation, includes short-term hospitalizations for suicide attempts followed by a two-year stay on a borderline unit.

Except for some notable distinctions in feelings and attitudes, the five versions of Hayley's experience were reasonably consistent. One major difference was that neither parent volunteered the information that Hayley and her sister had both been molested by a neighbor when they were little. Possibly this topic was not introduced because the sister took the experience casually; Hayley, however, suppressed the memory, regressed when she recalled it a year ago, and still has difficulty discussing it today.

Hayley is now enrolled in a graduate program with a clearly defined goal of teaching music to children, with whom she works very well. She describes herself as having changed from a "perfect fake robot" to a "happier" person with greater depth and closer relationships who is "enjoying an exciting period of [her] life." She manages her illness better because "the craziness is shorter and easier to get through" and continues therapy as a highly motivated outpatient. Hayley decided not to have her comments included here.

This interview is a faithful transcription edited primarily by the deletion of less relevant passages. It illustrates both what has changed for the better and what misunderstandings still persist. Clearly the experience was painful for both parents to recall. At two points, when talking about Hayley's faithful friends and about her husband's preparation for the marathon, Sandra began to cry.

Martin: Hayley was always very outgoing, gregarious, communicative. I had difficulty with her even before we recognized her sickness, and I denied her sickness right up to the end because she is very bright and I felt that she was manipulating us a great deal.

I had problems because our personalities conflicted. I'm sort of laid back, not very outgoing, and to my mind Hayley was very self-centered. Everything had to revolve around her. My other two children were very different in that respect. It's not that I didn't love Hayley, but she came on too strong. She was very much into herself at the expense of others. I felt that she hurt other people, not deliberately, but because she had to come first. She never recognized other people's needs. That used to get me angry. This was before I was aware that she had a problem.

Sandra: Hayley is very outgoing, very, very personable. Very talented as a concert musician and in other areas. She always needed an enormous amount of attention.

Hayley is the only member of the family who is adopted. Early on, I attributed a lot of her self-centeredness and incredible need for attention to that. She came to us when she was five weeks old. I tried so hard not to make her feel different that of course I made her feel different, although the other children didn't feel that she was favored. Hayley got nothing more in the way of things, but what I did do was excuse her behavior just a little bit more because when she was pushing, I felt that she was just testing. Some of that was from knowing too much. It's better to know nothing and just go and do instinctively what you must. I should have set firmer limits when she was being obnoxious, and I didn't. That I'll own.

I had become angry, too, because the agencies had encouraged us to tell Hayley that she was adopted very early on. The social sciences are always changing their advice, while in the meantime I may have wrecked somebody's life. But unquestionably that was a core piece of it. I remember Hayley playing with a doll when she was five years old and saying to it, "Why did your mommy throw you away—you were only five weeks old!" and then start to cry. We never presented the adoption that way, but that's how she perceived it. Everything else was seen through a glass darkly. Had she been older when she learned of the adoption, the bonding would have been there.

Hayley seemed to come to attention naturally because she was very precocious, very funny, so people paid attention to her all the time. She didn't pull on people's skirts; she was just always cute and saying funny things and used to getting that kind of attention from early on.

She either hated or loved others and felt that they either hated or loved her. She never talked about liking, no gray areas.

As she grew older in nursery school, she got along well with the other kids, but she was bossy and usually in charge. Through school she was very competitive for attention. If she wasn't the favorite, she would get very upset and make the teacher's life miserable. She would do whatever she could, including rebel, to get that attention. For a while she went around with the least desirable group of kids.

Then in fourth and fifth grade Hayley had a very traumatic and profound time. She had a teacher who did not respond to her negative methods of getting attention. I remember noticing how completely she changed because he wouldn't humor her. Suddenly she became sweeter, nicer, more amenable. She became more part of the group, and she loved being in that class. From that point on, all her striving was toward achievement.

In retrospect the first hint we had that something was not right was when she left that situation. For those two years the class had been almost like a family, an incredibly nurturing environment, and when she had to go on to sixth grade, she began to be depressed. She had a real problem with separation. Each of her hospitalizations started in May, when she couldn't face school ending.

But the depression was expressed inaccurately. Hayley would complain that she had no friends when she was still the center of the crowd, the lead in the school plays. That whole sixth grade year her teacher told me that something was strange because nothing that Hayley said about being excluded was true.

Ours is a very competitive school district, full of highly affluent families who value education. I teach at a community college and my husband works for a manufacturing company, so we were not in their class economically, and our values were very different. Our son used to cut the alligators off his shirts, and our other daughter played with children from the immediate neighborhood, which was less affluent. But Hayley always needed badly to belong to the right group, all of whom were very Ivy League and materialistic.

In junior high, Hayley said once that she had made up her mind never to be depressed again. She suppressed whatever was working on her and for three years was the belle of the ball. Every day she would come home and say, "This was the best day of my life!" She was very dynamic and charismatic, a cheerleader; on stage you couldn't look at anyone else, she was that *there*. She got very involved in the chorus, which performed on television a few times. She did well academically. But she always had this kind of intensity that scared me, a little bit of trying too hard, going too fast, working too much, everything was always the best. It was too good to be true, and I'd say so, but because I wanted it to be true . . .

Hayley became again a little frantic in ninth grade when she knew she was going over to high school, which was terrible for her. All her friends except two went to a different high school. During tenth grade she would come home and say, "I don't know who I am; I'm a fag; I have no friends." Without a group, she didn't know where she fit in, only that she wanted to.

I just kept seeing a more intense franticness. But still we were quite close. There was sibling rivalry, especially with her sister, but both of them saw their brother as Mr. Perfect. Hayley and her sister are 17 months apart and totally different. Hayley could be quite mean to her sister, but only later did I realize how much she resented her for the usual reasons.

Martin: I felt that our other children were more like me. Throughout this whole period, I wasn't aware of any kind of changes in Hayley. I thought she was just in a stage of life. I was into my business, my own life, and aside from my difficulty with Hayley, I wasn't that involved and didn't consider her problem serious. I admired all her gifts, but I disliked her self-centeredness.

Sandra: And I attributed a lot of that to her adoption having made her less secure. She sucked her thumb surreptitiously until she was in the sixth grade. But it didn't overly concern me because she seemed to be doing so well.

In high school I began to say to her that she should seek some counseling, and she didn't want to. A real focus of much of her anger and distress about not being like everyone else was that her brother chose to attend a state college. The clothes and cars were competitive, and the schools hypercompetitive, so that was a very painful time for all of us even though the other children didn't care about these things.

The really big trouble started when Hayley was preparing to go off to college. She said she didn't want to go to a state school, but it was really the fear of separation again. She started to see a therapist.

Hayley got only 1000 on her SATs and was destroyed, utterly destroyed by it. She was so frantic at this time anyway that this seemed to push her over the edge. Her friends were getting 1300, and she thought she was stupid. And *we* thought she was a spoiled, obnoxious brat, because that's how the problem was presenting itself. So we were getting angrier and angrier and not understanding that this kid was just having a hard time leaving, among other things.

Martin: I really wasn't noticing this. I may have been into denial. I felt Hayley wasn't being treated unfairly. My wife and I were starting to have conflicts because Sandra was starting to feel guilty that maybe she had fed into Hayley too much over the years and I disagreed with that. Even during Hayley's first hospitalization, I believed that she wasn't sick; I kept telling myself that she couldn't be sick, she was just looking for attention. Naturally she would be angry at my attitude as we kept having more and more confrontations. I could not believe that a girl with all this talent, with all this going for her, could be sick. If she would say that she wanted to be admitted to a hospital or something, I would always laugh at her and say, "That's absolutely ridiculous—there's nothing wrong with you!" So this subject was becoming difficult for me. Very, very tough.

Sandra: I can't tell you how hard it is to understand how torn up borderlines are. One minute Hayley would say she was terribly depressed; the next minute the phone would ring and she'd be all bubbly. A complete change that would make us think, "What is all this bullshit?" It sounded like, "My brother or sister is doing something—look at *me*, look at *me!*" Whenever the others needed something, she would be sure to need more. I began to really resent that neediness, which seemed very manipulative.

Hayley continued to have friends even though she began to neglect or be nasty to them. But that she still has many of those friends from that period is an indication of the loyalty she does engender.

Her senior year she wanted to graduate school early, just finishing up her credits with home teaching. The school was completely against that because she had become phobic and the worst thing would have been to stay home. I was pretty adamant about her taking AP courses or something, not understanding that she couldn't tolerate school any more because she felt like such a loser.

Hayley's therapist seemed to share our feeling that she wasn't as sick as she thought she was, and he wouldn't let her talk about suicide. She had chosen this therapist herself, and he had no idea what kinds of games she was playing with him.

Then one night she became so desperate about school that she overdosed on her medications. She came into our room and woke us up to say that she had taken the pills and felt tingly. At the hospital, the psychiatrist asked her if she was sorry she had done it, and she said no, so she was hospitalized in their psychiatric unit for six weeks and had to finish her senior year at home.

She had left us a letter that I wanted out of my sight forever as quickly as possible . . .

Martin: I was amazed at the contents of that letter. She really felt she was a burden and doing us a favor. That's when I started really going off the deep end too. I just couldn't believe that she could write something like that, that there would be no pain for us, that it would be best if she were out of the way. As if it wouldn't bother us.

I remember going to a parents' meeting at the hospital where she was finally helped. I used to get so angry. One of the kids committed suicide, and one of the patients shared the fact that this boy was in tremendous pain and so took his life. I stood up and said that I was pleased that it wasn't my daughter and that I felt more pain for the parents than I did for the boy. The girl who shared this really came back at me and said, "You have no idea what borderlines experience in the way of pain." I said, "I don't care what you experience—we all experience pain!" Even at that time I wasn't giving too much sympathy, because we all suffer.

But then I started looking into myself and realizing that borderlines to go through emotions very much more magnified or exaggerated in their heads than mine or my wife's. Then I had to really start letting go, and when I did that, I began to really relate to Hayley more. I was able to communicate with her better, and we started to open up a new relationship. I made myself more vulnerable, and we really started making progress.

Sandra: When Hayley got out of the hospital, she continued to see the therapist she had there, who diagnosed her as borderline.

We gave her an ultimatum: either she go to school locally or get a job, not hang around and get depressed. She started at the community college where I teach and hated it at first because it made her feel like such a loser. We didn't like that attitude. But she did very well there and eventually loved it.

All during this time she was very depressed. She went to Europe with an orchestra at the end of her first year of college; she was anxious about going but had a wonderful time. You can imagine how crazy this made us, with her functioning at this level, making new friends, being teachers' favorite, and saying that she was very depressed. And that May again, she was hospitalized after another suicide attempt.

After her two years of community college, she was going to apply to an Ivy League school. There were several essays to write, and she had trouble getting herself together to do it. I was so anxious for her to be on with her life again that I did not recognize that this was another transition she would have trouble with. I helped her with the essays, and she had a successful interview. Once accepted, she was so terribly ambivalent about going that I didn't know whether to cheer or cry. It brought on another episode. She locked herself in a motel room with a supply of pills and called an older friend and her therapist. They talked her out of suicide.

The next day we all went down to see the therapist. He felt that she needed hospitalization, and she had been talking about how she had to be admitted to the best program. I was terribly against it because I felt that she had to get well in the world. I didn't understand what hospitalization was all about and felt that it was a negative experience that would reinforce her illness. The first hospital had a patient who did a lot of cutting, and before that Hayley had never cut. I felt that this was copycat behavior. I wondered what hospitalization could accomplish. It was a terribly scary thing.

Martin: That one time that morning, I think Hayley really had almost destroyed the therapist, because he felt that she had been making progress. She had threatened to kill herself before he could call us. That was when I finally relented and realized how serious it was, that she had to go to the hospital. We had tried everything, and she wanted to go. It was difficult, though, because we knew it would be at least 15 months.

Sandra: If Hayley had been curled up on the couch there, we could have understood. But this was a kid who was out in the world, who had a boyfriend and was doing well in school and teaching music. She asked to delay her admission a few days because her students were giving a recital. It was just so bizarre.

Martin: I felt that Hayley was destroying the rest of the family. Her sister and brother were concerned for us, and we were concerned for each other. Although generally speaking, we supported each other, my wife and I were battling because we had different ideas about what direction we should take. So we were having problems, and the family was starting to fall apart. In a way it was almost a relief to get Hayley into the hospital, because we knew that she was going to the best program and that our insurance would cover it.

Sandra: Hayley was admitted to an acute unit to wait for a bed in the borderline unit. She was so afraid that she wouldn't get transferred that she cut herself.

Martin: I felt that this was very manipulative. A few months later I decided that as much as I supported Hayley, if she ever cut herself again—which destroyed me even more than her attempts with pills—I would not support her any more. It bothered me so much that I had to take that risk. And she never did again. you really have to put it right out before the patient. My wife was against it and said she couldn't have done it, so I had to.

I knew also that Hayley was extremely committed to anything she did and very strong-willed. I didn't know how to help her, so I decided to dedicate a marathon to her. I had never run before, but I trained for a year and ran the marathon for her. I really think it was an inspiration to her, along with our always being there for her but not feeding into it or feeling sorry for her as some of the other parents tended to do. You have to be tough with these kids at times. We gave her our love, but we also gave toughness. The therapist who heads the unit says Hayley will be borderline for the rest of her life, with ups and downs. But we're very thankful for what the hospital did for her.

Sandra: To me, the marathon was very moving. There's such a feeling of helplessness when someone you love is ill like that. You want so much to do something! I know Martin wanted to be with Hayley in her struggle any way that he could be, so he overcame an obstacle, a big one. It moved me so every time I watched him going out in the morning to be with his daughter, knowing that there was no way he would have done this on his own. Then the day of the marathon, Hayley couldn't leave the hospital, but he did complete it, and it was such a victory of his spirit. I perhaps felt it more than she did. I don't know what it meant to her then or ultimately. But it was a binding thing for Martin and me, and it meant a lot to the entire family even though the other children weren't home.

Martin: It was very difficult making the first call to tell her brother and sister about Hayley. They couldn't believe it.

Sandra: They were more concerned for us than they were for her.

Martin: I have developed a different relationship with Hayley after having gone through all this. So has her sister. But there was always more closeness between her brother and sister, and they felt as I had that Hayley was selfish, so they felt more sorry for us and were angry with her for doing this to us. They didn't like the hospital, but they were more than willing to come for family sessions and visits. Even her brother and sister-in-law came up as a couple to the house group to support her.

Sandra: When her brother got married, Hayley had not been hospitalized all that long, and they did let her out to attend, but that was a whole big deal too. Even during his wedding, our preoccupation was with Hayley. That was a very hard time. Martin's mother had been ill and died the day before the wedding.

Martin: Her brother handles it worse than her sister; he doesn't show it as much. Her sister is more responsive to Hayley's problems and more willing to sit down and discuss them. If I mention Hayley to her brother, he doesn't handle it as well. He shows more concern about me and wants to tune it out. His attitude is that Hayley should get her act on the road and get better, because enough is enough. I used to feel that way too. Now I know that maybe Hayley will never really get her act on the road completely, but as long as she keeps working at it she can live a normal life.

Sandra: With her brother, Hayley is at her worst. She is so uptight about being with him and so much wants his approval that she's more "on" than she ordinarily is. She's just too larger than life at those times. He's lower keyed and very down to earth. He tries to be the supportive older brother and has been very good with her on many occasions, but when she has done things to him in the past, he hasn't forgiven her that easily. There is not that level of communication that there is between Hayley and her sister now. They're extremely close. Her sister is a very compassionate kid with lots of friends, and now Hayley can value that. Many times when Hayley is having a hard time, she'll call her sister long-distance as one of the first people she can turn to. She knows that she'll get feedback that will be levelheaded, true, and honest. Her sister is extremely clear and open in what she feels. She is the most clearsighted in the family.

I see Hayley maturing. The patients who have a good network do the best, and she always had that. She may not have thought that her friends cared about her, but they did. And she has her friends from the hospital. We had problems with that at first, not wanting her to associate only with "mental patients," feeling that she has to live in the real world. But that is the best. These patients really do understand each other in a way that no one else can and are enormously supportive of one another.

Martin: Hayley has told me that it's important to maintain a network of support. I emphasize this to parents all the time, that they should try not to feel uncomfortable that the patients are dealing with other borderlines when they get out. Every time there is any kind of incident that causes them hurt, they contact each other, and it's been very helpful and beneficial to each of them. As far as I'm concerned, they can do that for the rest of their lives.

While they're doing that, we as a couple can share all these positive experiences with other parents whose kids are being discharged, who are going through this dilemma, to tell them that there is hope. It's beneficial for them to hear that, just as it was for us when we felt it was hopeless.

Sandra: I never felt that it was hopeless. I was despairing, but I never felt that **it** was hopeless.

Martin: That's what I meant. We felt hopeless and despairing ourselves. We were helpless, but that didn't mean that Hayley couldn't get better.

Sandra: I wouldn't allow the thought that she might not get better. She really is very different now. But it took a lot of work.

Family therapy in particular was horrible. I felt attacked a lot of the time by Hayley. The therapist never seemed very good; she would let things get out of control. We had one therapist for a few months whom I liked a lot, but then she left for private practice, and that really ticked me off because they shouldn't have started her with us. I never felt connected with the next social worker, a very young girl. Hayley loved her, but she lacked experience. This is not to say that it wasn't helpful. The whole thing was helpful, but I hated every minute of it. **Hated every minute of it.** It was very painful, and I don't like dredging up all that stuff. When Hayley first became ill, I did go into personal therapy myself; I just didn't like family therapy. It went on every week for the whole time she was hospitalized. After the therapy, we had family group, which *was* very helpful.

The treatment was an enormous investment of time, energy, and money that kept us very focused on this illness. I didn't want to make it the center of my life. Some families do, and we need people like that, but I don't want to join them. I wanted to go on and do other things rather than stay in it and reinforce Hayley's illness identity. I would like to see her grow out of that.

She was very anxious for us to continue therapy after the hospital. I said, "No—I've had it," and it's very hard for me to say no to Hayley, just as it's hard to say it to anyone who's not well.

It was painful to learn about family issues that contributed to the illness. Talk about blocking. I recognize how I wasn't real with my feelings very often. I thought I was responding genuinely, when in fact I was playing a role. It was very hard for me to understand that; I got all twisted up. It amazes me that Hayley's sister is as clear as she is. My feelings get layered with my shoulds, and guilt, and intellectualization, so I was not sure what I was feeling.

Martin: Mine were a little different. My relationship with Hayley got better even though we had tons of confrontations at the sessions that whole year, where she would attack me and accuse me of things. That we weren't there for her—which was absolutely ridiculous to me—that I drank too much, and maybe I did and became aware of that, which was good for me in a way, but these things were magnified in her mind. Hayley said, for example, that Sandra and I had too many arguments and that each time we had a fight, she would think we were going to separate. As a little girl she was terrified and wouldn't tell us.

Sandra: She also accused us—and I would believe what she said, can you believe that? She would say something, and I wouldn't see it as coming from this distorted perception of a borderline person. I thought that she described the way things actually were. At one point we went to an outside therapist for a few sessions because she had accused us of something about our relationship. The therapist said to me, "So you think that this is the way it was because this is what your daughter said?" I realized then how off the wall it was for her to say that we didn't have a good relationship. Like anybody else we've had problems, but we never considered divorce. That possibility was true for her but not necessarily reality, or my reality.

She was correct, though, about the drinking problem. Martin had an alcoholic personality, and there was that element at first.

Martin: Hayley's confrontation helped me change in that way and in other areas. Out of this whole horrible thing I felt I came out a better person because I got involved with people; I started doing volunteer work that I would never have done otherwise. There were pluses. But at times Hayley walked out on sessions after we had driven an hour and a half to get there. I wasn't going to feed into that, so we went home. She was smart enough to know that we needed to discuss and work it out.

Sandra: I found out that Hayley wouldn't die if we had a confrontation. That was a biggie. There is no question that ours was too symbiotic a relationship. If she was high, I was okay, and if she was down, I was too. I learned that I could separate from her enough to get angry and not pussyfoot. The therapy helped us unravel communication in this way. It helped me look at my role as the peacemaker. We thought that we really made an effort to communicate ideas and feelings, but it was probably just what we felt comfortable communicating and not necessarily anything negative.

There's a difference now. I have come a long way in that when Martin and I are by ourselves, I can really get angry and get it all out, and then it's over. Before, I buried a lot of negative feelings like anger and tried to make nice and good and the situation as pleasant and positive as possible. It came out in other ways, and how it came out I'm not sure.

Martin: When we were a young couple, I was stubborn and would never apologize. I would retrench, and Sandra would always come to me and open a line of communication again. And I would argue with my kids.

Sandra: But only when it got to a point. He would kind of ignore things until he blew up. And that was not great either.

Martin: I think over the last 15 or 20 years, as we got involved in certain religious groups, Sandra and I learned to communicate better. But basically in the beginning, I was not a communicator with my wife or my kids. I kept my feelings to myself too. It was a long slow process to get them out.

For many years, I had very low self-esteem. I never felt that Hayley had that same feeling because she always excelled in everything. Then I realized that I manipulated by being quiet. I would control people by hiding my feelings because I didn't have the confidence to express myself. Hayley pointed that out to me. She said, "Dad, just because I yell and play the violin and look so confident, that doesn't mean that I feel good about myself." So I learned that being outgoing could be a mask. I kept saying "Hayley, how could you possibly be doing these things to yourself?" not realizing how bad she felt about herself. We helped each other by learning that even though we acted differently, we both had the same insecure feelings.

Sandra: When her therapist told us that Hayley was borderline, he gave us a book. He tried to explain it, but it's a very difficult concept for people to understand because there are so many different aspects of it. I still can't explain it to most people. I don't remember whether or not I read the book—sometimes you want to face these things, and at other times you just want to hold them at arm's length. It's still something that I'm not all that comfortable with because I don't know exactly what it is.

Part of me wants to believe that Hayley is going to be fine. And I'm glad she got the help she did before she made any big life decisions. She's learned an awful lot. She's so insightful about so many things, certainly a lot more than I was at her age. It has come hard, but she's a sponge; she's very, very bright, and she has learned so much and is very strong-willed. I'm convinced that anything she wants to do, she can accomplish. If she wants to stay sick, she'll do that; if she doesn't, she'll get better. And there was a time that I wasn't convinced that she *wanted* to get better. When she was going to community college, she seemed to be holding on to it, although I could be wrong. Maybe she just wasn't ready to get help. That's what I mean by not knowing, which of it is the illness—or whether the illness is the not being ready to get on and to use the tools the hospital gave her.

We can measure her progress very well now because she was seriously injured in an auto accident a month ago. She had to forget about the summer school she was planning and come home to live for a while, without her car. We were really nervous that it would start her up all over again, but she seems to have pulled through fine.

Hayley seems to understand what is right for her now. She was seeing a therapist she felt was too supportive, so instead she switched to somebody from the hospital who is more confrontative. She knows that she'll be uncomfortable with this method but will also grow.

She continues to connect with people and is terrific with little tiny kids and their parents as well as with older people. She has always had that concern with people and that specialness. I won't say that everybody loves her, but most people do. She's funny, a great mimic, very personable.

Hayley is also a lot less self-involved now, more considerate and sensitive. Almost every week she visits her grandmother, and they have lunch or go shopping together. I know it's a bright spot in my mother's week because she lives alone and looks forward to these visits. Hayley's having made them a priority in her busy life shows how much she has grown in awareness of and empathy for other people.

Some of these patients seem to be so bright. It's as if just living in the world is too much for them, they're extra sensitive like poets. Hart Crane sounds borderline to me because of his intense sensations and emotions.

Martin: The bottom line is that Hayley does it herself now. She really works at it. We could reach out to her 24 hours a day, but if she's not committed to getting better, what's the sense? Hayley has learned that commitment. I feel very comfortable saying that.

Sandra: And we say it to everyone. We met families who did not want anyone else to know about the patient.

Martin: One of the couples we met at the hospital came back a number of times and were wonderful people, very helpful to us. Unfortunately their boy did commit suicide, years later. They had lived in terror because they could never share his condition with anybody; they were always covering up for his being in the hospital. The stigma was such a shame.

Sandra: They once went to a cocktail party, saw a doctor from the hospital, and left immediately.

We were very, very fortunate in being able to talk about Hayley's illness to many of our friends and relatives. They were supportive because everyone has some kind of trouble. And I need that kind of support at times. Once you accept it as part of life, it's not a shameful thing to have a child with problems like this. There's a lot of onus on mental disorders. And we couldn't help but wonder how we would feel if our son came home with a borderline woman, how fearful we might be of what this could mean down the road. We are aware of these kinds of things and also aware that families tend to be blamed.

I need it reinforced again and again that I did the best job that I could for Hayley. Whatever mistakes we made were not intentional, but as much as you say that intellectually, you never stop thinking, "What if . . . what if . . . if only. . . ."

II

What Causes Borderline Personality Disorder?

16

Four Psychoanalytical Viewpoints

No developmental theory of borderline psychopathology explains all the difficulties of borderline adults.

PATRICIA M. CHATHAM, PH.D.[1]

In this section, we will continue to define *what BPD* **is**, but much less directly. The next several chapters will consider each of the elements that has been proposed as a major contributing factor.

Except for the most polemical of affectophiles, almost all major theorists about BPD hypothesize that early family life or *developmental factors* help cause the illness. Having departed from classical psychoanalysis in both theory and practice, the purest "developmentophiles" share what Dr. Kernberg calls "many common features . . . at least part of the ideas I've tried to develop." These commonalities include a theory that "good enough" parenting in childhood enables the personality to develop into healthy maturity. Faulty interaction with parents or other caretakers can halt this psychological progression and cause BPD.

But the major psychoanalytical approaches to BPD are theoretically disparate and controversial. The discrepancy can be illustrated by comparing their explanations of one symptom, splitting. Readers can extrapolate from this specific example how varied are the viewpoints to be found even within a distinct branch of psychiatry.

The developmentophiles dwell deep in the heart of "blame the mother" territory; thus we must venture therein.

Object Relations Theory and the Work of Margaret Mahler

Classical analytic thinking emphasizes instincts and drives that influence a person's feelings or behavior without reference to the environment. Therapy is focused on the patient: her psychosexual development and psychology as demonstrated by her reactions to the analyst.

*Object relations theory** offers a broader framework of general development. It holds that immediately from birth, an infant relates actively and significantly with others to gratify needs. Rather than innate drives, this interaction, especially when frustrating, is the primary motivation for behavior. Therapy addresses the presence and reactions of the therapist as well as the patient, along with the psychology of their relationship.

The most influential object relations model for the early phases of infant development originated with Margaret Mahler and her colleagues. They hypothesized that the infant's "psychological birth" and development into healthy, mature functioning occur in three cumulative phases. The infant spends his first month or two of life in a state of *normal autism,* oblivious to everyone but himself. Over the next four or five months, the infant in the *symbiotic phase* recognizes his mother merely as an extension.

Mahler divided the *separation-individuation* phase into four overlapping subphases as follows:

- *Differentiation subphase* (5–8 months), in which the child becomes aware of people other than mother and can distinguish them.
- *Practicing subphase* (8–16 months), in which the child first crawls, then toddles away from mother but frequently returns to her to "check in."
- *Rapprochement subphase* (16–25 months), in which the toddler increasingly recognizes the world beyond mother and distinguishes himself from its inhabitants. His early sense of self as the center of the universe is deflated by the recognition that he is a very small, vulnerable person in a gigantic world.

Object can refer to either a person or the memory of a person or experience. It also refers to any experiences with other people that have been incorporated into the mind either consciously or unconsciously to form a structure within the ego.

This deflation of his autistic power and importance causes anxiety and ambivalence. Thus the child alternately clings to his mother, watching her every move, then darts away if she tries to confine or hold him. During this period, the mother must encourage the child to separate while providing continual emotional support that helps the child learn to tolerate her absence. Practice in separating and reuniting helps the child come to know himself, love and trust his parents, and view other people with appropriate ambivalence.

- *Object constancy phase* (25–36 months), in which the child endures longer separations from mother with the aid of *transitional objects* like teddy bears, dolls, or blankets that remind him of her. Eventually he develops an evocative memory of his loving mother; this soothing image helps him outgrow his need for transitional objects. The child likewise learns to cope with his ambivalence and frustration and recognizes that rage is neither permanent nor annihilating.

Throughout separation–individuation, the child has to resolve two central conflicts, that between autonomy and dependency and that between fear of engulfment and fear of abandonment. He must also overcome the tendency to see his mother as totally good or bad (depending on whether or not she is meeting his needs) and develop his object constancy, a sense that mother's disappearance is temporary, that she continues to exist when not present and will return.

Mahler considered the rapprochement subphase to be the key to the development of BPD. She believed that a mother who either distances herself prematurely or clings to her child for too long can cause the fears of abandonment and engulfment that torment borderlines.

Neither Necessary nor Sufficient

Some of the symptoms of BPD support this developmental theory. Borderlines often complain, for example, that they can't describe their thoughts and feelings. This would make sense if they were, in fact, stuck in a developmental phase at which they had hardly begun to think at an articulate level. And because development of speech defines the child as a distinct person, their communication difficulties could be related to conflicts about separation.

Borderlines also behave just like children in the rapprochement subphase. "When the psychopathology is raging in these patients and they're behaving in a really skewed and maladaptive way, their psycho-

logical functioning is regressed in the sense that it is primitively organized," says Dr. McGlashan.

> It's not sophisticated or integrated, and the nuances of perception and judg-
> ment and so on disappear. In some respects, the psychological organization
> of the person at that time mimics that of young children.

There are, however, increasingly compelling arguments *against* the
separation-individuation theory. Researchers have pointed out that
Mahler herself later qualified it. In 1971 she wrote that she had "come to
be more and more convinced that there is no 'direct line' from the
deductive use of borderline phenomena to one or another substantive
finding of observational research."[2] Six years later she used two case
histories to demonstrate that disturbance in the rapprochement subphase
was neither necessary nor sufficient to cause BPD.[3]

Another argument focuses on female development in particular, an
area of research about which many male psychiatrists are highly suspicious. "It's very difficult to discuss female development in a really technical way because it's highly influenced by ideology at this point," says
Dr. Kernberg. "That doesn't necessarily contribute to best understanding." This ideology is grounded, however, in ongoing empirical research in the psychology of women and female development, especially
that taking place at Harvard University under the direction of Carol
Gilligan, Ph.D. Catherine Steiner-Adair, Ed.D., a research associate at
the Harvard project who has written about the new findings,[4] notes that

> Mahler's observations were funneled through the language of psychiatry and
> medicine at a particular moment in their history. Other researchers have
> shown that there is nothing "autistic" and "symbiotic" about the early
> infant's interaction with its mother. In contrast to Mahler's separation-in-
> dividuation theory, which suggests that identity is gained through increasing
> experiences of autonomy and separateness, the model of identity develop-
> ment based on female experience is one of self-differentiation within the
> context of relationships. In the psychology of women, dependency is highly
> valued, something to be deepened and matured throughout life, and the
> developmental map is one from unequal dependent relationships, in which a
> child is clearly more dependent on an adult, to mature interdependency.

A process similar to separation-individuation is thought by its advocates
to be repeated in adolescence, a notion with which Steiner-Adair likewise disagrees:

There is no evidence at all that girls go through a similar kind of separation-individuation process in adolescence. Rather, they go through a much more complicated, difficult, ongoing struggle to find what is unique to themselves, again within the context of relationships with their mothers, fathers, friends. . . .

As noted in Chapter 12, Dr. Andrulonis believes that adolescent boys likewise attach crucial importance to relationships.

The Harvard Project on the Psychology of Women and the Development of Girls has thus far reported findings on subjects the youngest of whom are seven years old. By the age of seven, these girls could have been conditioned into abandoning their "natural" autonomy, which is the culturally approved ideal for males, to strive instead for dependency, the corresponding ideal for females.

What the Harvard researchers describe, however, appears genuine, not merely a phenomenon adopted to please. "The notion of a self bounded by the skin is a peculiarly male Western cultural ideal," says Linehan. "A relational self is positively linked to interpersonal sophistication, and to try to change people into individuated selves on the assumption that such a person is better is, I think, extremely arrogant."

Family and other empirical studies have likewise discredited separation-individuation theory. "Among other things, it's not very productive to imagine what goes on in the mind of a child too young even to talk to you," says Dr. Paris, who has conducted some of these studies. "In fact, it's ridiculous."

Finally, separation-individuation is also implicated in the development of other quite different psychiatric illnesses rather than being peculiar to borderlines.

Over the past several years, most theorists in fact have abandoned the notion of "phase-specific" development of BPD. Their framework now encompasses the entire family experience throughout childhood. Once a believer in separation-individuation, Dr. McGlashan, for example, has changed his mind:

It's erroneous to say that borderlineness derives from experiential trauma at an early age. However, I would add that what the emotional climate is and has been in the family is not irrelevant, and there's no question that this is particularly true with borderlines. Their histories are grisly, many of them, really grisly. But I think we really must in some respects start over again and try to figure out what causes what. Plenty of people grow up with grisly histories like that who manage to survive, who aren't borderline, who aren't psychotic, and what makes the difference? We just don't know.

To a lesser extent, Dr. Kernberg has likewise broadened this thinking along these lines.

Dr. Kernberg: Disowning What Is Bad

Dr. Kernberg agrees with other observers that borderline patients do often think, feel, and behave more like toddlers than adults. "I wouldn't pinpoint the origin of their illness exclusively to the rapprochement subcrisis," he says. "I do think that BPO derives from early childhood, most closely from separation-individuation, but that is a long period of development." During this period, he believes, the illness originates in an idiosyncratic mixture of constitutional and environmental factors.

A partly constitutional factor is excessive aggressive drive. The child's aggressive feelings and fantasies cause intrapsychic conflict and overreactions to the human mistakes of its parents.

Unlike classical psychoanalytic theorists, who believe that drives are innate, Dr. Kernberg stresses that drives also depend upon environmental influence. Aggression, for instance, is a predisposition influenced by intense interactions with other people and chronic, cumulative traumata. "The experience of pain originates aggression, and in vicious circles, that organizes aggression as a drive," says Dr. Kernberg. "I'm saying this to deal with the issue of whether aggression is primary or secondary. Both factors, nature and nurture, play a role."

For many borderlines, "nurture" has been largely missing. The primarily environmental factor leading to BPO is excessive frustration caused by inadequate parenting that does not satisfy instinctual needs and wishes.

Over the years during which she is trying to build a unique identity, the child develops hostility toward those upon whom her very life depends, anger so destructive as to be terrifying. Her experiences are mostly negative, and she doesn't know whether this is because she is bad, other people are bad, or both. At times it seems one way or the other. All she knows is that the few good experiences she has enjoyed are threatened by the bad ones and the hatred they evoke in her.

At first the child is unable to recognize that good and bad coexist in the same person. This defect in perception is later used actively as a defense. The child separates the two to protect the good from her onslaught of aggression, to relieve her guilt for hating the bad, and to avoid the fearful anxiety she feels when good and bad get too close.

Borderlines come to rely upon splitting everything in their world, including themselves. This adaptation to their predicament is terribly crippling. Splitting the world reduces its color to black or white. Splitting the self precludes the development of a realistic, stable identity. Splitting others prevents an awareness of their goodness from surviving their temporary human failures. The borderline's fragile ego leaves her unable to tolerate unpleasant feelings, apt to lose touch with reality, and prone to all the other symptoms of BPO.

The concept of splitting is central also to the theories of Dr. Masterson.

Dr. Masterson: Borderline Mothers and Six Horsemen

Drs. Masterson and Rinsley have worked together and separately using Mahler's formulations of normal development to understand the pathology of BPD. Over the past several years, Dr. Rinsley's thinking has evolved into a framework with which Dr. Kernberg feels quite akin technically. Meanwhile the theory and practice of The Masterson Method, described in the books, articles, and audio and videocassettes produced by that expert and his colleagues in The Masterson Group, have been more influential.

Dr. Masterson does not see the borderline as a level of functioning. He instead considers it a specific entity with an intrapsychic structure revealed clinically by what he calls "the borderline triad": separation-individuation leads to anxiety and depression, which lead to defense. The separation-individuation crisis is repeated in adolescence, often aggravated in borderlines by disruptions like a move to a new home or a divorce.

Drs. Masterson and Rinsley have both emphasized the pernicious influence of a mother who rewards clinging behavior and threatens abandonment as the child begins to separate. To separate from mother means losing her love; to remain with mother means losing herself. This conflict causes the child to give up her individuality and to vacillate between clinging dependency and omnipotent grandiosity. The clinging quality of the mothers themselves led Dr. Masterson originally to conclude that all borderlines had borderline mothers.

Dr. Masterson's views about borderline mothers in particular are not widely shared. Separate studies by Dr. Gunderson and by Dr. Paris have shown, in fact, that as children, borderlines experienced chronic emotional neglect from rather than clinging by their mothers. More recent studies, however, have confirmed Dr. Masterson's general notion that borderlines were both neglected and overprotected.[5]

Drs. Masterson and Rinsley have both since modified their position, acknowledging that the situations they had observed were those of the severely disturbed families of hospitalized patients who might not represent all borderlines. Dr. Masterson now suggests other possibilities for the origins of the illness: nature, nurture and fate.

- *Nature* is a child genetically unable to have an autonomous self.
- *Nurture* is the mother's capacity to identify and support individuation, which could be compromised by factors ranging from emotional difficulties to physical absence.
- *Fate* is separation stress that affects either the mother's availability or the child's capacity to experiment with her emerging self.

Each of the three contributes to the clinical syndrome, and the therapist may need to decide what role each has played.

The borderline's mother is not sufficiently available to provide emotional support for her emerging self. Feeling threatened by abandonment, the child fails to differentiate herself from the rest of the world into a unique identity. Torn between her needs for mothering and for independence, between the extreme possibilities of engulfment and abandonment, the child splits her mother into a good one who rewards dependence and a bad one who punishes efforts toward autonomy.

This split results in the borderline's having two prominent *feeling states*. What Dr. Masterson calls the *withdrawing object relations part-unit* (WORU) consists of the borderline's image of her mother as withdrawing or aggressive, an image of herself as bad and inadequate, and resulting feelings of anger and frustration covering profound *abandonment depression*. This is Dr. Masterson's term for the various intense feelings of borderlines. It has six components that he calls "the Six Horsemen of the Apocalypse": depression, rage, fear, guilt, hopelessness and helplessness, and emptiness and void.

The *rewarding object relations part-unit* (RORU) consists of the borderline's image of her mother as rewarding and supportive, an image of herself as nourished and beloved, and the resulting feeling of being good and compliant while behaving regressively.[6]

Like Dr. Kernberg, Dr. Masterson sees this split as the basis of other primitive defenses, problems with separation, and diverse maladaptations intended to maintain a positive relationship with the mother. Dr. Kernberg, however, disagrees largely with Dr. Masterson's approach:

Dr. Masterson uses a concept of Margaret Mahler which I find too restrictive, the focus on separation-individuation with a certain neglect of Oedipal conflicts and with a certain simplification of the internalized structures of object relations. Dr. Masterson's approach has valid elements, but I find it less comprehensive than mine.

Dr. Masterson declined to be interviewed for this book. His review of this writeup acknowledges the importance of Dr. Kernberg's contribution. Dr. Masterson explains, however, that Dr. Kernberg's view is in the neighborhood of the problem while his own is at the exact address, identifying, as it does, the borderline triad as the central feature of the disorder.

Drs. Adler and Buie: Beyond Loneliness

Another major psychodynamic approach to BPD is one based on Heinz Kohut's writings on self psychology as articulated by Drs. Adler and Buie, who have worked together since the mid-1960s.

The theories of Drs. Adler and Buie are grounded in separation-individuation, although they locate the origin of BPD earlier than the rapprochement subphase. They consider the illness to be caused by the child's belief that she has been, or will be, abandoned, and the sense of aloneness that results.

This fear results from parental, especially maternal, failure to provide sufficient holding and soothing, enough attention to and validation of the child's feelings and experience. The mother misunderstands and thus responds inappropriately to what the child needs, so the child develops an incomplete sense of being cared for. She has few good experiences to balance her feelings of neglect. Her primary feeling is a terror of utter aloneness, emptiness, hunger, coldness, and annihilation. The fear or actuality of such abandonment also produces rage.

The child thus neglected develops no coherent, enduring sense of a lovable self. Instead she feels an inner void that must constantly be filled with external sources of support. But the relationships she so desperately needs don't satisfy her. She develops no capacity for evocative memory to stabilize and sustain her through periods of solitude, fluctuation, and other stress.

The borderline therefore uses other people to help evoke soothing images or to perform other functions she does not have built in. Unable to recall sustained love, she becomes a reassurance addict seeking a fix of affection to help maintain her self-esteem. The loss or threatened loss of a relationship leaves the borderline feeling hollow and abandoned, bereft of self-esteem, and anxious to end these feelings through self-mutilation or suicide.

Ingrid's journal gives some idea of what impaired evocative memory is like, although hers reads more like an intellectual than an emotional experience. Feeling suicidal, she is writing at 12:30 A.M.

> Everyone goes home; there is no one here. I am alone with me. I wish I could know that if I needed someone they would be here. [A former therapist] is always there. How can she be replaced when the others are only here during the day?
>
> Mom is also there, but she is not here. I want to be there with Mom and with [the therapist]. I don't feel safe here. No one is here. [My roommate] is here, but she can't [be] here because she has to be with her. I will always be with me, but I am the most dangerous to me. [A patient about to be discharged] is here, but she will be there soon. When she leaves, she will be gone. Everyone is gone. They all go home. I want to go home. I want a home. If I can't be with me, then I shouldn't be. If I shouldn't be, then I have to find a way not to be. I can be OK when they are here, but they are there. I feel like I am in a room with a wall, and the wall is closed at night and I can't see anyone. And on the wall is death. Death wants me. Death is always here. The pictures [hallucinations] are here when everyone is there. I'm really scared. What if they don't come here and stay there? Please come here and be here when I need you. I wish death would be there, not here. So far away but within reach. But they are not within reach.
>
> Death is within reach when they are not. But if death is here, then no one will ever be there again.
>
> [This is followed by sketches of hanging and drowning figures, body parts, car crashes, and bottles of poisonous chemicals.]
>
> I can scream for help, but it is silent, and no one responds. No one hears!!! No one is here!

This panicky sense of emptiness and abandonment is different from loneliness. To be lonely, one must have clear memories of those who are absent. The borderline instead loses all memories of others at the time she needs them most. To most people, who invoke such soothing memories as automatically as they perspire when hot, this concept may be hard to understand. But as Ingrid's descriptions imply, someone who is "there" instead of with the borderline might as well no longer exist.

The borderline's predicament results in both her enormous need for relationships and her great fear of intimacy. The tension between this need and fear can cause rage, guilt expressed in self-punishment, departure from therapy as the relationship grows more intense, and anxiety that is relieved by acting out. The angry, impulsive, manipulative behavior of borderlines is their pathological attempt to elicit involvement and caring.

Rather than undo such destructive patterns, like Drs. Kernberg and Masterson, Drs. Adler and Buie concentrate on creating the soothing memories that never existed. The patient who has learned to comfort herself in solitude, they feel, is no longer borderline.

It is the lack of a holding image, rather than the difficult of integrating good and bad ones, that Drs. Adler and Buie consider crucial to understanding BPD. Their notion of splitting thus differs from that of Dr. Kernberg, as Dr. Adler explains:

> In their aloneness state, borderlines can't split because they have transiently lost all sense of both the positive and the negative qualities of important people. Only when they have solid representations of the holding, soothing qualities of others can they then split off the frustrating, enraging ones.
>
> We don't see splitting as a major issue in every single borderline; it's not as ubiquitous as Dr. Kernberg makes it out to be. And there are two kinds of splitting. The first kind is the true splitting Dr. Kernberg describes that takes place inevitably regardless of how the therapist, for example, is behaving. The second kind occurs only in a two-person framework such as therapy. Here the patient feels misunderstood and enraged at the therapist, then the two of them patch things up, and the patient feels understood and idealizes the therapist.

Dr. Gunderson likewise views splitting in such an interactive context.

"I am not as close to Drs. Adler and Buie as I am to some other thinkers," says Dr. Kernberg. "I think that in a way they underemphasize the analysis of aggression in these patients." Dr. Adler agrees in part, suggesting that he and Dr. Buie emphasize aggression just as much as Dr. Kernberg does but address it in therapy differently. In his turn, Dr. Adler explains that

> the major thing missing from Dr. Kernberg's work is what Dr. Buie and I call the core sector, the issues of aloneness that elicit the rage. Dr. Kernberg would talk about the rage in terms of the splitting, while we would talk about the rage of abandonment that goes with the aloneness issues.

The theories of Drs. Adler and Buie are increasingly being supported by the findings of Dr. Paris, Dr. Herman, and other investigators that many borderlines exhibit an aloneness state as a result of neglect or abuse.

Dr. Gunderson: Ambivalence and Reaction

Dr. Gunderson positions himself theoretically between Dr. Kernberg and Drs. Adler and Buie. He agrees with Dr. Kernberg, for example, that aggression is a central issue in BPD (although a developmental factor by no means peculiar to this illness)[7] and approaches it similarly. But like Drs. Adler and Buie, Dr. Gunderson views aggression primarily as a reaction to parental neglect and failure. His theory also incorporates the passive masochism of borderlines, and he emphasizes their positive motivation to establish and maintain good relationships, including those with their therapists.

Although a symptom like splitting is really beyond the realm of descriptive psychiatry, it has formed a basis for Dr. Gunderson's conceptualization of BPD. "I have tried to contribute to the understanding of splitting by dissecting it into different components," he says.

> Sometimes I write to correct misrepresentations rather than carve out some new definition of my own. Splitting as it's described by Dr. Kernberg, for instance, is a real phenomenon present in borderline patients. I too see it arising as a conflict around the management of aggression and the efforts to dissociate oneself from aggressive feelings.
>
> But I also think that many things that get called splitting actually don't reflect that kind of intrapsychic failure but have more to do with the interactive context in which a very radical shift in the borderline's attitudes are observed. Interactive splitting is a reaction to frustration, the effort to idealize caregivers, and then the disillusionment when the idealization isn't met.

The difference between this reactive splitting and that described by Dr. Adler is that according to Dr. Gunderson, "rather than vacillating between 'all-good' and 'all-bad' views of their objects . . . borderline patients fluctuate between levels of functioning."[8]

In this model, the variety and instability of the borderline's symptoms can be understood in terms of her relationship to an important person. The three levels of functioning from which particular symptoms arise each depend on the location of that person in the borderline's life, the symptoms that result, and the borderline's attempts to alleviate them.

Level 1, the highest, exists when the other person is present and supportive. Rather than being completely pleased and comforted by his or her presence, the borderline feels ambivalent. She is depressed because she wants more from the person but is afraid that such a request would lead to rejection. Instead she clings to the person, dissatisfied with both of them, feeling bored and lonely, acting dependent and masochistic.

The borderline regresses to level 2 when the person is frustrating her or appears likely to leave. She is afraid to precipitate the departure by expressing her rage. Instead she implies her hostility through sarcasm, belligerence, and accusations. The borderline tries to manipulate the other person (often through self-destructive acts) to regain contact and control.

Their behavior on level 1 shows that borderlines do not idealize but are at best ambivalent: people mean well and are capable of pleasing but nevertheless are vaguely unsatisfactory. Similarly, on level 2 a borderline does not see the other person as totally bad. Rather than arbitrarily reversing her opinion, she reacts to frustration by the important person. Her anger and devaluation allow her to feel some control over the person, to squelch her awareness of his or her positive qualities, and to convey distress in the hope of obtaining some response.

Dr. Gunderson notes that besides mistaking ambivalence for idealization, splitting as understood by Drs. Kernberg and Masterson poses other important problems. It does not take into account how the borderline's anger is being used and expressed under specific circumstances. It assumes that when switching between views of the other person as totally good or bad, the borderline reverses her view of herself also, which is not necessarily so. It does not explain why, when the other person is supposedly bad, the borderline doesn't leave him or her—"in fact, under such circumstances," writes Dr. Gunderson, "they cannot leave."[9] Try as she might, the borderline can't deny that she values and needs the "bad" person. In this respect, Dr. Gunderson suggests, borderlines can relate to others better than do patients with other personality disorders.

"The danger in seeing splitting as too much of an intrapsychic problem and not enough of an interactive one is that it underestimates the capacity of clinicians and other people to correct it," says Dr. Gunderson. "Moreover, the idea that an interpretation of the splitting can in itself be very useful is, I think, wrong."

The borderline sinks to level 3 when the other person is absent. She tries to avoid the panic associated with solitude by impulsively indulging in self-abuse, promiscuity, or some other reckless activity that creates contact with new people. (These activities differ from level 2 suicidal gestures, which are aimed toward restoring contact with the important person.) Failure to establish contact can deteriorate into dissociative or psychotic-like experiences such as *ideas of reference* (beliefs that random events are focused upon the self) or hallucinations.

This level corresponds to the concept of aloneness put forth by Drs.

Adler and Buie, and all behavior represents an attempt to ward it off. The borderline also feels completely bad for having failed or alienated the important person.

Dr. Gunderson characterizes his formulation as "more of a reshuffling or reordering of the same set of observations drawn on by others . . . than a radical departure from them."[10] Although unlike Dr. Masterson he does not focus on the split mother image and underlying abandonment depression, both of them emphasize the availability of loving care as a determinant of much borderline behavior. Dr. Gunderson writes of having found Dr. Kernberg's "views of treatment consistent with my experience, whereas his theories about the origins and definition of borderline patients often have seemed discordant."[11] He agrees with features of Dr. Kernberg's formulation, but his own is heavily descriptive as well as dynamic. Dr. Gunderson views borderline patients as being driven not primarily from within, as Dr. Kernberg would have it, but from both within and without.

The differences between these psychoanalytic formulations* of BPD again reflect the instability that characterizes the illness. They raise a number of questions about who borderlines are and how they are most effectively treated.

And as we'll see in Chapter 24, the psychoanalytic theorists have various ideas about what constitutes therapy with borderlines as well.

Notes

1. Patricia M. Chatham, *Treatment of the Borderline Personality* (New York: Jason Aronson, 1985), p. 196.
2. Margaret S. Mahler, M.D., Sc.D. (Med.), "A Study of the Separation-Individuation Process and Its Possible Application to Borderline Phenomena in the Psychoanalytic Situation," *The Psychoanalytic Study of the Child*, Vol. 26 (1971), p. 415.
3. Margaret S. Mahler, M.D., Sc.D. (Med.), and Louise Kaplan, Ph.D., "Developmental Aspects in the Assessment of Narcissistic and So-Called Borderline Personalities," in *Borderline Personality Disorders: The Concept, the Syndrome, the Patient*, ed. Peter Hartocollis, M.D., Ph.D. (New York: International Universities Press, 1977), pp. 71–85.
4. Catherine Steiner-Adair, Ed.D., "The Body Politic: Normal Female Adolescent Development and the Development of Eating Disorders," in *Making Connections: The Relational Worlds of Adolescent Girls at the Emma Willard School*, ed. Carol Gilligan, Nona P. Lyons, and Trudy J. Hanmer (Cam-

*Some of the other prominent psychoanalytic theorists not mentioned elsewhere in this book whose methods are oriented toward BPD include Wilfred R. Bion, D.S.O., B.A., M.R.C.S., L.R.C.P.; L. Bryce-Boyer, M.D.; Richard D. Chessick, M.D., Ph.D.; Peter L. Giovacchini, M.D.; Arnold H. Modell, M.D.; Harold F. Searles, M.D.; and Vamik D. Volkan, M.D.

bridge: Harvard University Press, 1990), pp. 162–82; and "New Maps of Development, New Models of Therapy: The Psychology of Women and the Treatment of Eating Disorders," in *Psychodynamic Treatment of Anorexia Nervosa and Bulimia,* ed. Craig Johnson, Ph.D. (New York: The Guilford Press, 1991), pp. 225–44.

5. J. Paris, M.D., and H. Zweig-Frank, Ph.D., "Parental Bonding in Borderline Personality Disorder," in *Borderline Personality Disorder: Etiology and Treatment,* ed. Joel F. Paris, M.D. (Washington, D.C.: American Psychiatric Press, forthcoming).

6. James F. Masterson, M.D., *Psychotherapy of the Borderline Adult: A Developmental Approach* (New York: Brunner/Mazel, 1976), pp. 58–59.

7. John G. Gunderson, "Interfaces Between Psychoanalytic and Empirical Studies of Borderline Personality," *The Borderline Patient: Emerging Concepts in Diagnosis, Psychodynamics and Treatment,* ed. James S. Grotstein, Marion F. Solomon, and Joan A. Lang, Vol. 1 (Hillsdale, N.J.: The Analytic Press, 1987), p. 43.

8. Ibid., pp. 51 ff.

9. Ibid., p. 53.

10. John G. Gunderson, M.D., *Borderline Personality Disorder* (Washington, D.C.: American Psychiatric Press, 1984), p. 39. Copyright © 1984 by John G. Gunderson.

11. Gunderson, "Interfaces," p. 40.

1 7

Some Other Background

*The psychological or social terms used to describe these breaks [in the brain], such as
loss of ego boundaries or lack of self-esteem, are metaphors used to describe
biological processes that we are just beginning to understand.*

NANCY C. ANDREASEN, M.D., PH.D.[1]

Like other psychiatric disorders, BPD has become the subject of various biological models of its origins and course.
Because of its complexity, BPD offers all kinds of clues that
will eventually lead to better understanding of the brain
and other body systems.

To examine some of these findings and the implications
for borderline patients and their treatment, we will first
need a rough map of affectophile territory and a working
knowledge of their language.[2]

The Limbic System and the
Basal Ganglia

Many aspects of mental illness, including some of the
symptoms of BPD, are thought to arise from the brain's
limbic system and its connections.

The limbic system is a group of brain structures that
collect and regulate information, either recirculating it or
sending it elsewhere in the brain. It is closely connected to
the *cerebral cortex,* which performs the "highest" brain func-

tions like reflecting and reasoning. The transmission of information among these structures enables us, among other things, to learn, remember, think creatively, and make decisions. One component of the limbic system, the *hippocampus,* is involved in short-term memory that is subsequently consolidated and stored.

The primary responsibility of the limbic system, however, is to regulate emotional behavior. It helps us to begin, stop, and organize various behaviors and particularly to tame our most aggressive impulses. Involved as it is with thought and feeling, the limbic system highlights our perceptions and thoughts with emotional nuances that help us isolate and concentrate upon essentials.

Thus the limbic system contributes greatly to each individual's personality; manner of understanding, remembering, reasoning, and judging; and patterns of behavior.

The limbic system is connected with many other parts of the brain. Among its various structures, the *amygdala* is believed to originate emotional behaviors. It also controls the *hypothalamus* and its intermediary, the *pituitary gland,* which regulates the hormonal functioning that influences thirst, sex drive, and appetite. Through such processes, our emotional states alter our hormone levels, preparing the body to react appropriately to environmental stimuli, and influence our physical health.

The *basal ganglia* lie on either side of the limbic system and are related to it neurochemically. Like the limbic structures, the basal ganglia are associated with the functions of the *thalamus* (a relay station for various parts of the brain that modulates movement, sensation, emotions, and behavior) and the hypothalamus. The basal ganglia integrate sensory information from the environment. As part of one of the brain's two motor systems, the basal ganglia also modulate body movement.

The Neuroendocrine System

The neuroendocrine system consists of several glands distributed throughout the body. It includes the pituitary, the thyroid, the adrenals, the sexual glands, and the part of the pancreas that produces insulin. The neuroendocrine system maintains its equilibrium through a feedback loop: hormones travel through the bloodstream between the hypothalamus, the pituitary, and the various other endocrine glands.

As the monitor of this system, the hypothalamus acts as a go-between for brain and body, regulating aggression, appetite, thirst, water balance, and growth rate.

Neurotransmitters

Brain function depends on the ability of *neurons* (brain cells) to communicate with each other through their tangle of intertwined filaments. To oversimplify an extremely complicated process: a *presynaptic neuron* (transmitting cell) sends an *action potential* (electrical signal) to the end of a filament, then secrets a chemical messenger into the *synapse* (the space between two cells). These messengers, called *neurotransmitters,* might be epinephrine, norepinephrine, dopamine, serotonin, tryptophan, gamma aminobutyric acid (GABA), naturally occurring opiates like endorphins, or dozens of other substances.

The neurotransmitter floats across the synapse and binds to a *receptor* on the surface of the *postsynaptic neuron* (target cell). The binding produces a chemical reaction in the postsynaptic neuron that causes it either to relay or to stop further transmission of the electrical impulse. The neurotransmitter is then either degraded by enzymes like *monoamine oxidase* or resorbed into the presynaptic neuron (a process called the *reuptake*).

Current neuroscience focuses largely upon identifying, mapping, and describing the functions of neurotransmitters. Abnormalities in various neurotransmitter systems are believed by neuroscientists and biological psychiatrists to be the causes of mental illness. Research is increasingly suggesting that more than one neurotransmitter may contribute to the development of a single psychiatric disorder and, conversely, that one neurotransmitter system may be abnormal across several different mental illnesses that have symptoms in common. Dr. Siever and Kenneth L. Davis, M.D., therefore suggest that neurotransmitter systems are associated more clearly with dimensions of behavior than they are with categories of illness.[3]

Most psychiatric drugs work in the synapse to affect neurotransmitter binding to receptors, thus increasing or decreasing signal transmission. A drug that *blocks* the neurotransmitter from reaching the postsynaptic receptor *stops* the transmission to the brain cells that depend upon it. A drug that *increases* the effectiveness of an *inhibiting* neurotransmitter likewise decreases neuronal flow. A drug that *blocks* the *reuptake* of the neurotransmitter by the presynaptic neuron prolongs its stay in the synapse and allows it again to bind to the receptor, thus increasing (*or inhibiting*) signal transmission.

A neurotransmitter infamous as the hypothetical cause of schizophrenia is *dopamine,* an important chemical messenger in many parts of the limbic system and basal ganglia. Schizophrenics are thought to have increased numbers of dopamine receptors in these areas of the brain, resulting in overactive transmission through excessively sensitive neurons.

Diseases of the basal ganglia like Huntington's chorea and parkinsonism cause symptoms similar to those in schizophrenia and some affective disorders. The dopamine circuits in the basal ganglia help explain one side effect of *neuroleptics* (antipsychotic drugs). By blocking dopamine from binding to its receptor, neuroleptics calm psychotic patients and diminish or eradicate their delusions and hallucinations while leaving them mentally alert. But these drugs can cause pseudoparkinsonism, a reversible condition, because they block dopamine not only in the limbic system but also in the basal ganglia, which modulate body movement.

The neurotransmitters that figure prominently in hypotheses about BPD are as follows.

NOREPINEPHRINE

Norepinephrine is carried by brain circuits called the *noradrenergic* system. Unlike dopamine circuits, the noradrenergic system rises from the brain stem to cover the organ like a web connecting almost half of its cells. Norepinephrine circuits are most heavily concentrated in the limbic system, where they transmit messages that help engender feeling states. The noradrenergic system may also contribute to muscle tension through messages it sends to the spinal cord in response to stress.

Its pattern of distribution through the brain makes it unlikely that norepinephrine plays a role in intellectual functioning. Instead it is thought to regulate the excitability of the cerebral cortex. Emotional stimulation causes norepinephrine to be released throughout this brain structure, helping explain why perceptions arouse feelings, why feelings color thought processes, and why some events do or don't attract our attention.

SEROTONIN

The *serotonergic system* is another web very similar in structure to the noradrenergic system; its circuits are heavily concentrated in the thalamus. Like norepinephrine, *serotonin* is therefore thought also to regulate widely scattered parts of the brain. As we'll see in the next chapter, abnormal levels of norepinephrine and serotonin may contribute synergistically to BPD.

Gamma-aminobutyric acid (GABA)

Unlike most other neurotransmitters, which are excitatory, *gamma-aminobutyric acid (GABA)* appears to be inhibitory. Nancy C. Andreasen, M.D., Ph.D., refers to GABA as "the brake in the brain."[4] As such GABA regulates or slows the noradrenergic and other brain systems that stimulate anxiety or other emotional arousal.

We noted earlier that neuroleptics exert a calming effect by blocking dopamine; antianxiety drugs do so by enhancing the effectiveness of GABA at its receptor.

GABA receptors are closely related to others specific to *benzodiazepines,* the most common antianxiety agents. Benzodiazepine receptors are most highly concentrated in the limbic system, especially in the amygdala.

Neuropeptides

In Chapter 11 we came across the *neuropeptides,* which include two families: a group of regulatory hormones like thyrotropin-releasing hormone (TRH), and the endorphins and enkephalins. The latter, which do not meet all criteria for neurotransmitters, act like opiates in the brain, attaching to specific receptors that modulate the perception of pain. These opiate receptors are located in the limbic system and the basal ganglia. Thus neuropeptides are also thought to play major roles in regulating emotional behavior.

Affective Disorder

Affective disorder* is a useful model to illustrate how the brain and its neurotransmitter systems give rise to the symptoms of mental illness.

In *DSM-III-R,* major affective disorder is divided into bipolar dis-

---

*DSM-III-R changed the term *affective disorder* to *mood disorder,* which has yet really to catch on in psychiatric literature and conversation.

order and *depressive disorders*. A constitutional emotional vulnerability in a person (sometimes shared by other family members) can cause discrete episodes of *classical* or *major depression,* also called *melancholia.* Such an episode may be triggered by environmental events but takes on a life of its own that is continual, impervious to outside stimuli, and in some people, completely incapacitating.

The melancholic person has many physical symptoms like sleep disturbance (either early morning awakening or sleeping too much), greater depression in the morning, appetite and weight changes, impaired concentration, low libido, and lack of interest in activities. An important symptom is loss of the ability not only to anticipate pleasure but also to experience it when placed in an enjoyable situation.

Episodes of melancholia in neurotic people tend to involve feelings of sadness, guilt, or remorse for having failed to meet their goals or live up to their standards. Whether withdrawn or agitated, the sufferer appreciates attempts by others to help. But feelings of defeat, failure, or worthlessness can lead to preoccupations with death and genuine, dangerous suicide attempts.

Responsive to antidepressant drugs, classical depression is thought to be primarily a biological illness arising from neurotransmitter abnormalities.

One hypothesis involving the *catecholamines* (the subcategory of neurotransmitters that includes dopamine and norepinephrine) suggests that depression is caused by a deficiency of norepinephrine. This is supported by the action of many antidepressant drugs to increase the amount of norepinephrine available for signal transmission.

Another supportive finding is that people with affective disorder, particularly depression, show symptoms of neuroendocrine abnormalities like changes in appetite, sleep regulation, and adaptibility to stress and change. A decrease in norepinephrine activity could impair a person's ability to regulate hormonal secretions, normally the function of the hypothalamus and pituitary. Depressed people often have high activity of cortisol, a substance produced by the adrenal glands. Thus the dexamethasone suppression test (DST), which measures the body's ability to control cortisol production, is sometimes used to diagnose depression. Other neuroendocrine abnormalities seen in depressed patients can be measured by the insulin tolerance test (of growth hormone levels), the TRH test, and other types of *biological markers* for depression.

Drs. Siever and Davis have proposed a specific model of altered noradrenergic activity in depression: nerve impulses are increased and erratic, but the amount of norepinephrine released per impulse is decreased, reducing the person's responsiveness to specific stimuli.[5]

A supplementary hypothesis about the cause of depression implicates low activity of serotonin. That there may in fact be two types of depression caused by a decrease in the activity of either neurotransmitter is again suggested by patient responses to antidepressant drugs. Some drugs work on only one neurotransmitter, and some patients respond to only one type of drug.

In the next chapter, we will examine research with borderline and depressed patients that is refining these hypotheses.

Antidepressant Medications

The atypical, cyclic, and MAOI antidepressants are the three major categories of these medications.

Cyclic antidepressants are very similar in structure to antipsychotic drugs, from which they were originally derived. These antidepressants act primarily on the noradrenergic or serotonergic systems. Prevented by the drugs from being resorbed, these neurotransmitters remain in the synapse and reattach to their receptors, thus prolonging signal transmission. The tricyclic amitriptyline can act on both systems; with some overlap, imipramine and desipramine act on norepinephrine, and chlomipramine acts on serotonin. Fluoxetine, the drug that most specifically and potently increases serotonin activity, has become well known by its brand name, Prozac, through media reports on its efficacy and occasional harmful side effects.

The enzyme MAO destroys many neurotransmitters, including norepinephrine. MAOI antidepressants block its action to increase the amount of norepinephrine available for transmission. Although their mechanism is different, then, the effects of MAOIs are similar to those of the cyclic antidepressants.

Because they can cause fatally high blood pressure if combined with certain foods or other medications, MAOIs must be taken cautiously. Their use is normally reserved for atypical forms of depression.

Nature or Nurture?

It seems, then, that various kinds of abnormalities in brain structure or functioning can contribute to the development of mental illnesses. But even in apparently straightforward cerebral terms, nature cannot be entirely distinguished from nurture.

A person's constitution obviously precedes all else. In order to be damaged by the environment, he or she must have innately vulnerable brain structures and hence processes. Dr. Siever offers an example:

> If you're a small child, your mother is an alcoholic, your father is absent, you're very affectively sensitive, and you tend to be impulsive, perhaps what works best for you to get attention and relieve distress is a temper tantrum. But you have to be the kind of child who would have tantrums in the first place. Maybe another child who is a little inhibited and not so affectively sensitive just keeps his frustrations to himself. Yet another child who is very affectively sensitive but also very anxious and inhibited may seriously withdraw and get depressed; this child might become increasingly anxious, develop phobias, and be unable to go out to school.

This inborn vulnerability is increasingly being described by psychiatrists as *temperament*. "It's a useful concept that we lost for many years due to the psychoanalytic overkill," says Dr. Soloff.

By affecting actions within the environment, temperament can indirectly alter the course of psychological development. The hyperactive or depressed children described by Dr. Andrulonis, for instance, might be especially difficult to care for. The resulting poor fit with their parents would worsen the family situation in which they had to grow up.

That people can thus create and recreate their environments makes it misleading to categorize psychiatric illness as purely biological in origin. "A focus on genetic determinism misses the point about our new understanding of the neurophysiological and neuropsychological development of the nervous system and its relationship to mental disorder," says Dr. Adler.[6]

As constitution can alter experience, so too experience may in fact alter constitution. Studies in neural plasticity have suggested that the nervous system is not fully formed at birth and may require certain environmental stimuli in order to develop fully. Brain structures responsible for perception, learning, memory, language, and other aspects of personality might themselves individually adapt to the environment during early growth and development. Separation-individuation difficulties, neglect and abuse histories, and other factors thought to contribute to BPD could trigger maladaptive responses by the developing brain.

Recent studies have in fact shown that uncontrollable catastrophic stress from either single or repeated events can alter brain chemistry, making people more sensitive to the adrenaline surges that characterize PTSD.[7] "Massive trauma may make a difference in neurotransmitter function," says Dr. Siever. "There is no doubt that in animals, the course of development can alter some of these systems."

Support for this hypothesis can be found also in experimental data about *kindling*. "Kindling usually refers specifically to certain areas of the limbic system," says Dr. Cowdry.

> If you repetitively stimulate an area chemically or electrically, you can evoke progressively larger neurophysiological responses, as though the area becomes sensitized. Ultimately you can provoke seizures with stimuli that used to cause merely a local response. So it's a process of progressive electrophysiological sensitization of particular areas of the brain. Kindling can presumably be done through early traumatic experiences, although there is no evidence of this.
>
> Certainly some of the childhood trauma research suggests that such experiences can influence the development of dopaminergic tracts maturing in early childhood. It's an interesting speculation for which it's going to be hard to get confirmatory data. But it's useful heuristically in that it helps us to integrate, to heal some of the mind-body split that has developed in psychiatry.

Thus the phrase "arrested development," often seen in psychoanalytical theory about BPD, may be literally true biologically: a person may have arrested neurophysiological development at one level, or cognitive development at another. The thought abnormalities seen in borderline patients could conceivably have resulted from faulty training in how to view the world or from subtle neurophysiological immaturity or deformity. But there is no way to measure brain activity to determine whether it is "primitive," to use another psychoanalytical term, in this sense.

"I have heard that adverse environmental experiences can affect neurophysiological development, but I'm not knowledgeable enough even to address that point," says Dr. Soloff. "That would be a wonderful connection from a scientific point of view because it would wrap up the whole picture." It could likewise enrich a psychoanalytical point of view: we have already seen Dr. Kernberg's insistence that inborn predisposition to aggression does not become organized into a drive until acted upon by an adverse environment.

From an emotional point of view, however, such proof might disturb borderlines. While it could lessen the stigma of BPD in the psychiatric profession (where behavior arising from biological illness is forgivable), it might brand borderlines in the minds of many laypeople as having a self-generated incurable illness.

Either view is an oversimplification. "Whatever I'm aware of as genetic for the psychiatric disorders is a susceptibility or bias, like the predisposition to ulcers, heart disease, or diabetes," says Dr. Siever.

We know that these illnesses run in families. But there is a range of genetic input in psychiatric illness, from the severe liabilities of chronic schizophrenia to the less disabling personality disorders and neuroses. In the middle are patients in a gray area who go in and out of symptomatic distress.

Everybody has predispositions, and to some degree we all learn to know our own blueprint. What makes us unique in a way is that we don't simply have inborn wiring and yet we are not just passive products molded by experience. It's the tension between what we bring to the environment and what the environment brings our way that makes for individuality as I see it. It's not a one-way street in either case.

One misconception is that what is caused "biologically" must be cured "biologically," that is, with drugs, and what is caused "psychologically" must be cured "psychologically." Actually there need not be such a one-to-one relationship between causation and treatment. That's why family members and patients are often relieved to find out that there is some biological component to mental illness. It doesn't mean that the illness can't be changed by either biological or psychosocial treatment.

Besides constantly changing to absorb new experiences, the brain remains plastic throughout life, able to compensate for traumata—hence the ability of some stroke victims, for example, to recover much of their lost ability.* Similarly, even the symptoms of BPD most likely to be biological abate over time, challenging the traditional view of personality disorders as immutable.

In fact, Richard I. Shader and his colleagues suggest an excellent (and apparently endless) analogy between the personality and bone. A bone's size, shape, and form are genetically programmed, but it requires nourishment from without as well as within in order to mature. Although it appears hard and fixed, bone is actually an extremely fluid system through which various substances continually pass, and which is constantly being dissolved and rebuilt.[8] Most importantly, bone can become brittle and fracture along a line that will always remain vulnerable. The injured person may need to favor a previously broken bone, relying more heavily on other bones, just as a borderline patient may have to develop better coping mechanisms and emphasize her areas of strength. Otherwise, a healing personality, like a mended bone, can function very nicely.

Not too long ago, it would have been outrageous to suggest that bad experiences could subtly deform brain structures. Equally outrageous,

---

*In an article in the *New York Times* (16 December 1990), Oliver Sacks, M.D., describes coaching the actors who were to appear in the film *Awakenings*. While working with Robert DeNiro, Dr. Sacks began seriously to wonder whether the intensity of his acting had actually altered DeNiro's nervous system into a pathological state.

but perhaps not unthinkable, is that possibly a therapeutic environment can reform them into a healthier state. For some reason, perhaps this one, some patients who have taken psychiatric drugs continue their progress in psychotherapy after the drugs are stopped.

A biological vulnerability, then, ought not to aggravate the border-line's sense that she is bad or defective. The appropriate attitude toward BPD and its treatment is one not of determinism but of determination.

Notes

1. Nancy C. Andreasen, M.D., Ph.D., *The Broken Brain: The Biological Revolution in Psychiatry* (New York: Harper & Row, 1984), p. 222. Copyright © 1984 by Nancy C. Andreasen. Reprinted by permission of HarperCollins Publishers.
2. Useful descriptions of the brain and the actions of psychotropic drugs can be found in Dr. Andreasen's book and in Solomon H. Snyder, *Drugs and the Brain* (New York: Scientific American Books, 1986); Jon Franklin, *Molecules of the Mind* (New York: Dell, 1987); and Richard M. Restak, M.D., *The Brain: The Last Frontier* (New York: Warner Books, 1979).
3. Larry J. Siever, M.D., and Kenneth L. Davis, M.D., "A Psychobiologic Perspective on the Personality Disorders," *American Journal of Psychiatry,* in press.
4. Andreasen, p. 239.
5. Larry J. Siever, M.D., and Kenneth L. Davis, M.D., "Overview: Toward a Dysregulation Hypothesis of Depression," *American Journal of Psychiatry,* Vol. 142, No. 9 (September 1985), p. 1028.
6. Gerald Adler, M.D., paper [negative] read at debate, "Resolved: The Etiology of Borderline Personality Disorder Is Predominantly Biological," 143rd annual meeting of the American Psychiatric Association, New York, 16 May 1990.
7. Daniel Goleman, "A Key to Post-Traumatic Stress Lies in Brain Chemistry, Scientists Find," *New York Times,* 12 June 1990.
8. Richard I. Shader, Edward L. Scharfman, and Daniel A. Dreyfuss, "A Biological Model for Selected Personality Disorders," in *Psychiatry,* Vol. 1, Section 1, ed. Arnold M. Cooper, Allen J. Frances, and Michael E. Sacks (Philadelphia: Lippincott; New York: Basic Books, rev. ed., 1990), chap. 3, p. 2.

1 8

The Components of
Temperament

"We are in a state of creative chaos."

REX W. COWDRY, M.D.[1]

The search for biological components of BPD is not an
easy one. "The problem is that we're working backwards,"
says Dr. Paris.

> We're starting with phenomena and looking at biology. Dr.
> Siever said it beautifully at an APA convention when he re-
> marked that the neurotransmitters haven't read *DSM-III*. If
> we had a good biology of behavior, we could reclassify these
> things. But meanwhile no matter what we measure, one-third
> of the patients don't fit. So we have to wait for something
> better.

At least some researchers wait so impatiently that they bend
the rules of good science. "In reading the neurobiological
literature, we need to keep in mind what conceptualization
the authors are using because it will color everything else,
including how they read their data," says Dr. Kutcher.[2]
Some of these conceptualizations of BPD are the subject of
this chapter.

A Specific Illness

One hypothesis is that BPD is a specific illness with a unique biology. But no one has identified the core that isolates it and gives rise to its particular features and symptoms.

BPD may be primarily a disorder of impulse control, one in which genetic and environmental factors cause symptoms like substance abuse that exacerbate it. Thus a symposium on the illness as an "impulse spectrum disorder" was conducted at the 1990 APA convention, at which Dr. Stone noted that

> I have recommended abandoning the term *borderline* for something like *impulse-ridden* or *action-prone* for a more homogenous group of patients.
>
> Impulsivity is a key factor in BPD. It is a behavioral correlate to the excessive central nervous system irritability and whatever neurophysiological abnormalities may exist and appear to underlie many instances of the illness.
>
> But we must not reify when speaking of impulsivity, which is not the sine qua non. Impulsivity or action orientation is a conceptually unifying common feature.[3]

Dr. Soloff agrees that it is incorrect to assume that impulsivity is *the* most important aspect of BPD:

> Our focus may be on impulsivity right now because the experimental evidence is strongest there that a single neurotransmitter, serotonin, is involved with it. Scientists find serotonin very sexy. If you investigate serotonin, you can always draw a crowd to lectures and also get research money. But we can't ignore the affective instability, which is very, very prominent in borderline patients even in the absence of impulsivity.

A hypothesis about impulsivity suggested by Dr. Siever and his colleagues is that a child's ability to control her feelings appears to be important to healthy personality development. Biological vulnerability can make a child's emotions intense and hard to regulate and her impulses difficult to control.

Borderlines compensate for this deficit by controlling other people to prevent them from provoking bad feelings. The self-mutilation and tantrums of borderlines both discharge their feelings and influence others not to incite them. These behaviors may be patterns that became fixed in their relationships with their early caretakers.[4] Maintaining the patterns into adulthood causes borderlines to be labeled "manipulative."

Like so many other aspects of BPD, a predisposition to impulsivity is not unique but seen also in other psychiatric illnesses.

A Hodgepodge

A second biological model is that BPD is a mixed psychopathology. This model allows researchers to look at one aspect of the illness at a time in the hope that someday they will collectively fit the puzzle together. Here we will review some of the major approaches, many of which likewise focus on impulsivity.

ACQUIRED DEVELOPMENTAL BRAIN DYSFUNCTION IN BPD

We have already raised the possibility that at least some borderlines have nonlocalized brain dysfunction. Dr. van Reekum has suggested that normal personality development may require a critical mass of ego or cognitive functioning that has been damaged so as to lead to BPD. "The notion of acquired developmental brain dysfunction is suggestive," says Dr. Links, "but at present we can't say that this causes BPD because to some extent it has been found in patients with antisocial personality disorder and schizophrenia as well."[5]

THE LIMBIC SYSTEM AND BASAL GANGLIA IN BPD

Borderline patients have shown abnormalities on certain biological tests, specifically the DST, the TRH test, and the rapid-eye movement (REM) latency test.[6] Applied as biological markers for affective disorders, the tests have produced inconsistent, confusing results. "But it's confusing only if you view these tests as specific for depression," says Dr. Cowdry. "I think it's generally felt that many of these biological findings have a broader and less specific meaning than that." Not surprisingly, the broader implication is that many borderline patients have problems with limbic system–neuroendocrine regulation that are as yet undefined.

Among other symptoms of BPD that imply malfunctioning of the limbic system are those resembling complex partial seizure disorders. And a study by Dr. Cowdry and David L. Gardner, M.D.,[7] has shown that some borderline patients appear to be less impulsive while taking carbamazepine, an anticonvulsant drug similar in structure to a tricyclic antidepressant that works primarily in the limbic system. "It's interesting that it seemed to be particularly the behavioral dyscontrol that responded most dramatically to the carbamazepine," says Dr. Cowdry.

> The drug seemed specifically to help people have less of a kneejerk reaction to dysphoric states or rage episodes. Several people described *reflective delay* on carbamazepine—being able to stop and think about the feelings rather than simply acting on them.

This improvement did not impress the patients, who understandably wanted to be free of their bad feelings entirely.

But it does raise an interesting hypothesis. The patients who responded to carbamazepine had no abnormalities of the temporal lobes or limbic system apparent in EEGs. Instead their limbic systems appeared to work differently. "Many of the psychosensory symptoms and the primitive storms of affect could be linked to low thresholds for excitation of limbic structures in the brain," says Dr. Cowdry.

> This is an interesting hypothesis, one that provides a mechanism for why early experience could produce neuronal changes through kindling. This kindling model of increasing sensitivity to the environment might explain increasingly profound dysphoric responses to abuse or neglect. Such kindled foci [localized areas of disease] might be suppressed by anticonvulsants. The question is how such a drug might work. Does it raise the threshold in limbic structures for activation, does it actually attenuate the mood state? I think it does clinically in people for whom it works.

Nobody believes, however, that BPD is actually a seizure disorder. "The carbamazepine is interesting and provides an intriguing clue," says Dr. Cowdry, "but it's not direct evidence."

Equally intriguing and indirect are other speculations about a variation on the kindling model suggested by Dr. Stone. Limbic activity is normally suppressed by arousal of the cerebral cortex. Impulsive responses to the environment are checked by the frontal lobes, which contain memory circuits offering a repertoire of responses from which to choose. "Without this message to pause and reflect," says Dr. Stone, "a stimulus just short-circuits down into an impulsive response. This explains why cortical arousal is lower in impulsive sociopaths and higher in neurotically depressed patients, in whom it is inhibitory."

According to Dr. Stone, the brain's basal ganglia appear to be involved with procedural or habit memory. These memories appear connected to very early patterns of experience that contribute to one's permanent sense of identity. If abuse occurs, that system gets overloaded with negative memories tied in very closely with primitive survival mechanisms.

"When a borderline feels stressed and threatened, the habit memory system easily bypasses the cognitive and frontal lobe influences," says Dr. Stone.

She feels that she has no time to allow her more adaptive responses to come forward. She is like a soldier in a jungle, shooting first and then asking questions. These habit memory systems can be very difficult to overwhelm. Borderline patients agree that their assumptions and response patterns are faulty, but they can't give them up. They have high drive levels, low thresholds for excitation, and inability to inhibit their responses. Aggressive scripts acquired in childhood become difficult to change.[8]

This model helps explain why borderlines have such difficulty maintaining realistic perspectives on their environments. When even vaguely reminded of previous bad experiences, borderlines react as if they were occurring all over again.

Whitney explains how a borderline can learn to overcome such handicaps.

It all comes down to processing. I used to just get hit with so much stimulus, and my moods would be up and down all day. Now I can look back and say, "This was when I felt bad; this made me feel bad, and this was why." Even if I feel particularly paranoid and sensitive, I know why it's happening. Knowing that these feelings will happen under stress reminds me that I don't have to act on them because they will go away.

This is one of the most difficult yet useful coping techniques a borderline can learn: to remind herself that each mood is subjective and temporary, that she felt better before and will do so again.

As Whitney's description implies, therapy must help the patient develop cognitive resources to overcome such impairments. One possible method has been suggested in the study by O'Leary and her colleagues referred to in Chapters 6 and 12.[9]

In comparison to normal controls, the performance of a group of borderline patients in this study was significantly impaired on memory tests requiring them to recall complex material they had recently learned. But when they were offered cues, the borderlines improved much more dramatically than the control subjects and remembered almost as well. This suggests that borderlines have a deficit not in learning but in recalling without cues.

Therapists often note that borderlines have difficulty remembering past experiences, including therapy sessions. This amnesia is often interpreted as a defense against material that causes anxiety or other unpleasant feelings. O'Leary and her colleagues suggest instead that borderlines have difficulty recalling *any* complex material. Possibly this is why borderlines can't maintain a sense of consistency about themselves and others and have trouble effectively applying what they have learned from experiences.

"So does this have therapeutic implications?" asks Dr. Cowdry, who coauthored the study. "Does cueing help their cognition? Can you strengthen their egos through cognitive training to help them control their behavior?" The group recommends that therapists try cueing and encouraging borderline patients to keep journals and other records as one way to find out.

The researchers also found the performances of the borderline patients to be significantly impaired on several perceptual tests of the ability to separate essential from extraneous visual material. This might suggest poor psychological differentiation and preoccupation with some stimuli to the exclusion of others.

NEUROTRANSMITTERS IN BPD

"Very fine animal literature indicates that serotonin is the inhibitory neurotransmitter—it's Doctor No," says Dr. Soloff. If a rat is taught to press a lever to get food, then its serotonin system is lesioned, then it is given shocks when it presses the lever, it won't unlearn the original reward lesson as quickly as a normal rat. The lesioned rat can't suppress behavior that it knows is punishable. "So the function of serotonin may be analogous to that of the conscience: to suppress behavior based on anticipation of future punishment for one's acts," says Dr. Siever.

Extrapolated to people, these findings suggest a possible reason that borderlines have difficulty suppressing their aggressive impulses when upset. Even though they have affective sensitivity and feel profoundly guilty, they can't stop themselves from using alcohol, behaving promiscuously, or binge eating.

A related finding from these animal studies is that serotonin affects the brain's ability to process novelty. If a rat's serotonin system is lesioned, it becomes violent and kills mice unless it has already become accustomed to them. "The serotonin system modulates or suppresses aggressive motor reactions to novelty," says Dr. Siever.

To test these findings in people, Emil F. Coccaro, M.D., Dr. Siever and their colleagues measured the indices of serotonin activity in three groups of men: depressed and personality-disordered male patients and normal control subjects.[10] The results were as follows:

- Both groups of patients appeared to have serotonin activity lower than that of the controls.
- The borderline patients had low serotonin activity that was associated with impulsivity. The patients with decreased serotonin activity were more likely to perform self-damaging acts; they also showed more intense anger and a greater tendency toward aggression than those with normal indices of serotonin activity. The lower the serotonin functions in these patients, the higher their aggression was in particular.
- The low serotonin activity in the depressed patients did not correlate with impulsivity but did with suicide attempts—their aggression may have been directed inwardly.
- The personality disordered patients showed no correlation between low serotonin activity and history or severity of depression. But both groups of patients did show a correlation specifically with suicidality.

"So although depressed patients share serotonin abnormality with personality disordered patients," says Dr. Siever, "something else might be modifying it that is different between the two groups." The researchers are investigating whether the "something else" might be norepinephrine, which seems to mediate our sensitivity and reactivity to the environment and to encourage outwardly directed risk taking and sensation seeking. "We have found low responsiveness of norepinephrine receptors in our depressed patients, who seem not very tuned in to the environment and have distorted vegetative functions," says Dr. Siever.

In classical depression, the impulsivity caused by low serotonin activity might not be expressed outwardly in response to the environment because norepinephrine activity is also low. A suicidal or other inwardly directed impulsive behavior might occur in response to a flooding of anxiety or agitation.

In borderline and other personality disordered patients, however, the norepinephrine activity may instead be *high,* creating their hypersensitivity to the environment. "Aggression induced by a shock is associated with an increase in norepinephrine," says Dr. Siever.

This is the opposite of the findings with serotonin. So the noradrenergic and serotonergic systems may act synergistically in borderlines. A person with suppressed serotonin causing disinhibition of aggression, plus enhanced noradrenergic activity causing greater readiness to be stimulated by the environment, is at greater risk to become irritable and behave impulsively.

Presumably the nature of the environmental stimulus and the robustness of the noradrenergic response would determine whether the impulsive behavior would be directed outwardly or toward the self. Borderline depression differs from the classical variety in part by this very reactivity.

Variation on a Theme

A third biological model is that BPD is a variant of another disorder. BPD has most recently been associated with affective disorder, with impulsive behavior viewed as a way to manage the negative feelings.

The affective disorder hypothesis was first advanced by Dr. Klein when he and Dr. Liebowitz began studying hysteroid dysphorics and their responses to antidepressants, especially MAOIs. The theory has produced an enormous body of literature showing that anywhere from 40 to 70 percent of borderlines also have episodes of major depressive disorder. "Removal of affective features from BPD is really at variance with the views of a number of investigators still looking at affectively laden subtypes of borderlines," says Dr. Liebowitz. "Without affectivity, the pure form of borderline would be more toward the antisocial, impulsive, aggressive aspects of the illness."[11]

Dr. Siever suspects that like impulsivity, affective sensitivity might be a commonality distributed across different psychiatric disorders. He notes that a subgroup of borderlines have *dysthymia* (chronic mild depression). Dr. Akiskal has studied this subgroup and other borderlines who have *cyclothymia* (mild bipolar disorder) or *bipolar II disorder* (a variant with milder manic episodes).

Dr. Stone believes that in individual borderline patients whose families show a high incidence of affective disorder, this component cannot be overlooked. "I have been misquoted for about 15 years as saying that BPD is an expression of affective disorder," he says.

I have never said that all cases or even a majority of them are as such. To view BPD as an affective spectrum disorder cannot account totally for its etiology. In individual pedigrees, however, the evidence of affective disorder is impressive. In some patients the borderline disorder can be seen as a forme fruste or deluded expression of fullblown bipolar II and bipolar disorder or recurrent depression. Some groups of borderline patients are so overwhelmingly affective that the burden of proof would be on the skeptic to show that affective disorder and BPD are not two sides of the same coin.[12]

The Skeptics Reply

Dr. Gunderson, however, would prefer to view the individual pedigrees in a larger context. "Dr. Stone's interpretations are debatable," he says.

> There is not evidence for manic depressive or alcoholic genes having important roles specifically in BPD. Borderline patients come from totally dysfunctional families from which we can't just extract risk genes.[13]

According to Dr. Gunderson, depressed borderline patients show families with more of the other personality disorders than BPD. "Also, when we control for current affective disorder," he says, "much of the linkage in terms of overlap in family history and perhaps also of drug responsitivity disappears."

> The more recent and methodologically sophisticated studies have shown that patients with other personality disorders have equal or more depression than borderlines. And depressed subjects have other personality disorders more often than BPD as a comorbid condition.[14]

The groups of depressed borderlines referred to by Dr. Stone and other reseachers may not be as large as many studies have implied. Dr. Soloff notes that the most accurate study of the incidence of affective disorder in BPD is one conducted by Minna R. Fyer, M.D., and her colleagues.[15] In groups of borderline patients from two hospitals, the researchers found that 34 percent and 45 percent of the borderline patients had affective disorder, an incidence no greater than would be expected. "That study is important because they controlled for the baseline incidence of affective disorder in their patient population," says Dr. Soloff. In so doing, the group eliminated the selection bias of much of the earlier borderline research, which had been conducted in clinics for depression.

Additional observations call into question some assumptions fundamental to this research.[16] Dr. Siever's hospital, for instance, has a special research program for depressed patients and another in a different unit for patients with personality disorders. To enter the depression study, the patients must show classic depressive episodes by structured interview and spend their first two weeks in the hospital medication-free.

During this period the purely depressed patients would usually stay the same or grow worse. But the majority of personality disordered patients who met criteria for depression would start to feel better within a few days, presumably because they liked the attention and caring they received from the hospital staff. "We had retrospective diagnoses of major depression for almost half of our personality disordered group, but by the end of the waiting period less than 10 percent of them still met Hamilton scores for depression," says Dr. Siever. "This means not that borderlines shouldn't get antidepressants, but that there is something fundamentally different in their mood reactivity."

"This result is really significant because it addresses the whole issue of the validity of the diagnosis of major depression," says Dr. Soloff. "It suggests that the diagnosis of depression in character disordered patients in general is highly suspect."

These findings have not checked the astonishing rate at which information on this issue continues to accumulate. "All of it points toward the lack of a strong or specific association," says Dr. Gunderson. "I have a paper in press with the *American Journal of Psychiatry* that updates my 1985 review and really lays the issue to rest."

BPD itself undoubtedly has an affective component that like its other features is neither necessary nor sufficient to explain the illness. Dr. Siever's reference to a "fundamental difference" is frequently echoed by other researchers. No other form of affective disorder is like borderline depression: for some reason, the emotional disturbance in borderlines takes a particular form.

Borderline Depression

The biological components of this form appear merely to *distinguish* it from melancholia. "Borderline depression is characterized by dysphoric states with discrete depressive symptoms," says Dr. Cowdry, "but unlike classical depression, there is a marked environmental responsivity, especially to other people."

Borderline depression is associated with what Dr. Klein calls *rejection sensitivity*. Borderlines feel great loneliness and alienation that alternate with their angry, needy, demanding reactions to the frustrations inherent in relationships. They are more likely than nonborderline depressed people to make frequent impulsive suicide attempts and to require hospitalization. Dr. Silk and his colleagues refer to nonborderline depression as a "sad/guilty" type and borderline depression as a "bad/mad" type.[17]

Unlike melancholia, borderline depression consists of an episode of dysphoric mood shifts within a general pattern of chaotic functioning. Some of the physical symptoms are similar but have different dynamics: weight change can result from binge-purging, for instance, and impaired concentration from substance abuse. Although depressed borderlines feel bad and worthless, they blame others for their emptiness, boredom, and other feelings of deprivation and remain irritable and agitated.

Underlying all this, as Dr. Cowdry suggests, is

> a certain absence of responsiveness to reward, to positive occurrences, that suggests that there may be problems with both repetitive behavior—that is, reward seeking—and also with the reward mechanism itself. Somehow rewarding events don't carry the same significance for most borderlines that they do for normal people. There is a chronic emptiness or sense of depression with a small *d,* that life is not very gratifying. Is that a cognitive problem? Is it part of having a dysfunctional attitude? Does it say something more prominent about these individuals' biological responsivity to rewards?

The importance of the distinction is that those involved with borderlines should not expect their depression to look like that of most people. "Depressed people just wither away, but borderlines are active and aggressive," says Ingrid. In fact, a study by Drew Westen, Ph.D., and his colleagues suggests that psychoanalytic therapists need to refine their theories about depression, which may interact with borderline pathology in a unique way.[18]

The relationship between BPD and affective illness may mean that there is a subgroup of depressed borderlines not clearly distinguished. Possibly some patients have both syndromes, either coexisting or with one subservient to and/or causing the other.

Or perhaps their relationship is just one thread in the pattern of factors thought to contribute arbitrarily to BPD.

In their 1985 review, Dr. Gunderson and Glen R. Elliott, Ph.D., M.D., suggest—and still maintain—that both BPD and affective disorder arise from a variety of innate and environmental factors that interact to become either one illness, the other illness, or some combination of the two.[19]

Biological Splitting

We have looked at the symptom of splitting from four developmental points of view, and before leaving the biology of BPD, we should add a more scientific explanation for it. "Splitting may be a kind of specialized state-dependent learning,"* says Dr. Siever.

> Borderlines have highly polarized dissociated affective states and use dissociation as a defense. When something triggers a positive representation, it may be stored with very good feelings. But the very bad feelings may be so overwhelming and devastating that when those are triggered, they must be kept dissociated. It's not that borderlines cognitively can't recall what another person is really like, but their representations become split off from each other in a sort of state-dependent fashion. The affective immediacy is gone because it doesn't have the same resonance.
>
> Splitting develops a psychological life of its own with borderlines. They can use these idealized images as protection against the negative feelings of rage or helplessness. So they've developed a whole psychological vocabulary.
>
> But in part this defense, like others, may evolve or be made more likely from some of the underlying temperamental factors. Someone with an unstable or impulsive temperament is more likely to use splitting as a defense. There's no doubt that abuse and trauma can lend themselves to using dissociation, but some people are nevertheless better at it than others.

Like those of most researchers in the biology of BPD, Dr. Siever's speculation actually blends temperament with environment. Most borderline specialists frown upon pure affectophilia.

The Hazards of Affectophilia

The heavy-duty biological theorizing about BPD indulged in by the affectophiles worries Dr. Gunderson. "To suggest that the etiology of BPD is predominantly and primarily biological is reductionistic," he says. "It obscures what is known and harmfully misleads the care of such patients and the humanistic integrity of our field."[20]

State-dependent learning is that which takes place under specific circumstances and is lost under any others. A patient can acquire a skill under the effects of medication, for example, and lose it when the drug is stopped.

Dr. Gunderson's point is that just because symptoms may arise from temperament or from traumata that can be registered neurophysiologically, this doesn't make the resulting illness *primarily* biological:

> The biological approach frightens me by its implication that borderlines are not accountable for their behaviors. That's dangerous and misleading. They are not bad people, but there is a complex interface between the problems of their backgrounds and the formation of their characters where holding them accountable for some of what they do is an essential component of treatment. If we can't bring that to bear in treatment, we convey Dr. Akiskal's sense that these people are victims of neurobiological dysregulations and that the greatest hope we can offer is pharmacotherapy.[21]

Borderlines may literally have been brainwashed into coping poorly, but with help they can be debriefed into a healthier way of life.

Notes

1. Rex W. Cowdry, M.D., and David L. Gardner, M.D., "Pharmacotherapy of Impulsivity in Borderline Personality Disorder," paper read at the 143rd annual meeting of the American Psychiatric Association, New York, 16 May 1990.
2. Stanley P. Kutcher, M.D., "Borderline Personality Disorder Heterogeneity: Pharmacotherapy and Psychotherapy Implications," paper read at the 143rd annual meeting of the American Psychiatric Association, New York, 15 May 1990.
3. Michael H. Stone, M.D., discussion of the symposium "Borderline Personality: Impulse Spectrum Disorder" at the 143rd annual meeting of the American Psychiatric Association, New York, 16 May 1990.
4. Larry J. Siever, Howard M. Klar, and Emil F. Coccaro, "Psychobiologic Substrates of Personality," in *Biologic Response Styles: Clinical Implications,* ed. Larry J. Siever and Howard M. Klar (Washington, D.C.: American Psychiatric Press, 1985), pp. 43–44.
5. Paul S. Links, M.D., and Robert van Reekum, M.D., "Constitutional Factors in Borderline Personality," paper read at the 143rd annual meeting of the American Psychiatric Association, New York, 17 May 1990.
6. See Henry W. Lahmeyer, M.D., Charles F. Reynolds III, M.D., David J. Kupfer, M.D., and Roy King, M.D., "Biologic Markers in Borderline Personality Disorder: A Review," *Journal of Clinical Psychiatry,* Vol. 50, No. 6 (June 1989), pp. 217–25; and Meir Steiner, M.D., Paul S. Links, M.D., and Marilyn Korzekwa, M.D., "Biological Markers in Borderline Personality Disorders: An Overview," *Canadian Journal of Psychiatry,* Vol. 33, No. 5 (June 1988), pp. 350–54.
7. Rex William Cowdry, M.D., and David L. Gardner, M.D., "Pharmacotherapy of Borderline Personality Disorder: Alprazolam, Carbamazepine, Trifluoperazine, and Tranylcypromine," *Archives of General Psychiatry,* Vol. 45 (February 1988), pp. 111–19.
8. Stone, "Impulse Spectrum Disorder" discussion.
9. Kathleen M. O'Leary, M.S.W., Pim Brouwers, Ph.D., David L. Gardner, M.D., and Rex W. Cowdry, M.D., "Neuropsychological Testing of Patients with Borderline Personality Disorder," *American Journal of Psychiatry,* Vol. 148, No. 1 (January 1991), pp. 106–11.
10. Emil F. Coccaro, M.D., Larry J. Siever, M.D., Howard M. Klar, M.D., Gail Maurer, Ph.D., Karen Cochrane, M.Ed., Thomas B. Cooper, M.A., Richard C. Mohs, Ph.D., and Kenneth L. Davis, M.D., "Serotonergic Studies in Patients with Affective and Personality Disorders," *Archives of General Psychiatry,* Vol 46 (July 1989), pp. 587–99.

11. Michael R. Liebowitz, M.D., paper [affirmative] read at debate, "Resolved: The Etiology of Borderline Personality Disorder Is Predominantly Biological," 143rd annual meeting of the American Psychiatric Association, New York, 16 May 1990.
12. Michael H. Stone, M.D., "An Integrated, Psychobiological Model of Borderline Personality Disorder," paper read at the 143rd annual meeting of the American Psychiatric Association, New York, 17 May 1990.
13. John G. Gunderson, M.D., discussion of the symposium "The Borderline Patient: Development, Therapy and Outcome" at the 143rd annual meeting of the American Psychiatric Association, New York, 15 May 1990.
14. John G. Gunderson, M.D., paper [negative] read at debate, "Resolved: The Etiology of Borderline Personality Disorder Is Predominantly Biological," 143rd annual meeting of the American Psychiatric Association, New York, 16 May 1990.
15. Minna R. Fyer, M.D., Allen J. Frances, M.D., Timothy Sullivan, M.D., Stephen W. Hurt, Ph.D., and John Clarkin, Ph.D., "Comorbidity of Borderline Personality Disorder," *Archives of General Psychiatry*, Vol. 45 (April 1988), pp. 348–52.
16. Siever, Klar, and Coccaro, pp. 52–53.
17. Kenneth R. Silk, M.D., Naomi E. Lohr, Ph.D., Laura Gold, Ph.D., Edna Pressler, M.A., Joel Nigg, A.C.S.W., and Drew Westen, Ph.D., "Standard Rating Scales and Depression in Borderline Personality Disorder," paper read at the 143rd annual meeting of the American Psychiatric Association, New York, 15 May 1990.
18. Drew Westen, Ph.D., M. Jay Moses, B.A., Kenneth R. Silk, M.D., Naomi E. Lohr, Ph.D., Robert Cohen, M.A., and Henry Segal, M.A., "Quality of Depressive Experience in Borderline Personality Disorder and Major Depression: When Depression Is Not Just Depression," paper read at the 143rd annual meeting of the American Psychiatric Association, New York, 15 May 1990.
19. John G. Gunderson, M.D., and Glen R. Elliott, Ph.D., M.D., "The Interface Between Borderline Personality Disorder and Affective Disorder," *American Journal of Psychiatry*, Vol. 142, No. 3 (March 1985), pp. 277–88.
20. Gunderson, "Etiology" debate.
21. Ibid.

19

Family Legacies

"If a herd of buffalo had wandered into my living room and died, we would have stepped over them and pretended they weren't there."

"PAIGE"

We have learned that for much of its history, inferences about BPD were drawn from what therapists learned in treatment sessions. Such inferences became theories about overinvolvement (the separation–individuation theory) and neglect (the aloneness theory) in the families of borderline patients.

Once the borderline concept was standardized and more precisely defined by *DSM-III* and Dr. Gunderson's work, researchers could conduct family studies to determine what the backgrounds of patients had actually been like. "The original observations and theories about BPD have been amply verified by empirical studies," says Dr. Gunderson. "These empirical studies severely implicate a seriously disturbed environment as a predominant etiological cause for BPD."[1] Suggested by the comments from parents that appeared in Chapter 14, such information can be obtained from genetic, family history, and family environment studies.[2]

Genetic Studies

To study genetic factors in an illness, researchers must first determine its *phenotype:* the outward manifestation of its biochemistry determined by the interaction of its genetic constitution with the environment. Having established the phenotype, researchers can then study the illness in twins and adopted children to tease apart its hereditary and environmental contributors.

It should be clear by now why researchers have not yet identified a phenotype for BPD. And in fact, the one small twin study of BPD that was published by Svenn Torgersen in 1984 indicates that "genetic factors may influence the development of the schizotypal, but not the borderline, personality disorders."[3] Presently there is little evidence to support a genetic hypothesis for BPD.

Family History Studies

Twin and adoption studies are required to prove that an illness is genetic. This can be *suggested,* however, by family prevalence or history studies, which record psychiatric disorders in the biological relatives of patients. Any illness that seems prevalent in the families of borderline patients may somehow contribute to BPD. An incidence of the illness itself among relatives would suggest that despite its complexity, BPD can be inherited.

The major family history studies of BPD have differences between (and in some cases flaws in) their methodologies but do show some consensus. The incidence of affective disorder in the families of borderlines, for instance, appears related to that of depression in the patients themselves. The most frequently cited study to show a positive correlation was done several years ago by Dr. Pope and his colleagues. These researchers found a subgroup of borderlines prone to major depressions whose families show an elevated incidence of *unipolar depression* (major depression without manic episodes).[4] More family studies comparing the borderline to other personality disorders might clarify whether this finding differentiates the illness.

Such research shows BPD to be linked to neither bipolar disorder nor schizophrenia.

Family studies have shown the incidence of BPD in the closest relatives of borderline patients to be higher than that found in the families of patients with closely related personality disorders. A recent study by Zanarini, Dr. Gunderson, and their colleagues found that 18 percent of close relatives of borderline patients met *DSM-III* criteria for BPD and 25 percent had a morbid risk of developing it.[5] Although the implications of these findings are unclear, they support the view that BPD is a valid disorder that "breeds true."

Interestingly enough, the illness appears to be equally distributed among male and female relatives. "Other studies besides ours have looked at the prevalence of BPD in families," says Dr. Links, "and found that men and women not identified to the mental health profession seem to evidence equal rates of the disorder." "I think that the fathers of borderline children are equally as disturbed as the mothers and that BPD is much more common in the fathers than has been published," says Dr. Andrulonis, "but I can't prove that yet." The findings of these researchers qualify Dr. Masterson's theory about borderline mothers and support the assumption that male borderlines are often misdiagnosed by therapists.

The studies also suggest that an inherited risk for BPD includes illnesses like alcoholism, other substance abuse, and antisocial personality disorder as well. Although common in families of borderline patients, these illnesses are not specific to BPD, and their implications are not clear. "It's hard to know what the relationship is," says Dr. McGlashan.

> I tend to think that alcoholism, for instance, has more to do with genetics. It's all speculative, but there's a higher incidence of alcoholism in affective disorders as well, and although we don't know what borderline is, we do know that there's a connection with affective disorders and also that certainly borderlines are substance abusing. So there may be some multiple genetic linkages there with substance abuse and affective disorder.
>
> If you had a family history of affective disorder as opposed to one of alcoholism, would you get a certain borderline lineage? Would you get a type of borderline who is more impulsive and substance abusing as opposed to the type who is more dysphoric, depressive, and self-destructive? That's the kind of study that needs to be done, but it would require very large numbers of patients.

The notion that the borderline is connected to other types of disorders of course recalls Dr. Kernberg's model. And with reference to families, it's an especially unfortunate one. "Consider what it must be like," says Dr. Gunderson, "to be raised by a borderline, antisocial, or alcoholic parent."

To pursue such findings, some researchers have tried instead to isolate the basic components or *substrates* of BPD and look for those in families. "Part of the unique character of the borderline may arise from two substrates, impulsivity, and affective instability," says Dr. Siever. Jeremy M. Silverman, Ph.D., Dr. Siever and their colleagues traced each of these symptoms in the families of borderlines as a distinct and independent personality trait.[6] The group found increased risk for each trait in the families, with comparatively few relatives having both of them.

In the serotonin study described in the preceding chapter,[7] the patients with the lowest serotonin activity had the greatest histories of impulsivity in their families; in fact, lowered serotonin activity was associated more closely with impulsivity in the family than with the presence of this trait in the patients themselves.

"It's possible, then, that a couple of threads contribute to becoming borderline," says Dr. Siever.

> A child could have liability to both affective sensitivity and impulsivity combined with adverse environmental circumstances. Disentangling the influences, however, becomes very tricky because usually "nature" and "nurture" are synergistic too. For example, alcoholic impulsive parents may pass on a genetic liability to impulsivity but also may be much more likely to act impulsively and abusively or become involved in incest with their children. I'm sure that the abuse plays a role independent of the genetics, but in real life genetic and social influences usually occur together.

An alternative proposal is that an as yet unknown inherited factor lends many of the symptoms of BPD their unique flavor and expression.

Family Environment Studies

The traditional theory that BPD results from a pathological upbringing is supported by comparatively few studies. One reason may be that borderlines' recollections of their childhoods may be judged too inaccurate for research purposes. Unless they can somehow corroborate patient descriptions, and until prospective studies of families can somehow take place, researchers must accept the possibility of such distortions as a given.

Like modifications in psychoanalytical theory, those family environment studies that *are* taking place have abandoned specific phases of development to focus more on chronic problems. They have already isolated several patterns that are associated quite specifically with BPD.

SEPARATION AND LOSS

Various studies show that between 25 and 65 percent of borderlines were separated from or lost a parent because of divorce, death, or illness requiring extensive hospitalization. This incidence of separations, many of which occurred when the borderlines were preschoolers or adolescents, is significantly higher than that seen in other psychiatric illnesses. It helps explain the borderline's terror of loss and her compulsion to seek care from others, to manipulate those who threaten to leave, and to withdraw angrily from those who remain unavailable.

OVERINVOLVEMENT AND NEGLECT

Some borderlines describe families with whom they remained enmeshed even though they could perceive the pathology. "I was a very outgoing child and had a lot of friends, but that got squashed somewhere along the way," says Whitney.

> Toward adolescence, I became more of a recluse. Relationships just became too painful because they would bring up all this rage that I didn't understand and couldn't handle. I would get jealous and angry and blow off my high school girlfriends and run away to my family where it was safe. It was a very protective environment. I knew the jealousy within a large family very well and how to deal with it. And I could isolate in my family, get lost among all those people. So eventually I started cutting all of my friends out of my life.

Borderlines contrast with other psychiatric patients in their negative views of family overinvolvement.[8] Family studies consistently show, however, that only a minority of borderlines have such families.*

The opposite extreme, which is far more common, is for the family to have operated in what Dr. Gunderson calls "a vacuum." Sometimes this happens because the bond between the parents is so tight as to exclude care of the children. It can take the form of either no conflict or, as some studies show, enormous hostility between the parents and toward their children.

One pattern quite specific to the families of borderline patients is that

---

*One of their interesting features is a widespread observation described by one psychiatrist that the names of borderline patients tend to have unusual spellings, as if the family had wanted to distinguish and claim the child from birth.

one parent (usually the father) is absent, aloof, or otherwise uninvolved
with the family while the other is overinvolved. The distant parent may
see the other's pathological dependency on the children but fail to protect them from it. This combination of overinvolvement and neglect of
course fits the classical pattern of separation-individuation theory articulated primarily by Dr. Masterson. "We do hear complaints from
borderlines that their parents were overprotective and interfered with
their autonomy," says Dr. Paris, "but I think it's only in combination
with neglect that this can be understood." This pattern, which has been
called *affectionless control,* is strongly related to depression. Animal and
trauma studies have shown that the next step down—a combination of
overinvolvement and intermittent abuse—has particularly devastating
consequences for the developing child.

ABUSE

Dr. Links and his associates in fact speculate that the family environment unique to borderline patients is that in which the parents' overinvolvement interacts with their highly malevolent attitude toward the
child.[9] The extent of this hostility has recently become apparent in the
high frequency of abuse that has been shown in the childhoods of borderlines.

We will examine this pattern in the next chapter. The point here is
how often the perpetrators manage to hide abuse as carefully as addicts
protect their drugs. "Some families function so well socially that they
look good by ordinary mental health criteria," says Dr. Herman.

> This may go along with a tremendous amount of hidden pathology, includ-
> ing a rigid code of appearances that keeps the children from getting help.
> Incest perpetrators, for instance, are often pillars of the community, even
> ministers—and they are also often batterers. We don't really have psychiatric
> diagnostic categories that capture or describe this kind of pathology very
> well. It's a social pathology that has to do with the abuse of power.

The contrast between outward appearance and inner reality must surely
exacerbate the abuse by further confusing the child. This invalidation
may hold true also for the comparatively innocuous situations in which
the borderline describes merely not fitting in, competing with a favored
or learning-disabled child, or enduring other difficulties common in
normal family life.

ISOLATION AND BRAINWASHING

Another reason abuse can be well hidden is the tendency of the families of borderlines to be isolated and self-contained. The children have no norms against which to judge the pathology of such families, in which feelings are not permitted. "One of the most striking things about growing up for me was that I was never asked how I felt about anything or discussed any feelings," says Melanie. This situation leaves children with no guidelines for controlling emotions. "If my mother got upset, she would run into her room and cry," says Alice.

> I never saw my parents get angry with each other and really deal with it. They would just walk in opposite directions. That didn't show me an acceptable way to deal with my feelings. If I had learned this, maybe things could have been different for me. Instead I would get angry with myself because I didn't know where else to put the feeling.

Feelings that do get through seem to be bad and must be kept secret. Her rage, jealousy, and other unpleasant emotions are part of the evil that the borderline perceives within herself. "My parents always made me feel like a bad person," says Robin. "Nothing I did was ever good enough; I never got praised for anything, and everything that went wrong was my fault." "My father called us stupid and treated us like possessions," says Whitney. "We thought we had no rights and never questioned anything."

BIPARENTAL FAILURE

Family studies in general and abuse histories in particular have helped redirect attention toward the borderline's parents as a couple. Nearly a decade ago, Hallie Frank, Ph.D. (now Zweig-Frank), and Dr. Paris described the implications of one of their borderline family studies: "theorists have given too much attention to the role of the mother and insufficient attention to that of the father and have failed to apply the family systems approach to psychodynamics."[10] The researchers' main finding at the time was that borderline patients remembered their fathers as neglectful.

Now Dr. Paris reports unequivocal findings that borderlines remember *both* parents as uncaring, possibly as a result of psychiatric illnesses of their own. "Since the number of subjects was large," he and Zwieg-Frank write, "and since the findings applied to both male and female borderlines, as well as to both outpatients in a general hospital and university students, the results seem generalizable to borderlines as a whole."[11]

In general, Dr. Gunderson says, borderlines come from "very actively conflicted, chaotic families who create a sustained environment of unpredictability and emotional turmoil." Many studies show preborderline children bringing to school what they have learned at home; they have performance problems that exacerbate their sense of badness and alienation and their desperate search for affection and nurturance.

The Legacy

Researchers conclude family studies of BPD by cautioning that the implications of their results are still unclear and suggesting directions for further research. Like Dr. Siever and his associates, who are trying to isolate biological substrates of BPD in families, Dr. Links and his colleagues are trying to specify developmental factors of the illness. "We've outlined that the next generation of research will have to try to understand more exactly what the etiological factors may be," says Dr. Links, "to measure them more precisely, and I think most importantly, to find factors that we could perhaps moderate to affect the etiology or the course of the disorder."

One such factor is the multigenerational transmission referred to earlier by Dr. Gunderson. Besides looking back at their families without blaming them, borderlines must also recognize and stop abuse or other negative factors they themselves may have passed on.

Emily, for instance, reenacted her family situation quite literally:

> Everything felt out of control, like there was no home base or security. It was frightening to go to bed at night and be scared of the next time my father would threaten me. I was angry with my mother for staying with my father and not protecting me; I wanted her to take me away. But she was even more subservient and docile then than she is now.
>
> And I ended up dominating her, taking on my father's traits. It was a dual thing, a role reversal in which *I* would threaten *her*. Growing up was really confusing and angry and volatile and destructive and horrible, and so was I. But my mother chose to be there, and I had to realize that. Even so, I treated her like a worthless piece of shit. I have a hard time coming to terms with that today. The guilt is endless, if I let it be.

Sharon and her mother, "Gillian," have each been diagnosed as DIB borderlines and express their symptoms similarly. Sharon accepts the diagnosis; like Paige, Gillian believes that she may instead have PTSD, and she remained conflicted about an interview until it was too late. The mother and daughter look alike and do the same work when they haven't quit or been fired. Each is supported by Sharon's stepfather. Both were sexually abused at age four. Both came from broken homes: Gillian's divorced parents farmed her out to uncaring relatives; Sharon's father divorced her mother in Sharon's infancy. The two women have had years of therapy both individually and together.

Sharon's descriptions of her mother imply both how difficult Gillian's life has been and how easy it was to recreate for her daughter:

> When I was small, my mother was on welfare, with the state threatening to take us kids, so she sent my brothers and sisters to live with relatives and kept me with her. She took out her pain on me by beating and neglecting me. Social services kept checking up on her about me. She was so furious with them for thinking her a bad mother that she behaved well in front of them and hit me afterwards. If I was happy around anyone but her, she would hit me for making her feel like a rotten mother.
>
> I would already have had kids if it weren't for this problem. I have changed enough by now to be a very gentle, giving mother. But the first time I got pregnant, my therapists urged me to go to Parents Anonymous. So I have had two abortions instead to give myself time to work everything out so that I won't hurt my kids.

Other borderlines reenact their family backgrounds more subtly. But however she does so, each borderline has grabbed that ball and run with it, having developed attitudes and expectations from her family experiences that nourish her pathology. Therapists therefore carefully highlight such symptoms. The descriptions of Emily and Sharon demonstrate that although they can't change their pasts, borderlines can take charge of their futures.

Notes

1. John G. Gunderson, M.D., paper [negative] read at debate, "Resolved: The Etiology of Borderline Personality Disorder Is Predominantly Biological," 143rd annual meeting of the American Psychiatric Association, New York, 16 May 1990.
2. Some of the major family studies on BPD on which this discussion is based include: Michael H. Stone, M.D., "The Borderline Syndrome: Evolution of the Term, Genetic Aspects, and Prognosis," *American Journal of Psychotherapy*, Vol. 31 (1977), pp. 345–65; John G. Gunderson, M.D., John

Kerr, and Diane Woods Englund, A.C.S.W., "The Families of Borderlines: A Comparative Study," *Archives of General Psychiatry*, Vol. 37 (January 1980), pp. 27–33; Hagop Souren Akiskal, M.D., "Subaffective Disorders: Dysthymic, Cyclothymic and Bipolar II Disorders in the 'Borderline' Realm," *Psychiatric Clinics of North America*, Vol. 4, No. 1 (April 1981), pp. 25–46; Armand W. Loranger, Ph.D., John M. Oldham, M.D., and Elaine H. Tulis, Ph.D., "Familial Transmission of *DSM-III* Borderline Personality Disorder," *Archives of General Psychiatry*, Vol. 39 (July 1982), pp. 795–99; Miron Baron, M.D., Rhoda Gruen, M.A., Lauren Asnis, M.S., and Sally Lord, M.S.W., "Familial Transmission of Schizotypal and Borderline Personality Disorders," *American Journal of Psychiatry*, Vol. 142, No. 8 (August 1985), pp. 927–34; Paul H. Soloff, M.D., and James W. Millward, M.D., "Psychiatric Disorders in the Families of Borderline Patients," *Archives of General Psychiatry*, Vol. 40 (January 1983), pp. 37–44; Patricia M. Schulz, M.S.W., Paul H. Soloff, M.D., Thomas Kelly, A.C.S.W., Merle Morgenstern, M.S.W., Robert Di Franco, M.S.W., and S. Charles Schulz, M.D., "A Family History Study of Borderline Subtypes," *Journal of Personality Disorders*, Vol. 3 (1989), pp. 217–29; Paul S. Links, M.D., Meir Steiner, M.D., Ph.D., and Gail Huxley, R.N., "The Occurrence of Borderline Personality Disorder in the Families of Borderline Patients," *Journal of Personality Disorders*, Vol. 2, No. 1 (1988), pp. 14–20; Joel Paris, David Nowlis, and Ronald Brown, "Developmental Factors in the Outcome of Borderline Personality Disorder," *Comprehensive Psychiatry*, Vol. 29, No. 2 (March/April 1988), pp. 147–50; Mary C. Zanarini, Ed.D., John G. Gunderson, M.D., Margaret F. Marino, M.Ed., Elizabeth O. Schwartz, M.S., and Frances R. Frankenburg, M.D., "*DSM-III* Disorders in the Families of Borderline Outpatients," *Journal of Personality Disorders*, Vol. 2, No. 4 (1988), pp. 292–302; Mary C. Zanarini, John G. Gunderson, Margaret F. Marino, Elizabeth O. Schwartz, and Frances R. Frankenburg, "Childhood Experiences of Borderline Patients," *Comprehensive Psychiatry*, Vol. 30, No. 1 (January-February 1989), pp. 18–25; and Joel Paris, M.D., and Hallie Frank, Ph.D., "Perceptions of Parental Bonding in Borderline Patients," *American Journal of Psychiatry*, Vol. 146, No. 11 (November 1989), pp. 1498–99.

3. Svenn Torgersen, CandPsychol., "Genetic and Nosological Aspects of Schizotypal and Borderline Personality Disorders: A Twin Study," *Archives of General Psychiatry*, Vol. 41 (June 1984), p. 554.

4. Harrison G. Pope, Jr., M.D., Jeffrey M. Jonas, M.D., James I. Hudson, M.D., Bruce M. Cohen, M.D., Ph.D., and John G. Gunderson, M.D., "The Validity of *DSM-III* Borderline Personality Disorder: A Phenomenologic, Family History, Treatment Response, and Long-term Follow-up Study," *Archives of General Psychiatry*, Vol. 40 (January 1983), pp. 23–30.

5. Mary C. Zanarini, Ed.D., John G. Gunderson, M.D., Margaret F. Marino, M.Ed., Elizabeth O. Schwartz, M.S., and Frances R. Frankenburg, M.D., "Psychiatric Disorders in the Families of Borderline Outpatients," in *Family Environment and Borderline Personality Disorder*, ed. Paul S. Links, M.D., M.Sc., F.R.C.P.(C) (Washington, D.C.: American Psychiatric Press, 1990), pp. 74–75.

6. Jeremy M. Silverman, Ph.D., Lynn Pinkham, M.A., Thomas B. Horvath, M.D., Emil F. Coccaro, M.D., Howard Klar, M.D., Stuart Schear, M.A., Seth Apter, M.A., Michael Davidson, M.D., Richard C. Mohs, Ph.D., and Larry J. Siever, M.D., "Affective and Impulsive Personality Disorder Traits in the Relatives of Borderline Personality Disorder Patients," *American Journal of Psychiatry*, in press.

7. Emil F. Coccaro, M.D., Larry J. Siever, M.D., Howard M. Klar, M.D., Gail Maurer, Ph.D., Karen Cochrane, M.Ed., Thomas B. Cooper, M.A., Richard C. Mohs, Ph.D., and Kenneth L. Davis, M.D., "Serotonergic Studies in Patients with Affective and Personality Disorders," *Archives of General Psychiatry*, Vol. 46 (July 1989), pp. 587–99.

8. Paul S. Links, M.D., M.Sc., F.R.C.P.(C), and Heather Munroe Blum, Ph.D., "Family Environment and Borderline Personality Disorder: Development of Etiologic Models," in Links, ed., *Family Environment*, p. 17.

9. Ibid., p. 15.

10. Hallie Frank, Ph.D., and Joel Paris, M.D., "Recollections of Family Experience in Borderline Patients," *Archives of General Psychiatry*, Vol. 38 (September 1981), p. 1034.

11. J. Paris, M.D., and H. Zweig-Frank, Ph.D., "Parental Bonding in Borderline Personality Disorder," in *Borderline Personality Disorder: Etiology and Treatment*, ed. Joel F. Paris, M.D. (Washington, D.C.: American Psychiatric Press, forthcoming).

20

The Metabolism of Abuse

*"We're definitely going to the other extreme and creating a real problem. I'm seeing patients who have been told by their therapists, 'You **must** have been sexually abused, and I'm going to keep at you until you remember!' "*

JOEL PARIS, M.D.

Childhood emotional, physical, and sexual abuse is unique among the factors thought to contribute to the development of BPD. No other factor raises so many issues about the diagnosis and dynamics of BPD, the feelings and perceptions of borderline patients, and the psychiatric profession as a whole. If splitting were not the best metaphor for BPD, childhood abuse might aspire to that status: it is emerging as *the* developmental factor *really* to be reckoned with.

Incestuous sexual abuse in particular is an experience still to be metabolized by therapists as well as by their patients. Besides being a hot topic, it may well go down in the history of the borderline concept as a watershed in its evolution.

The Benefit of the Doubt

Researchers might be expected to doubt the incidence of childhood sexual abuse reported by borderlines for two reasons. One is the latter's reputation for distortion; the other is a psychiatric tradition of misinterpreting sexual abuse descriptions as patient fantasies. Freud disavowed his original "seduction theory" that childhood sexual trauma leads to adult psychological disturbance because it implied an incidence of incest and molestation that he found incredible.[1] Now therapists are suggesting that the seduction theory ought to be dusted off and reexamined.

Among them are researchers whose patients have confirmed their reports of abuse. Out of 53 incest survivors in group treatment studied by Dr. Herman and Emily Schatzow, M.Ed., 74 percent obtained corroborative evidence of their sexual abuse from another source, and another 9 percent found corroborative evidence that was suggestive but not conclusive. Of the remaining 17 percent who found no additional evidence, the majority had made no attempt to obtain it. The authors expressed hope that their study would "lay to rest, if possible, the concern that such recollections might be based upon fantasy."[2]

Dr. Herman has also described the ability of incest survivors to distinguish between parental rules that were strict but fair (enforced by corporal punishment that they considered nonabusive) and those that were unfair.[3] And a study by Westen and his colleagues of the incidence of abuse in adolescent borderline patients likewise supports patient descriptions in several respects.[4]

Studies like these appear to have created a double standard for borderlines' childhood recollections. The rule is now that therapists must believe everything they are told about sexual abuse, and that only. Dr. Paris comments on this illogic:

> When borderlines say that their parents were uninterested in them, everybody still responds, "There they go complaining." I think that if we're going to believe abuse histories, we have to believe the rest of the childhood histories as well. Borderlines do exaggerate, but not that much.

Like "manipulation," "distortion" can exist largely in the mind of the observer.

Qualifying the Findings

What is now questioned instead is the methodologies of the abuse studies themselves. Along with definitions of abuse, designs vary between studies, making it hard to compare the findings. And although more recent studies have compared childhood abuse histories of border-lines to those of other psychiatric patients, "researchers haven't been asking these questions of families of people with no mental illness," says Dr. McGlashan. "That's a next step that may have been taken by one or two investigators already."

Within the borderline realm, "the studies don't take into account that people who are sexually abused tend to have many problems that go along with that," says Dr. Paris. "Their families are crazy, disruptive, chaotic, difficult, you name it." In this sense, focusing on sexual abuse alone distorts the situation. "The biggest factor in my pain is my mother's physical abuse and emotional neglect, much more so than the sexual abuse," says Sharon. "But that may be because I haven't dealt with the sexual abuse yet."

"I see sexual abuse as just another example of inconsistent parenting, the generational confusion as to who is responsible for what and where the boundaries are," says Dr. Hodulik.

One of the common dynamics that is not talked about is that these are terribly lonely, isolated, emotionally abused children, for whom some sexual molestation feels wonderful because somebody is paying attention to them, before it gets really bad.

Some studies have not distinguished sexual abuse from emotional or physical abuse and the witnessing of violence. Other therapists caution that this too distorts the situation: one of cumulative interacting traumata in which the influence of sexual abuse in forming borderline symptom patterns is nevertheless unique. "Sexual abuse is the most invisible and in other ways the most toxic form of trauma because of the tremendous confusion it engenders," says Dr. Herman.

If nonviolent, it can be distorted into a sign of love. Some perpetrators want a sexual response from the child as well, causing the victim to feel as if her mind and body have been colonized in a way that doesn't occur with physi-cal abuse. But it's really simplistic to try to scale these things, even though we do. You have to allow for a multitude of considerations.

The many considerations also include the nature of the sexual viola-tion itself. This is another reason Dr. Paris qualifies the findings:

The studies have failed to take into account the differences between the various kinds of sexual abuse. Instead they lump together all types of inci-dents, making for very high numbers. The amount of harm done varies enormously depending on who the perpetrator was, how often the child was abused, how long it lasted, what was actually done, and whether she could tell somebody and get help.

Molestation by someone other than a relative, for example, would be experienced as a loss of innocence without the betrayal of trust inherent in incest. Dr. Paris's group is now studying sexual abuse in borderlines while correcting for all of these factors, trying to see if its effects exceed those of general family pathology.

The Data

The findings about abuse histories in borderlines, and the implications of these data, are meanwhile very confusing. But even the more methodologically sound studies, many of which suggest that their findings are conservative, have found very high frequencies of such traumata in borderline patients—in some studies, up to 80 percent. Studies comparing reliably diagnosed borderlines to other psychiatric patients have found high rates of physical abuse in all the groups but higher rates of sexual abuse—ranging from about 30 to 70 percent of patients—in the borderlines.[5]

"The traumata that are visited upon most of the people who later become borderline are themselves quite nonspecific and insufficient alone to cause BPD," says Dr. Gunderson.

> Having said that, I am increasingly impressed by how important the abuse experiences are in the creation of BPD. It is possible for people to get a borderline personality without having abuse in their backgrounds, but it nonetheless comes closer to specificity in the etiology of this disorder than any other factor.

The tentative findings are that borderlines are distinguished from other psychiatric patients (including those with BPO) by

- *Sexual* and/or *multiple* abuse: sexual abuse by more than one person (who could be from within or outside the family) and/or sexual combined with physical abuse.
- Neglect as well as abuse (the latter being considered a more likely source of borderline rage), along with a weaker correlation with separation and family chaos.
- The early ages at which the abuse is experienced.

We might note here that although boys and girls in general are at equal risk for physical abuse, sexual abuse is estimated to be suffered by one out of three girls as opposed to one out of ten boys.[6] Sexual abuse also tends to be more prolonged than physical abuse. Drs. Herman and van der Kolk suggest that this factor may account for the prevalence of women among borderline patients.[7]

The patterns of abuse peculiar to either sex need to be teased apart just like its other forms. "Incest causes rage and guilt, but physical abuse does not necessarily cause guilt," says Dr. Stone. "Physically abused children may be more violent than self-destructive." Having grown up in an abusive environment, a boy might have societal reinforcements to distance himself from home and other people, while a girl might instead be encouraged to focus on relationships, increasing her risk for reenacting her victimization and for becoming borderline.

Seeing and Not Seeing

Why are childhood abuse histories in borderlines being studied only now? In this context, as in the sterotyping of borderlines, the psychiatric profession has again acted like the media—this time in "discovering" sensational behavior that has long been available for scrutiny. "I have kicked myself because I have heard sexual abuse histories from my patients for 15 or 20 years but didn't write about it," says Dr. Paris. "I am among those people . . . whose theorizing failed to give abuse the attention it very clearly deserves," writes Dr. Gunderson.[8]

Although many therapists knew and many others may have sensed that their borderline patients had been sexually abused, good data have appeared only within the past few years. This is partly because the definition of BPD has been increasingly tightened. "The older definition of BPD allowed for the nonabused affective-disordered group," says Dr. Stone. "We're seeing more abuse because we have redefined BPD more narrowly in terms of the angry, self-damaging acts, so the definition picks up the abused population."[9]

Dr. Stone suggests three other reasons that abuse is now being highlighted: sample bias in the recent studies showing high incidence; sample bias toward low incidence in the psychoanalytic practices out of which arose developmental theories about BPD; and possible increases in the incidence of abuse over the past several years resulting from more broken homes and stepparenting.[10]

A more obvious reason is that it simply hadn't occurred to many therapists to ask borderlines about their trauma histories. Paige uncovered a good example when she volunteered one summer as an aide at a geriatric state psychiatric institution. "At least eight out of ten women in my group were sexually abused as children," she says.

> They were diagnosed as mentally ill, and their abuse was never dealt with. At 70 or 80 years old, after shock treatments and lobotomies, here they were still talking about what daddy or uncle did in specific detail, with nobody listening.

"Certainly the general awareness of abuse in society has heightened clinicians' interest in and investigation of it," says Dr. Gunderson, "and it has also emboldened and encouraged patients to talk more about something that they might previously have felt was more secretive and foreign." The increase in awareness resulted primarily from the women's movement, which broadened the perspectives of male therapists.

Before feminism forced them to confront it, many therapists did not recognize the particular significance of sexual abuse in the development of BPD. Paige tried raising the issue with one of her therapists, for instance, only to be told that it wasn't important. "In 1985, Dr. Kernberg headed a discussion group at the annual convention of the APA," says Dr. Herman, who has since been invited to lead such a group herself.

> I asked whether he saw a high incidence of sexual abuse in his borderline patients. "Oh yes, I see it all the time," he said, "And I have no idea what to make of it." And then he turned to the next question.
> This is the hallmark of trauma. People see it, and they don't see it. They practice doublethink, disconnecting the knowledge of the experience from its affect and meaning.
> If you look at the psychoanalytical descriptions of many of the borderline defenses or behaviors and the countertransference reactions to them, it's as though the psychoanalysts are describing a traumatic reaction, but they have dissociated the trauma, just like their patients.

Dr. Kernberg replies that over the years since this meeting, his group's review of their data has made them very much aware of the significance of severe traumatic experiences, including abuse, in childhood. As a result, says Dr. Kernberg, "I have changed my views about this matter."

Confirming Theory

Although they have been slow to appreciate the significance of abuse, psychoanalytical psychiatrists are quick to note data that confound their formulations. Years ago they gave up their notion of borderline schizophrenia and revised classical theory to accommodate BPD. Now they have relegated separation-individuation to the mere starting point of a childhood hell prolonged enough to incorporate abuse histories. And like much other empirical evidence about the development of BPD, abuse data are validating some of the psychoanalytical formulations that preceded them.

Drs. Adler and Buie and Dr. Gunderson, for instance, have described borderline aggression as an angry, vengeful reaction to actual, not imagined, mistreatment.* They describe the mistreatment broadly in terms of its time frame and type. "It's essentially generic, the terrible things that happen to these children," says Dr. Adler. "It's part of the same awful continuum to be neglected as to be literally abused." Although he views such developmental factors generically, Dr. Adler has long been alert to the specific effects of abuse. "When a supervisee would present a new patient to me, I would often begin to formulate the antecedents in childhood experience," he says, "and it surprised me how often I would be correct."[11]

The current tendency to scan all of childhood for clues about BPD was prefigured by Stern's 1938 paper on borderlines, which specified that the factors influencing the development of the pathology, including cruelty and brutality, happened constantly over several years rather than being unique experiences.[12] All researchers agree that the childhood abuse of borderline patients was chronic. "Abuse in general is not a single incident," says Dr. Herman. "It's part of a family pattern of either chaos or coercive control."

Dr. Kernberg likewise distinguishes between isolated incidents and prolonged incest, which is an extremely disorganizing experience:

> In this case, incest is no longer a traumatic experience but rather reflects a distortion of *all* interaction processes—a deceptiveness and dishonesty infiltrating all human relationships. It's the tip of an iceberg of pathology. This

*Dr. Kernberg originally viewed aggression as being inborn; surprisingly few therapists are familiar with the reformulation he described earlier.

longstanding severe pathology exists also in the frequently observed physical abuse, drug abuse, alcoholism, and witnessing of chronic violence in the family.

Some therapists documenting and studying childhood trauma believe, on the other hand, that incest and other abuse can't simply be absorbed into existing theory, that it *remains* a traumatic experience and needs to be dealt with as such. While acknowledging separation-individuation and neglect theories, Dr. Perry, Dr. Herman, and their colleagues emphasize that abuse adds the element that was missing.[13]

What therapists *agree* on, then, is that

- A bad childhood environment contributes to the development of BPD.
- Many borderlines have suffered not only deprivation but also childhood trauma, especially sexual abuse.
- This traumatic environment existed for a long time.

What therapists *disagree* on is

- whether abuse has traumatic effects distinct from that of a poor family environment of neglect and loss;
- whether sexual abuse has a uniquely pernicious impact.

Some researchers who would affirm the last two points are trying to rewrite dynamic theory to credit the effects of trauma more fully.

Traumatic Splitting

Saunders and Arnold, for example, argue that many borderline symptoms are not defenses against intrapsychic conflict, as the psychoanalysts would have it, but rather internalizations of actual experiences of abuse.[14] Although this sounds comparatively simplistic, Saunders and Arnold characterize the symptoms as arising out of a relational matrix far more complex than that appealing to psychoanalytical thinkers. The authors therefore propose a theoretical reformulation.*

Their model is well represented by our touchstone symptom, splitting. Within the childhood abuse context, Saunders and Arnold reformulate splitting in terms of its

- *Timing.* Although the primitiveness of splitting suggests that it originates early in childhood, Saunders and Arnold argue that it can arise at

---

*Popular books on adult children of alcoholics likewise explain borderline symptoms as reactions to the trauma of growing up with alcoholic parents. Within this context splitting, for example, reflects the perceived discrepancy between the alcoholic parents' behavior when sober and when drunk.

any point before adolescence due to the devastating impact of chronic abuse within a "safe" family environment.

- *Relational context.* It is not the mother–child relationship that generates splitting, but rather that between the child and the male perpetrator of abuse. The abuse that results from her ignorance, powerlessness, or neglect in this particular situation is what gives the mother's unresponsiveness to the child its connotation of profound betrayal.
- *Status as a defense.* Splitting is less a defense than a repetition of the child's actual experience of abuse, denial, contradictions, and mixed messages. What Saunders and Arnold call "a learned template superimposed on contemporary experience" is activated in the borderline when she anticipates a repetition of her early relationships. The extreme reactions that helped the abused child deal with genuine dangers are inappropriate to similar situations in the present and are labeled pathological in the borderline adult. But if therapists and other outsiders have trouble integrating what they hear about abusers, ask these theorists, how can a child be expected to picture an abuser realistically, integrate her love for and hatred of him, and develop a stable identity of her own?

Splitting can also be explained in terms of another concept discussed by Saunders and Arnold that may apply to borderlines. *Traumatic bonding* is the term used by other researchers for the intense, inextricable attachment to someone who alternates loving connection or dependency with intermittent mistreatment.[15] As well as *perceiving* people as good and bad, the borderline may be *attracted* to those who genuinely alternate affection and abuse, each of which is then exaggerated in the borderline's mind.

Echoing Dr. Siever's earlier reference to splitting as state dependent, Dr. Herman agrees with the explanation just outlined:

> Why would a child fail to integrate idealized or terrifying images of her caretakers? The reason would have to be either constitutional or adaptive. Splitting is adaptive. Children must preserve some sense of connection at any cost, in this case by walling off the image of the abusive figure from the positive one. I think they do so in a state–dependent way, flipping between modes of affection and terror that accurately reflect their environments. They grow up constantly scanning their interpersonal environments to see if they're safe, reading subtleties of expression, posture, gesture, and so forth in an almost uncanny way. But if you ignore the original reason for this behavior, it looks perverse, incomprehensible, and ultimately pathological.*

---

*Linehan's explanation is that scanning results from the borderline's having grown up in an invalidating environment. "Constant invalidation prevents you from trusting yourself," she says. "Any normal person who was reinforced only for seeing and feeling as the environment does would learn to scan it as a result."

We saw in Chapter 11 how an abuse context can help explain borderline self-destructiveness. Saunders and Arnold have reformulated other
borderline symptoms like projective identification, aloneness, and identity diffusion as likewise being secondary to abuse, implicating memory
coding of maladaptive defenses, images of oneself as dirty or evil, dissociation, and other consequences of this trauma.

Controversy and Problems

Childhood abuse has become so hot a topic in BPD that some patients
are using it as a calling card. "Incest is fashionable," says Dr. Kernberg;
"a patient can cash in on it and get huge secondary gain." Examined
more closely, it falls short of implied expectations and creates several
problems.

Despite the impact of abuse on a child's psychological development,
many therapists feel that its specific role in BPD is being exaggerated.
Other psychiatric patients—and probably other people with no mental
illness—were abused as children. We have noted that 33 percent of girls
and 10 percent of boys are at risk for sexual abuse, yet only 2 percent of
the population is borderline. Other contributing factors may account for
the difference.

Many therapists suggest that a neglectful family environment is what
allows the abuse to happen; perhaps the interaction of both factors is
required to cause BPD. Dr. Paris and Zweig-Frank propose, for example, that "abuse may effect BPD through its association with dysfunctional families rather than via a post-traumatic mechanism."[16]

"A high incidence of trauma does not prove that even flagrant abuse is
the cause of BPD," says Dr. Paris. Nor does it account for the borderlines
with no trauma histories: even if 30–70 percent of borderlines suffered
sexual abuse, then equal percentages did not. In the better studies, the
cases of incest account for the lowest percentages.

And some borderlines with especially gruesome trauma histories are
less severely disturbed than others who suffered less abuse. "That's one
of the most puzzling things," says Dr. Paris, "that some borderlines
haven't had it that bad." "It may be," write Zanarini, Dr. Gunderson
and their colleagues, "that the day-to-day presence of an erratic but
nonabusive parent may be equally important in the etiology of BPD."[17]

Focused on sexual abuse histories as a feature distinguishing BPD
from other illnesses, therapists might underestimate the anguish of borderlines who were *not* physically or sexually abused. Out of the border-

lines I have interviewed, the greatest misery and least hope were expressed by Alison, who suffered neglect and enormous emotional deprivation. "Abused children at least are *there,*" she says. "Neglected children don't exist." "The patient I treated the longest, for 14 years, was not abused," says Dr. Adler. "She was much more neglected."

This is why knowledgeable therapists emphasize the *experience* of childhood traumata rather than the actual events. To do so can ultimately be far more validating. "Trauma is now nicely documented in BPD, but what makes someone borderline is the meaning that gets attached to those events," says Dr. Gunderson.

> To cause BPD, abandonment and abuse must occur within nonsupportive, often neglectful contexts that not only fail to help the child adapt to these traumata but also reinforce the harmful misleading messages they cause. The structure of the borderline personality grows out of conflicting views of oneself as a victim of trauma, which produces rage, and as the cause of trauma, which produces a sense of badness.[18]

In this context, the question of which type of trauma is the worst becomes meaningless. "It feels as abusive to a child to be neglected as to be literally abused," says Dr. Adler.

The subjectivity of the traumatic experience fully validates all of its manifestations from mild to severe. It keeps the therapy focused on the patient rather than on the events and explains why some borderlines, to use Dr. Paris' phrase, "haven't had it that bad." And emphasizing the *experience* of incest or molestation in particular gives full weight to sexual abuse while at the same time counteracting its inexcusable stigma. The last thing borderlines need is another black mark on their diagnosis.

Until recently, many therapists found it difficult to ask patients about sexual abuse. Unless a therapist sensitive to the effects of sexual abuse encourages her to discuss it, a patient is still unlikely to report it. We have already seen how difficult such disclosure was for Renée. But just as the DST has been misused in many patients because it seemed to mark depression, now therapists are anxious to latch onto trauma histories immediately and out of context. "We're now in a funny period where we're flipping from a denial to an intrusion phase in a cultural sense," says Dr. Herman.

> Having not recognized the PTSD stressor for so long, we're now pouncing on it like a smoking gun, with no consideration of the patient's ability to integrate this material. The old-fashioned catharsis or exorcism model that recovering the traumatic memories automatically cures the patient simply isn't true.

It may take years of therapy before an abused patient will be able to discuss her traumatic experiences. Therapists are now telling horror stories that premature disclosure of their sexual abuse has caused borderlines to suffer psychotic breaks. If he pressures a patient to confront that experience long before she is ready, a therapist might justifiably be viewed by her as just another abuser expecting her to "put out."

A Healthy Dialectic

Since their fall from power, the developmentophiles have not had an easy time. Invading their turf from one direction, the affectophiles challenge their emphasis on environmental contributors to BPD. Besieging them from another, the—what? traumatophiles?—insist that they have given this factor too little attention. But the controversy surrounding childhood abuse is necessary, as Dr. Herman explains:

> Sexual abuse has been taboo, repressed for so long that it is now entering our consciousness in a very dialectical, polarized way. It *has* to. If it threatens establishment views, it *should,* because therapists have really missed the boat in an important way, one that was predictable in a male-dominated profession with a female patient population. The polarization is healthy and useful as part of how people's ideas change, but it will need eventually to be synthesized.

Drs. Herman and van der Kolk in fact emphasize that if early developmental trauma in particular does alter biological systems, then bringing it to the forefront might help, as Dr. Soloff says, to "wrap up the whole picture."[19]

Zanarini, Dr. Gunderson, and their colleagues conclude a study of the childhood experiences of borderlines by observing that while the complaints of these patients are often exaggerated, "it may also be that they have substantially more reason for the intense pain that they implore others to acknowledge than has generally been recognized."[20] While enriching the process of inquiry, the abuse controversy means that at long last, borderline survivors are indeed being "paid back."

Notes

1. Judith Lewis Herman, M.D., and Emily Schatzow, M.Ed., "Recovery and Verification of Memories of Childhood Sexual Trauma," *Psychoanalytic Psychology*, Vol. 4, No. 1 (1987), p. 1.
2. Ibid., pp. 10–11, 2. Copyright © 1987, Lawrence Erlbaum Associates, Inc.
3. Judith L. Herman, M.D., "Trauma and Neglect in Borderline Personality Disorder," paper read at the 143rd annual meeting of the American Psychiatric Association, New York, 17 May 1990.
4. Drew Westen, Ph.D., Pamela Ludolph, Ph.D., Barbara Misle, B.A., Stephen Ruffins, Ph.D., and Judith Block, M.A., "Physical and Sexual Abuse in Adolescent Girls with Borderline Personality Disorder," *American Journal of Orthopsychiatry*, Vol. 60, No. 1 (January 1990), pp. 55–66.
5. The following studies have shown this range of results: Susan N. Ogata, Ph.D., Kenneth R. Silk, M.D., Sonya Goodrich, Ph.D., Naomi E. Lohr, Ph.D., Drew Westen, Ph.D., and Elizabeth M. Hill, Ph.D., "Childhood Sexual and Physical Abuse in Adult Patients with Borderline Personality Disorder," *American Journal of Psychiatry*, Vol. 147, No. 8 (August 1990), pp. 1008–13; Mary C. Zanarini, John G. Gunderson, Margaret F. Marino, Elizabeth O. Schwartz, and Frances R. Frankenburg, "Childhood Experiences of Borderline Patients," *Comprehensive Psychiatry*, Vol. 30, No. 1 (January/February 1989), pp. 18–25; Paul S. Links, M.D., Meir Steiner, M.D., David R. Offord, M.D., and Allan Eppel, M.B., "Characteristics of Borderline Personality Disorder: A Canadian Study," *Canadian Journal of Psychiatry*, Vol. 33, No. 5 (June 1988), pp. 336–40; Judith Lewis Herman, M.D., J. Christopher Perry, M.P.H., M.D., and Bessel A. van der Kolk, M.D., "Childhood Trauma in Borderline Personality Disorder," *American Journal of Psychiatry*, Vol. 146, No. 4 (April 1980), pp. 490–95. An overview appears in J. Paris, M.D., and H. Zweig-Frank, Ph.D., "A Critical Review of the Role of Childhood Sexual Abuse in the Etiology of Borderline Personality Disorder," unpublished manuscript.
6. Ogata et al., p. 1008.
7. Judith L. Herman, M.D., and Bessel A. van der Kolk, M.D., "Traumatic Antecedents of Borderline Personality Disorder," in *Psychological Trauma*, ed. Bessel A. van der Kolk (Washington, D.C.: American Psychiatric Press, 1987), p. 116.
8. John G. Gunderson, M.D., "New Perspectives on Becoming Borderline," in *Family Environment and Borderline Personality Disorder*, ed. Paul S. Links, M.D., M.Sc., F.R.C.P.(C) (Washington, D.C.: American Psychiatric Press, 1990), p. 153.
9. Michael H. Stone, M.D., "An Integrated, Psychobiological Model of Borderline Personality Disorder," paper read at the 143rd annual meeting of the American Psychiatric Association, New York, 17 May 1990.
10. Michael H. Stone, M.D., "Abuse and Abusiveness in Borderline Personality Disorder," in Links, ed., *Family Environment*, pp. 131–48.
11. Gerald Adler, M.D., paper [negative] read at debate: "Resolved: The Etiology of Borderline Personality Disorder Is Predominantly Biological," 143rd annual meeting of the American Psychiatric Association, New York, 16 May 1990.
12. J. Christopher Perry, M.D., M.P.H., Judith L. Herman, M.D., Bessel A. van der Kolk, M.D., and Lizabeth A. Hoke, Ph.D., "Psychotherapy and Psychological Trauma in Borderline Personality Disorder," *Psychiatric Annals*, Vol. 20, No. 1 (January 1990), p. 33.
13. Ibid., p. 42.
14. Eleanor Saunders, Ph.D., and Frances Arnold, Ph.D., "Borderline Personality Disorder and Childhood Abuse: Revisions in Clinical Thinking and Treatment Approach," Work in Progress, Working Paper Series, No. 51 (Wellesley, Mass.: The Stone Center for Developmental Services and Studies, Wellesley College).
15. Saunders and Arnold cite Don Dutton and Susan Lee Painter, "Traumatic Bonding: The Development of Emotional Attachments in Battered Women and Other Relationships of Intermittent Abuse," *Victimology: An International Journal*, Vol. 6, Nos. 1–4 (1981), pp. 139–55.
16. J. Paris, M.D., and H. Zweig-Frank, Ph.D., "Parental Bonding in Borderline Personality Disorder," in *Borderline Personality Disorder: Etiology and Treatment*, ed. Joel F. Paris, M.D. (Washington, D.C.: American Psychiatric Press, forthcoming).

17. Mary C. Zanarini, Ed.D., John G. Gunderson, M.D., Margaret F. Marino, M.Ed., Elizabeth O. Schwartz, M.S., and Frances R. Frankenburg, M.D., "Psychiatric Disorders in the Families of Borderline Outpatients," in *Family Environment and Borderline Personality Disorder,* ed. Paul S. Links, M.D., M.Sc., F.R.C.P.(C) (Washington, D.C.: American Psychiatric Press, 1990), p. 82.
18. John G. Gunderson, M.D., paper [negative] read at debate: "Resolved: The Etiology of Borderline Personality Disorder Is Predominantly Biological," 143rd annual meeting of the American Psychiatric Association, New York, 16 May 1990.
19. Herman and van der Kolk, p. 118.
20. Zanarini et al., "Childhood Experiences," p. 24.

2 1

The Social Smorgasbord

"Most people with BPD will present with whatever happens to be the symptom of the day. For example, several years ago when The Exorcist hit the movie screens, we saw a tremendous run in the clinics of people who were demonically possessed. Many of these people would have met the current criteria for BPD."

CRAIG JOHNSON, PH.D.

*T*he popular media would love for us to believe that BPD is a new illness exemplifying the 1990s. We often see the theory that our unstructured, fragmented, rapidly changing society is the perfect medium for the growth of borderline personalities. Dr. Hellerstein has even asked (perhaps rhetorically) whether any time but ours could even produce the illness.[1]

As examples of this theory, various modern celebrities have been referred to—however rightly or wrongly—as borderline. The paradigm of the condition is thought to be Marilyn Monroe; others so designated have included Samuel Beckett, Zelda Fitzgerald, Brenda Frazier, Jimi Hendrix, Janis Joplin, Kierkegaard, Gelsey Kirkland, T.E. Lawrence, Sylvia Plath, Anne Sexton, and Thomas Wolfe. Fictional and film characters have likewise been called borderline. These borderlines are free of stigma; their illness has only increased their popularity with the public.

The psychiatric community is well aware of the social aspects of mental illness, including BPD,[2] and their relevance to diagnosis. It is widely acknowledged, for instance, that one culture's pathology is another's normalcy; the same could actually be said for professions within a culture. Beyond this, therapists must acknowledge social influences almost by default: psychoananlytical theories can't be proven, but social factors can, and they give rise to many of the familial conditions inherent in developmental theories.

Personality disorders are especially susceptible to social influences because each diagnosis depends considerably on how the patient relates to her environment. Borderlines are, of course, hypersensitive in this respect, and at least superficially they do seem to represent cultural trends. And aside from defining and exacerbating the expression of its symptoms, social factors may well contribute indirectly to the development of BPD itself.

Our Borderline Society

Some theorists believe that mental illness represents, and therefore metaphorically expresses, social pathology. Thus the neurotic supposedly exemplified the repression of Freud's time and the schizophrenic the rejection of society for individual realities in the 1960s. In this context, BPD is a metaphor not only for psychiatry but also for society as a whole.

Everyday life elicits thoughts, feelings, and behaviors from many people that resemble borderline symptoms. As a result of constantly shifting, at times extremely questionable norms and values, people in general feel unconnected to the past and future and uncertain how to respond. Boredom, disillusionment, and cynicism arise out of hopelessness that society can improve.

Many people seek yet seem incapable of intimacy, tormented by the tension between love and hate that enlivens close relationships. Responding to psychoanalytical encouragement, more of them are acting out these and other emotions. Extreme examples are the rates of crime, child abuse, and substance abuse, which have risen rapidly.

The high incidence of homosexuality (as well as bisexuality and "perversion") in BPD evidences the confusion caused by the sexual revolution and the greater acceptance of alternative lifestyles. The contradictions in the illness reflect society's polarizations, mixed messages, and hypocrisy, the instability its mobility and fast pace.

Family life has unraveled in the past few generations. High divorce rates have caused fathers to disappear or yield to stepfathers (although the incidence of incest may not have correspondingly increased, stepfathers are far more likely than natural fathers to commit this crime). The extended family has shrunk into the nuclear family and now single-parent households. Family members live farther apart without keeping in touch. Because many more women work, day care staffs are replacing parents as the primary caretakers of infants and small children.

All this social disruption is a result of modernization, and as we have learned, BPD was first recorded by psychiatrists a generation or so after the onset of the industrial revolution. It seems, then, that BPD is to some extent a product of urban society.

This is the position of Dr. Paris, who believes that as major determinants of the behavior seen in personality disorders, sociocultural factors deserve more attention:

> This is quite speculative, but in traditional societies, people are given identities, have clearcut social roles, do what their parents do, and don't have to decide everything. Those societies exact a price in terms of psychiatric problems, but you don't see BPD. I can't prove this because I haven't done a proper survey, but it's an impression shared by many people that BPD has a lot to do with the rapid pace of modernization and change.

Dr. Paris associates BPD with the tripling of the suicide rate in young adults (mostly males) that has occurred over the past generation.

A Curious Perversion

Among the "many people" to whom Dr. Paris refers are, however, some dissenters. "The concept that personality disorders must be psychosocially determined is a very curious perversion of conceptualization in our field," says Dr. Akiskal. "Nothing can be further from the truth."[3] Of course no single factor determines these illnesses, but Dr. Akiskal's is not the only valid objection to generalizations about sociocultural influences.

Social factors affect everyone in the population, only 2 percent of which is borderline. The majority of psychiatric patients have *other* disorders. Although likewise exceptionally vulnerable, these patients are not showing borderline responses to social pathology, presumably because of constitutional and developmental differences.

Sociocultural influence is especially difficult to assess partly because it must be teased apart from such biological or environmental factors. Most borderlines are women, for example, the accepted explanation being that borderline men are culturally conditioned to express their illness differently. "But are these just culture-bound differences or actually a different kind of condition?" asks Dr. Siever.

> There are reasons to think that both the biological and developmental aspects of the disorder could be different. Maybe some of the brain neurotransmitter systems are modulated differently in males and females. Maybe developmental factors of abuse play a special role with women.

Similarly, we can ask what kind of factor abuse actually represents. "The rate of incest reflects male dominance in the culture," says Dr. Herman. But this observation does not make the social factor ultimately more important than the developmental one in causing BPD.

A social factor is one that borderlines actually *do* perceive and react to, not what theorists *think* they react to just because it's in the air. The average person might suppose, for instance, that by dramatically confusing and ill-defining their roles, the feminist movement exacerbated identity problems in women that made them prone to BPD. Or perhaps it prompted women to renounce natural interdependency for autonomy, thus making relationships more difficult to maintain.

But suppose the incidence of BPD were thought to have *decreased* during this time. The average person might then think that along with increased paternal involvement in child rearing, today's greater independence, more acceptable emotional expression, and enhanced self-esteem for women have benefited the entire family.*

Placing it in a social context makes the already diffuse borderline concept fizzle toward meaninglessness. Theorists see *everything* about today's society contributing to BPD. Society offers so enormous a smorgasbord of possibilities that one can pick and choose influences to support or refute any thesis. This is why history is subject to reinterpretation and why if borderline symptoms were described to almost anybody, that person could explain them culturally.

---

*Data actually suggest that the feminist movement has reduced psychiatric illness in women. "The problem is that borderlines may be an especially sensitive group of women who don't follow general trends," says Dr. Paris. "Since the 1960s, the frequency of suicide attempts among women has increased."

A New Epidemic?

Commemorating the 100th anniversary of the National Geographic Society a few years ago, Russell Baker's column in the *New York Times* identified, with brilliant precision, the reason that today's children don't know geography. Our increasingly permissive society, Baker explained, allows modern children to satisfy their natural curiosity about the human body simply by consulting television or other readily available media that feature nudity. Unlike previous generations of giggling voyeurs, today's children need not search for naked people in back issues of *National Geographic.*[4]

Baker's thesis is a delightfully plausible selection from the social smorgasbord that every middle-aged reader can cheerfully confirm. The same cannot be said for many reasoned theories about how social patterns affect this or that, which are sometimes equally questionable and always considerably less fun.

Millon believes that we have what he calls "a contemporary epidemic of BPD," one that he attributes largely to "two broad sociocultural trends that have come to characterize much of Western life this past quarter century."[5] One is the emergence of social customs that exacerbate faulty parent–child relationships, the other the diminished influence of other factors that in earlier times would have compensated for this problem.

Nobody knows for sure, however, whether this epidemic is new or whether therapists are finding more BPD because they are looking harder with better diagnostic criteria. References to an epidemic remind me of the "discovery" of bulimia nervosa in the late 1970s, when I was interviewing women who had hidden their binge-vomiting for up to 30 years.* That BPD wasn't as apparent several years ago doesn't necessarily mean that it wasn't widespread. Perhaps much acting out took place behind the same closed doors that hid the incidence of childhood sexual abuse.

More important for our present purpose, a thesis such as Millon's blurs the distinction between incidence and etiology. Millon's explanation implies that like other pathological aspects of modern life, the two

---

*In *Fasting Girls* (Cambridge: Harvard University Press, 1988), Joan Jacobs Brumberg likewise shows that anorexia nervosa, which is also considered a purely contemporary phenomenon, was prefigured by the habits of medieval ascetics and first emerged as a modern illness in the Victorian era.

trends he identifies are both unprecedented and among the most relevant social influences on BPD.

This premise ignores the crucial factor already mentioned by Dr. Gunderson: it is not events that contribute to the development of BPD, but how the susceptible person *experiences* them. (In a psychiatric conference lecture, I have likewise suggested that it is each patient's experience of a mental disorder itself, rather than just the symptoms, that it is crucial to understand fully.[6])

The same holds true for social factors. We assert confidently, for example, that no horror in history compares to the prospect of nuclear holocaust. Would that we could return to the Middle Ages and debate that point with a survivor of the Black Death! To suggest that modern society is uniquely stressful is grossly to underestimate the very sophistication that produced it.

A predisposition to BPD could be exacerbated by *any* fast-paced, unstructured society lacking alternative sources of solace and nurturance to compensate for deficiencies in family life. But ours is not the only such society to have existed over the past few centuries. To use an example that might surprise readers, let us go to Victorian England and see what *other* social factors unique to *that* society might have helped two women to develop BPD.

Two Victorian Borderlines

We meet Miss Wade living in London. Like many borderlines, she has felt compelled to communicate "what [her] life has been" and so has written a brief autobiography. Miss Wade grew up with nine other girls living with a woman who claimed to be her grandmother. She writes,

> I must have been about twelve years old when I began to see how determinedly those girls patronised me. I was told I was an orphan. There was no other orphan among us; and I perceived (here was the first disadvantage of not being a fool) that they conciliated me in an insolent pity, and in a sense of superiority. I did not set this down as a discovery, rashly. I tried them often. I could hardly make them quarrel with me. When I succeeded with any of them, they were sure to come after an hour or two, and begin a reconciliation. I tried them over and over again, and I never knew them wait for me to begin. They were always forgiving me, in their vanity and condescension. Little images of grown people!
>
> One of them was my chosen friend. I loved that stupid mite in a passion-

ate way that she could no more deserve than I can remember without feeling ashamed of, thought I was but a child. She had what they called an amiable temper, an affectionate temper. She could distribute, and did distribute pretty looks and smiles to every one among them. I believe there was not a soul in the place, except myself, who knew that she did it purposely to wound and gall me!

Nevertheless, I so loved that unworthy girl that my life was made stormy by my fondness for her. . . . When we were left alone in our bedroom at night, I would reproach her with my perfect knowledge of her baseness; and then she would cry and cry and say I was cruel, and then I would hold her in my arms till morning: loving her as much as ever, and often feeling as if, rather than suffer so, I could so hold her in my arms and plunge to the bottom of a river—where I would still hold her after we were both dead.

The rest of Miss Wade's account complains of the "slights and wrongs . . . trials and vexations . . . innumerable distresses and mortifications" she endures from others, her perception of which eventually causes her to destroy her one chance for happiness with a gentleman to whom she is briefly engaged.

As the quality of her writing might suggest, Miss Wade is not a real person. She is a creation of Charles Dickens; her account forms Chapter 21, "The History of a Self-Tormentor," in Book Two of his novel *Little Dorrit*.[7] In Miss Wade, Dickens transcended his characteristic ineptitude in creating female characters to portray what appears to be a borderline with symptoms of narcissistic personality disorder.

Therapists might argue that it's ridiculous to use a fictional character to suggest that a psychiatric illness existed in another society. But a fictional character is really no more subjective than a therapist's report of a case and no less legitimate than much of what has passed for research on BPD in this century. An unusual creation for this most perceptive and socially conscious novelist, Miss Wade might be more representative of some of her contemporaries* than could any few case histories.

But we're not concerned here with the analysis of one borderline, or even with whether she actually existed. The issue is whether such a person *could* have existed in the Victorian age, and if so, whether her illness *could* have been aggravated by sociocultural factors that do not affect modern borderlines.

Miss Wade has no family and refers to herself only as what she is not—"not a fool" and "not like other people." She accepts her work as a governess and her later engagement less by choice than as "despicable" situations simply placed before her.

---

* *Little Dorrit* was first published in 1857. Although the action is set 30 years earlier, Dickens specifies in his preface that the society depicted in the novel very much reflects his own time.

At different points, Miss Wade threatens to run away "alone, [walking] night and day" and to "burn my sight away by throwing myself into the fire." Her rage, envy and misery appear alternately as "black despondent brooding" and as sullen obstinacy used as "a sharp retort" that "made [her] feel independent."

Having been "altogether bound up [first] in the one girl" and later with her fiancé, Miss Wade is "tormented beyond endurance" by jealousy. " 'You don't know what I mean by hating,' " she says in reference to a soundrel who rejects her. " 'You can't know.' " Spying upon this man and his bride-to-be is, she says, "one of the few sources of entertainment left to me."

Miss Wade finds " 'no pleasure in anything but keeping me as miserable, suspicious, and tormenting as herself,' " agrees another character, one of several in the novel whose statements corroborate the impression created by her account. She is " 'fitful and uncertain to a fault,' " says a second character, and someone who " 'writhes under her life,' " says a third. " 'A woman more angry, passionate, reckless, and revengeful never lived.' "

The reader is inclined to question this last statement, however, when Miss Wade comes upon a younger woman who is more prototypically borderline. Tattycoram is a foundling adopted by a kindly couple, the Meagleses, to be a maid for their sweetly spoiled daughter. Like "Pet," the daughter's nickname, "Tattycoram" was fondly invented by the family to replace "Harriet Beadle," the foundling hospital's equivalent of "Jane Doe."

All that the family asks of Tattycoram is reflective delay—that she "count five and twenty" before blowing up. Tattycoram has tantrums because although she recognizes that Pet's parents " 'make a fool of her, they spoil her,' " she hates and envies Pet for thinking of " 'nothing but herself.' "

> "She was younger than her young mistress, and would she remain to see *her* always held up as the only creature who was young and interesting, and to be cherished and loved? No. She wouldn't, she wouldn't, she wouldn't!"

The Meagles' patience with her implies that Tattycoram already has much of what she wants and simply projects her own selfishness upon Pet. But Tattycoram feels a sense of injustice that " 'occasionally gets the better of better remembrances,' " as Mr. Meagles says, " 'you must have the unfortunate temperament of the poor, impetuous girl herself, before you can fully understand it.' "

"A sullen, passionate girl!" writes Dickens. When Miss Wade comes upon her, Tattycoram seems possessed: sobbing, raging, plucking at her lips "with an unsparing hand" and "pinching her neck, freshly disfigured with great scarlet blots" because she has been left alone. She claims that her misery does not " 'signify to any one' " and cries, " 'I am ill-used, I am ill-used, I am ill-used!' " Reminded by Miss Wade of her dependent position, Tattycoram replies, " 'I don't care for that. I'll run away. I'll do some mischief. I won't bear it; I can't bear it; I shall die if I try to bear it!' "

Both women view this unbearable state as a sickness. Miss Wade stands "with her hand upon her own bosom, looking at the girl, as one afflicted with a diseased part might curiously watch the dissection and exposition of an analogous case." While acting out the feelings that Miss Wade has repressed, Tattycoram complains that at times she does not wish to control herself:

"Go away from me, go away from me! When my temper comes upon me, I am mad. I know I might keep it off if I only tried hard enough, and sometimes I do try hard enough, and at other times I don't and won't."

Unlike Miss Wade, Tattycoram knows that her feelings contribute to her distortions, and rather than hating consistently, she splits people. In this scene, for instance, Tattycoram "rage[s] and battle[s] with all the force of her youth and fulness of life" and sinks to the floor in a repentant heap. Having thus relieved her feelings, Tattycoram decides instead that *she* is evil and the Meagleses are good. She continues:

"What have I said! I knew when I said it, it was all lies. They think I am being taken care of somewhere, and have all I want. They are nothing but good to me. I love them dearly; no people could ever be kinder to a thankless creature than they always are to me. Do, do go away, for I am afraid of you. I am afraid of myself when I feel my temper coming, and I am as much afraid of you. Go away from me, and let me pray and cry myself better!"

No wonder Tattycoram is afraid of Miss Wade: the latter validates all her distortions and helpless rage.

Miss Wade literally seduces Tattycoram from her family: she is told by Mr. Meagles that he is " 'old enough to have heard of such' " behavior as lesbianism. She has " 'passion fiercer than yours, and temper more violent than yours,' " he warns Tattycoram. But the latter is " 'bursting with hate of the whole house,' " stamping her foot and anxious to be " 'torn to pieces,' " as she later declares, rather than return. She and Miss Wade therefore begin sharing their misery, as another character later observes:

As each of the two handsome faces looked at the other, Clennam felt how
each of the two natures must be constantly tearing the other to pieces. . . .
each proudly cherishing her own anger; each, with a fixed determination,
torturing her own breast, and torturing the other's.*

In sheltering Tattycoram, Miss Wade suffers the fate dreaded by all
borderlines: that of repulsing someone close to her by exposing her true
self. Horrified by this embodiment of what she might someday become,
Tattycoram seizes responsibility for her distortions and returns to the
Meagleses, declaring, " 'I am bad enough, but not so bad as I was indeed.' " From seeing in Miss Wade her " 'own self grown ripe,' " Tattycoram may instinctively have grasped the possibility that her rage and
impulsivity will eventually subside, as happens to many borderlines (others of whom do, in fact, "mature" into narcissists). Still capable of feeling
"glow and rapture," Tattycoram enjoys that state upon her welcome
home.

Where did Dickens come up with these women? Why did he so
carefully depict borderline symptoms in two minor characters in a long,
difficult novel? Could he have thought that they might be familiar to his
readers?

Clearly Dickens based some of his important characters on people he
knew, including his parents and sister-in-law as well as some recognizable public figures. He referred to the "fasting women and girls" of his
time, as anorexics were then called, and quite possibly he came across a
few Miss Wades and Tattycorams as well. (Their symptoms were apparent enough for Falret to have described them explicitly.) For several
reasons, Dickens' time as well as ours was well suited to aggravate borderline pathology.

A Turbulent Age

The Victorian age was a turbulent epoch of massive legislative reforms
and local and distant revolutions. Emphasizing foreign and imperial affairs, Britain fought wars with Russia, China, Afghanistan, and Dutch
South Africa while maintaining the territorial expansion that created the

---

*According to Dr. Paris, Miss Wade fulfills *DSM-III-R* but not DIB criteria for BPD because she
threatens to but does not actually self-mutilate. Could using another person instead of a razor to hurt
oneself qualify as self-mutilation in this context? No, says Dr. Paris, "it is exactly on the interface of inner
suffering and acting out that social factors are operative . . . the inner structure of character does not
change, just the behavioral manifestations." But surely its different expressions over time and between
cultures do not illegitimatize the dynamics of the symptom itself.

Empire. Back home, the extension of railway lines transformed commerce and industry and profoundly affected the lives of all classes. Along with the development of steamships, the railways enormously increased communication that stimulated the exchange of ideas and provided for a rapid development of civilization and culture. The scientific and medical discoveries of the age alone still profoundly influence our lives today.

But as Dickens wrote of the French Revolution, his own age was "the worst of times" as well as "the best of times," one whose social truths were exposed by the great popular novelists, poets and essayists.

Although Dickens' characters alone make a great case for the merits of acting out, we usually think of the Victorians as repressed. But as Steven Marcus has documented in *The Other Victorians*,[8] repression was merely a veneer over a thriving underground of prostitution (especially of children), perversion, pornography, crime, and opium dens. Evidence clearly indicates that the sexual abuse of young children was widely recognized, tolerated, and even encouraged.[9]

The shift from farm to factory in the 19th century destroyed many families, leaving their children homeless. Unprotected in an unstable society, girls as young as five were commonly lured into brothels to be raped. Impoverished children not earning money as sex objects labored at other jobs. Dickens himself never fully recovered from having been removed from school by his family and packed off to London to work in a rat-infested shoe blacking factory while his father loafed at home. In the city Dickens lived alone in a rented room, spending his share of his salary on pastries, bullied by homosexual advances from his co-workers, humiliated beyond endurance, his dreams shattered.

Although apparently intact, Victorian family life for middle- and upper-class children was not necessarily more nurturing. Some were overindulged into helplessness like Pet; some were consigned to nannies; many had lost their mothers in childbirth. Marriages were arranged; husbands were unfaithful, and the more fortunate illegitimate offspring spent their entire childhoods in exile at hellish boarding schools.

Still other children had upbringings that were abusively strict. Art critic John Ruskin, for example, describes the hours he spent each Sunday in the sitting room staring at the patterned carpet while his parents silently read Scripture. But organized religion, which dominated everyday Victorian life, had been staggered by works like Charles Lyell's *Principles of Geology* (later to be complemented by Charles Darwin's *The Origin of Species by Means of Natural Selection*), which made it impossible still to interpret the Bible literally.

The aspect of Victorian life most relevant to Miss Wade and Tattycoram is their illegitimacy and its implications within that society.

" 'What your broken plaything is as to birth, I am,' " Miss Wade tells Mr. Meagles. " 'She has no name, I have no name. Her wrong is my wrong.' " This bond of misery is the source of their vague sense of identity: Dickens describes Tattycoram as being like glass "uncertain of hue" where "deep-stained" and "now like fire and now like harmless water drops" where clear. It defines their sense of badness and alienation and is the source of their great suspicion. " 'I used to think, when I got into that state, that people were all against me because of my first beginning,' " says Tattycoram, " 'and the kinder they were to me, the worse fault I found in them.' "

This perception, like those of many borderlines, is a bit of truth perceived accurately but blown emotionally all out of proportion. Before they even select a child, the Meagleses expect her to have a " 'temper a little defective.' " A perceived need to allow for such presumed deficiencies may likewise have inspired the kindnesses bestowed upon Miss Wade. In rejecting this human frailty in people who treat them well, both women hurt others but most of all themselves.

I haven't the space here to document the richness of these characterizations, much less to discuss in detail the borderline symptoms set forth. Nor does this brief sketch of Victorian society convey the profound stresses of the time. But Miss Wade and Tattycoram do illustrate how one social factor in particular could indeed interact with an "unhappy temper" and a deprived childhood to cause BPD.

The distinction between the sense of badness that haunts modern borderlines and that felt by Miss Wade and Tattycoram is that the latter is grounded in a clearly defined social circumstance. As such it shows how the argument for the modernity of BPD could be turned around. Modern America is (supposedly) a classless society in which no particular importance is attached to being born out of wedlock. In a society in which illegitimacy carries no taint, a prescient Victorian psychiatrist might have asked, how could someone feel evil enough and uncertain enough of her identity to be diagnosed as borderline? If we looked at modern borderlines from that perspective, if we did not know that an overwhelming sense of badness could exist ill-defined, with no clearcut social precipitant, we might likewise be unconvinced.

Earlier Modernism

Marcus refers to the dominant character type of the 19th-century middle class as showing "covert and unacknowledged contradictions of character and of the structure of individual self-hood that are connected in very deep and complex ways with the historical character of the society in which they were played out and with its large contradictions."[10] He traces an intellectual discourse that extends over most of the 19th century, ending with Walter Pater's conclusion to the 1873 edition of *The Renaissance*. This "specimen of modernism" is paraphrased by Marcus as stating several contemporary themes, among them that "our mental existence fines down to no more than a succession of discrete, evanescent impressions. Individual identity is unstable; communication with others is an impossible illusion."

Throughout most of the 19th century, Marcus argues, the great Victorian thinkers shared an uncannily accurate "prefiguration in thought and culture of what in the last thirty years or so we have begun to see being acted out in the lives of large numbers of individuals in advanced or late capitalist society and certain institutions peculiar to it." The time period of large-scale acting out is basically the same one pinpointed by Millon—but the *social forces* that Marcus considers responsible were first set forward in the writings of Thomas Carlyle, who was born in 1795.*

It is hardly coincidental that the sociocultural factors apparently most relevant to BPD began exerting their influence in the 19th century, when borderlines were first well described. Certainly these conditions have been aggravated over the last generation, but to suggest that ours is the only "borderline society" is to close off a potentially fruitful line of etiological inquiry.

If we consider the masses of people whose lives were completely transformed during the Victorian age, if we look at other societies in which turbulence and confusion perhaps took different forms (or comparable social factors overwhelmed simpler people), we really must wonder whether the borderline epidemic is, in fact, one that we can own.

Notes

1. David Hellerstein, "Border Lines," *Esquire* (November 1982), p. 133.
2. A review of some social factors that could contribute to BPD appears in Roy R. Grinker, Sr., Beatrice Werble, and Robert C. Drye, "Society, Culture and the Borderline," in *The Borderline Syndrome: A Behavioral Study of Ego-Functions* (New York: Basic Books, 1968), pp. 163–71. See also J. Paris, M.D., "Suicidality in Borderline Personality Disorder," early draft of chapter in *Borderline Personality Disorder: Etiology and Treatment* ed. Joel F. Paris, M.D. (Washington, D.C.: American Psychiatric Press, forthcoming); and "Personality Disorders, Parasuicide, and Culture," early draft of article in press at *Transcultural Psychiatric Research Review* (1991).

*Dickens' having created Miss Wade and Tattycoram in the 1850s but located them a generation earlier lends timelessness to their symptoms that transcends social factors entirely.

3. Hagop S. Akiskal, M.D., paper [affirmative] read at debate, "Resolved: The Etiology of Borderline Personality Disorder Is Predominantly Biological," 143rd annual meeting of the American Psychiatric Association, New York, 16 May 1990.

4. Russell Baker, "Naked Ignorance," *New York Times*, January 16, 1988.

5. Theodore Millon, Ph.D., "On the Genesis and Prevalence of the Borderline Personality Disorder: A Social Learning Thesis," *Journal of Personality Disorders*, Vol. 1, No. 4 (1987), p. 355.

6. Janice M. Cauwels, Ph.D., "Eating Disorders: Shared Symptoms, Unique Experiences," paper read at The Michael M. Axinn Fourth Annual Memorial Conference, "Eating Disorders: A Current Perspective," North Shore University Hospital–Cornell University Medical College, Manhasset, N.Y., 19 May 1989.

7. Quotations in this discussion are from Book 1, Chapters 2, 16, and 27, and Book 2, Chapters 9, 20, 21, and 33 of *Little Dorrit*.

8. Steven Marcus, *The Other Victorians: A Study of Sexuality and Pornography in Mid-Nineteenth Century England* (New York: Norton, 1985).

9. Florence Rush, "A Victorian Childhood," *The Best Kept Secret: Sexual Abuse of Children* (Englewood Cliffs, N.J.: Prentice-Hall, 1980), pp. 56–73.

10. Steven Marcus, *Freud and the Culture of Psychoanalysis: Studies in the Transition from Victorian Humanism to Modernity* (Boston: Allen & Unwin, 1984), p. 193. Additional quotations in the text are from pages 205 and 208 of this edition, all by permission of Routledge.

2 2

Final Common Pathways

"Keep in mind that many borderline patients develop this disorder without identifiable traumatic childhood stresses. The disorder is a final common pathway. It is not easy to become borderline."

JOHN G. GUNDERSON, M.D.[1]

Now we must switch gears. We have examined the definition of BPD, the attempts to discriminate it from other illnesses, and the particular schools of thought about its origins. In doing so, we have been following a historical pattern, as Dr. Stone observes: "Over the past several years, the definitions of BPD have become tighter, while the etiology has meanwhile expanded to include all kinds of things."[2] The most accurate way to view the illness, as Dr. Gunderson says above, is as an integration of these separate areas of study.

As might be expected at this level of complexity, *integration* does not mean *consensus*. Integration has resulted merely in etiological models of BPD that are broader than those we have seen so far and yet offer an advantage over them. "One stimulating aspect of BPD is that it really is at the intersection between developmental explanations and neurological hypotheses," says Dr. Cowdry. "The challenge is that of trying to fit those hypotheses together rather than viewing them as antagonistic and mutually exclusive." Here is yet another meaning of *borderline*. Besides being a model of where psychiatry has been over the past century, BPD also offers a model of where it can ideally go.

It is within this context that the developmentophiles, the affectophiles, and everybody in between cease their squabbling and start to look their best.

Biological Psychoanalysts

On the one hand, psychoanalytical psychiatrists acknowledge the influence of constitutional factors in the development of BPD. The nature of their theorizing makes this unavoidable. "However seductive they may seem," writes Dr. Stone, "psychoanalytic theories have not been able to demonstrate rigorously the influence of psychodynamic factors, and there seems no alternative but to underline the importance of constitutional and sociocultural factors."[3]

We have already seen Dr. Kernberg emphasize the importance of nature as well as nurture. "Undoubtedly some subgroups of borderline patients have genetic predispositions," he says.

> One subgroup suffers from minimal brain dysfunction, which may be very important in creating spatial distortions during early separation-individuation. The sense of time and space are very much influenced by cognitive functions. There are constitutional differences in reactivity to anxiety, to stimuli, the degree to which an individual hypo or hyperreacts—what used to be called temperament. So etiological factors are not isolated summations but somehow function in an integrated way affecting personality development.

It is hardly surprising that the experience of events contributing to the development of BPD can vary so dramatically. These possibilities explain both borderlines' insistence that their emotions are uniquely intense and therapists' emphasis on their distortions.

Psychoanalytical Biologists

But it is perhaps surprising that psychiatrists interested in biological research, on the other hand, acknowledge the importance of developmental factors in BPD. Dr. Andrulonis, for example, who enjoys high prestige among the affectophiles, feels that environmental factors are definitely more important than any type of organic or genetic factors in BPD whether in males or females. Tragic histories of abuse, neglect, separation, and rejection predominate in my research over the organic factors.

Other biologically and phenomenologically oriented investigators likewise emphasize psychodynamic—even traditional—approaches to patient care. This too may be unavoidable, depending on how much success they have had in uncovering biological markers, tracing substrates, or administering pharmacotherapy to borderline patients.

Putting It All Together

Just about any specialist in BPD will therefore have some working model of the illness that combines the elements we have studied. What is interesting is how the different therapists integrate them.

Dr. Stone's list of contributing factors includes a compromised central nervous system, aggression that is either innate or caused by violence or abuse, abnormal neurotransmitter levels, incest, alcoholism, and bipolar disorder. These all lead to irritability and result in a decreased ability to modulate emotions.[4]

Like Dr. Gunderson's earlier comments about trauma, a more detailed model offered by Fred Pine, Ph.D.,[5] emphasizes the borderline's experience of being overwhelmed, which has no one-to-one relationship with actual events. It can be described as follows:

The child who will become borderline has some early handicap, perhaps neuropsychological problems or early illness and pain. She is left with a low ability to screen out environmental events to a comfortable level of experience or to sort out the experiences that get through.

This inborn deficit reduces her capacity to cope with an excess of unpleasant stimuli to which she is exposed during childhood. She is afflicated with overwhelming, ongoing traumata from any of a variety of sources: intrusive or destructive parents, the pain or illness itself, too much neglect that results in overwhelming neediness.

All of this constitutes a stimulus overload: the child is overwhelmed by psychic stress. She has no way to control this barrage because it is too amorphous to contain and because she has no language yet with which to label it. Thus overwhelmed, she cannot develop the ego functions necessary to reach healthy maturity.

The most important of these is the development of trust in her caretakers and, by extension, the world. This lack of trust may underlie all the other developmental failures. Most children learn during periods of contentment, or at least while they anticipate gaining some control over bad feelings or events. The borderline has no time to enjoy such good periods. Unable to relieve, much less gratify, her needs, she cannot believe that she will ever feel better, so she instead uses any means available to meet them immediately or to still her anxieties.

Most of us learn to manage our bad feelings by experimenting with techniques that might work better and thereby developing effective, mature psychological defenses. Panic-stricken by her overwhelming emotions, the borderline instead clings to her infantile coping mechanisms. It is too risky to try anything else.

Others experience distress as a signal to activate their coping mechanisms. Because the borderline does not trust in prospective relief for her distress, it just causes more distress. The borderline therefore cannot learn to master her overwhelmed feelings and to control her behavior. Her rage remains untamed.

Thus preoccupied with her own needs and the resulting pain, the borderline sees other people primarily in terms of whether or not they can gratify her. Clinging to the only techniques she knows, as though survival itself depended on them, she cripples her development into maturity and self-esteem. In this sense, BPD could be defined as an immaturity of ego functions, a distorted version of a survival instinct.

Dr. Soloff believes that there are at least four elements of BPD. In his model, three of these are innate aspects of a genetically heritable disposition, namely neurotransmitter vulnerability that leads to a susceptible temperament. This handicap is comprised of

- Affective instability, what Dr. Klein calls *affective dysregulation*. "This is biological, probably rooted in either catecholamine or serotonergic mechanisms," says Dr. Soloff. "We're not sure about that piece of the puzzle."
- Cognitive distortions, including thought pathology under stress. "These are a subject of great controversy," says Dr. Soloff. "They are most likely a dopaminergic phenomenon because the symptoms respond to low doses of neuroleptics."
- Impulsivity. "Here we have the strongest evidence of a link to serotonergic transmission," says Dr. Soloff.

To produce BPD, this biological potential interacts with a fourth element—pathological interpersonal relationships—that is strictly non-biological and psychodynamic. "Where this comes from is unclear," says Dr. Soloff. "My earlier studies indicated loss of a parental figure due to divorce or death, but today we have much better studies showing neglect and shocking abuse." A terrible childhood in which she is treated as a manipulated object causes the borderline to believe that she is unlovable and subject to abandonment in Dr. Masterson's sense of the word. This results in the chaotic, unstable, overly dependent, masochistic interpersonal style toward which psychodynamic therapy is directed.

This fourth element is the hardest to overcome, as Dr. Soloff explains:

> Some things hold true across the board, and Dr. Kernberg has put his finger on some of them—that's why I give him all the credit in the world for some of the contribution. All of these patients have low self-esteem, all are rejection sensitive, and all of them use various interpersonal mechanisms to deal with that. At the heart of the learned part is some psychodynamic process that makes these people feel unlovable and worthless, and that doesn't change with all the medication in the world. That's why after ten years of using psychopharmacological approaches to the borderline patient, we can still stand beside Dr. Kernberg and say, "There's still a lot of work for you to do," and after 40 years of psychoanalytic approaches, he has said to me more than once that the mood instability and impulsivity don't change in his patients, that they still have troubles.

This chapter is brief partly because 100 years of research have left so much more to be done with BPD that a discussion of the possibilities alone could become another book.

Charting the Pathways

Meanwhile we can summarize what is known at this point about the possible causes of BPD:

- No single contributing factor is necessary or sufficient for the development of BPD; together the factors have cumulative, interactive effects.
- Whatever causes BPD does not necessarily maintain the illness; nor must the type of treatment match the type of inferred cause.
- Both genetic and environmental factors contribute to BPD, but they are probably not specific to this illness.
- Phase-specific psychoanalytical explanations for BPD are suspect, especially in light of recent data about chronic trauma histories of borderline patients.
- Family factors are important contributors to BPD, but it is not known whether they are genetic, environmental, or both.

- BPD overlaps with affective disorders; except for studies suggesting a dopaminergic process in the illness,[6] there is no indication that it is linked to schizophrenia.
- Social factors may influence both the development of BPD and the actual expression of its symptoms.

These and other models of BPD raise questions implied earlier: do the different routes all create the same illness, or is BPD actually a group of similar but separate illnesses? "As BPD is currently defined, a number of etiologic routes could result in the same cluster of symptoms," says Dr. Siever. "As we understand more about its etiology, we may be able to distinguish disorders resembling BPD from the more etiologically specific illness."

At least the final common pathways all lead in the same direction; all that remains is to follow them. At this point, researchers in BPD tend to refer to their sponsor. "You should include an editorial piece about how the NIMH has to make more money available for the study of borderline patients," says Dr. Soloff. *"Absolutely* quote me on that."

Notes

1. John G. Gunderson, M.D., paper [negative] read at debate, "Resolved: The Etiology of Borderline Personality Disorder Is Predominantly Biological," 143rd annual meeting of the American Psychiatric Association, New York, 16 May 1990.
2. Michael H. Stone, M.D., "An Integrated, Psychobiological Model of Borderline Personality Disorder," paper read at the 143rd annual meeting of the American Psychiatric Association, New York, 17 May 1990.
3. Michael H. Stone, M.D., "Introduction," in *Essential Papers on Borderline Disorders: One Hundred Years at the Border*, ed. Michael H. Stone, M.D. (New York: New York University Press, 1986), p. 4.
4. Stone, "Integrated, Psychobiological Model."
5. Fred Pine, Ph.D., "Borderline Pathology: Developmental Aspects," paper read at the 143rd annual meeting of the American Psychiatric Association, New York, 15 May 1990.
6. David L. Gardner, M.D., and Rex William Cowdry, M.D., "Pharmacotherapy of Borderline Personality Disorder: A Review," *Psychopharmacology Bulletin*, Vol. 25, No. 4 (1989), p. 520.

III

What Can Be Done About Borderline Personality Disorder?

23

Shortening *"Bucket Brigades"*

"Patients have the right and the responsibility to do consumer shopping."
AMY BAKER DENNIS, PH.D.

We noted in Chapter 2 that the term *bucket brigade* can refer to the tendency of borderlines prematurely to leave a series of therapies. In two outcome studies of psychotherapy, Dr. Gunderson and his colleagues found this pattern to predict that borderlines would eventually do well in treatment.[1] In the earlier study (which followed outpatients), Drs. Waldinger and Gunderson suggest that some patients might need this form of preparation before settling down to meet the challenges of intensive therapy.

I have heard consistently from previously hospitalized borderlines, however, that they hated resident rotation, which required them to change therapists during the course of their stay. A borderline can be "prepared" for intensive work simply by receiving supportive therapy first, either from the same therapist or in the process of switching practitioners only once.

The bucket brigade pattern might also mean that borderlines are so sensitive to their interactions with therapists that it is harder for them to find a treatment situation that "fits." And like most patients, borderlines probably don't know the difference between psychoanalysis and primal scream; it doesn't occur to them to learn about psychotherapy options before scheduling consultations. The process of starting psychotherapy thus becomes one of repeated trial and error. Possibly those borderline patients who keep trying eventually do well because of determination.

Motivated patients in particular need not waste time with the wrong therapists. It is up to them instead to do "consumer shopping," as Dennis calls it, before buying. Learning about the alternatives before she tries her first outpatient therapy—and if it doesn't work out, requesting an intelligent, thoughtful referral from her therapist to someone whose work he *knows well*—might help the borderline shorten her bucket brigade.

This final section discusses the various treatment options available to borderlines in particular. (Other readers considering psychotherapy should first consult one of the more general guides to the subject.[2]) I have assumed that many readers either have been diagnosed as borderline or have good reason to think that they have BPD.

This chapter and the next focus upon outpatient psychotherapy. Not surprisingly, *"there is no treatment of choice for borderline patients,"* as Dr. Soloff has written in italics,[3] and theoretically there is little consensus. But certain treatment techniques appear to be widespread, and some of them will be summarized here to help educate the borderline patient about what to expect.

Like family backgrounds, the treatment of BPD is a crucial topic that occupies surprisingly little space in the psychiatric literature. Except for Dr. Masterson's publications, what little material exists has not been very sound, specific, or helpful. That this situation is improving is indicated by such examples as the treatment manual recently published by Dr. Kernberg's group and the analyses of five borderline case histories contributed by Drs. Waldinger and Gunderson.[4]

We noted in Chapter 4 the discovery by psychoanalysts that borderlines could not tolerate classical treatment techniques. The trend from the 1940s to the 1960s was to reject this modality for these patients in favor of a more supportive approach.[5] This in turn has given way to an emphasis (at least in the literature) on expressive therapy. First I will describe the supportive and expressive (or what Dr. Masterson calls *reconstructive*) approaches separately as two forms of therapy used with borderline patients.

Supportive Therapy

Supportive refers to the therapist's stance in that form of psychotherapy, which Dr. Gunderson suggests is used with 95 percent of borderline patients. Supportive therapy is conducted once a week, possibly over years, and is often decreased gradually rather than terminated abruptly. It focuses on the practical realities of daily life: seeing them clearly, defining them, and thinking logically about them.

The supportive therapist directs the borderline patient away from her maladaptive coping mechanisms while encouraging and reinforcing better ones. If a patient copes with anxiety by rearranging all her furniture, for example, the therapist might encourage this harmless defense rather than examining the anxiety itself. To this end, he intervenes with advice, persuasion, and inspiration. The therapist may also educate the patient and add structure to the treatment sessions by defining her symptoms or dynamics.

The focus of supportive treatment is conscious or preconscious functioning. The therapist does not explore the patient's past or interpret and help her resolve unconscious conflicts. He avoids using techniques like free association, which borderlines can find very disorganizing, and does not encourage *regression* (a return to more immature and primitive patterns of thinking or reacting).

In all these respects, the therapist behaves actively like a real person and may in fact connect with the patient emotionally and encourage contact between sessions. If the patient develops a negative transference* toward him, the therapist will point out why her perception is incorrect but will not interpret her hostility. Gratified by his support, the patient generally feels good about the therapist and carries this positive attitude over to her relationships in the real world.

Supportive therapy helps suppress disturbing thoughts and feelings and increase the patient's stability. It can improve a patient's self-esteem and the quality of her relationships. The patient and therapist may also work toward more specific goals with the option to continue the therapy after these have been met.

Another option is for the patient to move into expressive psychotherapy.

Expressive Therapy

Expressive refers to the patient's role in this type of treatment. Expressive therapy with borderlines is probably *written about* 95 percent of the

---

*Misperceiving in the therapist attributes actually possessed by important people in her life, the patient reacts to him accordingly in a *positive* (affectionate) or *negative* (hostile) transference.

time because of its complexity. While supportive therapy may be harder
for the therapist to conduct, expressive therapy is harder for the patient
to tolerate. It requires more time and effort—three or more sessions a
week for several years, with or without long-term hospitalization—and
its goals are considerably more lofty.

In expressive therapy, *everything* is examined and interpreted:
thoughts, feelings, behavior, unconscious conflicts, dreams, whatever
the patient reveals. Unlike that of classical analysis, however, its immediate concern is with the present, not childhood experiences. Only over
time does the therapy proceed to more *genetic* interpretations—that is,
explanations of how the patient's pathology developed. Initially the
therapist might focus on why acting out feelings, for example, is ineffective and self-destructive; once the patient gained control over her behavior, he would help her analyze her compulsion to act out.

Without necessarily using supportive interventions, the expressive
therapist first limits any self-destructive behaviors that threaten him, the
patient, or the treatment. He strengthens the *therapeutic alliance:* the cooperation of the patient whose trust and good will toward the therapist
motivate her to work with him as a team.

The patient is encouraged to talk about whatever comes to mind.
Thus exposed, her inner world can be interpreted so that its dynamics
may be understood. The therapist confronts the patient with her
thoughts, feelings and behaviors, demonstrating that her defenses need
to be outgrown. Regression might be encouraged as essential to the
process of restructuring.

By increasing her insight and helping her resolve intrapsychic conflicts (or deficits), the therapist ultimately hopes to restructure the patient's personality into a state of psychological maturity. This will help
the borderline solidify her identity, tolerate aloneness, and maintain relationships.

Although less involved than in supportive treatment, the therapist is
still more active than he would be with a neurotic patient. His interpretations remind the borderline patient that he is present with her in reality
and otherwise help structure the sessions. But the therapist maintains an
anonymous, neutral, calm attitude whose unresponsiveness frustrates the
patient and prompts her to develop either positive or negative transferences. The therapist uses such feelings and his own reactions to them as
tools for better understanding the patient. By tolerating her hostility, he
helps dilute her anger and direct its energy more constructively.

In one sense, supportive therapy with borderlines appears to be a last
resort used because these patients are too damaged psychologically to
tolerate much more. But expressive therapy has not been demonstrated
conclusively to outdo it.

As a topic in the psychiatric literature, supportive therapy gave way to the more expressive mode largely as a result of Dr. Kernberg's influence. Dr. Kernberg developed his therapeutic approach while participating in and later directing the Menninger Foundation Psychotherapy Research Project.[6] On the basis of this study and his own clinical experience and investigation into severe forms of psychopathology, Dr. Kernberg considers his methods to have been proven empirically.

The Menninger Project

As a formal research study, the Menninger Project was conducted from 1959 to the publication of its final report in 1972. The project involved two groups of 21 patients each. The healthier group was treated with classical psychoanalysis, while the sicker group—composed of what would now be called borderline patients—received psychoanalytically oriented psychotherapy. The more severely disturbed patients in this second group had supportive psychotherapy, and the rest had expressive psychotherapy. "So I had the opportunity to study volumes of notes documenting the progress of 42 patients undergoing these three types of long-term treatment," says Dr. Kernberg.

Statistical analysis of this case material showed that the sickest patients benefited from neither supportive psychotherapy nor classical analysis. They did best with expressive psychotherapy bolstered by support outside the sessions from hospitalization or adjunctive therapy. "That gave me a tremendous assurance in my own thinking about it, which went along the same lines," says Dr. Kernberg, who began writing a series of papers later assembled into the book *Borderline Conditions and Pathological Narcissism.*[7]

The distinction between supportive and expressive psychotherapy is somewhat arbitrary (and here oversimplified). From this point on in the discussion, *supportive* and *expressive* refer to modes within psychotherapy that is *primarily* intensive, expressive psychoanalytic psychotherapy. How these two approaches are used in treatment with borderlines is here summarized nicely by Dr. Kernberg:

> The large majority of authors feel that at different times the therapy should be more supportive or expressive. I don't. I feel that one has to differentiate supportive *effects* of treatment from *techniques,* and that the use of purely expressive techniques permits a more supportive effect than do supportive techniques. For example, the analysis of primitive defensive operations strengthens the ego because these operations have an ego weakening effect.

Of course, certain measures in my approach might be called supportive, such as contract and limit setting or the establishment of parameters of technique. But these are only temporary devices that then are to be resolved by interpretive means.

In general a number of authors also try first to build up a supportive relationship before starting to interpret. I believe that by interpreting the negative transference it is possible to increase the therapeutic alliance and the patient's capacities to work in the treatment situation. But I don't find these to be major differences.

Like his view of aggression, Dr. Kernberg's conceptualization of supportive and expressive elements appears to be misunderstood and his methods thus incorrectly practiced by many therapists. And like his writing, his description here conveys little of the warmth his patients must experience. "My sense is that when Dr. Kernberg is working well clinically, he is more supportive than he writes about," says Dr. Adler. "In videotapes of his sessions, he is a caring, involved man."

"I agree absolutely," says Dr. Gunderson.

I have written about the disparity between what Dr. Kernberg writes and what he does. I think that he doesn't honor certain aspects of his approach because on an ideologic basis, it breaks with psychoanalytic tradition of the analyst being an impassive, objective observer. Most borderline patients need a therapist who is quite interactive and anything but a blank screen, who uses the force of his personality and commitment as well as various forms of more overt support to keep such patients attending to the task.

The similarities among the psychodynamic psychotherapies to which Dr. Kernberg refers include other principles as well.

The Initial Contract

Psychotherapy begins with the therapist's explanation of the therapeutic process, the patient's responsibility in sessions, the appointment schedule, the procedures for paying fees and missing appointments, the vacation arrangements, and so forth.

Because they tend to test therapists, borderline patients need more structure than this: clear ground rules with specific consequences of not following them. The therapist and the borderline patient therefore negotiate a more explicit contract that specifies the responsibilities of each and the various means by which the patient can meet hers. If the patient is chronically suicidal, for instance, she may agree in advance to go to an emergency room when in danger. Or the patient might agree to maintain whatever financial arrangements she has made to pay for the sessions.

The patient must understand that the contract is not intended as a reflection on her. It merely helps to control her destructive behaviors and keep the progress of therapy smooth and stable. The patient should also recognize that regardless of how bad she feels, she is not entitled to any special departures from the therapist's usual policy. Not following the agreed-upon contract is simply not in her best interest.

One aspect of treatment that may puzzle borderline patients is limitation of their self-mutilation, binge-vomiting, or other forms of acting out. Therapists differ among themselves and between patients in how much of this behavior they will permit, and some won't allow it at all. If she has come to treatment for help with these symptoms, the patient may wonder, how can she be expected first to cure them?

The rationale is that such actions discharge feelings. It saves a useless and destructive step if the patient simply tells the therapist what the contemplated action is trying to say. (If she can't control her behavior, she may benefit from hospitalization, some other form of crisis intervention, or dialectical behavioral therapy, which will be discussed in Chapter 28.)

Another question might be, why can't I call my therapist between sessions if something is wrong? Why should he dump me on strangers in an emergency room or at the end of a crisis hotline when I most need help? The reason is that a real emergency requires more assistance than one therapist can provide. The patient who overdoses intending to call her therapist is seeking secondary gain—a saving response from him. If she would rather not cut her wrists than deal with emergency room personnel, then she is not really in crisis.

Borderlines might not like the previous two paragraphs. They should therefore consider that expressive psychotherapy will bombard them with such callous statements, and worse, and decide for themselves whether such treatment is really what they want.

If the patient violates the contract by acting out self-destructively, the therapist can confront her and explain the behavior, implement specific principles for managing it,[8] enlist the aid of outside therapists, end the session, or as a last resort, end the treatment.[9] She should note also that the contract may require renegotiation and modification as therapy proceeds.

Consultation and Confidentiality

A crucial aspect of treating borderline patients that should be included in the initial contract is consultation. "I feel strongly about outside supervision when you're treating borderlines," says Dennis:

> I don't care how good you are—they force whatever part of you is chaotic and crazy to get mixed up in their problems. You need somebody objective and outside of you to show you this. Always, always, always have supervision.

It is essential that the therapist have one or more colleagues available with whom he can discuss the patient's case. Linehan, whose entire staff meets regularly for this purpose, explains that

> many mistakes are being made by therapists doing ineffective treatment with no way out. Therapy with borderline individuals is so unbelievably stressful that the mental health of the therapist has to be a concern also. A patient who will not give permission for consultation should not be treated.

Consultation raises the equally crucial issue of confidentiality, one that may not always be properly respected. Some therapists view information they receive from patients as having been literally given to them to do with as they please. Others apparently believe that a license to practice psychotherapy is a sacrament and that information should be kept confidential only from laypeople.

"Confidentiality involves not just what is said but also the quality of the talk, whether it is pejorative," says Linehan.

> Consultation involves discussing the patient anonymously as a genuine issue, with respect and compassion. What can happen instead is that the therapist ends up gossiping. The job of the consultant is to help the therapist maintain compassion and avoid blaming the patient and speaking pejoratively about her.
> Consultation does not mean disclosing everything. Patients often say extremely intimate, sensitive things that are not necessary to repeat in order to treat them. I would never repeat some things patients have told me to anyone for any reason.

Like consultation, hospitalization raises issues about what can be repeated appropriately to other therapists. Ingrid's therapist reassured her that session contents were confidential, then discussed an embarrassing but innocuous incident with the other staff. As a fledgling mental health professional, Ingrid has since concluded that *"There is no confidentiality.* **None.** Being a staff member *myself* now in a *different* environment, I am sure that *there is no confidentiality."* Hospitalization likewise poses the problem of who might gain access to patient records.

I have interviewed psychiatric patients and those with many other conditions for a decade without ever having encountered as much raw fear of exposure as that expressed by borderlines. Stigmatized by her diagnosis, her perceptions discredited and her rights to privacy perhaps disregarded, a borderline patient may be terrified to have her case discussed even with another therapist.

The large number of borderline patients itself underlies the importance of reconciling consultation and confidentiality. "Discussing consultation gives you the opportunity to call for a reexamination of confidentiality by the profession," says one psychiatrist. Therapists might reaffirm their commitment to patient privacy while meeting the primary goal of protecting the patient's life.

We have seen that Gerry attempted suicide when faced with a legal, appropriate communication about his psychiatric status to his ex-wife. To avoid such surprises, the therapist might well discuss confidentiality as part of the initial contract. Specifying what consultation entails, the therapist can ask how the patient feels about it. He can also explain that life-threatening situations authorize him to take necessary protective action even if it means her exposure.

The patient and therapist should each agree in advance exactly what the therapist has and has not been authorized to do.

Smart Shopping

Even to begin psychotherapy requires considerable initiative on the part of the borderline patient, as Dennis explains:

A borderline can call up a therapist and interview him over the phone: what's your perspective? How do you treat borderlines? What do you know about them? How do you feel about treating them? What kind of success have you had with them? What do you think about involving my family? These are some really important questions a patient can ask therapists so that she doesn't get ripped off.

Borderline patients can, of course, add other questions about whatever particularly concerns them.

Another matter given insufficient attention, as Dr. Gunderson emphasizes, is the need to find a therapist who "fits." "Not all therapists can treat borderlines, and not all therapists who specialize in these patients can treat every kind of borderline," says Dennis. "It has to be a very good marriage."

The patient who is told that the therapist doesn't treat borderlines or that he considers the two of them ill-suited should not feel rejected. On the contrary, she is fortunate that the therapist has recognized and admitted to limitations that would have made treatment a disaster. "Therapists don't often turn people away, and that's very sad," says Dennis. "Instead they think, 'I've had all this training—I should be able to manage anything.' That's nonsense."

One of the most unfortunate problems the prospective patient may encounter is that therapists most prepared to work with borderlines sometimes share the diagnosis. Some people choose psychotherapy as a profession because of unresolved conflicts of their own, and some therapists feel most comfortable when their patients are acting these out. Dr. Masterson, among others, has suggested that therapists who marry former patients (which most of their colleagues would condemn) may be expressing the typical borderline fear of separation.*

One way to try to avoid a poor fit or a disturbed practitioner is for the patient to consult three or four therapists before deciding with whom she wants to work. The patient and therapist can then agree upon a trial period of treatment (perhaps a few months) after which they will decide if they want to continue. Despite her discomfort with separations, the borderline patient is far better off with this arrangement than she would be spending years in a bad situation.

Bad treatment is especially hard for a borderline patient to recognize as such because besides distorting others, she lacks an *observing ego,* the ability to stand back and examine herself rather objectively. And because borderlines are difficult to work with, many therapists assume that problems in treatment always originate with the patient.

The patient should therefore educate herself about psychotherapy[10] in advance and try to discuss any troublesome matters with her therapist. Consultation is also a right of the patient: she can seek the advice of a second therapist, who will speak with both of them and make recommendations accordingly.

---

*Theory has changed since the days when Carl Jung married a former patient and had an affair with another still in treatment (who later became an analyst) and Freud remained friends with several patients of his.

The borderline patient should not fall into the rut described by Carla in Chapter 1 of taking care of her therapist. She has more than enough to do to take care of herself.

Bucket Brigades

The outcome study by Drs. Waldinger and Gunderson surveyed descriptions by highly experienced therapists of their treatments of borderline patients. The authors found that only 54 percent of the borderlines continued therapy longer than six months, and among those who remained in long-term treatment, more than half left against their therapists' advice. "Even in the hands of experts," the authors write, "the patient who gets much better is the exception rather than the rule."[11] But they also found that the longer patients stayed in treatment (some of which was classically psychoanalytical), the more they improved. Many patients made considerable gains in their ego functioning, behavior, relationships, and sense of self.

In the 1989 study by Dr. Gunderson and his colleagues, 60 percent of a sample of hospitalized borderline patients discontinued treatment within six months. The study revealed three reasons for dropping out: anger at being confronted rather than supported too early on in therapy, insufficient support from families, and lack of motivation and active resistance to treatment.

Dr. Stone similarly reports that 40 percent of his borderline patients drop out within six months.[12]

Although potentially discouraging to therapists, this information is intended to reassure borderline patients. Obviously no borderline who finds treatment difficult is unique. It is appropriate for her to approach psychotherapy with healthy skepticism as well as optimism. Leaving treatment doesn't make her a bad patient or a hopeless case. Perhaps she isn't ready; perhaps it was the wrong situation; perhaps her bucket brigade will be longer than she might wish.

Or perhaps treatment is not appropriate for her at all.

No Treatment?

Some therapists consider long-term psychiatric treatment to be potentially *iatrogenic* for borderline patients—that is, likely to make them worse.[13] As alternatives they propose treatment that is short-term (or at least intermittent) or conducted in settings like day hospitals. For some patients, treatment is not recommended at all.

What kinds of patients might not benefit from psychotherapy? Dr. Frances, Clarkin, and Samuel Perry, M.D., appear to qualify Dr. Gunderson's findings, suggesting as they do that borderline patients with histories of treatment failures are poor candidates. Treatment may also be inappropriate for masochists or narcissists who are prone to respond poorly and for patients who view it as a means to another end (like a lawsuit), who are antisocial or have criminal histories, who pretend illness, who have regressed badly in therapy, or who are poorly motivated.[14]

Dr. Stone might add those patients who have no positive aspects to their real lives to fall back on, build upon, or look forward to. Paradoxically, a patient must be "more than half well to tolerate depth-therapy," he writes. "When morbidity is to health as the desert is to one of its small oases, the terrain is not likely to become green."[15]

As we'll see in this section, however, psychotherapy is not the only alternative available to borderlines. Too little is known at this point about why therapy succeeds or fails to suggest that new or alternative treatment methods might not be promising. What *is* known is that the outcome of therapy ultimately depends on the patient herself. Strengthening that self is a goal shared by all her prospective choices.

Notes

1. Robert J. Waldinger, M.D., and John G. Gunderson, M.D., "Completed Therapies with Borderline Patients," *American Journal of Psychotherapy*, Vol. 38, No. 2 (April 1984), pp. 190–202; John G. Gunderson, M.D., Arlene F. Frank, Ph.D., Elsa F. Ronningstam, M.Sc., Stuart Wachter, M.D., Vincent J. Lynch, M.S.W., and Pamela J. Wolf, B.A., "Early Discontinuance of Borderline Patients from Psychotherapy," *Journal of Nervous and Mental Disease*, Vol. 177, No. 1 (1989), pp. 38–42.
2. See, for example, Otto Ehrenberg, Ph.D., and Miriam Ehrenberg, Ph.D., *The Psychotherapy Maze: A Consumer's Guide to Getting in and out of Therapy*, rev. and updated (New York: Simon & Schuster, 1986); Gerald Amada, Ph.D., *A Guide to Psychotherapy* (New York: Madison Books, 1985).
3. Paul H. Soloff, "Borderline Disorders," in *Handbook of Outpatient Treatment of Adults*, ed. Michael E. Thase, Barry A. Edelstein, and Michel Hersen (New York: Plenum, 1990), p. 323.
4. Otto F. Kernberg, M.D., Michael A. Selzer, M.D., Harold W. Koenigsberg, M.D., Arthur C. Carr, Ph.D., and Ann H. Appelbaum, M.D., *Psychodynamic Psychotherapy of Borderline Patients* (New York: Basic Books, 1989); Robert J. Waldinger, M.D., and John G. Gunderson, M.D., *Effective Psychotherapy with Borderline Patients: Case Studies* (New York: Macmillan, 1987).
5. Thomas A. Aronson, M.D., "A Critical Review of Psychotherapeutic Treatments of the Borderline Personality: Historical Trends and Future Directions," *Journal of Nervous and Mental Disease*, Vol. 177, No. 9 (1989), pp. 513–15.
6. Otto F. Kernberg, M.D., Esther D. Burstein, Ph.D., Lolafaye Coyne, Ph.D., Ann Appelbaum,

M.D., Leonard Horwitz, Ph.D., and Harold Voth, M.D., "Psychotherapy and Psychoanalysis: Final Report of the Menninger Foundation's Psychotherapy Research Project," *Bulletin of the Menninger Clinic,* Vol. 36, Nos. 1 and 2 (January–March 1972).
7. Otto F. Kernberg, M.D., *Borderline Conditions and Pathological Narcissism* (New York: Jason Aronson, 1975).
8. See, for example, Eric M. Plakun, M.D., "Psychotherapy with the Self-Destructive Borderline Patient," in *Difficult Clinical Situations,* ed. Allan Tasman, M.D., and William Sledge, M.D. (Washington, D.C.: American Psychiatric Press, forthcoming).
9. For a discussion of these matters, see Michael A. Selzer, M.D., Harold W. Koenigsberg, M.D., and Otto F. Kernberg, M.D., "The Initial Contract in the Treatment of Borderline Patients," *American Journal of Psychiatry,* Vol. 144, No. 7 (July 1987), pp. 927–30.
10. See, for instance, Ehrenberg and Ehrenberg, Chapter 10, "Resistance or Incompatibility?"
11. Waldinger and Gunderson, p. 197.
12. Michael H. Stone, M.D., "Introduction," in *Essential Papers on Borderline Disorders: One Hundred Years at the Border,* ed. Michael H. Stone, M.D. (New York: New York University Press, 1986), p. 3n.
13. Aronson, pp. 520–21; David F. Dawson, M.D., "Treatment of the Borderline Patient: Relationship Management," *Canadian Journal of Psychiatry,* Vol. 33, No. 5 (June 1988), pp. 370–74.
14. Allen Frances, M.D., John Clarkin, Ph.D., and Samuel Perry, M.D., *Differential Therapeutics in Psychiatry: The Art and Science of Treatment Selection* (New York: Brunner/Mazel, 1984), p. 217.
15. Stone, "1970s and 1980s," in *Essential Papers,* p. 432.

24

Psychodynamic Treatment Dogmatic and Pragmatic

"First use common sense. Everything else follows."[1]

OTTO F. KERNBERG, M.D.

The most obvious treatment option available to border-lines is psychodynamic psychotherapy. Readers may wish to review the psychoanalytical formulations of BPD described in Chapter 16 before proceeding to this brief summary of their practical applications in treatment. A quick look back at the abuse histories discussion in Chapter 20 might be useful also.

Like its neighbors, this chapter encourages borderlines to consider which treatment approach they might find most compatible.[2]

Dr. Kernberg: Integrating Fragments

The main target of Dr. Kernberg's treatment approach is the patient's splitting of herself and her world. Therapy helps the patient assemble her fragmented perspectives into a more complex and realistic one. Dr. Kernberg uses himself as a prime example, confronting the patient with her attempts to split him and demonstrating that despite her best efforts, he remains consistently whole.

In treatment, Dr. Kernberg emphasizes three techniques:

- *Interpretation*. More than any other theorist, Dr. Kernberg relies on interpretation. He begins immediately to confront and clarify the patient's behavior in the present and moves slowly into genetic interpretations at more advanced stages of treatment.

Along with Dr. Gunderson, Dr. Kernberg believes that the borderline patient's distortions are both a reaction to past experiences and a defense used in the present. So he first examines the patient's distortions of his comments. A patient projecting her own hostility, for instance, may "hear" every interpretation as an attack. Clarification helps the patient use the interpretation correctly and control her tendency to distort.

- *Transference analysis*. Dr. Kernberg sees the borderline patient's negative transference—her hostility, aggression, splitting, envy, and projected paranoia—as the primary manifestation of her illness. He interprets it throughout treatment from beginning to end. The other side of the split—the patient's tendency to idealize the therapist—is also quickly interpreted as a defense against her deeply rooted hatred of him.

This policy is another example of how Dr. Kernberg's descriptions of his approach need to be distinguished from his practice. "A therapist who followed too literally Dr. Kernberg's call for early transference interpretation and confrontation would be underestimating the amount of support borderline patients require in the earlier stages of treatment," says Dr. Gunderson.

Dr. Kernberg believes that the patient has two levels of transference. One is a primitive type arising from her distortions of childhood experiences. As analysis helps her develop more mature defenses, her transference becomes a higher type based on actual experiences. The patient then sees both her parents and the therapist more realistically.

Transference is linked closely to both the patient's current conflicts in the real world and the overall goals of treatment.

- *Maintenance of technical neutrality*. Dr. Kernberg is more strict than other theorists about maintaining a position of technical neutrality, which he defines as "concerned objectivity." To study the patient's interactions with others as scientifically as possible, the therapist must remain in the background. Although he insists that the therapist show warmth and empathy to the patient, Dr. Kernberg avoids contaminating their relationship with his own personality and needs.

To protect the neutral stance, Dr. Kernberg does as little structuring as possible within the therapy, relying instead on outside supports to help the patient. If the patient acts out, the therapist may deviate from neutrality as briefly as possible, explaining the need for more structure, analyzing the patient's destructive behavior, and assigning her responsibility for it.

The circumstances that might elicit such a deviation include, in order of importance: any life-threatening danger, interruption of the treatment, lies or silence from the patient, contract breaches like refusal to meet with an adjunct therapist or take medication, and acting out, especially in sessions. Dr. Kernberg does permit some relatively harmless acting out. Although an anorexic patient would be required to maintain a minimum weight, for example, a bulimic patient might be allowed to continue occasional binge-vomiting if it caused no serious complications.

Dr. Kernberg requires patients to be completely honest about any feelings or behavior that could compromise treatment. He makes clear that his job during sessions is to provide the patient with tools to use at other times to solve her problems. Thus a suicidal patient, for example, is expected to seek outside help when in danger. If she attempts suicide and instead calls Dr. Kernberg, he will do everything possible to save her life, then end her treatment.

These and other conditions of the treatment contract are explained firmly and explicitly. The patient is assured confidentiality unless she becomes suicidal. She must either work or attend school as well as socialize and cannot make therapy the center of her life. Any medication she requires is prescribed by another psychiatrist.

The patient's responsibility is to speak freely about whatever is on her mind; the therapist's is rigorously to confront, clarify or interpret, providing a model the patient can use to control, observe, think about, and better understand herself. This process of analysis within a holding environment is called *containment,* a term Dr. Kernberg borrowed from Dr. Bion.[3] Dr. Kernberg focuses on what occurs in therapy and addresses the patient's symptoms directly. His firm resistance to the patient's attacks decreases her fears of her rage and impulses.

By exposing the patient's intrapsychic conflicts and helping her resolve them through insight, Dr. Kernberg helps her attain the goals of treatment: to control her feelings and behavior better; to create more accurate, complete perspectives that improve her sense of identity and her relationships with others; to develop greater self-esteem; and to pursue important goals more steadily and realistically.

Dr. Masterson: The Method

Dr. Masterson's treatment focuses on undoing the borderline triad that created the pathology. The therapist confronts the patient's maladaptive defenses; absorbing the confrontation, the patient controls these defenses. This allows her abandonment depression to be worked through, freeing her self to separate. The patient recreates in therapy an elaborated and distorted version of her relationship with her mother through her transference acting out (not, as Dr. Kernberg believes, through her transference).

Dr. Masterson divides this therapeutic process into three stages:[4]

- *The testing stage.* Early in treatment, the patient acts out to test the trustworthiness and competence of the therapist. Confronting her and illustrating how her behavior is self-defeating, the therapist makes it seem less desirable. By repeating this function for her, he secures the patient's trust so that a therapeutic alliance can be formed.

Unlike Dr. Kernberg, Dr. Masterson does not emphasize the early use of interpretations. By controlling her acting out, he engages the patient in describing her feelings and helps her to accept interpretations later. These interpretations help the patient understand how distortions resulting from real past experiences affect her relationship with the therapist. The therapist's confrontations set the patient to work analyzing and interpreting her behavior itself.

At this point, the patient shifts from transference acting out to transference. She can see both the therapist as he is in reality and the qualities she projects onto him. She no longer uses primitive defenses and acting out to ward off the abandonment depression, which proceeds to emerge.

- *The working-through stage.* Once the therapeutic alliance is secure, the patient works through her abandonment depression. During this stage, the therapist switches from an emphasis on confrontation to a reliance on interpretation.

- *The separation stage.* The patient works through the final stages of separation of her self-image from that of the therapist. This process occurs in normal development when the adventuresome toddler seeks emotional "refueling" from the mother, who responds by appreciating and approving of her independent activities.

Without revealing personal information, Dr. Masterson takes a supportive role as a "real" person. He encourages the patient's individuality through appropriate discussion of the reality aspects of new interests and activities, sharing with her his own knowledge of whatever pastimes she has rediscovered. He validates her new feelings and perceptions, empathizes with her disappointments, congratulates her on success, and maintains the implicit expectation that she will behave like an adult.

Dr. Masterson thus supplies the patient with a role model upon which she can base new, more satisfying relationships. As a result of her growth into individuality, the patient emerges from therapy with a more realistic view of her mother and their earlier interactions and a new, more autonomous sense of self.

Drs. Adler and Buie: Support and Soothing

Like Dr. Masterson, Drs. Adler and Buie divide treatment into three phases;[5] with Dr. Adler's approval, I have designated them as:
- *The aloneness phase.* The therapist helps the patient develop holding, soothing images. Drs. Adler and Buie view the patient's hostility as realistically grounded in inadequate mothering and other disappointing relationships. This hostility is worked through early in treatment to allow the patient's positive transference to emerge. The process requires both participants to survive their rage and the therapist to contain and interpret the patient's projections and provocations. This enables the patient reliably to experience the soothing and holding the therapist provides.
At this point, Drs. Adler and Buie assert that the patient is no longer borderline but deals instead with narcissistic issues. Rather than fearing aloneness and annihilation, she grapples with the incompleteness and the feelings of worthlessness that characterize narcissistic pathology.
- *The narcissistic phase.* Drs. Adler and Buie address these issues, including the patient's idealization, using Kohut's framework for narcissism. Unlike Dr. Kernberg, Drs. Adler and Buie see idealization as an expression of developmental arrest. Progressively disillusioning the patient until she sees the therapist realistically is central to their approach.
Dr. Waldinger likens this distinction to "a figure-ground problem in drawing." Drs. Adler and Buie see the positive transference as the background and the negative transference as an overlay. Dr. Kernberg sees the reverse.[6]

Drs. Adler and Buie do not interpret the patient's idealization for some time because it helps keep her in treatment. Unlike neurotic patients, borderlines can't establish a therapeutic alliance because they have difficulty observing themselves realistically and seeing the therapist as a separate person. Instead the patient continues therapy because the therapist supports, comforts, and appears to understand her. The alliance is secured only toward the end of treatment. The therapist who believes that it is established earlier, say Drs. Adler and Buie, is only fooling himself to avoid the aloneness that the borderline patient makes him feel.

But within this phase Drs. Adler and Buie eventually help the patient work through her idealization using what Kohut called *optimal disillusionment:* gradually the patient recognizes the therapist's human imperfections without being overwhelmed by disappointment. This disillusionment is interpreted in relation to past disappointing experiences. The patient now develops a reasonable sense of completeness and self-worth.

- *The integrative phase.* The therapist validates the patient's positive qualities and achievements to help her consolidate and incorporate her progress in therapy. As a result she loves, respects, and trusts herself and has developed appropriate values and ideals.

The therapist must constantly "be there" for the patient as a comforting, empathic person impervious to her rage. Arrested at a preverbal developmental stage, the borderline patient may not respond well to interpretations; in fact, she may experience them as insults to her narcissism. Although Drs. Adler and Buie focus on relevant issues like aloneness and self-esteem, the content of their interpretation is only as important as its context, as a mother's words are only as important to an infant as her voice. Drs. Adler and Buie therefore offer the patient both an interpretive approach and tremendous support, ranging from hospitalization to phone calls, extra appointments, audiotapes, and postcards while on vacation. Above all, they offer the understanding that she is essentially alone and has difficulty depending upon the therapist as someone who will not abandon her.

As Dr. Masterson validates the separating patient's new ideas and feelings, Drs. Adler and Buie emphasize her positive qualities and boost her self-esteem. Increasingly throughout treatment, they provide the new experience of genuine caring rather than simply role-play good parents. The patient is known, esteemed, and even loved by her therapist. When appropriate, the therapist remains part of the idealizing transference that sustains her, without necessarily interpreting her wish to see him as the perfect caregiver. Through this experience, the patient learns to understand, esteem, and love herself.

Drs. Adler and Buie are thus the least confrontative, warmest, and most giving of the major theorists. But however supportive, their therapy also addresses the patient's hostility. "An emphasis on supportive versus expressive therapy minimizes how Dr. Buie and I approach it," says Dr. Adler.

> We feel that all therapy requires different degrees of support versus going after the affect, that is, interpreting the hatred and rage as well as the positive feelings of the patient. We pay a lot of attention to the support the patient needs in terms of being able to form a relationship that can then sustain analysis of the aggression. My hunch is that ultimately we would do so as effectively as Dr. Kernberg, if not more effectively, because our approach is based upon a sense of a supportive environment that can tolerate the aggressive intensity.

Emphasis on such a holding environment raises an important issue: the number of mental health professionals encountered by many borderlines and the splitting that results. Ideally outpatient therapists and the staffs of hospitals, day treatment centers, and emergency rooms would interact, creating a larger favorable environment for borderline patients that is disappointing only now and then.

Conflict and Deficit

By now it might be apparent that psychodynamic treatment of BPD follows one of two major approaches: that used by Drs. Kernberg and Masterson and that used by Drs. Adler and Buie. These do not correspond precisely to the distinction between supportive and expressive therapy discussed earlier. Drs. Kernberg and Masterson work within a model of *conflict* in which the borderline is primarily concerned with splitting good from bad. They therefore reply on the content of interpretation and the resulting insight to undo the patient's destructive coping patterns.

Drs. Adler and Buie instead rely primarily on a model of *deficit* in which the borderline lacks evocative memories of soothing people and experiences. They use interpretation and address the patient's conflicts about relationships as part of the process of helping her develop such missing ego structures.

The implications for a borderline patient considering treatment are extremely important. Although the conflict-deficit distinction is an oversimplification, therapists in either camp would address any number of situations differently. If a patient called him instead of behaving self-destructively, for instance, Dr. Kernberg would explore the symbolic or defensive value of the action and, depending on his evaluation, decide how to proceed. Drs. Adler and Buie would express gratification about the contact and comfort the patient before trying to understand and interpret the action.

The major practitioners maintain a very intense debate over the merits of their respective techniques, and both approaches have loyal followers. Rather than be mutually exclusive, either approach could be used with different patients or at different times in the treatment. It behooves the patient, then, to learn where a prospective therapist stands on this and other issues.

Dr. Gunderson: A Middle Course

Like his model of BPD, Dr. Gunderson's treatment approach steers a middle course between the two sides. He believes that the therapist should address the borderline patient's hostility early on in treatment but without interpreting it too much. Instead he helps the patient control her rage and explore what triggered it. Although he views borderline aggression as both innate and reactive, he treats it as the latter. The patient learns that her anger is specifically reactive, inappropriate to the circumstances, and thus amenable to change.

Dr. Gunderson identifies four stages of psychotherapy with borderlines:[7]

- *Boundaries.* The patient tests the treatment boundaries implied by policies about scheduling, phone calls, fee payments, and so forth. This is similar to Dr. Masterson's testing phase except that Dr. Gunderson is more supportive and prepared to demonstrate to the patient his availability and commitment.
- *Negativity and control.* The patient begins to recall important past experiences, and the therapist helps her connect them to the present reality of therapy using confrontation and interpretation within a supportive environment. This stage also resembles the corresponding phase in Dr. Masterson's treatment, but rather than focusing on abandonment depression, Dr. Gunderson analyzes the patient's aggression. He clarifies for her how her dependency, masochism, devaluation, envy, and manipulation represent attempts to control him. The patient works through her anger and becomes more stable. She explores her disillusionment with the therapist and incorporates the positive qualities he shows her.

- *Separation and identity.* Like Drs. Adler and Buie, Dr. Gunderson notes qualities likely to emerge in this stage that make the borderline patient appear narcissistic. But Dr. Gunderson sees these features occurring along with corrective disillusionment, so that the patient is actually becoming more realistic, tolerant, and humble. The patient consolidates the gains she has made in role functioning and social relationships. She is better able to tolerate frustration and has explored her identity with encouragement and support from the therapist.
- *Termination initiative and letting go.* During the final phase, the prospect of ending therapy causes the patient to regress slightly. Issues she has worked through emerge to be reexamined and reintegrated.

Dr. Gunderson is careful to qualify the results to be expected from successful treatment, noting, among other things, that "rather than a resolution of old conflicts and defenses, successful treatment of borderline patients opens up new and more adaptive possibilities for action."[8]

Like Drs. Masterson and Adler and Buie, Dr. Gunderson actively tries to reparent the patient (as opposed to Dr. Kernberg, whose techniques do so more implicitly). He too creates a holding environment and supports new ideas and feelings resulting from the patient's increased awareness of her complex personality. Although Dr. Gunderson emphasizes the analysis of defenses less than Dr. Kernberg does, he believes that the patient must see how she not only distorts her relationship with the therapist but also contributes to the pathological aspects of her relationships in the real world.

Dr. Gunderson recognizes that at any given moment, the therapist must assess how anxious the patient is, how well disposed toward the therapist and able to relate to others, and thus how capable of understanding and using interpretations. These changes in her capability result from both the patient's conflicts and deficits and her movement between the three levels of functioning that come into play during therapy.[9]

The patient functions on level 1 during uninterrupted phases of psychotherapy, when she feels supported. She longs for closeness and feels depressed and empty but remains stable and can accept interpretation. "At this level, the therapist can work with the patient feeling confident that she seems more allied with common goals," says Dr. Gunderson. But she is unsure of the therapist and fears being dependent on or controlled by him, causing her alternately to be passively compliant, withdrawn and defiant, or otherwise resistant.

Once the patient has come to need the therapist, she reverts to level 2 when he seems inattentive, inaccurate, or withholding, when the therapy is suspended, or when a session merely ends. The frustrated patient feels helpless and grows angry, withdraws, or tries to prevent separations.

She may dismiss the therapist's attempts to clarify but responds to confrontation and limit setting.

Because treatment provides structure, the patient seldom reverts to level 3 in sessions unless she has not established ties with the therapist.

Despite their influence, these and other psychoanalyatic treatment approaches to BPD are being challenged for paying insufficient attention to childhood trauma. Unless a trauma history is specifically addressed, say some therapists, the patient cannot recover.

Treatment for Trauma

To find out precisely what *does* aid recovery from childhood trauma, Drs. Perry, Herman, and their colleagues questioned groups of borderline and other psychiatric patients about their treatment. The borderline patients in particular told the researchers that it did not help for their therapists to avoid talking about the trauma history.

To some extent, the patients considered it important for the therapists to demonstrate faith in the possibility of recovery. But what was most helpful, they explained, was to obtain validation of their emotional reactions to trauma through talking. They advised the therapists to clarify and interpret a patient's experiences in light of her previous trauma to decrease her confusion.[10]

This is precisely what is being emphasized by researchers studying childhood abuse. Saunders and Arnold argue that therapy with childhood abuse victims based on traditional formulations is inaccurate. Such an approach also decreases the patient's trust while increasing her anxiety, sense of badness, fear of her own anger, and resistance to treatment. (Dr. Kernberg's treatment in particular has been characterized as actually being accusatory.[11])

If the true causes of her feelings and behavior are identified, the patient instead feels the relief of having been validated and of finally understanding thoughts, feelings, and behaviors that have made no sense. Her "pathological" or "primitive" characteristics no longer cause her to feel terribly ashamed and defensive against "blame" from the therapist. A reformulation within the context of childhood abuse, say Saunders and Arnold, makes the therapist more empathic and better informed.[12]

"Treatment involves more than just validation of the abuse," says Dr. Herman.

It's sharing with the patient a whole conceptual framework about what trauma is and what exploitation does to people. They did their best as children to cope with extremely abnormal environments. Now they can do better. But we can't take away their poor coping techniques until they have learned other ways to relieve ther incredible internal emotional pain. So in a way, we develop a retraining program. The early stages of treatment are more cognitive, more focused on self-care and self-protection, and much less interpretive in terms of classical Kernbergian confrontation.

Although any theory ought to be shaken out and reexamined frequently, the discrepancy between "traditional" psychoanalytic thinking about BPD and this reformulation may be more apparent than real. "Much of what Dr. Kernberg says about treatment is very useful once you add this essential missing piece," says Dr. Herman. And regardless of the approach, one goal of treatment is to help the patient take charge and give up the roles of victimizer and victim.

"We have all had cases in which talking about abuse had dramatic beneficial effects for the patient," says Dr. Paris. "In that respect, I agree that there is a post-traumatic element involved—it's part of a bigger picture, but it certainly has helped us as therapists." Unless traumatic memories are recovered, validated, and integrated as a precondition of other change, the patient may leave therapy. Perhaps trauma therapy as well as supportive therapy is needed to prepare some borderline patients for more intensive work.

That not all therapists have availed themselves of such "help"—that they have instead confronted patients about aggression without acknowledging the suffering that caused it—may be another reason borderline patients so often launch themselves on bucket brigades.

Eclectic Therapy

Treatment that emphasizes childhood abuse is a pragmatic approach to some of the problems posed by the borderline patient. Even more pragmatic—yet probably most difficult—is simply to combine various elements of these different approaches in response to the needs of individual patients. This is the method used by Drs. Stone and McGlashan, for instance, who thereby follow a principle set down by Melitta Schmideberg in 1947: "The technique should be adapted to the patient and not the patient to the technique."[13]

Dr. Stone advises that "borderline patients have a way of reducing us to our final, common, human denominator, such that allegiance to a rigidly defined therapeutic system becomes difficult to maintain. They force a shift in us, as it were, from the dogmatic to the pragmatic."[14] In an article on this topic, he offers a wonderful example of a single session with a borderline patient in which the therapist's responses draw upon the theories of Searles, Kernberg, Kohut, Giovacchini, Freud, Donald Klein, Liebowitz, Soloff, and others.[15]

Dr. Stone might be called "dogmatically pragmatic," for he believes that an eclectic approach is necessary to treat borderline patients effectively. His includes psychoanalytical psychotherapy; supportive, cognitive and behavioral therapy; pharmacotherapy; and bibliotherapy (often with books loaned from his own library).

Similarly, Dr. McGlashan is guided by the principle mentioned earlier that borderlines are more different than they are similar. "You have to tailor the treatment," he says. "For some borderlines, an approach like Dr. Kernberg's is the treatment of choice. For many of them it's not."

Electic thus differs from dogmatic therapy in degree: a practitioner considers a particular approach to be suitable either some or all of the time.

Treatment Success

Each major theorist claims success for his methods (in fact, Drs. Adler and Buie describe their treatment as "definitive"). Dr. Waldinger suggests various possibilities to explain this discrepancy:[16]

- As has been frequently observed, each theorist emphasizes the methods and phases of treatment that most distinguish him from the others, when actually the basic approach is quite similar.
- The similarity—perhaps a factor not yet identified—is what makes all the treatments effective.
- As they are sifted through a succession of therapists, borderline patients end up with the best match. That therapist then describes the methods that work based on that particular group of patients.

This possibility corresponds to a point made by Dr. Aronson that the atmosphere created by each approach elicits the very symptoms that the theorist sees as central and suppresses those that are not.[17] Dr. Adler suggests, for example, why aloneness issues don't appear in Dr. Kernberg's work:

My hunch is that they're not there in part because the patient won't bring them out unless she is convinced that the therapist cares, has the capacity to hear about that kind of horrible pain, and will not foreclose important parts of his or her personality in response.

In addition, Dr. Kernberg defines at the beginning of treatment that the patient is expected to make use of auxiliary mental health professionals at moments of crisis or during his unavailability, thus diluting the emerging, intense transference that leads to the aloneness experiences.

The appearance of only selected symptoms seems to confirm the validity of the approach, which of course is already the one best suited to address them.

For practical purposes, this discrepancy need not be resolved. The most appropriate treatment for any borderline patient is whatever works. The point is that the patient herself should think about and try to find it.

Notes

1. Otto F. Kernberg, M.D., "Psychodynamic Treatment of Borderlines," paper read at the Psychodynamic Psychotherapy with Borderline Patients seminar, sponsored by the The New York Hospital–Cornell Medical Center, Westchester Division, New York, 12 January 1991.
2. More detailed descriptions may be found in the following articles, upon which this discussion is based: Charles Swenson, M.D., "Kernberg and Linehan: Two Approaches to the Borderline Patient," *Journal of Personality Disorders*, Vol. 3, No. 1 (1989), pp. 26–35; Robert J. Waldinger, M.D., "Intensive Psychodynamic Therapy with Borderline Patients: An Overview," *American Journal of Psychiatry*, Vol. 144, No. 3 (March 1987), pp. 272–74; Thomas A. Aronson, M.D., "A Critical Review of Psychotherapeutic Treatments of the Borderline Personality: Historical Trends and Future Directions," *Journal of Nervous and Mental Disease*, Vol. 177, No. 9 (1989), pp. 515–20; Gerald Adler, M.D., "Psychodynamic Therapies in Borderline Personality Disorder," in *Review of Psychiatry*, Vol. 8, ed. Allan Tasman, M.D., Robert E. Hales, M.D., and Allen J. Frances, M.D. (Washington, D.C.: American Psychiatric Press, 1989), pp. 49–64; and Leonard Horwitz, Ph.D., "Divergent Views of the Treatment of Borderline Patients," *Bulletin of the Menninger Clinic*, Vol. 49, No. 6 (November 1985), pp. 525–45.
3. Swenson, p. 32.
4. James F. Masterson, M.D., "Psychotherapy of Borderline and Narcissistic Disorders: Establishing a Therapeutic Alliance (A Developmental, Self, and Object Relations Approach)," *Journal of Personality Disorders*, Vol. 4, No. 2 (1990), p. 185.
5. Dan H. Buie, M.D., and Gerald Adler, M.D., "Definitive Treatment of the Borderline Personality," *International Journal of Psychoanalytic Psychotherapy*, ed. Robert Langs, M.D., Vol. 9: 1982–83 (New York: Jason Aronson, 1982), pp. 51–87.
6. Waldinger, p. 271.
7. John G. Gunderson, M.D., *Borderline Personality Disorder* (Washington, D.C.: American Psychiatric Press, 1984), pp. 54–63.
8. Ibid., p. 62.
9. John G. Gunderson, "Interfaces Between Psychoanalytic and Empirical Studies of Borderline Personality," in *The Borderline Patient: Emerging Concepts in Diagnosis, Psychodynamics and Treatment*, ed. James S. Grotstein, Marion F. Solomon, and Joan A. Lang, Vol. 1 (Hillsdale, N.J.: The Analytic Press, 1987), pp. 48–55.
10. J. Christopher Perry, M.D., M.P.H., Judith L. Herman, M.D., Bessel A. van der Kolk, M.D., and Lizbeth A. Hoke, Ph.D., "Psychotherapy and Psychological Trauma in Borderline Personality Disorder," *Psychiatric Annals*, Vol. 20, No. 1 (January 1990), pp. 35, 39.

11. Daniel B. Wile, "Kohut, Kernberg, and Accusatory Interpretations," *Psychotherapy*, Vol. 21, No. 3 (Fall 1984), pp. 353–64.
12. Eleanor Saunders, Ph.D., and Frances Arnold, Ph.D., "Borderline Personality Disorder and Childhood Abuse: Revisions in Clinical Thinking and Treatment Approach," Work in Progress, Working Paper Series, No. 51 (Wellesley, Mass.: The Stone Center for Developmental Services and Studies, Wellesley College).
13. Melitta Schmideberg, "The Treatment of Psychopaths and Borderline Patients," *American Journal of Psychotherapy*, Vol. 1 (1947), p. 46.
14. Michael H. Stone, M.D., "Treatment of Borderline Patients: A Pragmatic Approach," *Psychiatric Clinics of North America*, Vol. 13, No. 2 (June 1990), p. 267.
15. Stone, pp. 268–69.
16. Waldinger, pp. 272–74.
17. Aronson, p. 518.

25

Psychotherapy Among Company

Avoid loaded contexts; never hospitalize.

DAVID F. DAWSON, M.D.[1]

The stereotype of the psychiatric hospital is an impersonal institution that protects society from patients dangerous to others or themselves. To borderlines, however, hospitals are places to be safe for the short term and to progress toward recovery in the long term. For some of these patients, a borderline unit not only feels but also looks like a home and family. Unless someone is acting out, visitors can be surprised that such a unit resembles a college dormitory.

We learned in Chapter 1 that borderlines comprise a considerable percentage of psychiatric inpatients. Michael B. Rosenbluth, M.D., characterizes the literature on hospitalization of borderlines as "first generation" and notes that like the patients themselves, its authors have trouble looking beyond the present.[2] Yet they have no choice: therapists now predict that borderlines will replace schizophrenics as the chronic occupants of psychiatric hospitals, whose programs were not designed with them in mind.[3]

The trial-and-error modifications intended to accommodate borderlines has increased the risks that hospitalization poses for these patients, other inpatients, the staff, and even the program itself.[4] Yet hospitalization can not only save a borderline's life but also turn it around. Some patients admit as much, but all insist that for at least part of the time, hospitalization is hateful.

It is also controversial. One argument has to do with how long the hospital stay should be. Dr. Rosenbluth divides the opposing sides on this issue into those therapists who support only short-term hospitalization for borderlines and those who think that short-term is good but long-term is much better.[5] But short- and long-term hospitalizations are seldom clearly distinguished. Most therapists view short-term as lasting up to a few months while long-term might last a minimum of six months and extend to two or three years.

There are no rules about when either type of hospitalization is appropriate and not enough data to test impressions. "As a whole," writes Laura J. Miller, M.D., "the indications for hospitalization sometimes violate 'common sense.' "[6] Those summarized here have been conflated from several sources.[7]

Short-term Hospitalization

Short-term hospitalization is more common for borderlines than long-term because of the crises that punctuate their illness and the costs of keeping them longer. In fact, many therapists believe that effective treatment with borderline patients requires ready access to a hospital.

The purposes of short-term hospitalization for a borderline might be to

- confront the patient with denial of her illness to prepare her to begin outpatient therapy
- revise, recommend, or tailor outpatient therapy
- diagnose complex mixtures of psychopathology
- introduce medications or other forms of treatment
- protect the patient from self-inflicted danger during crises or regressions
- avoid other high-risk situations
- help the patient out of a psychotic episode
- provide rest for the patient and/or her family
- offer sophisticated consultation that helps clarify or resolve a stalemate in outpatient therapy. (Conversely, the patient's outpatient therapist can explain her behavior to the hospital staff and help them clarify their intense reactions to her.)
- interrupt persistent negative therapeutic reactions, in which progress is followed by regression

- accustom an overinvolved family to hospitalization to elicit their support for long-term treatment
- identify the patient's attempts to exploit social agencies by pretending disability.

The Benefits of Long-term Hospitalization

Although Dr. Gunderson, for example, describes long-term hospitalization as incorporating the implied goals of short-term, it is often viewed as a different treatment modality.

Its advocates consider long-term hospitalization a laboratory: the patient's individual therapist can study how she interacts with staff and other patients as well as with him. The hospital staff meet regularly to pool their impressions of borderline patients whose emotions have been released by limitations on their acting out. The result is what Dr. Swenson calls a "personality x-ray" that clearly reveals the character pathology.

Long-term hospitalization of a borderline patient might be appropriate to address
- unbearable or uncontrollable emotions
- intense negative therapeutic reactions
- sustained or frequent psychotic episodes or a concurrent diagnosis of multiple personality disorder
- transference psychosis
- declining motivation or hopelessness
- dangerous and sustained risk of suicide
- malignant self-destructive, impulsive, or debilitating behavior that escalates despite increased structure in outpatient therapy
- less dangerous behavior that interferes with treatment
- regressive or self-destructive impulses that the patient denies or will not discuss in outpatient therapy
- inability to establish ties with a series of outpatient therapists
- repeated countertransference mismanagement, in which the therapist has behaved inappropriately and crossed the usual boundaries
- several frequent, sustained previous treatment efforts. "One of our patients had 145 [sic] previous hospitalizations," says Dr. Swenson. "Eight to 12 is typical." Some borderline patients use hospitalizations to escape from or get back at their therapists.
- use of symptoms to elicit caretaking from everyone: for some borderlines, suicidality becomes a way of life

- weak social or family supports, a neglectful or disturbed family situation, and the resulting lack of structure to support outpatient therapy
- skills insufficient to function independently in the real world, several failed relationships or job losses, inability to care for physical needs
- exploitation of the health care system like abuses of elective surgery or prescription drugs or frequent changes of physician.

The Disadvantages of Long-Term Hospitalization

The above list makes it sound as though borderline patients could hardly avoid long-term hospitalization. But this form of treatment offers many disadvantages as well, such as

- incredibly high costs. Reimbursement problems increasingly make long-term hospitalization a treatment of last resort.
- stigmatization
- disruption of the patient's life, including her outpatient therapy. "It's very hard for a patient to pick up the threads of her life afterwards," says Dr. Paris.
- loss of freedom
- exposure to sicker patients
- staff disagreement about treatment.

The borderline patient may be manipulating the staff, or they may be having countertransference reactions to her. Or the staff may be expressing what Dr. Gunderson calls "genuine differences in opinion which derive . . . from the well-considered, but genuinely different perspectives thoughtful staff may have about the same phenomena."[8] Dr. Gunderson feels that too often patients are blamed for such disagreements.

- risk of traumatization.

"You go into the hospital and you're locked up, and you can't get away from what you tell people, and you can't get away physically," says Ingrid.

It's very scary to be in a place where you know they can commit you and keep you locked up for months and months and months and if you ever wanted to do anything, they could restrain you. You have absolutely no control over anything. They can stop you from using the phone, or writing to people—you give up whole control, and it's very scary.

This fear increased Ingrid's resistance because she believed that the more the staff knew about her, the longer they would confine her.

Robin realized Ingrid's fear of being restrained:

> The first step would be to put me in the quiet room. If I wouldn't cooperate, or if I acted out while I was in there, they would restrain me. Six or eight large men would jump on me and hold me down, which is really terrifying. If I wouldn't stop struggling, they would tie me in bed. If I still didn't calm down, they would inject me. Then for the next few days I would have bruises all over me.

Such practices actually protect borderlines and help them learn self-control: some patients in fact liked the quiet room because they felt safe there. But Ingrid and Robin are describing one of the most renowned treatment programs in the country. For a patient like Paige who happens into a bad situation, such confinement could become a nightmare.

• damage to self-esteem.

The unit director admits that many patients echo this complaint expressed by Robin:

> On the unit they have a philosophy that made me feel even worse about myself than I did before. They give you a list of symptoms and things you do to other people, and you feel that you're doing it on purpose. And they confront you. It's accusatory.

• effects of institutionalization.

Previously hospitalized borderlines describe situations that were unrealistic and insulted their common sense. The staff enforced rules while permitting no reasoning and invested the smallest occurrences with enormous psychological significance. "One day I ran into the unit chief a few times in the hallway, and finally he stopped me to ask why we kept meeting each other," says Whitney. "I looked him straight in the eye and said, 'Doctor, sometimes a cigar is just a cigar.' "*

"If something happened and you were 5 percent responsible, you'd have to look at that 5 percent," says Ingrid. "Sometimes it's better to look at the other person's 95 percent."

Although intended to foster realistic interaction, this environment is clearly unlike real life. "The whole therapy thing keeps you from living in a way," says Ingrid. "Real life is a different way of communicating that you have to learn and that is not taught on the unit."

• difficulty in leaving.

*Freud's response to questions about the symbolic significance of his fondness for cigars.

Along with the level of caring, this unrealistic situation is one reason that borderlines become terrified of the prospect of discharge and often regress both beforehand and afterward. "When they told me I was leaving, I trashed my room," says Rebecca.

It really scared me because I felt that all the supports I had gained in the hospital would disappear. I couldn't believe how intensely I felt I would be abandoned by people. I also questioned constantly whether I could hold my own if I felt suicidal again out there. I was constantly crying, not wanting to say goodbye to my peers. The staff had to be kidding!

Although therapists emphasize that hospitals are holding environments, they have long disregarded the effects of being ejected to create a new environment in the real world.

Various hospitals are now experimenting with programs to help the borderline patient wean herself from the unit at a comfortable rate. The inpatient might, for instance, take extended passes, attend school, or begin work. She might help plan her discharge, agree to a series of prospective release dates, switch to a day hospital (actually a night hospital would make more sense), move into supervised housing, or negotiate specified visits and/or phone calls back to the unit. The hospital might keep a bed open for a limited time after discharge so that the patient can return immediately if necessary.

• risks of regression.

This is the most controversial disadvantage of long-term hospitalization in particular. The issues appear to be whether inpatient treatment of the borderline does, in fact, cause regression and if so, whether this benefits or harms the patient.

The admonition by David F. Dawson, M.D., quoted above is repeated by other therapists. Dr. Masterson believes that except for adolescent or low-functioning borderlines, inpatient treatment should be minimal because "hospitals are caretaking environments that promote regression."[9] Dr. Paris agrees that a hospital is the worst place for a borderline. "It's not at all clear that hospitalization is necessary unless the patient is in a coma after overdose or otherwise needs medical care," he says. "Running around trying to prevent suicide just drags the therapist down."

"There is much evidence anecdotally and even some in the research that borderlines don't do well in hospitals," says Dr. Links.

The mental health profession sets up a context that may enhance the presentation of the disabilities. The analogy would be with a physical handicap.

You don't keep the patient in bed; rather you try to help him by changing the environment to accommodate and mobilize him. If borderlines have difficulties in interpersonal functioning, a hospital setting that encourages them to be dependent and responds to expressions of incompetence might be the worst thing if that's part of the disability.

Borderlines still end up in hospital and get treated there, and at the moment there probably isn't a better setting. I don't want to give the wrong impression. Some of them might need long-term hospitalization, that's fair enough. But by looking at new settings for intervention, we might be better able to gain their cooperation and get them to function more cooperatively and competently.

An interesting feature of this argument is that Drs. Dawson, Paris, and Links all practice in Canada. "Here we probably have less opportunity for long-term hospitalization just by the nature of the funding, so borderlines tend to have short hospitalizations," says Dr. Links. "This serves a purpose at least to protect the patient." But he agrees with my reminder that therapists view short- and long-term hospitalizations as different treatment modalities, perhaps explaining some of the skepticism on the part of Canadian psychiatrists about what inpatient treatment can accomplish.

Dr. McGlashan has concluded, on the other hand, that institutionalization is not as much of a danger for borderlines as many people think. "It's true that borderlines want to be hospitalized to be taken care of and coddled," he says.

But our experience was that when indulged in this respect, with no discharge date, eventually the patients said, "So what's this? What's so great about it?" They realized that the world out there has a lot more exciting things going on, that this resting and being cradled in the arms of your therapist is not all it's cracked up to be, and that it's actually more fun being an adult.

The majority of the men got into a fight with somebody here and took off, in typical adolescent style, leaving AWOL or signing out against medical advice. Many of the women went the same way. But however they did it, they got themselves out. They got into more mature functioning in a way because they wanted to.

Dr. McGlashan's study has shown that borderlines who left in this manner were doing as well 15 years later as those discharged more appropriately. Although their departures reflected impulsivity, they apparently also shared a striving for independence and autonomy.[10]

Dr. Gunderson suggests that harmful and disruptive regression is probably the result of poorly designed programs.[11] From the patient's viewpoint, it might seem to matter little why she has regressed, but the reason is important. Whether regression occurs is less important than what its effects might be.

Therapists' views on this issue depend on whether they consider the goals of hospitalization to be stabilization and attachment or the breaking down and reconstruction of the personality. In other words, the controversy is the distinction between supportive and expressive therapy writ large. If regression is considered essential to the patient's treatment, the staff will be prepared to work with it effectively; if it is not, and therefore not properly addressed, it will be at best useless and at worst harmful. Improperly handled, borderline regression can be a devastating experience.

A Typical Day on a Borderline Unit

The recollections of their hospitalization presented here are from borderlines who were successfully treated in a prestigious long-term unit designed for such patients. Its specificity to this particular unit and patient qualify the following description by one of them of what the program was like.

While in outpatient therapy, Whitney made repeated suicide attempts to elicit attention from her psychiatrist and to be hospitalized briefly:

> I wanted to be in the hospital, but I also wanted my psychiatrist to take care of me and to come and go as I pleased. With any short-term hospitalization, your doctor is your primary caretaker, and he decides when you go out and don't. Mine gave me eight-hour passes, and I had a private room. By the third hospitalization, he figured out that he had been making it too comfy and I was living my life there.

Whitney's psychiatrist then announced that he wasn't doing his job of keeping her out of the hospital and that the situation had to change. "I was devastated because I was so attached to him, and that was when I realized that I had to either go long term or kill myself," she says. Her psychiatrist recommended the unit on which Whitney spent 11 months.

Whitney's initial reaction to this hospital was typical of newly admitted borderlines:

> The minute I got there I wanted to leave. I put in my 72-hour letter [request for discharge] the next day. They expected me to stay in a four-bed room,

which I thought was horrendous, and there was no air conditioning or other comforts. I was also told I would be restricted for six weeks. There was no way I wanted that. And it was a confrontational unit. Instead of being babied, I had my behaviors thrown in my face. It scared me to death, even more than being alone.

The average age I think was 25, with a range from 20 to 30. There were a few teenagers and one male while I was there.

It was therapy from the minute you got up until you went to sleep. It was exhausting at times. You had to be out of bed by eight, or they would come, get you up, and lock the door for the day. You would have breakfast and have to be escorted to activities by a peer on the unit to get you to interact with them. That was hard for me, so they put me on the buddy system pretty quickly to get me to be less afraid of people and to open up.

Then you had your individual therapy session, a meeting with your vocational counselor, then a meeting in the afternoon, then one at night, and one-to-one meetings with staff members. Once a week there would be peer group with the staff and other patients, where you talked about how your week had gone. It was very intense. How you did in that peer group determined whether or not you got passes for the week.

Even just sitting down on the unit and talking, if you or somebody else were having a hard time, it just felt like therapy 24 hours a day. Very, very intensive.

My activities were leisure things because I always had such a hard time relaxing. I also had a TA staff member who would talk with me periodically about my leisure activities. I could never finish something, so I went into things like ceramics. It sounds like the mental patient thing to do, but it did teach me a lot because I stuck with something. It was totally frustrating at first—I didn't want to do it; I begged to get out of it, but I was made to stick with it. I ended up really getting a lot of pleasure out of it.

They also put me in seasonal sports because I hate sports. They thought it was because I never did them as a kid. But I still don't like sports, although it was fun at times.

I had seasonal crafts too, and I worked in the patient-run thrift shop handling food and clothing donations. We earned work credits and got gift certificates to a classy department store. Eventually I had a volunteer job off grounds.

In the meantime people were at all different stages of treatment, and everything, *everything* under the sun was a community issue.

One time a girl refused to go to peer group and was carried into the quiet room. It was very upsetting, especially because right afterwards I had to collect myself and go to a volunteer job off grounds. It felt really horrible, as if I was living two lives. Sometimes when people acted out, I would be hit in the face with being in a mental hospital. Other times I could go for days without realizing where I was.

If this description surprises readers, Ingrid will be gratified. "More than anything else, I want people to know what the hospital is like, and what therapy is like, and what kinds of things are worked on," she says.

> To get rid of the stigma. To make people less scared of it, so they wouldn't overreact to it, so that I could talk about it. People can be honest about rehabilitation centers, but to have been in a hospital for two years . . . I wish people could understand that borderlines can get beyond all that and get better.

Group Therapy

Obviously many of the advantages of hospitalization can be derived from psychodynamic group therapy, whether inpatient or outpatient.[12] Like a hospital unit, group therapy creates more interactions than individual therapy does. Within a group, the borderline patient can work on her interpersonal as well as individual issues.

Like family therapy, group therapy has its own huge literature, very little of which is specific to borderline patients. "Nevertheless," writes Dr. Gunderson, "it is common clinical wisdom that group therapy is a valuable adjunct to ongoing individual psychotherapy."[13] It appears clearly indicated in particular for patients with histories of incest.[14]

Dr. Gunderson explains the discrepancy between clinical practice and published data in terms of the difficulty of getting borderlines to enter groups and stay put. He suggests that one way to do so is to make participation in group therapy a condition of individual treatment.

Group therapy for borderlines is viewed as an adjunct, not an alternative, to individual treatment. Some therapists believe that the group should be designed specifically for borderlines, while others think that these patients need the majority of the group members to be better controlled and to have stronger egos. Apparently psychotic and neurotic patients, who tend to be more inhibited, benefit from having borderlines in their groups.[15]

Compared to individual therapy, group therapy offers borderline patients the following advantages:

- It dilutes the intensity of the one-to-one relationship with the therapist, making it easier to sort out transference from realistic reactions.
- The patient can more easily control her distance from a group and can take "time off" from treatment by withdrawing. Leonard Horwitz,

Ph.D., describes a borderline patient who regulated her emotional involvement with a group by falling asleep when an upsetting issue was discussed.[16]
- It forces the borderline to confront her envy of others and her need for exclusive attention.
- Patients who have trouble recognizing their maladaptive behaviors can overcome their denial by observing them in others.
- The social structure provided by the group anchors the patient in reality and helps her control her behavior.
- Isolated patients can benefit from the stimulation, interaction, and support they obtain from the group.
- If the patient's own therapist leads or co-leads the group (which is not necessarily recommended), he can better recognize his unwarranted emotional reactions to individual patients.
- Confrontation by peers can be more believable and acceptable than that by a therapist, whom the borderline is more likely to distort. And peers are often better than therapists at spotting manipulation and other borderline tactics. These features, however, make group meetings painful. Even patients who report that peer confrontation was the most valuable aspect of their treatment found least helpful the humiliation involved.
- Recovering patients can serve as role models.

Conversely, a badly managed group can encourage borderlines to regress. "I don't want attention in my eating disorders group all the time, but if I'm feeling particularly bad, it would be nice if someone recognized it without my having to act out," says Ingrid. "This group just makes me feel miserable all over again—in real life, you get encouragement for doing okay."

Other disadvantages to group therapy are as follows:
- Borderline candidates for group therapy—and therapists to lead them—must both be selected very carefully. An unskilled therapist can easily be sucked into group pathology.
- The same exasperating qualities that borderlines need most to work on might make group therapy a bad idea. Many borderlines are self-absorbed and unempathetic; like Gerry, who admits that he "just didn't care," they may not give enough attention and support to other group members.
- Other people's problems that are upsetting or irrevelant may cause isolated patients to become even more withdrawn.
- The group members may start taking care of each other.

One reason group therapy for borderlines has not been emphasized may be that whether its features are advantages or disadvantages seems to depend entirely on the particular group. The same could be said of any group, of course, the difference being that borderlines could exert far more influence on both members and leaders.

An interesting example is a study conducted by Norman D. Macaskill, M.R.C. Psych., nearly a decade ago.[17] Dr. Macaskill asked eight female DIB borderlines who felt they had benefited from group therapy to complete questionnaires indicating which aspects of it they found most and least helpful. Two features stood out as being most helpful. One was the opportunities to help others in the group, suggesting that group therapy has a unique effect of counteracting borderline self-centeredness, demandingness, and envy. The other was that of learning about their own behavior and feelings through empathic interpretation that made the group members feel great relief at being understood.

This appreciation contrasted with the patients' dislike of learning how they appeared to others and working out difficulties with fellow group members. Feedback from each other seemed painful, irrelevant, and useless compared to interpretations from the therapist. It was as though the patients were having individual therapy within the group: they benefited from the "holding" quality of the therapist-patient relationship, not from their interaction with peers. Yet something about group membership gave the patients hope for the future.

Dr. Macaskill observes that his findings corroborate Dr. Kernberg's theory: early interpretation of hostility and narcissistic features has a supportive and strengthening effect. It is not the technique but how it is applied that determines whether it is soothing or intrusive. The study also suggests that group therapy for borderlines should be carefully designed to prevent their transforming it into what they want it to be.

It may become necessary further to develop group treatments—or the alternative modalities mentioned by Dr. Links—simply because third-party payers will increasingly demand more proof of treatment efficacy than is presently available for hospitalization. Such alternatives might be refined to offer many of the benefits of hospitalization while decreasing the expenses and risks. That so much research needs to be done in this area implies that many possibilities exist. Meanwhile it remains important to recognize that some borderlines spend time in "dormitories"— not snake pits.

Notes

1. David F. Dawson, M.D., "Treatment of the Borderline Patient: Relationship Management, *Canadian Journal of Psychiatry*, Vol. 33, No. 5 (June 1988), p. 372.
2. Michael Rosenbluth, M.D., "The Inpatient Treatment of the Borderline Personality Disorder: A Critical Review and Discussion of Aftercare Implications," *Canadian Journal of Psychiatry*, Vol. 32, No. 3 (April 1987), p. 233.
3. Laura J. Miller, M.D., "Inpatient Management of Borderline Personality Disorder: A Review and Update," *Journal of Personality Disorders*, Vol. 3, No. 2 (1989), p. 122.
4. Ibid., pp. 125–26.
5. Rosenbluth, pp. 228–29.
6. Miller, p. 124.
7. Additional sources include Charles R. Swenson, M.D., "Psychodynamic Approach with Hospitalized Borderline Patients," paper read at the Psychodynamic Psychotherapy with Borderline Patients seminar, sponsored by The New York Hospital-Cornell Medical Center, Westchester Division, New York, 12 January 1991 (subsequent comments by Dr. Swenson are from this lecture); Harold W. Koenigsberg, M.D., "Indications for Hospitalization in the Treatment of Borderline Patients," *Psychiatric Quarterly*, Vol. 56, No. 4 (Winter 1984), pp. 247–58; Wayne S. Fenton, M.D., and Thomas H. McGlashan, M.D., "Long-Term Residential Care: Treatment of Choice for Refractory Character Disorder?" *Psychiatric Annals*, Vol. 20, No. 1 (January 1990), pp. 44–49; John G. Gunderson, M.D., *Borderline Personality Disorder* (Washington, D.C.: American Psychiatric Press, 1984), pp. 131–50; Lawrence J. Brown, "Staff Countertransference Reactions in the Hospital Treatment of Borderline Patients," *Psychiatry*, Vol. 43 (November 1980), pp. 333–45.
8. Gunderson, pp. 149–50.
9. James F. Masterson, M.D., *The Search for the Real Self: Unmasking the Personality Disorders of Our Age* (New York: The Free Press, 1988), p. 207.
10. Thomas H. McGlashan, M.D., and Robert K. Heinssen, Ph.D., "Hospital Discharge Status and Long-Term Outcome for Patients with Schizophrenia, Schizoaffective Disorder, Borderline Personality Disorder, and Unipolar Affective Disorder," *Archives of General Psychiatry*, Vol. 45 (April 1988), p. 367. See also Robert K. Heinssen, Ph.D., and Thomas H. McGlashan, M.D., "Predicting Hospital Discharge Status for Patients with Schizophrenia, Schizoaffective Disorder, Borderline Personality Disorder, and Unipolar Affective Disorder, *Archives of General Psychiatry*, Vol. 45 (April 1988), pp. 353–60.
11 Gunderson, p. 135.
12. For an overview, see Thomas A. Aronson, M.D., "A Critical Review of Psychotherapeutic Treatments of the Borderline Personality: Historical Trends and Future Directions," *Journal of Nervous and Mental Disease*, Vol. 177, No. 9 (1989), pp. 522–23.
13. Gunderson, p. 170.
14. Judith Herman, M.D., and Emily Schatzow, M.Ed., "Time-Limited Group Therapy for Women with a History of Incest," *International Journal of Group Psychotherapy*, Vol. 34, No. 4 (October 1984), p. 606.
15. Gunderson, pp. 171–72.
16. Leonard Horwitz, Ph.D., "Group Psychotherapy of the Borderline Patient," in *Borderline Personality Disorders: The Concept, the Syndrome, the Patient,* ed. Peter Hartocollis, M.D., Ph.D. (New York: International Universities Press, 1977), p. 405.
17. Norman D. Macaskill, M.R.C. Psych, "Therapeutic Factors in Group Therapy with Borderline Patients," *International Journal of Group Therapy*, Vol. 32, No. 1 (January 1982), pp. 61–73.

26

Turning Points and Followups

"Treatment is not the only path to better adaptation. All of the followup studies have indicated that on the whole borderlines get better, if you can keep them alive. But the ways they get better are innumerable and highly individual."

THOMAS H. McGLASHAN, M.D.

As an educated consumer, a borderline contemplating the prospect of treatment needs to consider whether psychotherapy will actually help her. To find out if a particular type of therapy is effective for an illness, researchers conduct long-term followup studies of patients. "Followup gives the lie to all of our fancy findings," says Dr. Soloff. "We have to do followup to see what happens when treatment ends—does it carry over, has the patient truly learned a new way?"

Problems in Methodology

"I'm not aware of any evidence for psychotherapy working with borderlines," says Dr. Akiskal. "I know of no study that meets today's criteria for methodological rigor in psychotherapy research."[1] One reason none of the psychodynamic approaches to BPD has yet been proved effective is that followup studies are tremendously difficult to conduct properly. In response to Dr. Akiskal's comment, Dr. McGlashan says,

The bottom line is that it is pragmatically impossible to design a study to test the efficacy of psychoanalytic psychotherapy, or basically just about any form of interpersonal psychotherapy, that would satisfy the level of methodological rigor used in drug studies. Biological psychiatrists are extraordinarily cavalier when they say that everything has to reach the drug study standard.

They're right in terms of its being necessary to demonstrate scientifically that psychotherapy is efficacious. But the methodological controls would require hundreds of thousands of hours of work. Theoretical necessity does not make such research possible.

Methodological soundness demands a randomized controlled outcome study. To evaluate psychotherapy with borderlines, researchers would randomly assign some patients to the treatment being studied and others to a second modality that might be viewed as a standard or "placebo."

The study would require DIB borderlines who have no other mental illnesses that might affect their prognoses. It would continue for the several years required to restructure a personality; a brief followup might fall short of turning points in treatment.

But a study of that length would allow life factors to intrude and affect the patients' prognoses independent of their therapy. Various patients might stumble upon (or lose) a suitable relationship, win a lottery, become paralyzed in an auto accident, or just react to more mundane occurrences impossible to distinguish from treatment effects. "We have learned that to study outcome alone is not enough," says Dr. Kernberg. "To differentiate treatment from life, we must study whether outcome is related to process."

Its length would make a properly controlled long-term study unethical. The control group of borderlines would spend years getting less than optimal treatment or none at all. Psychotherapy cannot be thus withheld from patients, just as placebos can be given only temporarily during medication trials.

The study would be limited to one type of treatment because adjunctive therapies would confound the results as variables. But we have seen how widely varied psychoanalytic approaches alone can be. Even if the study focused on a clearly defined modality, evaluations would be necessary to insure that the therapists conducted it correctly. Independent judges would need to monitor each patient's treatment by continually studying videotapes of sessions.

These (and other) difficulties would apply to prospective followups of therapy with any types of patients. Borderlines, of course, pose special problems. "My impression is that there is less prospective research on BPD than on other psychiatric disorders," says Wayne S. Fenton, M.D.

A major problem is the difficulty of eliciting and sustaining cooperation from borderline patients over long periods of time. This may be especially true in short-term treatment settings, where a revolving-door situation develops in which the patients often leave angry. The heterogeneity of the patients also makes research difficult.

Dr. Fenton's own prospective study of borderline and schizotypal young adults is focused on both trauma histories and neurobiological underpinnings, following their developmental influences. This is different from studying treatment efficacy, which cannot be demonstrated by these means.

But even just showing the course of BPD in a specific group of patients is useful, especially when combined with other findings. "The argument whether or not treatment helps is in a way more political and ideological than really technical as far as I can tell," says Dr. Kernberg.

> I very much agree that we need empirical research, but that's only one part. The second part is clinical experience, and the third part is investigation into the psychopathology, into the mechanisms of what happens. I think you have to put these together.

In and of themselves, the major long-term followup studies of BPD conducted thus far have yielded valuable results. Among these was pleasantly surprising evidence that even the sickest borderlines eventually get better. This finding implicitly qualified the standard view of personality disorders. "A defining feature of a personality disorder is that the pattern of adaptation be chronic and relatively inflexible to treatment and life stress," says Dr. McGlashan. "But our findings show that borderlines undergo changes with time."

Dr. Kernberg had concluded as much years earlier. Describing the Menninger Project, he says,

> One has to remember that this project started in 1954; it is the first generation of psychotherapy research. We have become much more sophisticated, but with all its limitations, it had some significant findings indicating that technique influences the outcome in long-term psychoanalytic psychotherapy with very sick patients. That's an empirical valid finding.

Although this project was smaller and less rigorous methodologically than the outcome studies that followed, it completely convinced Dr. Kernberg that borderlines could get better.

The Major Long-Term Followup Studies

Other therapists learned as much in the mid-1980s, when a series of large-scale long-term followup studies of previously hospitalized borderlines began to appear from major treatment facilities. These include:

- *The Austen Riggs Study* (1985; 1989). Eric M. Plakun, M.D., and his colleagues at the Austen Riggs Center in Massachusetts followed 63 *DSM-III* borderlines over an average of 14 years.[2] Seventy-six percent of these patients achieved moderate to good outcome at followup.[3] Noting a considerable range from low to high functioning, however, Dr. Plakun began further study of potential predictors of outcome. The researchers reported that they saw no reason to assume that treatment did not contribute to the patients' improvement. They did not report a suicide rate.
- *The Chestnut Lodge Study* (1986). Considered the most elegant to date, Dr. McGlashan's study at Chestnut Lodge followed 81 *DSM-III*/DIB borderlines over an average of 15 years. Overall about 80 percent of the patients attained moderate to good outcome. The suicide rate was 3 percent. The patients who survived tended to function well by the time they reached their forties but remained susceptible to relapses in their late forties to early fifties, most often after losing a relationship.[4]
- *The PI-500 Study* (1986; 1990). Borrowed from the title of another study, "500" refers to 550 patients from the New York State Psychiatric Institute, 205 of which were *DSM-III* borderlines, traced by Dr. Stone and his colleagues over an average of 16 years. The incidence of suicide among the borderline patients was 9.4 percent. In addition to the life course identified by Dr. McGlashan, Dr. Stone found a greater variety of other patterns leading to generally positive outcomes for two-thirds of the patients.[5]
- *The Montreal Study* (1987). This study by Dr. Paris and his colleagues followed 100 DIB borderline patients for an average of 15 years, by which time 75 percent were no longer diagnosable as borderline. All scales of the DIB showed reduced symptoms. The suicide rate of 8.5 percent was, however, comparable to Dr. Stone's.

The importance of this study is that unlike the other three, which involved patients from more privileged families, it followed borderlines treated at the Jewish General Hospital in Montreal. The study therefore included patients from a wider range of socioeconomic and educational backgrounds who Dr. Paris feels represented their borderline population as a whole. The patients also received a wider variety of followup treatments. That the results of this study were consistent with those of its predecessors therefore lent their data considerable support.[6]

The major discrepancy between the studies is the low suicide rate found by Dr. McGlashan and the comparable higher ones found by Drs. Stone and Paris. Dr. McGlashan implicates the selection factor:

> The patients who went to PI did so early in their psychiatric careers. PI was often the first or second admission for them. For our patients it was often the fourth, fifth, or sixth admission, so they had been ill longer. Quite possibly the seriously suicidal ones had indeed been successful and killed themselves. Our group would therefore have been purged of the highly suicidal patients, so we found a low frequency of suicide.

The risk of suicide is worst when a borderline is in her twenties; Dr. Stone therefore attributes the discrepancy to the younger ages of the patients in the PI-500.[7]

The findings, then, are that roughly 9 percent of previously hospitalized borderlines commit suicide, most while in their twenties. Like antisocial patients and substance abusers, borderlines who survive improve as they reach their thirties and forties. One major goal of therapy is therefore simply to keep them alive long enough for the illness to subside.

Beyond this, the findings are controversial. The studies suggest that even long-term hospitalization does not make borderlines worse, but nobody knows for sure whether long-term intensive psychotherapy makes them better. Dr. Kernberg's conviction that it does is based on positive clinical as well as followup data, his observation of which, he says, "is what keeps me going."

Dr. Stone and his colleagues write that the findings of the four studies "call into question long-held claims about the psychotherapeutic treatment of choice, specifically about the need for exploratory therapy."[8] But psychotherapy in the generic sense, he writes elsewhere, especially when flexible and eclectic, "is frequently effective and even life saving with selected borderline patients."[9]

Dr. McGlashan evaluates the results of his study conservatively:

> I think that the information that comes out of the studies we did is a careful description of the life course of borderline patients who have been through an intensive inpatient treatment program. That's all you can say. You can't say that their life course resulted from that. When I was doing followup interviews, actually talking to these people, depending on the individual and

the particular story, I had my hunch as to which ones really benefited from the experience and which ones didn't, who got better because of the treatment and who got better some other way.

But merely knowing that they *did* get better helps cheer clinicians and motivate them to stick with borderline patients through the hard times.

Who Might Recover?

In conducting followup studies, researchers test several variables that might predict which patients are most likely to recover. But in the four studies described above, most of the variables tested predicted nothing, those that did were weak predictors, and the results were inconsistent.[10]

The factors listed here have been reported by other therapists as well as by the authors of these followup studies. They should be viewed simply as possible guidelines for treatment focus.

WHAT MAKES BORDERLINES WORSE

One feature often mentioned as worsening the prognosis for borderline patients is the presence of antisociality, malignant narcissism (which includes antisocial features), paranoia, or some combination of these that gives rise to hostility, aggression, manipulation, and lying. "The less ordinary honesty is preserved, the worse the prognosis," says Dr. Kernberg, who calls antisocial features one of the two most important prognostic indicators he has experienced.

Other coexisting conditions that can worsen the prognosis are substance abuse (in the patient or family history, except for alcoholism controlled by membership in Alcoholics Anonymous), depression, premenstrual syndrome, eating or anxiety disorders, or full-blown obsessive-compulsive disorder.

The presence of all eight *DSM-III-R* borderline symptoms or a preponderance of inappropriate anger, affective instability, or self-damaging acts does not bode well. Neither does a history of incest.

These factors should not be considered harbingers of doom, however, because progress in these areas in particular would proportionately *improve* a patient's prognosis.

WHAT MAKES BORDERLINES BETTER

The other prognostic indicator favored by Dr. Kernberg is the capacity for deep relationships with other people. "The more the patient is capable of real investment in commitment to others, hanging in there in relationships that are nonexploitive, nonparasitic, even if they are sick and neurotic," he says, "the better the prognosis." Likewise, the greater the borderline's ability to empathize, to control aggression in relationships, to enjoy sex (in this context, even "perverse" sexuality is better than none), and to evoke soothing memories, the brighter her prospects.

Borderlines are also likely to improve if they have natural advantages: high IQ, talent and capacity for creative accomplishment, exceptional attractiveness (in women), likableness, and self-discipline. Other positive signs are emotions that are distinct but controllable, especially the capacity to enjoy and remember pleasure (as opposed to needing frequently repeated excitement).

Core Gundersonian borderlines have a better prognosis because the DIB evaluates their previous level of functioning and screens out patients with schizotypal traits. Borderlines whose parents had intact marriages have had better outcomes than those whose family conflicts are indicated by divorce.

Patients functioning the best when admitted to a hospital (as indicated by the number and length of their previous admissions) are most likely to improve over time. A minor but intriguing finding by Dr. Plakun is that self-destructive behavior by borderlines during, but not preceding, hospitalization predicts better outcomes in terms of social and intimate functioning. Dr. Plakun notes that in 1965, Winnicott had described this phenomenon: the beneficial effects of allowing negative feelings to emerge within the contained holding environment of therapy, even if they must be managed by acting out.[11]

SUICIDE

The accepted suicide rate for BPD is comparable to those of other severe illnesses. "BPD may be a fashionable diagnosis," says Dr. Soloff, "but it's also as lethal as major depression or schizophrenia."

The risk of suicide, which is greatly increased in borderline alcoholics, peaks at around age 30. Dr. Paris' research finds suicide in borderlines to be predicted by previous attempts, higher education,[12] and better childhoods overall (reflecting the discrepancy between their expectations and their illness).[13] He notes also, however, that these patients also kill themselves unexpectedly, and it is uncertain whether treatment makes a difference.[14]

Dr. Paris believes that therapists should not focus on a patient's suicidality: some borderlines use the prospect of killing themselves as a temporary coping technique. Difficult as it may be, the therapist should just accept the risk and proceed with treatment. "To be derailed by chronic suicidality is to lose sight of the real work of psychotherapy," Dr. Paris writes. "Paradoxically, only by tolerating chronic suicidality can suicidality be successfully treated."[15]

Turning Points

The borderlines interviewed for this book provide their own short-term mini-followup that illustrates how difficult it can be to capture the effects of therapy. People concerned about them tend to want specific, if not simple, answers, so these patients have tried to identify actual turning points in their treatment.

Rebecca describes a change that occurred after she and another girl tried to elope from a hospital after a family visit. By concidence, Rebecca's parents took a different route home; the girls were spotted running across that road, and her brothers jumped out of the car and tackled them. At that point, Rebecca says, she began really to cooperate with the staff. "Another major turning point was becoming an active worker in the hospital bookstore," she says. "This experience helped me develop strong self-esteem and the courage to expand and achieve goals vocationally."

But like many psychiatric patients—borderline or otherwise—Rebecca still wonders about the *process* of recovery and complains that no one ever describes it:

> I was always fascinated by talking to people about borderline personality disorder, whether anybody has been able to pinpoint what the change is from feeling so desperate and not wanting to live to where they want to live again and get on with their life. What happens? Books never say. There is no direct answer. I don't know if it's building up self-esteem or lifting the depression.
>
> One thing I do know for sure, you have to keep busy. You just can't sit with your illness. I don't care what anybody says. You have to move physi-

cally or mentally. Otherwise you just obsess and go deeper where you don't want to let anybody else in.

In contrast to Rebecca's avoidance of obsessing, Emily believes that self-examination is a key ingredient:

> I think it's the will of the person to really benefit from therapy and to get better. I reached that point in the hospital about halfway through. I realized that I couldn't point my fingers at everybody else all the time, that something was wrong with me and that I couldn't look outside of myself to get better. Yes, you have to reach out for treatment and help, but to get better, you must look inside yourself and be honest, and that is very foreign to you.

Although Ingrid had cried out for help in all kinds of ways, she spent three years in psychiatric hospitals lying to her therapists. "It was a way of making contact without letting people get too close," she says. "I told psychological truths." Her turning point was almost an accident: her therapist decided to present Ingrid's case in a conference:

> When she explained that to me, I suddenly realized that it was all over. My therapy sessions and one-to-ones with the staff were all going to be video-taped, and everyone on the unit would be sitting down in meetings and comparing notes about me. I knew they would piece things together and figure out how much I had been lying to everyone. So I came into my next session with a list of ten things I had been lying to my therapist about.

Alice identifies a second turning point that occurred after a relapse:

> One turning point was when three or four people were discharged from the unit and I decided that for the first time I was going to deal with the losses. When I decided to face things rather than run away from them, my treatment really started to progress.
>
> But I really hadn't totally made the decision to get better. Even from the day I left the hospital, I was sure I would be dead within the first week, then the first year. I don't think I really decided to give up suicide until after I tried. During my second hospitalization, I made a decision not to be self-destructive any more. At some point you have to give up the unhelpful options. For three years I haven't thought about suicide. I don't want to be dead or have scars on my arms—there's no point in it. It didn't help me.
>
> It's a very conscious decision too.

These comments imply that recovery proceeds in stages marked by plateaus from which the patient must decide to boost herself to the next level. They suggest also that a patient may mistake a plateau for recovery and therefore have some pleasant surprises.

Back in the Real World

Alice's relapse after discharge is part of a pattern common among borderlines, one of several that have been articulated by Dr. Swenson and his colleagues. A few years ago, The New York Hospital-Cornell Medical Center, Westchester Division, held a symposium for those borderlines who had been hospitalized over the previous eight years and the present and former staff members who treated them. Sixty former patients attended, described their experiences, and completed questionnaires about the quality of their lives since discharge.

According to these data, two-thirds of the patients show consistent patterns of misery at different times. All of them enter the hospital with levels of misery close to 100. Six months into their treatment, the level is 50–60, and at discharge it ranges from 70–90.

The first year after discharge is hell. Six months into it, the misery levels are 80 and higher, although with much less acting out. But from two to eight years after hospitalization, a dramatic trend occurs in which the misery levels drop to 0–30.

Dr. Swenson cautions that this information comes from a self-selected group of borderlines who improved more than the patients who didn't come back. But it agrees with data from other short-term followup studies in which the global outcome scores a few years after hospitalization are also considerably higher than therapists might ever have expected.

The borderline patients reported that what helped them the most was to have someone who believed in them and to maintain friendships from the unit. For those capable of it, working was extremely important. The patients didn't remember much specifically about their therapy. Their evocative memories consisted mostly of particular incidents in which a staff member said, "Cut that out," or "Get your act together," or the like.[16]

Recovered or Coping?

Not surprisingly, all of the results described in this chapter have been greeted with great fanfare. But the optimism now being voiced by therapists creates some risks. Proof that the borderline can improve may produce impatience for her to do so. "The most important thing to recognize is that this problem took years to create, and there will probably never be a quick cure for it," says Linehan. "So there is a real need for patience and compassion all the way."

Another risk is that of unrealistically raising the hopes of borderlines and those concerned about them.

In the context of followup, "better" can mean functioning reasonably close to normal. Describing the borderline patients in their followup study, Dr. Paris and his colleagues write that "their work history, social relationships and family adjustment are all less than ideal, but not notably different from what one would see in an average outpatient clinic population."[17]

What this implies—and what researchers like to use as shorthand—is that patients will eventually be no longer diagnosable as borderline. Immediately this measurement suggests a qualification. As we well know, *DSM-III-R* is based on symptoms, not dynamics, and for many borderlines, apparently these are all that change. "The more flagrant symptoms go away, but I don't think the unhappiness does," says Dr. Siever. "The borderlines just aren't bothering people as much." Dr. Soloff agrees:

> The reason borderlines get better—and this is a clinical impression but also based on some understanding of the dynamics—is that the impulsivity dies down. They're not in hospitals or cutting themselves or overdosing or doing other impulsive behaviors any longer. Instead they have settled down into rather dependent kinds of relationships.
>
> Some of them have traded their overt demandingness and their acting out for physical signs and symptoms. They seem to become hypochondriacal. This is just some patients. But those individuals are not healthy and happy; they are still somewhat impaired. In that sense, character pathology isn't cured. People learn to cope.

From the viewpoints of their therapists or any other outsiders, symptom reduction could be viewed as a great improvement not felt by the patients themselves.

As Dr. McGlashan's opening quotation states, the paths to recovery are "innumerable." Perhaps treatment actually restructures the borderline's personality. Another possibility is that she simply grows up. Or a borderline could use a band-aid approach by avoiding situations that produce her symptoms. As Dr. Paris points out, some borderlines preclude difficulties by either withdrawing socially or establishing symbiotic relationships that are immature and close enough to satisfy their neediness and dependency.[18] But this could hardly be called true recovery.

Similarly, Dr. McGlashan and Robert K. Heinssen, Ph.D., have suggested that borderline symptoms dissipate not because of maturation but rather through simple burnout. People with Cluster B personality disorders are overtly out of place and relentlessly elicit rejection by or control from others. Over several years, this persistent negative social feedback may eventually convince them to behave better.[19]

The attention drawn to the followup study results shows both how desperate therapists become while treating borderlines and how unaware they might actually be of life's realities for middle-aged American women. Dr. Kernberg is the only therapist I know of who emphasizes that a woman's options for fulfillment decrease dramatically as she ages.* Ironically, life for borderlines gets better just when life for many women—especially those heavily invested in relationships—grows worse.

How high a quality of life could a middle-aged woman reasonably expect after an adulthood spent as a borderline? Some of Dr. McGlashan's data suggest that middle-aged borderlines remain highly susceptible to relapse after a loss. More studies of older borderlines may reveal a second suicide peak following menopause. And borderlines who remain single into their forties are likely to spend the rest of their lives confronting the "abandonment" they have fought so desperately to avoid.

Therapists can't expect to escort borderline patients into middle age, tidy up their symptoms, and then sigh with relief that the worst is over. The point at which patients are no longer borderline is one at which therapists might have to roll up their sleeves and tackle some new heavy-duty work.

Psychotherapy with borderlines in particular must focus upon relationships. At some point, however, a therapy that is realistic and humane would have to switch gears. The therapist must help the patient accept that for demographic rather than psychiatric reasons, she is likely to spend the rest of her life without an intimate relationship.† Real life is not like the extended family in *Thirtysomething,* and the borderline on her own will find her social opportunities severely circumscribed by discrimination against older single women.

The borderline must therefore make peace with herself and resolve to

---

*Here Dr. Kernberg means borderline patients who are highly narcissistic. But some of Dr. McGlashan's data appear to contradict Dr. Kernberg, who himself cautions therapists not to let middle-aged female patients automatically assume that life has already passed by.

†Removed from the full context of *Love Poems* (1969)—and her own series of affairs—Anne Sexton's "The Ballard of the Lonely Masturbator" well evokes the resulting isolation; the poem was published five years before Sexton's divorce and subsequent suicide at age 45.

build meaning into her life as relentlessly as her options for doing so dwindle. She can confront aging armed with longstanding stable friendships, family ties, fulfilling work, enjoyable leisure activities—any healthy context within which she has defined herself and can relish her freedom to live as she chooses.

Like any other bad news in this book, the above is not intended to discourage. It should instead alert the borderline that she will not be a treatment failure if she reaches middle age still struggling with unpleasant feelings. Nor will she be worthless, or even flawed, just because she is not involved in a committed relationship.

But borderlines should contemplate and plan for their emotional futures as astute yuppies anticipate comfortable retirements. The phenomenological truth is that borderlines will lose superficial attractiveness as they age just like everybody else. Behavior that elicits compassionate responses now will eventually look ridiculous, and their present means of manipulation will be completely stripped away.

The followup studies suggest only that no matter how bad she feels now, a borderline's efforts to recover have a good chance of success. They do *not* imply that a borderline can anticipate improvement with passive complacency. That a natural course for BPD has been suggested by these studies does not mean that any borderline can afford to wait it out.

The price paid for less misery need not be greater loneliness—but the time for the borderline to renounce self-destruction, decide what she wants out of life, and strengthen herself to pursue it, is *now*.

Notes

1. Hagop S. Akiskal, M.D., paper [affirmative] read at debate, "Resolved: The Etiology of Borderline Personality Disorder Is Predominantly Biological," 143rd annual meeting of the American Psychiatric Association, New York, 16 May 1990.
2. Eric M. Plakun, Paul E. Burkhardt, and John P. Muller, "Fourteen-year Followup of Borderline and Schizotypal Personality Disorders," *Comprehensive Psychiatry*, Vol. 26, No. 5 (September/October 1985), pp. 448–55.
3. Eric M. Plakun, M.D., "Narcissistic Personality Disorder: A Validity Study and Comparison to Borderline Personality Disorder," *Psychiatric Clinics of North America*, Vol. 12, No. 3 (September 1989), p. 612.
4. Thomas H. McGlashan, M.D., "The Chestnut Lodge Follow-Up Study, III: Long-Term Outcome of Borderline Personalities," *Archives of General Psychiatry*, Vol. 43 (January 1986), pp. 20–30; "The Prediction of Outcome in Borderline Personality Disorder: Part V of the Chestnut Lodge Follow-Up Study," in *The Borderline: Current Empirical Research*, ed. Thomas H. McGlashan, M.D. (Washington, D.C.: American Psychiatric Association, 1985), pp. 63–98.
5. Michael H. Stone, M.D., Stephen W. Hurt, Ph.D., and David K. Stone, "The PI 500: Long-Term Follow-up of Borderline Inpatients Meeting *DSM-III* Criteria, I. Global Outcome," *Journal of*

Personality Disorders, Vol. 1, No. 4 (1987), pp. 291–98. See also Michael H. Stone, M.D., *The Fate of Borderline Patients: Successful Outcome and Psychiatric Practice* (New York: The Guilford Press, 1990).

6. J. Paris, R. Brown, and D. Nowlis, "Long-term Followup of Borderline Patients in a General Hospital," *Comprehensive Psychiatry*, Vol. 28, No. 6 (November/December 1987), pp. 530–35.

7. Stone, *The Fate of Borderline Patients*, p. 283.

8. Stone, Hurt, and Stone, p. 297.

9. Michael H. Stone, M.D., "Treatment of Borderline Patients: A Pragmatic Approach," *Psychiatric Clinics of North America*, Vol. 13, No. 2 (June 1990), p. 278.

10. Joel Paris, M.D., "Followup Studies of Borderline Personality Disorder: A Critical Review," *Journal of Personality Disorders*, Vol. 2, No. 3 (1988), p. 193. See also Michael H. Stone, M.D., "The Course of Borderline Personality Disorder," in *Review of Psychiatry*, Vol. 8, ed. Allan Tasman, M.D., Robert E. Hales, M.D., and Allen J. Frances, M.D. (Washington, D.C., American Psychiatric Press, 1989), pp. 103–22.

11. Eric M. Plakun, M.D., "Prediction of Outcome in Borderline Personality Disorder," *Journal of Personality Disorders*, Vol. 5, No. 2 (1991), pp. 99–100.

12. Joel Paris, M.D., David Nowlis, Ph.D., and Ronald Brown, M.D., "Predictors of Suicide in Borderline Personality Disorder," *Canadian Journal of Psychiatry*, Vol. 34 (February 1989), pp. 8–9.

13. Joel Paris, M.D., "Empirical Investigation of the Role of Development in the Etiology and Outcome of Borderline Personality Disorder," in *Family Environment and Borderline Personality Disorder*, ed. Paul S. Links, M.D., M.Sc., F.R.C.P.(C) (Washington, D.C.: American Psychiatric Press, 1990), p. 126.

14. Joel Paris, M.D., "Completed Suicide in Borderline Personality Disorder," *Psychiatric Annals*, Vol. 20, No. 1 (January 1990), p. 20. See also C. Wesley Dingman, M.D., and Thomas H. McGlashan, M.D., "Characteristics of Patients with Serious Suicidal Intentions Who Ultimately Commit Suicide," *Hospital and Community Psychiatry*, Vol. 39, No. 3 (March 1988), pp. 295–99; David L. Gardner, M.D., and Rex William Cowdry, M.D., "Suicidal and Parasuicidal Behavior in Borderline Personality Disorder," *Psychiatric Clinics of North America*, Vol. 8, No. 2 (June 1985), pp. 389–403.

15. J. Paris, M.D., "Suicidality in Borderline Personality Disorder," in *Borderline Personality Disorder: Etiology and Treatment*, ed. Joel F. Paris, M.D. (Washington, D.C.: American Psychiatric Press, forthcoming).

16. Charles R. Swenson, M.D., "Psychodynamic Approach with Hospitalized Borderline Patients," paper read at the "Psychodynamic Psychotherapy with Borderline Patients seminar, sponsored by The New York Hospital-Cornell Medical Center, Westchester Division, New York, 12 January 1991.

17. Paris, Brown, and Nowlis, "Long-term Followup," p. 534.

18. Paris, "Critical Review," p. 195.

19. Thomas H. McGlashan, M.D., and Robert K. Heinssen, Ph.D., "Narcissistic, Antisocial, and Noncomorbid Subgroups of Borderline Disorder: Are They Distinct Entities by Long-Term Clinical Profile?" *Psychiatric Clinics of North America*, Vol. 12, No. 3 (September 1989), pp. 668–69.

27

Targeting Symptoms

Medication does not cure character but may modify its biologic basis in the long-term pursuit of change.

PAUL H. SOLOFF, M.D.[1]

*H*aving seen what might be expected from psychodynamic psychotherapy, readers can proceed in the next few chapters to consider two forms of therapy newer to borderline patients. Each looks especially promising both in and of itself or as an adjunct to enhance psychotherapeutic effects.

*O*ver half of hospitalized borderline patients receive medications, usually antipsychotics or antidepressants, although there is no treatment of choice.[2] An estimated 63 percent of borderline outpatients have had previous exposure to pharmacotherapy.[3] This is a relatively recent phenomenon. "It used to be easier to study the personality disorders because we didn't have to worry that the patients were on medications," says Dr. Siever.

> Now everybody comes into our hospital on medications; all the borderlines are on Prozac; and they don't want to get off them. Ten years ago, somebody who was borderline would not have been considered for medication at all.

It may seem odd for psychiatrists to medicate an illness when they don't know what it is. Predictably for BPD, the guidelines emerging from medication trials are confusing, and the data are still considered soft. But some guiding principles about pharmaco-therapy for borderline patients appear to have emerged.[4]

Bias Against Pharmacotherapy

Those borderline patients for whom medications have not been pre-scribed may see therapists who have reservations about their use. Psy-chotherapists may resist prescribing drugs* for borderlines in the belief that pharmacotherapy will damage the therapeutic relationship. They may fear that the borderline patient will be disappointed about psycho-therapy and will lose her motivation to participate. On the other hand, if medication quickly relieves some of the borderline patient's symptoms, it may activate deeper conflicts prematurely. The patient may use the prescribed drug to manipulate the therapist, act out her feelings, or dis-tract the two of them from the real work of psychotherapy. Even with-out such complications, therapists fear that medication may cause state-dependent learning.[5]

Dr. Masterson is opposed to the use of medications because he be-lieves that "drugs indicate to the patient that the therapist is willing to take care of her and will make life easy for her."[6] This assumption is contradicted, however, in a study by Dr. Waldinger and Arlene F. Frank, Ph.D. These researchers found that by relieving symptoms, creat-ing an impression of therapist involvement, and supplying a substance to take as well as verbal nurturance, pharmacotherapy often strengthened the borderline's relationship with her therapist and seldom weakened it.[7]

To date, the bias against pharmacotherapy for borderline patients re-mains just that, with no support from empirical evidence. "In skilled hands," writes Dr. Soloff, "the two approaches are entirely complemen-tary."[8] Thus Dr. Kernberg often tells psychiatric residents not to assume that expressive psychotherapy alone is sufficient: for some borderline patients, medications are entirely appropriate.[9]

But even those therapists who use pharmacotherapy do so as an ad-junct to psychotherapy. "Solely biologic treatment of borderline patients is abysmal," says Dr. Soloff. Part of this practice reflects the belief that drugs relieve symptoms temporarily, while psychotherapy creates per-

---

*Psychiatrists alone can prescribe medication. Psychologists and social workers often request them or *psychopharmacologists* (those who specialize in pharmacotherapy) to consult with and prescribe for their patients as necessary.

manent change. Ironically, we have seen that there is no scientific evidence that psychodynamic psychotherapy has any effect at all. Several studies show, however, that medications can benefit borderline patients, and much faster.

Researchers cannot assume that psychotherapy rather than pharmacotherapy reaches the source of BPD because no one has proven what causes the illness. "Perhaps the core is mild psychosis," write Solomon C. Goldberg, Ph.D., and S. Charles Schulz, M.D., "and the psychologic mechanism is the patient's way of dealing with the world through his or her altered perceptions."[10]

Medications can potentially benefit borderline patients in two ways. One is the relief of specific symptoms of BPD like anxiety or self-mutilation. The second is the treatment of another major illness that may exist along with the borderline condition. To review this usage first, we must once again raise that psychiatric specter, diagnosis.

Axis I and II Illnesses

All of the disorders listed in *DSM-III-R* are divided into two groups called Axis I and Axis II. Presented as chronic conditions featuring ingrained *traits* for which psychotherapy is clearly indicated, the personality disorders comprise Axis II. Viewed as more acute, time-limited, biological *states* for which pharmacotherapy is appropriate, other mental illnesses are included in Axis I. Whether a person has an Axis I or Axis II disorder determines which form of treatment is preferred and which is used as an adjunct.[11]

Because a patient can have a personality disorder and an Axis I disorder, or more than one Axis I or II disorder, therapists must distinguish any true coexisting disorders from symptoms that resemble them.

At this point, the task becomes more confusing. Although Axis I disorders are "acute," so to speak, and Axis II disorders are "chronic," the situation can be somewhat reversed with respect to Axis II *symptoms*. Both Axis II borderline depression and Axis I classical depression, for instance, feature episodic states arising out of longstanding predisposition.

Any borderline patient can present a bewildering array of depressive, anxiety, or psychotic symptoms, each of which can fluctuate in severity or appear and disappear over time. And researchers must use observation, standard tests, and feedback from others involved with the patients to try to specify and confirm their subjective descriptions of these symptoms.

"The distinction between Axis I and II is somewhat arbitrary, with many exceptions," says Dr. Cowdry.

> But it has been very helpful in reorienting theory and treatment away from an either-or situation toward recognition that an Axis I disorder can be superimposed on an Axis II disorder. Its most important practical effect has been to identify that people can have BPD and major depressive episodes, with specific implications for targeting treatment.

An overall treatment approach to a borderline patient with an Axis I disorder must be to target both illnesses. In itself, however, pharmacotherapy offers some options depending on individual cases. A borderline patient who is severely depressed or who has a strong family history of affective disorder is likely to be treated for her melancholia. Depending on which antidepressant is used, the patient may also gain better control over her behavior. If a patient has Axis I depression that is not overwhelming, another type of medication might likewise ease it while relieving suspiciousness, paranoia, and anxiety as well. "So it's really an issue of weighing all the evidence," says Dr. Cowdry,

> recognizing that in very few cases are we really going to be able clearly to identify a medication first choice. What we can instead do is lay out a road map to treatment with decreasingly likely approaches, with the expectation that we're going to be surprised along the way. In my experience, response is usually very difficult to predict.

One reason for this difficulty is that borderline responses to medications are idiosyncratic among psychiatric illnesses.

Target Symptoms

Pharmacotherapy is therefore used also to treat *groups* of symptoms of BPD. More or less disregarding whether the symptoms are state or trait, therapists aim toward those that are primarily affective, cognitive, or impulsive.

To do productive psychotherapy, a borderline patient must have her emotions, thoughts and perceptions well enough under control to allow for new learning. Dr. Stone suggests one hypothesis of how pharmacotherapy can help.

When medications are used to trim down the near-to-boiling-point heat in these brain systems, it becomes easier for the patient to work in psychotherapy to overwhelm them. It allows her time to achieve cognitive control over her maladaptive responses. The medications and the psychotherapy work synergistically as therapeutic methods. This offers our best hope at present for lasting recovery.[12]

This model suggests another reason that patients sometimes show dramatic improvement from medications that they maintain after the drugs have been stopped. (Conversely, however, medications can stop working after a time.)

Besides helping borderline patients engage in therapy, pharmacotherapy can also help keep them there. If the patient severely regresses, a temporary use of medication may spare her from hospitalization or preclude her impulsively quitting treatment.

Another measure of the complexity of BPD and the difficulties it creates is that every major class of psychotropic drugs has been tried in borderline patients. In some borderlines, these drugs work exactly as they do in other psychiatric illnesses. In other patients, the effects are broadly nonspecific—one drug can act upon a variety of borderline symptoms, and no one knows why.

Depending on the symptoms, most therapists prefer to prescribe one drug at a time for borderline patients. If indicated, a combination of drugs would most likely include a low-dose neuroleptic.

Neuroleptics

More is known about neuroleptics in the pharmacotherapy of borderlines than about any other type of medication. The consensus is that low-dose neuroleptics can relieve several acute symptoms of BPD: depressed mood, sleep disturbance, anger, hostility, impulsivity, suspiciousness, anxiety (and phobic anxiety), obsessive-compulsion, and preoccupations with physical symptoms. Some researchers have found the drugs to decrease parasuicidal episodes.

Neuroleptics also relieve cognitive symptoms like dissociation, confusion, illusions, and ideas of reference. It's difficult to tell whether or not the drugs affect borderline psychoses because the episodes are temporary. But their effect upon many of the symptoms of schizotypal personality disorder as well as BPD suggests that more than the antipsychotic action of neuroleptics is at work.

This is likewise suggested by the status of neuroleptics as "the border-line antidepressants." Neuroleptics sometimes relieve depression in borderlines better than tricyclic antidepressants do and thus tend to be the first drug prescribed even for borderlines who seem prominently depressed.

Antidepressants

This guideline is supported by a four-year study by Dr. Soloff and his colleagues comparing an antidepressant, amitriptyline, and a neuroleptic, haloperidol.[13] The researchers found that borderline patients who have major depression are *not* more likely to respond to an antidepressant than patients who have BPD alone.

A more recent study by Dr. Cornelius, Dr. Soloff, and their colleagues shows five borderline patients likewise responding well to fluoxetine even though four of them were free of major depression. Besides its efficacy in treating depression in this small group, fluoxetine also improved impulsivity and had mixed or no effects upon other symptoms.[14] Fluoxetine appears to have become "all the rage," as Dr. Cowdry says, among people involved with borderline patients. Families of extremely ill patients who have improved dramatically on the medication have created what another psychiatrist calls "a Prozac cult."

Although he describes Dr. Soloff's four-year study as "pioneering" and "vitally important," Dr. Cowdry disagrees with the particular finding about depressed and nondepressed borderlines:

> Major depressive disorder is a loose diagnosis, and amitriptyline was not necessarily the optimal tricyclic to use. Using a narrower definition of a classical affective episode and an antidepressant with a different spectrum of side effects might have shown a different pattern. My own clinical experience and our study using an MAOI, Parnate, found a near significant trend for borderline patients with a history of major depression to show a better response.

Dr. Soloff replies that their study findings are not terribly discrepant, depending on where the line of significance is drawn. Invoking esoteric statistical principles, researchers could quibble about whether Dr. Cowdry's data represent a *near significant trend,* as he says, or a *nonsignificant finding,* as Dr. Soloff maintains instead. "I agree absolutely that major depressive disorder is a loose diagnosis and that a narrower definition would give a different response," says Dr. Soloff.

That's a major problem with the treatment of affective states in BPD. Another is that biological psychiatrists get trapped into all-or-nothing thinking. They're used to curing depression, which is not what happens in borderline patients. The baseline in a borderline patient by definition includes severe mood swings and depressive periods. Biological psychiatrists pound away at these patients with drug after drug after drug, and they're very disappointed that the end result is not a low enough score on a depression rating scale to be a cure. To them, partial remission means still depressed.

So part of it is the psychiatrist's perspective. When the literature says that borderline patients respond more poorly to all antidepressants even if they have a comorbid major depression, it may be contaminated by the perspective of the investigator looking for a cure.

Although used widely by depressed patients, amitriptyline actually tends to worsen many symptoms in some borderline patients. The drug has increased suicidality, paranoia, impulsivity, demandingness, assaultiveness, and distorted thinking and has caused overall deterioration. Another tricyclic, desipramine, has likewise been found to be ineffective in borderline patients or to make symptoms worse.[15]

These odd response patterns have many possible explanations, one of which is that what borderlines describe as depression is really an atypical affective disturbance. The psychiatrist's usual response in such tricky circumstances is to try MAOI antidepressants, but these drugs seem not to be well indicated for borderlines. "MAOI studies have results that are just not as glowing as the conclusions are," says Dr. Kutcher. "My first choice would not be an MAOI because of the risk factor and lack of proof of benefits."[16]

The potential for adverse reactions to MAOIs, the toxicity of tricyclics in overdoses, and the lack of clearly demonstrated effectiveness mean that antidepressants alone are not the ideal drugs on which to start many borderline outpatients. Borderlines clearly suffering from Axis I major depression may need to be hospitalized in order to take these medications.

Of course, with BPD the opposite is also true: some patients benefit from the combination of a neuroleptic drug with an MAOI antidepressant.

Anticonvulsants and Psychostimulants

Dr. Soloff has suggested that anticonvulsants and psychostimulants appear worth investigating in borderlines who show neuropathology in their tests or histories. In Chapter 18 we learned about the beneficial effects of the anticonvulsant carbamazepine. "The effect of carbamazepine on neurotransmitter pathology is more general than just suppressing seizure activity," says Dr. Soloff. The drug can cause melancholia as a side effect, however, and so is not commonly prescribed to patients who have Axis I depression.

Antimanic Drugs

Carbamazepine is also an antimanic drug, as is lithium carbonate. Lithium enhances serotonergic function to diminish and help prevent recurrence of the symptoms of bipolar disorder. Besides calming agitation, it seems to normalize mood so that patients do not swing between mania and depression.

A study of lithium carbonate conducted by Dr. Links and his colleagues found that although the borderline patients noticed no improvement in their symptoms, the therapists who rated them observed a decrease in their irritability, suicidality, and anger. Such a discrepancy between subjective and objective perceptions occurs quite commonly in medication trials with borderline patients.[17]

Antianxiety Drugs

The benzodiazepine family of antianxiety drugs commonly causes dependence and can increase impulsivity and aggression in borderline patients. These drugs are therefore not generally used alone in borderlines, especially for those with histories of substance abuse.

Problems with Pharmacotherapy

While relieving certain symptoms of BPD, pharmacotherapy automatically activates others that may cause trouble. The medications can take on enormous symbolic significance that makes them particularly difficult to use with borderline patients. Frequently borderlines argue with their therapists about medication, refuse to take it, complain of side effects, or try to control their dosages themselves.

The borderline patient may misinterpret the introduction of medication as a sign that the therapist is abandoning her as a hopeless case or getting rid of her with a quick fix. She may feel that her lifetime of pain is not being taken seriously by a therapist who wants simply to medicate it away.

Associating the medication with her therapist, the borderline may use it to act out her feelings toward him. A patient who views her medication as a transitional object representing a therapist she cares about may experience an improvement similar to a placebo effect. On the other hand, almost half of borderline patients abuse their prescribed medications;[18] substance abusers *may* be more likely to do so, but no one is quite sure about this.

Dr. Soloff points out that the patient's family may complicate her pharmacotherapy. Some family members will welcome any therapy that even modestly improves the patient's behavior. Others will view a patient's response to medication as proof of physical abnormality that reduces their guilt and sense of responsibility for her illness. Still others will argue that the patient is bad, not mad, so that medication will be useless. Whatever the response, it will certainly affect the therapist's attempts to start and maintain the patient on drugs.

What to Expect During Pharmacotherapy

The importance of their support is one reason the patient's family may be enlisted to cooperate with pharmacotherapy. Another is that because borderlines often can't describe their feelings and may distort them, the therapist should be able to consult the family (as well as friends and hospital staff) for feedback on any changes.

What else can a borderline patient expect in a pharmacotherapy trial? An ideally conducted trial might be described like this:

A borderline patient who has settled into psychotherapy is approached by her therapist about trying medication. Depending on the patient, the therapist proposes either that she herself assume responsibility for taking the drug as an outpatient or that she be hospitalized at least until the medication has had a chance to take effect. If some risk is involved in outpatient pharmacotherapy, the therapist gives the patient frequent prescriptions for small amounts of the drug.

The therapist prepares and reassures the patient about the recommended experiment. Because she may have a biologically based temperament that predisposes her to BPD, he explains, the two of them are going to *try* using medication to alleviate certain of her symptoms. The therapist emphasizes that there is no guarantee that the drug will work and that its use in no way implies that psychotherapy has failed. The patient understands that medications are prescribed on a trial-and-error basis because of the state of the art, not because the therapist doesn't know what he is doing. Throughout the trial, the therapist remains supportive; he responds to the patient's realistic concerns about taking drugs and clarifies those of her fears that are distortions.

The medication trial is conducted as a case research study of one patient, who helps her therapist evaluate any changes in her feelings, thoughts, and behavior and reports any side effects that occur (thereby practicing the objective self-scrutiny she needs to learn in psychotherapy anyway). Taking the drug and periodically evaluating its effects also add a bit of structure to the psychotherapy that the patient finds helpful. Relying also on structure provided by her family and her social situation, the patient is able to cooperate in her medication trial.

Dr. Waldinger and Frank have studied the psychodynamics of medication use in psychotherapy with borderlines and have analyzed their complexities.[19] Their findings suggest that a borderline patient's attitudes toward her medications fluctuate just as rapidly, dramatically, and unpredictably as do her feelings toward her therapist. One day the drug soothes her; the next she believes that the therapist is trying to abandon or literally poison her. (Ironically, the patients who fluctuate most severely in this respect are the most likely to benefit from the medication.) Following the principle applied to borderline symptoms in general, the therapist therefore does not assume that he understands the meaning of the medication to the patient at any given time. He is prepared for changes in the patient's attitude and carefully monitors his own reactions to them.

The therapist may have the drug prescribed by a psychopharmacologist. One disadvantage of enlisting such assistance is that the team may split or the patient may play the two therapists against each other, cultivating the mutual suspicion between many analysts and pharmacologists. Another is that any time lags in sustained communication between them may prove dangerous to her.

But Dr. Waldinger and Frank also list advantages of team treatment other than distracting the patient from the medication's symbolism: a psychopharmacologist offers the primary therapist both expertise and a source of consultation about the treatment; he also keeps the pharmacotherapy out of the psychotherapy so that it doesn't conflict with other issues.

If the patient shows potential to abuse her medication or actually does so, the therapist does not threaten her. Instead he explains that ultimately no one, including him, can stop her from overdosing if she really wishes to do so. He points out that the patient herself cannot ultimately control the results of medication abuse: instead of dying, she may survive an overdose in an irreversible coma or some other undesirable condition. Although borderline patients tend not to manipulate their diets or mix drugs while taking MAOIs, for instance, Dr. Liebowitz cautions each patient that doing so can cause a stroke and invites her to accompany him to the neurology service to observe paraplegic patients.[20]

Pharmacotherapy is presently used for short-term maintenance of borderline patients; there are no good studies on their long-term drug treatment at this point. The therapist therefore monitors the treatment carefully. After the patient has taken enough medication for a long enough time (or after she has abruptly and profoundly changed symptoms), the therapist tries discontinuing the drug to see if it is still necessary.

The entire process remains experimental. "We have hypotheses about the types of medications that may be useful and some preliminary data to go on," says Dr. Cowdry, "and from there we recognize the heterogeneity and treat each patient as an individual."[21]

Advantages of Pharmacotherapy

Asked which of the various drugs are most effective with borderline patients, Dr. Cowdry has replied that "everything has worked and nothing has worked."[22] The pharmacological results that I have simplified here are actually quite confusing.

But this is one of the advantages that pharmacotherapy offers the treatment of borderlines. Either by themselves or in combination with certain biological tests, patients' responses to drugs may ultimately help identify what kind of pathology BPD actually represents. Pharmacotherapy can also help

- further distinguish BPD from Axis I illnesses. Like depression, for instance, the anxiety seen in BPD may be unique. "It's probably not the same anxiety as in anxiety disorder," says Dr. Kutcher, "but more like psychotic anxiety, with a different basis."[23] Borderlines also require much lower doses of neuroleptics and respond to them much more quickly than do schizophrenics. "Even patients with schizotypal features and a family history of schizophrenia tend to respond to relatively low doses," says Dr. Cowdry.

- further distinguish BPD from other personality disorders. "Most studies show BPD to be distinct from schizotypal personality disorder," says Dr. Soloff. "Fixed traits in schizotypal patients are probably temporary states in borderlines related to their emotional distress."
- isolate subgroups of borderlines. The popularity of this practice was demonstrated in a debate on the etiology of BPD conducted at the 1990 APA convention.[24] "The challenge is really to subdivide borderlines meaningfully and treat them with drugs," said Dr. Akiskal in defense of biological causation. "We have very strong evidence that pharmacotherapy works within many of these individual groups."
- illuminate the therapist-patient relationship, providing what Dr. Cowdry calls "grist for the mill of psychotherapy." Although frustrating, any conflicts also provide opportunities for better understanding the patient.

While pharmacotherapy for borderlines is increasingly coming into its own, much careful research is still needed. The long-term effects of drugs on psychological symptoms as well as body systems require study. Drugs now in use must be compared more comprehensively to each other and to psychotherapy; new ones must be tried, and subgroups of borderline patients more carefully distinguished. These prospects are not as cut and dried as they may sound. "Currently the pharmacologic management of BPD holds promise," write Dr. Kutcher and D.H.R. Blackwood, M.R.C. Psych., "yet its clinical application still remains very much an art."[25]

Notes

1. Paul H. Soloff, M.D., "What's New in Personality Disorders?: An Update on Pharmacologic Treatment," *Journal of Personality Disorders*, Vol. 4, No. 3 (1990), p. 241. Copyright © 1990 The Guilford Press.
2. Paul H. Soloff, M.D., "Psychopharmacologic Therapies in Borderline Personality Disorder," in *Review of Psychiatry*, Vol. 8, ed. Allan Tasman, M.D., Robert E. Hales, M.D., and Allen J. Frances, M.D. (Washington, D.C.: American Psychiatric Press, 1989), p. 66.
3. David L. Gardner, M.D., and Rex William Cowdry, M.D., "Pharmacotherapy of Borderline Personality Disorder: A Review," *Psychopharmacology Bulletin*, Vol. 25, No. 4 (1989), p. 515.
4. These appear in the following papers—and those by Drs. Soloff and Gardner and Cowdry, cited above—on all of which this discussion is based: Rex William Cowdry, M.D., "Psychopharmacology of Borderline Personality Disorder: A Review," *Journal of Clinical Psychiatry*, Vol. 48, No. 8 suppl. (August 1987), pp. 15–22, and "Roundtable Discussion," pp. 23–25; Stanley P. Kutcher, M.D., "Borderline Personality Disorder Heterogeneity: Pharmacotherapy and Psychotherapy Implications," paper read at the 143rd annual meeting of the American Psychiatric Association, New York, 15 May 1990; "Update on Borderline Personality Disorder: An Interview with Rex W. Cowdry, M.D.," *Currents in Affective Illness*," Vol. 6. No. 9 (September 1987), pp. 5–11; S. P. Kutcher, M.D., and D.H.R. Blackwood, M.R.C. Psych., "Pharmacotherapy of the Borderline Patient: A Critical Review and Clinical Guidelines," *Canadian Journal of Psychiatry*, Vol. 34, No. 4

(May 1989), pp. 347–53; Paul H. Soloff, M.D., "Neuroleptic Treatment in the Borderline Patient: Advantages and Techniques," *Journal of Clinical Psychiatry*, Vol. 48, No. 8 suppl. (August 1987), pp. 26–31; Rex William Cowdry, M.D., and David L. Gardner, M.D., "Pharmacotherapy of Borderline Personality Disorder: Alprazolam, Carbamazepine, Trifluoperazine, and Tranylcypromine," *Archives of General Psychiatry*, Vol. 45 (February 1988), pp. 111–19; Paul H. Soloff, "Borderline Disorders," in *Handbook of Outpatient Treatment of Adults*, ed. Michael E. Thase, Barry A. Edelstein, and Michel Hersen (New York: Plenum, 1990), pp. 309–32; Michael H. Stone, M.D., "The Role of Pharmacotherapy in the Treatment of Patients with Borderline Personality Disorder," *Psychopharmacology Bulletin*, Vol. 25, No. 4 (1989), pp. 564–71; John G. Gunderson, M.D., "Pharmacotherapy for Patients with Borderline Personality Disorder," *Archives of General Psychiatry*, Vol. 43 (July 1986), pp. 698–700; and Paul S. Links, M.D., and Meir Steiner, M.D., "Psychopharmacologic Management of Patients with Borderline Personality Disorder," *Canadian Journal of Psychiatry*, Vol. 33, No. 5 (June 1988), pp. 355–59.

5. Soloff, "Neuroleptic Treatment," p. 26.
6. James F. Masterson, M.D., *The Search for the Real Self: Unmasking the Personality Disorders of Our Age* (New York: The Free Press, 1988), p. 206.
7. Robert J. Waldinger, M.D., and Arlene F. Frank, Ph.D., "Clinicians' Experiences in Combining Medication and Psychotherapy in the Treatment of Borderline Patients," *Hospital and Community Psychiatry*, Vol. 40, No. 7 (July 1989), p. 716.
8. Soloff, "Psychopharmacologic Therapies," p. 78.
9. Michael H. Stone, M.D., "Treatment of Borderline Patients: A Pragmatic Approach," *Psychiatric Clinics of North America*, Vol. 13, No. 2 (June 1990), p. 269.
10. Solomon C. Goldberg, Ph.D., and S. Charles Schulz, M.D., "Pharmacotherapy for Patients with Borderline Personality Disorder" [letter], *Archives of General Psychiatry*, Vol. 45 (February 1988), p. 196. Copyright © 1988, American Medical Association.
11. Charles R. Swenson, M.D., and Marcia Johnston Wood, Ph.D., "Issues Involved in Combining Drugs with Psychotherapy for the Borderline Patient," *Psychiatric Clinics of North America*, Vol. 12, No. 2 (June 1990), pp. 297–98.
12. Michael H. Stone, M.D., discussion of the symposium "Borderline Personality: Impulse Spectrum Disorder" at the 143rd annual meeting of the American Psychiatric Association, New York, 16 May 1990.
13. Paul H. Soloff, M.D., Anselm George, M.D., R. Swami Nathan, M.D., Patricia M. Schulz, M.S.W., Jack R. Cornelius, M.D., Jaclyn Herring, M.S., and James M. Perel, Ph.D., "Amitriptyline versus Haloperidol in Borderlines: Final Outcomes and Predictors of Response," *Journal of Clinical Psychopharmacology*, Vol. 9, No. 4 (August 1989), pp. 238–46.
14. Jack R. Cornelius, M.D., M.P.H., Paul H. Soloff, M.D., James M. Perel, Ph.D., and Richard F. Ulrich, M.S., "Fluoxetine Trial in Borderline Personality Disorder," *Psychopharmacology Bulletin*, Vol. 26, No. 1 (1990), pp. 151–54.
15. Paul S. Links, M.D., M.Sc., Meir Steiner, M.D., Ph.D., Ingrid Boiago, B.A., R.N., and David Irwin, M.D., "Lithium Therapy for Borderline Patients: Preliminary Findings," *Journal of Personality Disorders*, Vol. 4, No. 2 (1990), p. 180.
16. Kutcher, "Heterogeneity."
17. Links et al., p. 180.
18. Robert J. Waldinger and Arlene F. Frank, "Transference and the Vicissitudes of Medication Use by Borderline Patients," *Psychiatry*, Vol. 52, No. 4 (November 1989), p. 417.
19. Waldinger and Frank, "Transference," pp. 416–27.
20. Michael R. Liebowitz, M.D., "A Medication Approach," *Journal of Personality Disorders*, Vol. 1, No. 4 (1987), p. 326.
21. Rex W. Cowdry, M.D., "Pharmacotherapy of Impulsivity in Borderline Personality Disorder," paper read at the 143rd annual meeting of the American Psychiatric Association, New York, 16 May 1990.
22. "Update on Borderline Personality Disorder," p. 7.
23. Kutcher, "Heterogeneity."
24. "Resolved: The Etiology of Borderline Personality Disorder Is Predominantly Biological," debate conducted at the 143rd annual meeting of the American Psychiatric Association, New York, 16 May 1990.
25. Kutcher and Blackwood, "Pharmacotherapy," p. 351.

28

"The Only Game
in Town"

*The lives of suicidal, borderline individuals are unbearable as they are currently
being lived.*

MARSHA M. LINEHAN, PH.D.[1]

Before the publication of *DSM-III*, personality disorders
could not be reliably measured, so psychologists did not
think of them as such. Today, however, the parasuicidal
symptoms of BPD are the target of a comprehensive treatment approach grounded in behavioral psychology.

The appearance of Freud's ideas in America was followed shortly by that of the behavioral model of mental
illness, which denounced them as unscientific. Behavior-
ism is the study of behavior (responses) and its relationships
with both the brain and the environment. The discipline is
concerned with thinking, emotions, and cognitive styles
(ways of organizing and using information) as well as observable behavior affected by both biology and learning
(experience).

Behaviorists stress analysis of factors in the here and now
(including previous actions or environmental events) that
both elicit behavior automatically and reinforce or punish
it. They apply methods developed in scientific psychology
to behavioral change through learning, which is assumed
to occur outside of awareness. The initial task of behavior
therapy is to uncover the factors influencing day-to-day
activities, but behaviorists believe that at least for serious
disorders, insight alone is rarely sufficient.

Behavior therapy has been used effectively for depressive, panic, anxiety and impulse control disorders; addictions; and sometimes even severe illnesses like schizophrenia.

When behavioral psychologist Linehan began working with women whose symptoms included repeated suicide attempts, she thought of them as parasuicidal. "A research associate of mine and the NIMH review committee both pointed out that these women resembled borderline patients," she says. "Once the diagnostic criteria were established, I began focusing on the category of personality disorders, which is characteristic of psychiatry, taking the dimensional approach used by psychologists."

Although a behavioral therapist, Linehan might also be called a "phenomenologist's phenomenologist." She has an extremely sharp eye for symptoms and dynamics of BPD that other therapists often miss or misinterpret and a gift for describing them with figures of speech. Linehan writes that borderline individuals are like people with third-degree burns over 90 percent of their bodies. Lacking emotional skin, they feel agony at the slightest touch or movement.[2] Helping a borderline patient to regulate her emotions is like teaching a person to build a tornado-proof house just as the storm hits.[3] Arguing, as does Dr. Akiskal, that our culture needs more tolerance for diversity, Linehan tells her borderline patients that they are like tulips in a rose garden who must learn how to be tulips, not roses.

An analogy frequently used by Linehan is that a borderline individual is like a person standing barefoot in the middle of a hot coal bed. "My feet hurt so bad," she says to her therapist, "pour water on them to cool them." An ineffective therapist will grab a hose and douse the borderline person's feet. An effective therapist will say, "No—you've got to run." If the borderline person remains immobilized by pain, the competent therapist will then jump onto the coal bed and push her off.

We have already seen Linehan's description of apparently competent person syndrome. It is one of the theoretical elements of her dialectical behavioral therapy (DBT), an offshoot of cognitive behavioral therapy that Linehan formulated with borderline patients in mind. The "dialectics" underlying Linehan's theory and method is her understanding of our familiar example, splitting, one that we can add to our list of explanations for that symptom.

DBT is the only form of psychotherapy for borderline patients that has empirical controlled scientific data (in press at the *Archives of General Psychiatry*) showing that it works. Dr. Swenson has introduced DBT in Dr. Kernberg's department, a continent away from Linehan's, and predicts that it will flourish in many treatment programs during the 1990s. But all therapists honing in on DBT look to Linehan for guidance. She runs the only program in Seattle designed specifically for borderline patients and is "usually the only behaviorist who treats BPD" anywhere, so she describes her work as "the only game in town."

Developmental Theory

Like the others we have seen, Linehan's theory of how BPD develops combines biological and environmental factors. Borderline individuals have an innate deficit in emotional regulation that produces their hypersensitivity to normal stimuli, their inability to modulate negative feelings, and their difficulty decreasing the intensity of their emotions back down to a normal level.

A child with this biological dysregulation grows up in an invalidating environment similar to that created by high expressed emotion families. Like Drs. Adler and Buie, Linehan believes that each borderline individual endured an unempathic and perhaps abusive childhood environment that precluded her learning to soothe herself.

The borderline person's family had an oversimplified idea of how to solve life's difficulties and therefore would not tolerate negative feelings. "Borderline individuals learn to feel ashamed because they are taught that they are the cause of their problems, all of which are easy to solve," says Linehan.

> They become convinced that they could act better and not get upset but that they just don't want to behave properly and are therefore terrible people.
>
> This is the essence of their experience of life, and it's really hell. Once in a while they recognize that they really are doing the best they can and become enraged that no one appreciates that. Then they flip back to seeing themselves as not trying hard enough, as morally reprehensible. They can't get to middle ground—but then, neither could their environments.

The child does not learn how to cope with intense feelings, problems in relationships, or other situations that most people manage quite well. She also has actual gaps in her learning experience, part of what makes her competence inconsistent. "I ask really strange questions that most people had answered years ago," says Andrea.

Unequipped with coping skills that most people take for granted, the child develops borderline patterns. Having internalized the messages of her family, she fails to trust the validity of her own emotions. Inconsistent, unpredictable, and often out of control, these emotions preclude her developing an identity because her experience is constantly being redefined. Alienated from others, she cannot maintain stable relationships. The borderline person resorts to addressing such problems and managing her emotional life through dysfunctional behaviors that ultimately prove self-destructive.

Like researchers emphasizing trauma histories, then, Linehan sees borderline symptoms as being largely adaptations to experience. She states more definitely, however, that such symptoms are much less pathological, the distortion in particular far less common, than most therapists think.

Linehan defines DBT by its theoretical basis (dialectics) and its treatment targets and strategies.

Dialectics

For every statement made about BPD, the opposite is also true. . . . Linehan's model formalizes the dialectic inherent in the illness.

As the philosophy suggests, dialectics is that all things existing in reality are whole, interconnected, heterogeneous, and composed of opposing forces: thesis and antithesis. Because reality is whole and nothing exists in isolation, identity is fundamentally tied to interrelationships. The essence of reality is change, which occurs as a continual process. Within each whole, the tensions between thesis and antithesis are continually resolved or synthesized, then repeatedly give rise to a new set of opposing forces and synthesis. Out of this inconsistency and process, truth develops over time.

As Linehan explains it,[4] dialectics has two contexts. One is the inherent tensions that must be balanced and synthesized while conducting therapy with borderline patients. The therapist uses the opposites inherent in the therapeutic relationship to effect change.

Linehan's principal dialectic here is that change can occur only in the context of acceptance, and acceptance is itself change. The therapist must therefore radically accept and validate the borderline patient as she is while simultaneously teaching her to change.

The second context is the need for the therapist to teach the borderline patient new, more balanced or dialectical ways of thinking, feeling, and acting. The therapist helps the patient change her rigid, dichotomous, extreme ways of responding.

Linehan organizes the prominent behavior patterns of BPD along three dialectical poles:

- *vulnerability vs. invalidation.* This central dialectical dilemma refers to the borderline person's intense emotional vulnerability and her tendency to invalidate herself and her own experience.
- *active passivity vs. apparently competent person.* The tendency of borderline individuals to approach problems passively and to demand help from the environment at times of stress is offset by their tendency to appear deceptively competent.
- *unremitting crises vs. inhibited grief.* Borderline individuals experience relentless personal catastrophes in a self-perpetuating cycle. Overloaded by these repetitive traumas and losses, the borderline person becomes unable to react appropriately, instead squelching bad feelings or dissociating.

Linehan believes that unawareness of these three patterns is what causes many of the problems encountered by therapists who work with borderline patients.

Splitting

The borderline person's rigid black-and-white ways of thinking, feeling, and relating are essential to Linehan's theory. "Often the behavior of both the patient and the therapist is explained as the splitting of the patient," she says. "I separate the two."

Intense emotional states can generate extreme thinking, behavior, and cognitive rigidity in anyone. Borderline individuals differ from other people in that they react easily and intensely over long periods of time. Combined with cognitive rigidity and the tendency of emotions to self-perpetuate, these extremes trap the borderline individual at either thesis or antithesis until the emotion becomes so intense that she flips back to the opposite pole. Because the validity of these emotional experiences have been, and perhaps still are, denied by those around her, the feelings become even more intense as the borderline person tries to elicit an appropriate response.

Linehan sees staff splitting as a completely different process. "My opinion is that staff split themselves up and start acting borderline," she says. "They then often blame this on the patient." Such splitting occurs because borderline patients are in extraordinary pain and have very strong beliefs about what they need and want from a therapist. An intense desire to help is aroused in the therapist, who tries every possible response, but unsuccessfully. The patient gets upset, asks for more help, and either doesn't accept it or derives no benefit from it.

Therapists can't tolerate borderline patients' pain or their own extreme failures to help effectively, so they blame the patients. Splitting occurs when some staff members are in the over-helping stage of feeling sorry for the patient and others have burned out and reached the blaming stage of wanting to be tough on her.

Treatment Targets and Strategies

In order of importance, DBT is directed toward:
- high-risk suicidal behaviors;
- responses or behavior by either the patient or the therapist that interfere with treatment;
- behaviors that preclude a reasonable quality of life;
- post-traumatic stress responses;
- enhanced respect for self;
- acquisition of four sets of behavioral skills;
- additional goals of the individual patient.

The short-term goal of DBT is to reduce self-destructive behavior. The long-term goal is to learn better coping and problem-solving skills and to tolerate and find meaning in present reality. These goals are the targets of several treatment strategies.

The core of DBT treatment balances validating with problem-solving strategies. In validating, the therapist searches for and responds to the inherent wisdom of the patient's perceptions and behavior, which Linehan calls "the nugget of gold in the cup of sand." In problem solving, the therapist teaches the patient new ways of thinking and acting as well as emotional regulation. The communication style in DBT balances irreverence with therapist vulnerability to influence by the patient. Case management strategies balance intervening in the patient's environment as necessary with a consultant strategy.

The consultant strategy is different from the conferences among DBT therapists about which Linehan commented in Chapter 23. Rather than acting as consultant to other therapists involved with the patient, advising them how to work with her, the DBT therapist acts as consultant to the patient about how to interact with others. "We are actually known as a tough therapy program because of my consultant strategy," says Linehan.

We make the patient the middle person and don't intervene for her. If we get a call from the police, an emergency room, or a crisis clinic, we say,

"Follow your usual policies, and let me talk to the patient." Then we ask the patient, "What did you do, and now what are you going to do to change that situation?" Or we go to an inpatient unit to sit behind the patient and help her decide how to deal with everybody else.

Practicing Linehan's relationship strategy, the therapist accepts the patient, enhances the alliance, addresses any problems, and uses the relationship to help effect change. The therapeutic relationship is conducted as a "real" one from which the patient can generalize to others.

Like the turning points mentioned earlier by borderline patients, Linehan's therapy is a process of ascending several levels. She describes these levels as suspended over an abyss. On each of them is a teeter totter with the therapist at one end and the patient at the other, representing thesis and antithesis. Each time the therapist and patient reach a balance, they ascend to another level, which synthesizes the opposites of the previous level in a process of growth and development.[5]

Such balances are sought in both group and individual DBT.

Group Therapy

Group DBT is held once weekly for two to two-and-a-half hours. In its setting (a classroom), its methods, and its homework assignments, the therapy resembles a course as much as it does an ongoing support group. The therapist instructs, models roles, conducts skill rehearsals, and offers feedback and reinforcement.

DBT teaches borderline patients four sets of skills, all of which are derived from standard behavioral therapy:

- *Core skills* for self-management and problem solving. These include
    —*observing*. This skill is similar to the psychoanalytical concept of the observing ego. The patient learns to sit with even the strongest feelings and fantasies and study them.
    —*describing* one's experience
    —*participating* fully in it
    —acting *nonjudgmentally*
    —acting *mindfully,* that is, one step at a time
    —acting *effectively,* finding what works (rather than what is fair) and does not interfere with long-term gain.

"The therapy could be described as common sense broken into little steps," says Renée:

I think the core skills are the most important. First of all, we were learning to identify what we were feeling. Then we learned to take that apart into increments that we could manage and make changes on. The most important thing about it was that we'd take the feelings and start to see them as separate from ourselves: bad feelings don't make bad people.

The next step is the coping skills. This is where the common sense part comes in, a lot of self-care really, like distractions and tolerating the stress.

The first year of therapy is divided into three four-month modules, one of which is devoted to each of the three sets of coping skills:

- *Emotion regulation*. These are longer-term skills for the patient to use when her emotions become intense but are still controllable. They include variations on relaxation and cognitive exercises derived from Zen Buddhism and from self-help principles that can be used to control states of mind.
- *Distress tolerance*. These emergency skills are applied when the patient feels compelled to act self-destructively. They include various applications of thought or behavior to control the emotions.
- *Interpersonal effectiveness*. This module teaches assertiveness and social skills for coping with conflict.

Having completed the first-year skill training group, a patient graduates to the second-year group, which serves as a transition to the third-year process group. "The second year is different because you learn more and different skills in the same areas and you build upon the skills you already have," says Andrea. "We process different things, help each other out more than we used to, and focus more now on interpersonal skills."

Individual Therapy

The borderline patient meets with her DBT therapist once (or perhaps twice) a week for two-hour sessions over the course of a year. The treatment proceeds in stages. Because the therapy is adjusted to meet the patients' needs at any particular time, its stages are overlapping and circular rather than chronological like those already described by the psychoanalytical theorists:

- *Orientation*. The therapist educates the patient about what to expect from therapy.
- *Assessment: analysis of problem behaviors*. This stage helps guide the implementation of treatment strategies and methods as well as the

focus of individual sessions; it is repeated each time problem behavior recurs.

- *Skill enhancement/reality tolerance training.* Most treatment time is devoted to this stage. Balancing the tension between acceptance and change, the sessions focus on crises, decision making, or problems. "The most important thing for the patient to recognize is a fundamental assumption that she didn't cause her problems, but she has to solve them," says Linehan.
- *Generalizations-integration-termination.* This stage teaches the patient to ask for help outside of therapy while maintaining her independence. In the eleventh month, sessions start tapering off unless the patient has contracted for more therapy. To do so, she must already have shown progress.

A patient who feels compelled to harm herself between sessions is instructed to call the therapist for consultation. This phone call is not intended to perpetuate crisis and elicit sympathy. The patient is expected to wait until she is ready to think about what skills she can apply to feel better, because that will be the therapist's first question, followed by active coaching.

A patient who has already hurt herself is not allowed to call for 24 hours because her problem has already been solved dysfunctionally. "You're supposed to catch the feelings and try your skills first, and then call your therapist," says Andrea.

> If I've done something self-destructive, I don't want to talk to him anyway. Otherwise I can call him up and get advice. What the therapist does that I can't do for myself is calm me down and tell me what skills I should be using. When I'm really stressed out, it's hard to think of them, and I can't attach what I've learned to my reality.

Linehan creates a therapeutic atmosphere of great involvement with the patient by teaching, challenging, encouraging, and praising. Her warmth and support help nourish the patient's self-esteem and better enable her to correct her embarrassing ignorance of skills fundamental to adult life. Linehan views anything less than this level of support as yet another invalidating environment.

But Linehan also establishes a firmly structured holding environment and an intellectual expectation and response similar to Dr. Kernberg's containment.[6] She is prepared to meet the patient's various challenges solidly and consistently, to help her feel cared for and in control. Linehan addresses all situations systematically: helping the patient analyze her behavior, suggesting what factors might be influencing the problem, and generating, trying, and evaluating behavioral changes.

"Linehan's approach is didactic, supportive, orienting, but at the same time also demanding," says Dr. Kernberg. "It's not simply regressive, teaching patients, but expects them in turn to respond with certain behaviors."

It appears also to be an effective approach, judging from the changes Andrea has noticed in herself:

> The program tries to reestablish how you think and handle situations so you don't act too emotionally extreme and don't let everything get you depressed. In the group you're not isolated because everybody has different strange experiences. You're really focused away from self-destruction and toward learning to handle situations. It's a very positive environment.
>
> The individual therapist helps you with personal problems and issues. You talk about what you've done, whether self-destructive or whatever, and there's a lot of support. Eventually you learn the skills and have to be very repetitive in your use of them. You're able to apply them to situations that come up, and you feel better. Not everything causes you to slice your wrist that one day would have. You build a better and better set of experiences; you can handle criticisms and suicidal feelings and develop a more positive outlook.
>
> I can now deal much better with my family, my boyfriend, my job, my diagnosis, my financial pressures, and my tendency to judge myself harshly. I have much less stomach upset and do much less self-mutilation and other destructive things than I used to.

DBT Compared to Other Forms of Treatment

Depending on whether they subscribe to a model of conflict or one of deficit, psychoanalytical therapists might take a dim view of DBT. Psychoanalysts think that skills taught in DBT are available in the air around the patient once her intrapsychic problem is resolved. "The dynamic criticism of DBT would be that it's very supportive and intrusive," says Dr. Soloff, "and as soon as the therapist is out of the picture and nurturance and dependence are broken, the patient will be back to her old mechanisms." From this perspective, DBT is a process of applying band-aids rather than treating wounds.

"That's always the criticism of behaviorists, that there will be symptom substitution," says Linehan. "Our data and the cognitive behavioral literature show that this doesn't happen."

Perhaps it is fairer to compare DBT to an adjunctive treatment like pharmacotherapy. It certainly causes fewer problems than medications while similarly improving the patient's emotional control. Dr. Soloff adds other considerations:

Linehan is very clear that her form of treatment helps reduce behaviors that are self-destructive, but her patients still feel lousy. They feel empty, hollow, and depressed, and they still have the impulses.

On the other hand, the patients who are successfully treated with medication, and there are not all that many who are *successfully* treated with medication, don't feel the impulses or mood swings but they still feel empty and hollow and at times want to hurt themselves. So Linehan can't treat the biologic elements so neatly with her behavioral approach, and I can't treat the psychodynamics with drugs. It's clear that there are elements of both in each patient.

Such comparisons would of course be more meaningful in a followup study of DBT and other treatment methods. Linehan has completed a one-year outcome study of her approach compared to whatever standard forms of treatment a control group of borderlines finds on their own. Her data show that DBT reduces the frequency and severity of parasuicide, the number of inpatient psychiatric days, and (surprising even to Linehan) the patients' anger. The dropout rate (presently 16.5 percent) is lower than that seen with other treatment formats. "We have no effect in one year on depression, hopelessness, suicidal ideation, and reasons for living," she says.

The New York Hospital–Cornell Medical Center, Westchester Division, also has the makings of a useful followup study because both Dr. Kernberg's and Linehan's treatment approaches have been standardized into manuals.[7] "We have one borderline unit using psychoanalytically oriented psychotherapy and hospital milieu treatment, very much influenced by my thinking, and an independent one where the borderline patients are treated with Linehan's technique," says Dr. Kernberg. "So we are comparing two alternative methods of treatment for a patient population that is quite representative."

Dr. Soloff has reservations about how successful DBT can be if used by other therapists:

Linehan has very clear ideas, sets very firm limits, and has an intensity about her that is charismatic. The magic may be Linehan herself and not the method. A therapist who is not a charismatic figure, who hasn't her fervor, might not be able to replicate it.

Linehan replies that Dr. Soloff's is a common observation. "But in our research study, my outcomes were not better than those of the other therapists," she says.

What I'm not sure about, though, is whether therapists could get the same results working elsewhere. The therapeutic culture, which is extraordinarily

important, must be taught directly, and even well-trained behavioral therapists require a year or two really to learn it.

And to do my therapy, you have to be flexible, able to think faster than
the borderline patient does, and consistently compassionate no matter what.

Perhaps rather than comparing DBT to other treatments, therapists
should consider combining them.

DBT Combined with Other Forms of Treatment

Dr. Swenson in fact points out that because borderlines have maladaptive dynamics whose symptoms are expressed behaviorally, their psychoanalytic treatment could be enhanced by the application of DBT.
Dr. Kernberg's model of treatment could easily incorporate Linehan's.
More liberal than many psychoanalysts, Dr. Kernberg sees DBT as a
useful, if incomplete, explanation for and approach toward the more
self-destructive symptoms of BPO. Linehan, however, suggests that behavioral and psychodynamic approaches are simply different theoretical
models for the same phenomena, neither being deeper or more complete than the other.

Yet the similarities between the two approaches suggest that any good
treatment of borderlines should include a firm, explicit contract, an
emotional holding environment, and a rigorous analytical approach. Dr.
Swenson suggests three possibilities for combining them:

• Start the borderline patient with DBT to help her control herself and
  function better, then switch to expressive therapy.
• Because expressive therapy is suited for only a minority of borderlines,
  combine DBT instead with supportive therapy.
• Use expressive therapy as the primary treatment and DBT as an adjunct, with its validating atmosphere somewhat diminished as a result.

Renée finds that this last option has worked well for her. "The analytic stuff has been a whole lot more helpful to me because I seem to
have a different level of insight than the other group members," she says.
"I keep hearing the same comment over and over from them: that if they
observe their self-destructive feelings, they will get lost in them, and
things will be worse." Renée is a high-functioning borderline patient,
however, so her experience may be unique. Linehan's research has compared DBT group therapy combined with psychodynamic individual
therapy to DBT individual therapy; the patients who received the latter
made far more progress.

Dr. Waldinger suggested earlier that features common to all therapy may be what makes each different type work. "I think there is basically a consensus on treatment," says Dr. Paris. "Linehan's method sounds almost the same as what Dr. Gunderson wrote in 1984." But unlike Dr. Gunderson's approach, DBT was created to address parasuicidal behavior specifically; it appears to accomplish that particular goal.

Hidden Disabilities and Obvious Skills

In doing so, DBT has made a significant contribution. Linehan has identified and addressed basic impairments in borderline individuals that often preclude their effectively using other forms of treatment. In so doing, she has started toward the goal of better understanding borderline disabilities that has already been mentioned by Dr. Links.

Linehan's model is so clear and logical that I fear having made it seem like a structure into which patients are pigeonholed. Actually the treatment is pragmatic: its individual elements are like any other tools, intended to be taken up and set aside according to the individual patient's needs at particular points in time. Similarly, the behavior patterns identified by Linehan are intended to be used for assessment: the therapist is never to assume their existence in any given borderline patient.

DBT is an important contribution particularly from the viewpoints of borderline patients themselves. Dr. Swenson reports that teaching the obvious has helped patients who have had difficulties in their unit for years. These patients have latched on to the simplest of concepts as lifesavers, as if to ask, "Why didn't anybody ever teach me this before?"

Like the attention now devoted to trauma histories, the advent of DBT has provided both new insights about and badly needed validation for borderline patients. "On the one hand, we probably teach borderline patients more than anyone else, all the time," says Linehan. "But I'm told that the biggest difference is that we also completely believe in them."

Notes

1. Marsha M. Linehan, Ph.D., "Overview of DBT: Targets, Strategies, and Assumptions in a Nutshell," chapter 7, in *Acceptance and Change of Borderline Patients: A Cognitive-Behavioral Treatment Manual* (New York: Guilford, forthcoming).

2. Marsha M. Linehan, "Dialectical Behavior Therapy: A Treatment for Borderline Personality Disorder," manuscript copy of article printed as "Dialektische Verhaltenstherapie bei Borderline-Personlichkeitsstorungen," *Praxis der Klinischen Verhaltensmedizin und Rehabilitation,* 2, Jahrgang/Heft 8, (Dezember 1989).

3. Marsha M. Linehan, Ph.D., "Dialectical Behavior Therapy for Borderline Personality Disorder: Theory and Method," *Bulletin of the Menninger Clinic,* Vol. 51, No. 3 (1987), p. 270.

4. For more details, see Linehan, "Dialectical Behavior Therapy," and "Cognitive and Behavior Therapy for Borderline Personality Disorder," in *Review of Psychiatry,* Vol. 8, ed. Allan Tasman, M.D., Robert E. Hales, M.D., and Allen J. Frances, M.D. (Washington, D.C.: American Psychiatric Press, 1989), pp. 84–102, upon which this discussion is based.

5. Linehan, "Dialectical Behavior Therapy."

6. Charles Swenson, M.D., "Kernberg and Linehan: Two Approaches to the Borderline Patient," *Journal of Personality Disorders,* Vol. 3, No. 1 (1989), p. 26. This article is the source of my references in this chapter to Linehan's treatment compared to Dr. Kernberg's and the possibilities for combining the two, some of which Linehan has corrected in my text.

7. Otto F. Kernberg, M.D., Michael A. Selzer, M.D., Harold W. Koenigsberg, M.D., Arthur C. Carr, Ph.D., and Ann H. Appelbaum, M.D., *Psychodynamic Psychotherapy of Borderline Patients* (New York: Basic Books, 1989). Marsha M. Linehan, Ph.D., *"Dialectical Behavior Therapy for Treatment of Parasuicidal Women: Treatment Manual,"* unpublished manuscript, University of Washington, 1984.

29

The Most "Difficult" Therapeutic Relationships

The reasons why borderlines are such difficult therapy cases do not reside exclusively within the patients. . . . Therapists get themselves into difficulties because of their own problems, blind spots, and character styles, as well as insufficient knowledge and inadequate training.

JEROME KROLL, M.D.[1]

Recently I attended a professional conference on BPD at which I had looked forward to meeting one of the speakers, a highly regarded therapist with whom I share a friend and who proved to be quite cordial.

While his audience chuckled appreciatively, this speaker described typical borderline acting out. It is crucial, he said, to establish an initial contract and set firm limits to control such behavior.

In diagnosing and assessing the borderline patient, the speaker continued, it is important to ask about prior treatment experiences to determine how the patient has destroyed her previous therapies. Twice during his brief lecture, he referred to the prototypical borderline's having "destroyed her therapy" without any qualification.

Unbeknownst to him, the audience included a spy from the real world who proceeded to address this issue during the question-and-answer session.

"I would like to know how you determine whether it

was the patient who destroyed the therapy," I said. "You yourself stressed the need for an initial contract and firm limit setting, and a therapist who would allow the acting out you describe to continue for a year or so [I was careful to specify] is obviously incompetent."

"That's **much** too harsh," exploded the speaker. He explained heatedly that I was being entirely too hard on therapists, that mine was an example of "black-and-white thinking."

I sent this therapist my writeup of our exchange and received in response a letter assuring me that neither he nor his colleagues "unilaterally attribut[e] treatment failure" to either the borderline patient or the therapist alone:

> We find, on [the] one hand, that borderline patients have typical ways of destroying their treatment; on the other hand, we also find that more experienced therapists are more capable of keeping borderline patients in treatment. Therefore, I think both patient and therapist contribute to successful and unsuccessful treatment collaboration.

These two sentences are contradictory. How can both parties be said to contribute to successful or failed treatment collaboration if the therapist's job consists of thwarting a patient hell-bent on destruction? This description implies that the patient is the bad guy and the therapist the good guy whose failures are excused by lack of experience.

But to say that the borderline patient "destroys her therapy" demeans the therapist as well by implying that he sits by helplessly watching her act. It not only reinforces the stigma attached to BPD but also feeds into the popular derogation of therapists as "professional friends" who collect three figures an hour merely for listening. As such it sets the patient a bad example of irresponsibility.

Therapy can be destroyed for any of a number of reasons. The therapy of borderline patients in particular is often destroyed by badly managed countertransference. Because other therapists are quick to excuse treatment failure with borderlines, such mismanagement can be hard to distinguish from outright incompetence.

In the general sense mentioned in Chapter 6 (and that used most often in discussions of BPD), countertransference is the therapist's positive or negative emotional responses to the patient.* But even this broad a concept may be too narrow. Psychiatry needs a term to describe the strong emotional responses from therapists to the very *idea* of borderline patients, a more articulate equivalent of the **"UGH!"** we saw in Chap-

---

*It is so common for therapists to react intensely to borderlines, however, that in some psychiatric circles *neutrality* toward a borderline patient is viewed as countertransference.

ter 1. In the above example, it could be applied to the speaker's outrage at my having appeared to take lightly the difficulty of treating borderlines.* Such a term would remind us that therapists set themselves up, in a sense, to react to borderline patients.

Profoundly influenced as it is by countertransference, treatment with borderline patients arouses controversy about who acts and is acted upon to create difficulties, who is responsible, who victimized, and who ultimately to blame.

A Most Essential Subject

In and of itself, countertransference is a predictable aspect of treatment that the therapist recognizes and transcends to remain detached and neutral. Dr. Gunderson places it on "a continuum with normal and even helpful aspects of therapy."[2] Emotions elicited by the patient's projective identification, for example, can be enormously useful gauges of how she herself is feeling.

But whether countertransference is helpful or not depends upon its consequences. Feeling an emotion is different from allowing it adversely to affect thought and behavior, but many therapists succumb to such influence unwittingly.

Countertransference can sneak up on a therapist in many forms. Therapists feel simultaneously trapped, hurt, enchanted, and exasperated while working with borderlines. "We have seen colleagues respond to these pressures through disorganization, chronic fatigue, franticness, guilt, chronic eating, or increased drug and alcohol use," write Dennis and Randy A. Sansone, M.D.[3] In other words, treating a borderline can make a therapist act like one. Or he may permit the patient to behave more like one by allowing her harmfully to act out.

"What typically happens," says Dr. Paris, "is that a therapist gets overinvolved trying to help too much; the borderline turns on him and becomes really vicious, and the therapist can't handle it and feels burned for life."

Countertransference is so pervasive a problem in therapy with borderlines that like a reminder of these patients, the subject itself arouses negative feelings. Les R. Greene, Ph.D., and his colleagues believe that countertransference phobia has adversely influenced the direction of research in BPD. Rather than investigate and describe treatment with

---

*Ideally the speaker would have referred to "how and why the patient's previous therapies failed," and I would have referred to the therapist's having "acted incompetently in this particular case."

these difficult patients, therapists have instead defensively focused on diagnosing BPD. Researchers as well as clinicians involved with border-lines may long have found it more rewarding "to name them than to tame them," when actually countertransference should be a prime target of investigation.[4]

Yet almost every professional book on BPD includes a chapter on countertransference, usually somewhere at the beginning. Because this book was written for nonprofessionals, the chapter is close to the end. And it discusses countertransference less from the viewpoint of the ther-apist than from that of the layperson. This different perspective, how-ever, makes the subject no less essential.

Unlike other psychiatric patients who elicit countertransference, the borderline is more prone to be genuinely victimized even by the thera-pist's positive feelings. However countertransference compromises ther-apy, the patient gets the worst of it. The therapist may have to endure ugly feelings, but a response in kind is betrayal by someone the patient is expected to trust. The therapist may feel impotent, but he presumably remains correct in his wellness, while the patient, who feels helpless, remains problematic in her illness. The therapist may be frustrated by difficulty, but the borderline continues to pay for badly managed treat-ment.

Countertransference can produce invalidation of the patient's percep-tions. The therapist may automatically misinterpret any reference by the patient to his feelings as evidence of resistance, distortion, or aggression. If she seeks advice from another therapist, the consultant may just as automatically side with her own. "Borderlines can be hurt by psychia-trists very easily," says Dr. Paris.

On the one hand, they do tend to split and devalue, and I've had patients who said I was the worst psychiatrist they had ever seen. But the fact is that one can't also assume that their complaints are invalid either.

Therapists can have unresolved conflicts, past experiences, or needs to be caring, loved, and powerful that give rise to countertransference and that preclude their recognizing it in themselves.

One consequence of countertransference is polarization: it shows how borderlines highlight the emotion-laden issues and value systems that split groups of people apart. This chapter considers the implications of three ideas that have polarized therapists:

- The therapist/patient is the source of countertransference difficulties.
- Borderlines can/cannot control their behavior and therefore do/do not make therapists dislike them.
- Borderlines do/do not contribute to their own victimization.

The Therapist/Patient Is the Source of Countertransference Difficulties

Current enlightened thinking dictates that countertransference problems result from the interaction between borderline patients and therapists, an unbalanced give-and-take in which one or the other may be more responsible for therapeutic difficulties at any given time. In reality, however, one is more likely to see the discrepancy expressed in the letter quoted above. Going along with the tendency to see BPD as a patient rather than as her illness is one of personifying the source of countertransference problems as either patient or therapist.

Some therapists have a vested interest in the notion that borderlines destroy their therapy. Psychoanalysts, for instance, believe that borderlines need to defeat their helpers. (Dr. Gunderson argues instead that therapists underestimate how much borderlines sincerely want to benefit from therapy and that the tendency of these patients prematurely to quit treatment has unreasonably given them a bad name.[5]) But such a conviction relieves the therapist of having to scrutinize his own interaction with the patient and allows him to indulge, as Dr. Kroll writes, "his need to be in control and to be correct." Even to argue that problems arise because therapists respond to borderline pathology, Dr. Kroll continues, "misses the point by reflecting the problem back upon the patient."[6]

We could return the ball to the other court by arguing that once he has diagnosed a patient as borderline, a therapist's expectation that he will experience countertransference can become a self-fulfilling prophecy. Borderlines are, of course, skilled at sensing what other people expect. A therapist's anticipation of emotional involvement and therapeutic difficulty can create a charged atmosphere to which the borderline responds by regressing and acting out.

Strictly (and ethically) speaking, the therapist *must* ultimately accept responsibility for countertransference difficulties. "What I've learned the hard way," says Dr. Paris, "is that if you permit the patient to destroy the therapy, you're not doing your job." The therapist's job is to conduct treatment properly (or if necessary, terminate it) regardless of how he feels or how the patient behaves.

Borderlines Can/Cannot Control Their Behavior and Therefore Do/Do Not Make Therapists Dislike Them

"It's okay to say that therapists hate many of the borderline patient's behaviors," says Dr. Waldinger.

> It's the truth. And it's worth a try to show borderlines this problem. But describe it in a way that does *not* confirm the borderline's fear that *she* is hateful. Talk about specific behaviors that drive therapists away.

Dr. Waldinger makes a good point, and his remarks imply another important one: one reason borderlines fear that they are hateful is that sometimes they are hated for symptoms they can't help.

Examples can be drawn from the class on personality disorders we heard from earlier. Significantly enough, the psychiatrist opened the class by asking the select group of residents what kinds of trouble they had encountered in working with borderline patients. Here are abbreviations of their responses in chronological order:

"Liking them."

"Having them be honest."

"The lability."

"The way they get psychotic . . ."

"Their distortions of interpersonal relationships and interactions . . ."

"The terrific anger and demandingness . . ."

"Being scapegoated by the hospital staff for having a borderline patient."

"The constant threat of self-destruction. There's a scythe hanging in the air."

Their replies quoted at greater length in Chapter 2 indicate that the residents reacted to the question with some emotion. But possibly excepting dishonesty and demandingness, none of the borderline symptoms they list is intended to create "trouble" for the therapist. The "threat" of self-destruction refers to a possibility, not an action. "These patients are always blackmailing you," says Dr. Paris, "saying, 'If you don't do it my way, I'm going to kill myself.'" *Blackmail* is a legitimate source of negative feelings—but therapists react emotionally to *suicidality* whether or not the patient uses it as coercion.

Addressing the subject of countertransference more directly, other therapists describe additional reasons that the treatment of borderline patients is problematic:

- The patient's chronic, unpredictable, self-destructive behavior. Not just the idea of self-destruction but the specific symptom—eating disorders, alcoholism, cutting that leaves permanent scars—can alienate a therapist particularly sensitive to it.
- The crisis-to-crisis nature of therapy.
- The borderline's invitations to the therapist to manage her life, to prove that he cares, alternating with rejection of his help. Dr. Waldinger attributes this behavior to borderlines' dilemma with closeness and distance. "They want perfect caregivers yet devalue most of the people they get close to," he says. "This puts therapists in a particular bind because people enter the mental health field to help others." Another explanation is that "help" from an "expert" who has never felt pain comparable to hers might seem to the borderline to invalidate her experience.
- The intensity of the patient's feelings—and their tendency to be punctuated by indifference.[7]
- The patient's lack of progress. A borderline who does not improve in treatment makes the therapist feel "impotent" (the adjective most commonly used), guilty, and angry and often causes him to withdraw. "Unlike people treating many cancers, for instance," says Linehan, "we cannot accept our inability to cure BPD without blaming the patient."
- The borderline's ability to expose the therapist's personality. "Borderline patients compel . . . our real selves to show—our humanity, our strengths and foibles, and sometimes our opinions about matters of the day," writes Dr. Stone. Although he believes that "we should not be afraid of such exposure," other therapists find it disconcerting.[8]

Again, only one symptom listed—invitations to caregivers—is a deliberate action by the patient. Objectively the symptoms of all psychiatric disorders are alike, but subjectively the symptoms of BPD are uniquely disturbing. What actually causes the "trouble" is not that the symptoms exist but that therapists dislike having to deal with them.

Both lists illustrate that the issue of whether borderlines are "bad" or "mad" is a red herring within the context of countertransference. To focus on the patient's control of her behavior not only misses the point but is especially misleading given the inconsistency of her capabilities.

The issue is not whether the patient sought the therapist's emotional response but what the feeling is, how well the therapist handles it, and whether he might put it to therapeutic use. Unfortunately, therapists sometimes act on their emotions—even positive feelings—in ways that are not therapeutic at all.

Borderlines Do/Do Not Contribute to Their Own Victimization

An article published by Dr. Gutheil in May 1989 deals with the relationship of BPD to boundary violations—especially sexual abuse—by therapists.[9] The letters and arguments that followed raised important points about countertransference, victimization, blame, and responsibility.

Dr. Gutheil's article states specifically that he wishes to make three points:

- Borderlines are particularly likely to evoke various kinds of inappropriate behavior, including sexual misconduct, from therapists.
- Out of the "miniscule fraction" of false accusations of sexual transgressions by therapists, the majority are made by borderlines.
- Therapists educated about patterns of errors in therapy and countertransference responses can avert the serious outcomes that result.

Later Dr. Gutheil notes that many of the patients involved in the legal cases he has studied were previously abused and might possibly have been involved in repetition compulsion.

Dr. Gutheil makes clear that in describing sexual misconduct, he is neither "indicting the patient (blaming the victim)" nor "explaining away, exonerating, or excusing the therapist's behavior," simply because "sex with a patient is never acceptable." Some of his language (like his references to borderlines who "seduce, provoke, or invite therapists into boundary violations") could suggest otherwise if taken out of context; thus Dr. Gutheil prudently repeats his position later in the article.

Publication of this article in the *American Journal of Psychiatry* elicited a series of letters that appeared in the issues of October and November 1989 and January, July, September, and October 1990. Some of these letters scapegoat Dr. Gutheil for bias and sexism that pervade the psychiatric profession but that his article does not express. Those writers who did not understand and support Dr. Gutheil's position accuse him of not recognizing that he *has* blamed borderlines for their therapists' behavior just as rape victims are blamed for that crime.

The most sustained attack appeared in January 1990 in a letter by Judith V. Jordan, Ph.D., and her colleagues, who treat many patients with histories of sexual abuse. They argue, among other things, that Dr.

Gutheil ought to consider "the difficulty these women have in protecting themselves from victimization."[10]

Therapists of either sex experience countertransference toward patients of either sex. But because it is most often a male therapist's response to a female patient (especially when difficulties around erotic feelings are involved), countertransference has feminist implications. In a deeply felt and logically reasoned letter published in September 1990, Patricia Illingworth, Ph.D., squelches the angry objections to Dr. Gutheil's article. She points out that much sexism is based on the assumption that women are victimized because they cannot take care of themselves. This view, she notes, has been used also in the contexts of slavery and apartheid to justify oppression. Sexism succeeds because women believe what their oppressors tell them and assume the roles of incompetents.

Self-oppression, says Illingworth, is a form of psychopathology; to disregard this fact, she writes, "is also to diminish the recognition of the harm experienced by women in a sexist society and, ultimately, to weaken the legitimate claims of feminists."[11] By describing how some women patients help oppress themselves, Illingworth concludes, Dr. Gutheil (a self-professed feminist) has instead strengthened these claims.

In the next issue of the *Journal,* a patient named Ann, who sees herself as having "some similarities" to the borderlines Dr. Gutheil describes, points out that to be subject to rigid boundaries in therapy is to trade powerlessness for support. "No wonder there is rage," she writes, describing how she and her therapist instead struggle with boundaries.[12]

We might add that rigid boundaries preclude growth, while flexible ones encourage it. But in doing so we would join these letter writers in overlooking an important point.

Each of these letters is insufficiently focused upon *borderlines*. Illingworth appears to describe the pathology of self-oppression that sexism can nourish in any and all women. But most women don't invite assault, rape, or other forms of victimization, and the rules of everyday social interaction can't be applied to a formulaic situation like that of therapy.

Most psychiatric patients don't invite victimization either. But borderlines are far more sensitive than most patients to influence from their therapists.

And borderlines show what Dr. Kroll calls "a *pattern* of frequent interpersonal entanglements" that cause various degrees of victimization, usually with "the cooperation of a person with complementary psychopathology."[13] This is the pattern that Linehan calls active passivity, the temperamental or learned helplessness of someone who believes that all difficulties must be magnified to be taken seriously. The activity is what Dr. Kroll describes as borderlines' ability to make other people act upon, advise, care for, or assume responsibilities for them.[14]

Borderlines work hard to be helpless. They complain about their victimization partly because this behavior is so ingrained that they cannot recognize its masochism. Or they may be trying to relieve their guilt. "Often when a borderline says that she is a victim," says Linehan, "she really does not believe it but is just trying to get you to convince her that she is not bad."

But as we have learned, the other pole of active passivity is the apparently competent person syndrome. Dr. Gutheil's article makes an additional point that neither he nor the letter writers fully articulate. Besides having needs and creating problems unique among psychiatric patients, borderlines also have severe impairments that are inconsistent, unpredictable, and poorly understood. They might be the abused woman's tendency to believe that she is the worthless, inert thing implied by her abuser's behavior. But for borderlines crippled instead by neglect or loss—or even for all borderlines—they might be something else.

Paige's bad luck with the mental health profession, for example, included her outpatient therapist, who tried to replace her mother. "She used to come to my house; I was invited over to hers—it's very hard for me even to think about," says Paige. "I knew more about her life and problems than she ever knew about mine." Although Paige recognized and disliked her therapist's overinvolvement, she cooperated with it as she did with her regimen of inappropriate medications.

Similarly, in Chapter 1 Carla described her attempts to protect a series of therapists from being hurt by her self-destructiveness. Carla can't accept responsibility for not harming herself but does try to monitor the therapeutic relationship, thereby assuming responsibility that is not hers.

To complain, as Dr. Gutheil does to one of his detractors,[15] that borderline patients are not ciphers, puppets, incompetents, or children, to point out that the therapists and patients he describes both were voluntarily in bed, is to imply that the patients might have seized control of the situation or at least refused to cooperate. To do so is, in turn, to ignore that borderlines are inconsistently competent, as Dr. Gunderson and Linehan stress, and that many of them nevertheless end up having to take care of their therapists.

Issues involving borderlines are thus different from those relevant to both other female patients and women with no mental illness, and they require the attention called to them by Dr. Gutheil. But to bring a feminist perspective to the treatment of borderlines *without allowing for their particular impairments* can be to oversimplify the situation *and* to hurt these patients with continued invalidation and unrealistic expectations.

The typical borderline patient is not yet equipped to take care of herself in the way Illingworth implies. Like other women, she owes it to herself to abandon the role of victim and assertively accept responsibility, seize control, and make choices. But like being depressed, taking responsibility is not the same experience for borderlines as it is for other psychiatric patients and well people. At least the process of accepting responsibility does not proceed in the same way or at the same rate. The borderline starts at a lower level of functioning. Using the same tools employed by other women, she can catch up to them and proceed to take over her life. Up to that point, however, while the borderline remains vulnerable, her therapist is obliged to protect her from victimization by him. To a lesser extent, he is of course obliged thus to protect all his patients, but the nature of her pathology causes the borderline to work against him.

As Ann's letter suggests, it's not easy anyway to protect and respect another person simultaneously. Ann describes flexibility in her therapist's rules—but she is not certain of her diagnosis. The boundaries of "secure understanding" that she reports sharing with her therapist are not necessarily strong or structured enough to create a holding environment for a borderline.

To the borderline, the fine line between support and invalidation also separates caregiving (including protection) from patronization. It is the latter that Illingworth correctly condemns and the former that the fragile borderline needs. In this sense, within or outside the context of countertransference, the borderline patient is indeed a special case.

This kind of situation and others that involve borderlines therefore require more thought than simple distinctions between empowerment and victimization. Accepting responsibility for herself is alone insufficient to empower a borderline or make her better. The more often responsibility is prematurely demanded of borderlines, the greater their compulsion helplessly to cry wolf, and the less likely they are to gain appropriate validation of their present realities aimed toward eventual change.

The delicate balances required in therapy with borderline patients are ultimately maintained, as Ann's letter suggests, through their wrestling with their therapists over boundaries.

In many ways, borderline behavior caricatures traditional notions of femininity. Their struggles with male therapists reflect those of centuries of women imprisoned by the inescapable "power" and "rightness" of men. Their manipulative, seductive behavior is grounded in traditional female survival tactics. It is hardly surprising that therapists respond emotionally to borderlines, that they feel frustrated when therapy goes sour:

male therapists, of course, share the focus on professional achievement that preoccupies most men, and the borderline patient makes it harder for the therapist to *do his job*.

Harder, but not impossible. The borderline patient simply lacks the power to "destroy therapy" all by herself.

Avoiding Destruction

What the borderline may have, however, is the power to avoid such destruction. Borderline patients motivated to make their treatment work should try as hard as possible to keep the following in mind:

There is no such thing as a "special" relationship with a therapist. Such interaction in a therapeutic relationship is inappropriate, unproductive, ultimately painful, and otherwise harmful. It demonstrates that the therapist actually cares little for the patient and illustrates a point once made by Anna Freud. "One of Anna Freud's students reported to me her having said, 'When the patient thinks the analyst is a fool, it's not always transference,'" says John A. Atchley, M.D., who treats eating-disordered patients, including borderlines. "That's a very important point for people to remember—that even psychiatrists can behave like fools."

The inappropriate relationships borderlines establish with therapists are like those they have with other people of "complementary psychopathology"—immature, unhealthy, and ultimately unsatisfying. They waste time, affection, and energy that the borderline could more happily direct elsewhere.

If her therapy is destroyed—for whatever reason—the borderline herself will be the loser. Sexual misconduct or other questionable practices by the therapist do not mean that she is unique, beloved, attractive, or even worthwhile. Taking "revenge" for such conduct through a lawsuit merely casts in stone her status as a victim. The best "revenge," for the borderline who thinks in those terms, is to discuss questionable behavior with the therapist, seek consultation herself, and, if necessary, change therapists.

Ideally the borderline patient should raise the issues of countertransference and consultation with a therapist immediately upon beginning treatment. *And she should never,* **never** *contract with a therapist who refuses to discuss these issues and commit himself when necessary to seek consultation on her case.* The only treatment for countertransference difficulties is a colleague's objective scrutiny of the situation before it is too late.

Notes

1. Jerome Kroll, M.D., *The Challenge of the Borderline Patient: Competency in Diagnosis and Treatment* (New York: Norton, 1988), p. 219.
2. John G. Gunderson, M.D., *Borderline Personality Disorder* (Washington, D.C.: American Psychiatric Press, 1984), p. 48.
3. Amy Baker Dennis, Ph.D., and Randy A. Sansone, M.D., "The Clinical Stages of Treatment for the Eating Disorder Patient with Borderline Personality Disorder," in *Psychodynamic Treatment of Anorexia Nervosa and Bulimia,* ed. Craig Johnson, Ph.D. (New York: The Guilford Press, 1991), p. 142.
4. Les R. Greene, Judith Rosenkrantz, and Deborah Y. Muth, "Borderline Defenses and Counter-transference: Research Findings and Implications," *Psychiatry,* Vol. 49 (August 1986), p. 255.
5. Gunderson, pp. 96, 92.
6. Kroll, p. 219.
7. Dennis and Sansone, pp. 141–42.
8. Michael H. Stone, M.D., "Treatment of Borderline Patients: A Pragmatic Approach," *Psychiatric Clinics of North America,* Vol. 13, No. 2 (June 1990), p. 273.
9. Thomas G. Gutheil, M.D., "Borderline Personality Disorder, Boundary Violations, and Patient-Therapist Sex: Medicolegal Pitfalls," *American Journal of Psychiatry,* Vol. 146, No. 5 (May 1989), pp. 597–602.
10. Judith V. Jordan, Ph.D., Alexandra Kaplan, Ph.D., Jean Baker Miller, M.D., Irene Stiver, Ph.D., and Janet Surrey, Ph.D., "More Comments on Patient-Therapist Sex" [letter], *American Journal of Psychiatry,* Vol. 147, No. 1 (January 1990), p. 130.
11. Patricia Illingworth, Ph.D., 'Further Views on Patient-Therapist Sex" [letter], *American Journal of Psychiatry,* Vol. 147, No. 9 (September 1990), p. 1259.
12. Ann, a patient, "A Patient's View of Doctor-Patient Boundaries" [letter], *American Journal of Psychiatry,* Vol. 147, No. 10 (October 1990), p. 1391.
13. Kroll, p. 51.
14. Ibid., p. 46.
15. Thomas H. Gutheil, M.D., "Patient-Therapist Sex" [reply letter], *American Journal of Psychiatry,* Vol. 146, No. 11 (November 1989), p. 1519.

3 0

The Emotional Roar

If we had a keen vision and feeling of all ordinary human life, it would be like hearing the grass grow and the squirrel's heart beat, and we should die of that roar which lies on the other side of silence. As it is, the quickest of us walk about well wadded with stupidity.

GEORGE ELIOT, *MIDDLEMARCH* [1]

*W*hile drafting a proposal for this book, I sought information from several competent therapists familiar with my work who encounter borderline patients frequently. Most of these therapists discouraged me from pursuing the topic. One psychologist in particular appeared stunned by the prospect and kept repeating, "No. No."

"Borderlines were bad enough before," laughed a patient at one point, "and now you've gone and *educated* them!"

I fail to see how any treatment dependent upon the patient's remaining ignorant can be therapeutic. I fail also to see how therapists can expect borderline patients to accept responsibility for behavior that is not intellectually as well as emotionally understood.

The second responsible act is to enter therapy; the first is to learn about one's illness and the treatment options. The danger of doing so in this case is one of nourishing an illness identity. But *well enough understood*, BPD is ultimately so mysterious and irreducible as to frustrate such effort. Perhaps if borderlines knew more rather than less about their illness, they could more easily grow beyond it.

Other therapists were less worried about themselves

than about me. They expressed concern that I might become a target of borderline rage and frivolous lawsuits. I had by that time published two short pieces about BPD, neither of which should have enraged anybody but both of which did. Fortunately, the few borderlines whose responses eventually reached me completely lost interest upon learning that I was "just a writer."

I suspect that my inferior status might likewise elicit anger from therapists if any patients decide to clobber them (verbally or literally) with this book. Borderlines have never before had a book like this available to them. I am counting on them instead to put it to constructive use.

Imagine how much insight might be gained if borderline patients began reporting how their own experiences compare to those described here.

The information might disturb them because of its contradictions and complexity. On the one hand, information helps structure the chaos in which borderlines live. On the other, an imbroglio isn't easily reduced to formulaic thinking.

I hope borderlines can accept that psychiatry has strengths and weaknesses, that therapists have human frailties but usually try their best, that as imperfect and frustrating as the whole situation may be, it keeps improving the prospects of patients as time goes by. In the process, I hope they give up some fantasies and distortions inherent in their pathology without feeling insulted themselves. The book is intended to empower, not demean.

I hope too that those involved with borderlines can absolve these patients of blame for being "difficult," believe that they do not distort as much as many people think, and accept that their motives should never be taken for granted.

And I hope that ultimately researchers will better distinguish pathology from adaptation and simple human variety. Greater tolerance of "intense" living within a profoundly relational context may be called for. The same intensity that disturbs others may be what ultimately saves a borderline, as Emily's comments imply:

On a positive note, there's a fight in a person who is diagnosed, for truth, to have things acknowledged. There's a lot of positives there. It's important to be with a person who understands and who can help you. It's very strange because it can be as good or as bad as it can be. It's up to you to make that decision. It can be really good, because you can get out of it. You can. But you have to turn it around and channel it and fight continually. It's hard. It gets very difficult. Sometimes it feels that it's not going to work, because you've got so many addictions or negative patterns of behavior that continually come up on you, but the more you push and the longer you do it, the more you put behind you. It makes you a more insightful, stronger person, and you can have wonderful relationships. It's just getting past all the negative feelings that you felt for so long and realizing that there is another world within this hell, the hell that you've been in for so long, that there is something out there. But you have to believe that, have faith, really. You really do.

Tulips do not come from another planet. They may be different from roses, but they can still share the garden.

Once upon a time, reading inspired thought. In these days of simplistic self-help, it instead substitutes for thinking. Books are supposed to supply answers—correct or incorrect, as long as they are quick.

Because there are very few answers about BPD, this book has instead raised questions. It has also illustrated what researchers believe still needs to be asked. One interesting phenomenon is the ongoing attempts to learn whether psychiatric illnesses would be more accurately grouped by dimensions rather than categories. To further explore the categorical approach in the meantime, researchers call for BPD to be compared more thoroughly to the other personality disorders. They are subdividing borderlines into groups who can be more precisely targeted with different types and levels of treatment. More studies of twins, adopted children and, prospectively, those at high risk for BPD are anticipated. Aggression might well become a popular research topic.

The controversies about BPD as a schizophrenic, then an affective, illness variant may eventually be "wrapped up," as Dr. Soloff would say, by a hypothesis put forth by Dr. Siever and his colleagues: unlike those in schizotypal personality disorder, psychotic-like symptoms in BPD arise temporarily within particular affective contexts like depression, anxiety, and anger.[2]

I suspect that the proponents of deficit theories about BPD can look forward to a steady rise in status. One reason is the increased focus on childhood trauma and its interaction with a context of neglect in particular. Another is the interest expressed by several researchers in reconstructing their understanding of the illness. Of particular importance is the increased awareness that borderline impairments are genuine and poorly understood. Along with the argument that psychiatric treatment is an artificial, "loaded" context rather than a laboratory setting for reality, this recognition should produce some interesting data.

Dr. Gunderson has noted the contrast between the previous status of

BPD as a wastebasket diagnosis and the excitement and energy with which researchers now tackle this widespread illness.[3] Regardless of where the research leads, this impetus cannot help but decrease the borderline stigma.

*W*hen bulimia nervosa became a hot topic, many researchers assumed the logical: bulimics binge because they can't control their eating; then they vomit only to stay thin. When it occurred to Johnson and others to *ask,* however, they learned that some bulimics eat only in order to vomit. (I have interviewed patients who drink and vomit water instead of food.)

Now borderline symptoms traditionally attributed to resistance, aggression, and other psychoanalytical constructs are being reexamined as neurobiological or traumatic in origin. Although it is not true, as Alison claims, that BPD is the illness of not being taken seriously, perhaps much of what borderlines say and do has not been taken seriously *enough.* Borderlines are often either not asked about their own dynamics or heard but not believed. Although the two are by no means mutually exclusive, perhaps it is time to suspend interpretation and encourage more questions instead.

I titled this chapter "The Emotional Roar" for two reasons. The quotation from *Middlemarch* that opens it seems like an accurate (if inadvertent) description of what it's like to be borderline, enduring an emotional roar that no one else can—or wants to—hear. Continuing the analogy, it is we outsiders whose perceptions and emotions are wadded with our "stupidity" (comparative dullness). Those afflicted with "keenness" gain valuable information to which we have no access. (And as Linehan emphasizes, many people therefore insist that it doesn't exist.)

Thus Dr. Gunderson refers to his patients' having "uniformly fostered in me more humility than confidence in what I might understand about them."[4] The researchers represented here keep in mind that their most important source of information, and the ultimate beneficiaries of all their efforts, are borderline patients themselves.

The other reason for the chapter's title has been implied throughout this book. The key to the borderline experience is Linehan's description of these patients as the emotional equivalent of third-degree burn victims. (To add the key to borderline behavior, their instability: each borderline is like a burn victim alone on a flimsy raft in the middle of the ocean, buffeted unpredictably and trying frantically to keep from being splashed.)

The point is that I *know*—as do readers of this book and, most of all, therapists—that borderlines are unimaginably miserable. The intensity of borderline emotions is almost mythical: therapists describe it far more eloquently and in much greater detail than I have space for here. There is no action left for any borderline to take that will drive home this point more completely. Acting out does nothing for relationships except disgust other people and drive them away.

*What BPD **is*** for each person it afflicts is ultimately *what she makes it.* The only real cure for this illness is the assumption of responsibility for her life by the borderline herself. "The problem," says Dr. Siever, "is that this goes against the experience of many borderline patients."

> My experience is that you have to empathize with the affective sensitivity of the borderline but have the patient examine her sole reliance on maladaptive, impulsive, aggressive ways of managing those feelings and help her find other ways. Even if helped by medications, patients must also relearn more adaptive responses to their environments.
>
> *Their* experience, on the other hand, has taught that if they're not noisy about their needs, they will be ignored. If psychotherapy were a question of sitting down and telling them that there are better ways of handling things, it would be very easy. But it often goes in one ear and out the other.

More inspiring in this context might be the borderline's preoccupation with uniqueness. It is not its depth but the nature of the borderline's pain—her own experience and her manner of explaining it—that is unique. The borderline can really communicate her special value only by describing, as best she can, where her pain comes from, how it disables her, and whatever else about herself a therapist needs to know.

An emotional roar only deafens people. All a borderline need do is try to talk.

Notes

1. George Eliot, *Middlemarch: A Study of Provincial Life,* Book 2, Chapter 20.
2. Larry J. Siever, M.D., David P. Bernstein, Ph.D., and Jeremy M. Silverman, Ph.D., "Schizotypal Personality Disorder: A Review of Its Current Status," *Journal of Personality Disorders,* Vol. 5, No. 2 (1991), p. 189.
3. John G. Gunderson, M.D., "Afterword," in *Review of Psychiatry,* Vol. 8, ed. Allan Tasman, M.D., Robert E. Hales, M.D., and Allen J. Frances, M.D. (Washington, D.C.: American Psychiatric Press, 1989), p. 124.
4. John G. Gunderson, M.D., *Borderline Personality Disorder* (Washington, D.C.: American Psychiatric Press, 1984), p. xi.

Affiliations

The affiliations of therapists who are quoted and/or whose work is featured in this book are listed below (articles cited in the notes list the affiliations of their authors on the title pages).

Gerald Adler, M.D.
Director of Medical Student Education in Psychiatry, Massachusetts General Hospital
Training and Supervising Analyst, Boston Psychoanalytic Society and Institute
Lecturer in Psychiatry, Harvard Medical School

Hagop S. Akiskal, M.D.
Professor of Psychiatry, University of Tennessee, on leave until October 1992 as Senior Science Advisor, Office of the Director, National Institute of Mental Health, Rockville, Maryland

Paul A. Andrulonis, M.D.
Medical Director, Division of Child and Adolescent Community Services, Philadelphia Child Guidance Center and
The University of Pennsylvania Medical School

Frances Arnold, Ph.D.
Assistant Attending Psychologist, McLean Hospital, Belmont, Massachusetts
Instructor in Psychology, Harvard Medical School

John A. Atchley, M.D.
President Emeritus, American Anorexia/Bulimia Association
Assistant Professor of Psychiatry, New York State Psychiatric Institute
Assistant Attending Psychiatrist, College of Physicians and Surgeons, Columbia–Presbyterian Medical Center, New York, New York

Dan H. Buie, Jr., M.D.
Training and Supervising Analyst, Boston Psychoanalytic Society and Institute

John F. Clarkin, Ph.D.
Director, Psychology Department, The New York Hospital—Westchester Division
Professor of Clinical Psychology in Psychiatry, Cornell University Medical College

Rex William Cowdry, M.D.
Chief Executive Officer and Chief of the Clinical and Research Services Branch, NIMH Neuropsychiatric Research Hospital, Washington, D.C.

Amy Baker Dennis, Ph.D.
Consultant, Center for the Treatment of Eating Disorders and National Anorexic Aid Society, Columbus, Ohio
Private Practice Psychologist, Affiliated Psychologists of Michigan, Bloomfield Hills, Michigan

Wayne S. Fenton, M.D.
Director of Research and Assistant Clinical Director, Chestnut Lodge Research Institute, Rockville, Maryland

Allen J. Frances, M.D.
Chairman, *DSM-IV* Task Force
Editor, *Journal of Personality Disorders*
Professor of Clinical Psychiatry, College of Physicians and Surgeons, Columbia–Presbyterian Medical Center, New York, New York

John G. Gunderson, M.D.
Director of Psychotherapy and Psychosocial Research Program, McLean Hospital, Belmont, Massachusetts
Associate Professor of Psychiatry, Harvard Medical School

Thomas G. Gutheil, M.D.
Co-Director, Program in Psychiatry and the Law, Massachusetts Mental Health Center
Associate Professor of Psychiatry, Harvard Medical School

Judith L. Herman, M.D.
Training Director, Victims of Violence Program, Department of Psychiatry, Cambridge Hospital
Associate Clinical Professor of Psychiatry, Harvard Medical School
Founding member, Women's Mental Health Collective, Somerville, Massachusetts

Charles Hodulik, M.D.
Director of Inpatient Psychiatry, Madison VA Hospital
Clinical Assistant Professor of Psychiatry, University of Wisconsin Medical School

Craig Johnson, Ph.D.
Executive Director, Department of Psychology, Laureate Psychiatric Clinic and Hospital, Tulsa, Oklahoma
Associate Professor of Psychiatry, Northwestern University Medical School, Chicago

Otto F. Kernberg, M.D.
Associate Chairman, Department of Psychiatry, and Medical Director, The New York Hospital—Westchester Division
Professor of Psychiatry, Cornell University Medical College

Donald F. Klein, M.D.
Director of Psychiatric Research and Director of the Department of Therapeutics, New York State Psychiatric Institute
Professor of Psychiatry, College of Physicians and Surgeons, Columbia–Presbyterian Medical Center, New York, New York

Jerome Kroll, M.D.
Professor, Department of Psychiatry, University of Minnesota Medical School, Minneapolis

Stanley P. Kutcher, M.A., M.D., F.R.C.P.(C), Diploma of Child Psychiatry
Head, Division of Adolescent Psychiatry, Sunnybrook Health Science Center, Toronto, Ontario, Canada
Associate Professor, Department of Psychiatry, Physical, and Rehabilitation Medicine and School of Graduate Studies, University of Toronto

Michael R. Liebowitz, M.D.
Director, Anxiety Disorders Center, New York State Psychiatric Institute
Professor of Clinical Psychiatry, College of Physicians and Surgeons, Columbia–Presbyterian Medical Center, New York, New York

Marsha M. Linehan, Ph.D.
Professor of Psychology and Adjunct Professor of Psychiatry, University of Washington, Seattle

Paul S. Links, M.D., M.Sc., F.R.C.P.(C)
Director of Research, Department of Psychiatry, Hamilton Civic Hospitals
Associate Professor, Department of Psychiatry, McMaster University, Hamilton, Ontario, Canada

James F. Masterson, M.D.
Director, The Masterson Group, New York, New York
Adjunct Clinical Professor of Psychiatry, The New York Hospital—Payne Whitney Psychiatric Clinic

Thomas H. McGlashan, M.D.
Director, Yale Psychiatric Institute
Professor of Psychiatry, Yale School of Medicine

Theodore Millon, Ph.D.
Professor, Department of Psychology, University of Miami, Coral Gables, Florida
Visiting Professor, Department of Psychiatry, Harvard Medical School and McLean Hospital, Belmont, Massachusetts

Joel Paris, M.D., F.R.C.P.(C)
Senior Psychiatrist, Institute of Community and Family Psychiatry, Sir Mortimer B. Davis–Jewish General Hospital
Associate Professor of Psychiatry, McGill University, Montreal, Quebec, Canada

Fred Pine, Ph.D.
Professor, Department of Psychiatry, Albert Einstein College of Medicine–Montefiore Medical Center, New York, New York

Eric M. Plakun, M.D.
Director of Admissions and Member of the Senior Staff, The Austen Riggs Center, Stockbridge, Massachusetts
Clinical Instructor in Psychiatry, Cambridge Hospital

Mark J. Russ, M.D.
Assistant Attending Psychiatrist, The New York Hospital—Westchester Division
Assistant Professor of Psychiatry, Cornell University Medical College

Eleanor Saunders, Ph.D.
Unit Psychologist, Charles River Hospital, Wellesley, Massachusetts
Assistant Attending Psychologist, McLean Hospital, Belmont, Massachusetts

Larry J. Siever, M.D.
Director, Outpatient Division, Bronx VA Medical Center
Professor of Psychiatry, Mount Sinai School of Medicine, New York, New York

Paul H. Soloff, M.D.
Professor of Psychiatry, University of Pittsburgh, Western Psychiatric Institute and Clinic

Robert L. Spitzer, M.D.
Chief of Biometrics Research, New York State Psychiatric Institute
Professor of Psychiatry, College of Physicians and Surgeons, Columbia–Presbyterian Medical Center, New York, New York
Special Advisor, Task Force on *DSM-IV*

Catherine Steiner-Adair, Ed.D.
Research Associate, Center for the Study of Gender, Education and Human Development, Harvard University
Private Practice Psychologist, Middlesex Family Associates, Lexington, Massachusetts

Michael H. Stone, M.D.
Professor of Clinical Psychiatry, College of Physicians and Surgeons, Columbia–Presbyterian Medical Center, New York, New York
Visiting Professor of Psychiatry, Albert Einstein College of Medicine, New York, New York

Charles R. Swenson, M.D.
Director, Program for Personality Disorders, The New York Hospital—Westchester Division
Associate Professor of Clinical Psychiatry, Cornell University Medical College

Robert J. Waldinger, M.D.
Director of Training and Education, Massachusetts Mental Health Center, Boston, Massachusetts
Assistant Professor of Psychiatry, Harvard Medical School

Mary C. Zanarini, Ed.D.
Assistant Director of Research, Psychosocial Program, and Assistant Psychologist, McLean Hospital, Belmont, Massachusetts
Instructor in Psychology, Harvard Medical School

Index

abandonment, fear of, 64, 77, 79, 81,
171, 191, 196, 197–98, 249, 271,
326
see also separation-individuation
phase
abandonment depression, 196, 202,
291, 295
abuse, 94–96, 139, 151, 161, 168, 199,
211, 219, 226, 232, 235, 239–52,
254–55, 256, 269, 271, 288, 365
absence of, 248–49
chronic, 245, 247
controversial aspects of, 248–50
emotional, 94, 95–96, 239, 241,
249
hidden, 234, 235, 257
incidence of, 239–40, 242, 243
multiple, 242
nonabusive corporal punishment
vs., 240
nonabusive parent vs., 248
physical, 64, 86, 94, 95, 130–31,
150, 153, 234, 237, 239, 241,
242, 243, 246
psychotherapy for, 297–98
recent focus on, 243–44
research on, 240–43
self-mutilation and, 128, 130–31,
132

suicidality and, 122
theoretical implications of, 245–48
traumatic splitting and, 246–48
verbal, 164
see also family environment; sexual
abuse; victimization
accountability without blame, 167
accusatory interpretations, 297, 306
acquired developmental brain
dysfunction, 142, 217
acting out, 21, 28, 29, 53, 85, 119,
144, 198, 257, 263, 265, 324,
325, 373
brain and, 134
destructively toward others,
124–25
in hospitalization, 18, 19, 63, 302,
306
in psychotherapy, 278, 281, 284,
290, 291, 321, 337, 356, 357,
358, 360; *see also* boundaries,
psychotherapeutic
sociocultural, 254–55
see also self-destructive behavior;
self-mutilation; suicidality
active passivity, 117, 346, 364–65
addictions, 26, 73, 87, 132, 135, 139,
343
see also substance abuse

borderlines (*continued*)
  stereotypes of, xiii, 7, 24, 114–15, 124–25,
    243, 282
  symptomatic behavior of, 16, 17–19, 21,
    75–76, 114–37, 191–92, 198–99, 216–17,
    361–63; *see also specific symptoms*
  see also families; male borderlines
borderline schizophrenia, 43, 48, 54, 55, 60,
  245
Borderline Spectrum, The (Meissner), 65*n*
borderline triad, 195, 197, 291
boredom, 65, 79
boundaries, psychotherapeutic, 295
  countertransference violations of, 304,
    363–67
  flexible vs. rigid, 364, 366
  initial contract in, 280–81, 283, 290, 353,
    356, 357
  limit setting in, 51, 278, 280, 281, 304, 356,
    357
  structure provided by, 277, 278, 280–81,
    289, 297, 338, 366
brain, 27, 35, 132, 267, 269
  acting out and, 134
  affective disorders and, 208–10
  basal ganglia of, 205, 207, 208, 219
  cerebral cortex of, 204–5, 207, 218
  depression and, 209–10, 218, 221
  environmental influences on, 134, 210–14,
    250
  gender differences in, 141
  kindling in, 212, 218
  limbic system of, 141, 204–5, 207, 208,
    217–20
  neurons of, 206
  neuropeptides in, 132–34, 206, 208
  PTSD and, 211
  synergistic activity in, 222
  traumatic injury to, 140, 142
  see also neurotransmitters
brain dysfunction, acquired developmental,
  142, 217
  see also organic brain dysfunction
brainwashing, 227, 235
Brown, Saul L., 168
Brumberg, Joan Jacobs, 257*n*
Bryce-Boyer, L., 202*n*
bucket brigade, metaphor of, 31, 275, 285, 298
Buie, Dan H., Jr., 7, 40, 197–99, 200, 201–2,
  245, 344, 376
  therapeutic approach of, 292–94, 295, 296,
    299–300
bulimia nervosa, 20, 22, 26, 78, 125, 132, 225,
  257, 281, 290, 372
  as self-mutilation, 134–35
Bychowski, Gustav, 48, 82

Canada, 142, 308, 318–19, 325
carbamazepine, 218, 336
"Carla," 15, 20, 29–30, 39, 119, 122, 128–29,
  285, 365
Carlyle, Thomas, 265
catecholamines, 209, 270
catharsis, 249
cerebral cortex, 204–5, 207, 218
Chatham, Patricia M., 57, 189
chemicals, self-mutilation with, 130–31
Chessick, Richard D., 202*n*
Chestnut Lodge, 40, 167
  followup study of, 318, 319–20
Chicago Psychoanalytic Institute, 52
children, 211, 233, 236, 257
  BPD in, 139–40, 144–47
  gender differences in, 144–47
  personality disorders in, 139
  of Victorian era, 263–64
  see also abuse; family environment; object
    relations, theories of; trauma
chlomipramine, 210
Clarkin, John F., 65, 66*n*, 286, 376
classical (major) depression, 209, 221, 222, 224,
  225, 230, 321, 331, 332, 334–35, 336
Coccaro, Emil F., 221
cognition, *see* distortions, cognitive; memory;
  thinking
cognitive behavioral therapy, xiv, 66, 135*n*,
  146, 299, 343
  see also dialectical behavioral therapy
cognitive criteria, diagnostic:
  of DIB, 79, 80
  proposed for DSM-IV, 67–69, 90
Coid, Jeremy, 132–33
cold pressor test, 133
Cole, Jonathan O., 16
competence, inconsistent, 116, 169, 344
  apparently competent person syndrome in,
    117–20, 343, 346, 365
  psychotherapists' views on, 118, 119–20
complex partial seizure disorders, 218
concerned objectivity, 289
conduct disorders, 145, 146
confidentiality, 154, 282–83, 290
conflict vs. deficit concepts, 278, 294–95, 296,
  351, 371
confrontation, 278, 281, 285, 298, 303, 306,
  310, 312
constitutional factors, *see* temperament
constitutional psychopathic inferiority, 47
consultant strategy in DBT, 347–48
consultation, 4, 5, 281, 282–83, 284, 303, 338,
  359
  for countertransference boundary violations,
    367